FROM PUBLIC DEFIANCE TO GUERRILLA WARFARE

From Public Defiance
to Guerrilla Warfare

*The Experience of
Ordinary Volunteers in
the Irish War of
Independence 1916-1921*

Joost Augusteijn

IRISH ACADEMIC PRESS

This book was set in 10.5 on 12 point Erhardt for
IRISH ACADEMIC PRESS
Kill Lane, Blackrock, Co. Dublin, Ireland
and in North America for
IRISH ACADEMIC PRESS
c/o ISBS, 5804 NE Hassalo St, Portland, Oregon 97213.

© Joost Augusteijn 1996

A catalogue record for this title
is available from the British Library.

ISBN 0-7165-2607-7

This book is printed on an acid-free and a wood-free paper.

Printed in Ireland
by Colour Books, Dublin

Contents

List of Graphs, Tables and Maps

Abbreviations

AARC   Archdiocese of Armagh, Records Centre
BMH   Bureau of Military History, Ireland
CBHC   Clew Bay Heritage Centre, Westport, Co. Mayo
CBS   Crime Branch Special
CI   County Inspector of the RIC
CO   Colonial Office Papers (contains the monthly confidential reports of the Inspector General and the County Inspectors of the RIC)
IG   Inspector General of the RIC
IWM   Imperial War Museum, London
MA   Military Archives, Dublin
MR   Monthly Confidential Report
NAD   National Archives, Dublin (former State Paper Office and Public Record Office, Dublin)
NLI   National Library of Ireland
O'MN   O'Malley Notebook, in UCD AD
PRO   Public Record Office, London
PRONI   Public Record Office, Northern Ireland
TCD   Trinity College, Dublin
UCD AD   Archives Department, University College, Dublin
WO   War Office Papers

The notes generally relate to the information in an entire paragraph. When necessary it is indicated to which particular aspect mentioned in the paragraph concerned they refer.

In the quotations I have substituted the official terms for the somewhat irregular abbreviations of military units and positions which were used by the original authors.

Preface

This study would not have become what it is today without the aid and encouragement of many individuals and institutions. In the first place I want to mention the untiring support and guidance of my Ph.D. supervisors, Professors M.C. Brands and J.T. Leerssen. In the course of my research countless people in various parts of Ireland assisted me, and almost unfailingly greeted me with the hospitality for which Ireland is renowned. Among them were veterans of the Irish War of Independence and other survivors who were willing to share their experiences with me, and to whom I wish to express my sincerest gratitude (their names are listed in the bibliography). Numerous people were helpful in locating veterans or graciously gave me access to original papers of the IRA in their possession; of these I particularly wish to thank the members of the Third Tipperary Brigade Commemoration Committee (notably Sean Watts attached to the Killenaule Community Project, and John Hassett), Fr Colmcille Conway from Callan, Fr Christy Dwyer of St Patrick's College, Thurles, James Doyle from New Ross, Bob Lambert from Rosslare, Jarlath and Anne Duffy from Carrowholly, who allowed me to use their upstairs closet containing a large collection of IRA papers and welcomed me in their home at all hours of the day and night, Michael MacEvilly who also scrutinised the text regarding events in Mayo, Captain Martin Bell, and Marcus Bourke from Dublin, Dr Dermot Devlin from Maghera, and Fr Murray and all at the parochial house in Armagh City. Furthermore, I wish to single out Mary-Rose O'Brien from Dublin, for her continuous enthusiasm and support. My gratitude to her also extends to her brother Cronan (John) and aunt, Peggy Flynn, in Cross, Co. Mayo for their hospitality.

My research was facilitated by the generous assistance from the Irish Department of Education through two scholarships at Trinity College, Dublin under the cultural exchange agreement between Ireland and the Netherlands. My time as a scholar at Trinity between 1989 and 1991 was greatly enhanced by the stimulating environment I encountered. I wish to mention Professor David Fitzpatrick, Dr Peter Hart, Professor Tom Garvin from UCD, Ciaran Nicholson, Dr Tom Crean and all members of the

Trinity History Workshop. David Fitzpatrick and Peter Hart read a draft version of my thesis, pointing out errors and gave invaluable advice. The librarians and staff of a myriad of archival institutions in Ireland, Northern Ireland and England, listed in the bibliography, have been unfailingly help-ful. Furthermore, I want to extend my appreciation to my close friends, family and in-laws for their unwavering encouragement to pursue this work, in particular my brother Arnout, who has been subjected to the effects of studying Irish history for many years. My thanks also to Brad Phillips, Steven Murray and Ine van Tol for their help with correcting my not always flawless exploits in the English language. Marcus Bourke's unselfish contribution in time and energy was indispensable in making my thesis suitable for publication. Finally, my greatest debt is to my wife Maureen, who aided and endured all stages of the making of this book, and without whose presence on this earth this study would never have been started or completed. I therefore dedicate this work to her.

Introduction

In the atmosphere of political struggle for Home Rule which dominated Ireland from the 1880s, most Catholics grew up with the notion that Ireland was a separate nation dominated against its will. This idea became gradually 'a fact of life', particularly in an environment where history and the historic battles between the Irish and the English were topics of discussion. The history of Ireland was seen as a continuous struggle to free the nation from the oppressive hand of Britain.[1]

Moreover, some of the new generation became convinced that a good Irishman should be ready to fight for an independent Ireland in the tradition of his ancestors. During the first decade of this century these young men moved away from the traditional nationalist organisations and joined more militant ones. The mood in Ireland and Europe in the early twentieth century contributed to their radicalisation, and the atmosphere created by the introduction of the Home Rule Bill in 1912 and the Ulster Protestants' reaction to this led to the founding of the Irish Volunteers in 1913.[2]

The Home Rule Bill was accepted but not implemented due to the need for political unity which followed the outbreak of the First World War.

1 Many leading activists from the War of Independence describe such a background, particularly emphasising the role of the teaching of Irish history at Christian Brothers Schools, see for instance Michael Moran, 'With Michael Kilroy during Easter Week 1916 and the years before'; C.S. Andrews (1979), 61; Liam A. Brady, *Derry Journal*, 1 & 4 May 1953; Brodie Malone, Moane/Malone, Tape; Thomas Heavey, 'Statement'. Some Unionists identified the teaching of Irish history as the main source of the 1916 Rising, Rt. Rev. Mons. Michael Curran, 'Statement', NLI, ms. 27,728(1).
2 The official Irish name of the organisation was Óglaigh na h-Éireann, but this was mainly used as a letterheading. Practically all members referred to themselves as Irish (National) Volunteers. This was a direct reference to the militias founded at the end of the 18th century in response to internal and external threats. Often initiated by the gentry, many of them had a strong sense of Irish patriotism and citizenship. They were an important factor in the extension of powers of the Irish Parliament in the 1780s. Thereafter the term Volunteers continued to have strong associations with Irish citizens taking control of their own destiny.

Although disappointing the aspirations of Irish nationalists, the delay was widely accepted. This changed when a relatively small group of radicals within the ranks of the Irish Volunteers attempted to take advantage of Britain's wartime commitment by staging a revolt during Easter 1916. The heroic failure of this uprising and the harsh treatment of the rebels changed the mood among large numbers of Irish nationalists away from constitutional to more radical means.

In the following two years the Irish Volunteers grew dramatically in strength and their strand of republicanism gained overwhelming political support in Ireland, as witnessed by Sinn Féin's success in the 1918 election when it won 73 out of 105 seats. Initially hoping to attain independence through political agitation and international pressure, the movement became increasingly violent. Sporadic attacks by individual Volunteers developed into a concerted guerrilla war during 1920, eventually forcing the British Government into a truce and a settlement with the IRA (Irish Republican Army)[3] in 1921.

This book is an attempt to depict how ordinary people changed from active nationalists into guerrilla fighters between the Easter Rising of 1916 and the Truce of 10 July 1921. Most joined after 1916 when the Volunteers functioned as a public association with a civil structure; but the organisation was soon transformed into an underground army. Only a small percentage of members in a limited number of areas actually made the transition to the use of violent means. Analysing the causes of this variation is the second objective of this book.

To give an idea of the extent of this growing willingness to use violence we look at what the real level of violence was and how it developed in different parts of the country. The number of indictable offences recorded by the police serve as a first indication of the activity of the Volunteers after the Rising.[4] This gives only a general picture of Volunteer operations, as they include all types of cases: political as well as non-political and violent as well as non-violent. The only offences separately enumerated were those which sprang from agrarian strife, mainly in the sphere of tenant-landlord relations. Nevertheless, as a steady level of 1,500-1,700 offences was recorded for several years prior to 1918, it can be assumed that the large increase in that year and thereafter was directly or indirectly caused by the activities of the republican movement.

3   After the establishment of Dáil Éireann in January 1919 some Irish Volunteers began to call themselves soldiers of the Irish Republican Army. Thereafter the terms Irish Volunteers and IRA became interchangeable. As a result of the initial voluntary nature of the Volunteers this conversion created some tension among those who saw the organisation as a people's movement. See C.S. Andrews (1979), 116.

4   Indictable offences in Ireland, IG MRs 1916-21; Charles Townshend (1975), Appendix IV.

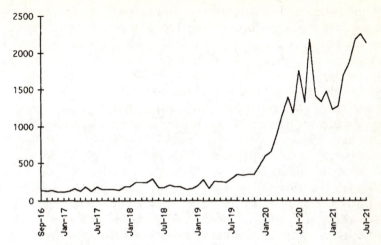

Graph 1: Criminal Offences in Ireland, 1916-1921

Offences shot up to 2,213 in 1918 and 3,112 in 1919 from previously established levels. Extremely strong growth is recorded in 1920. Although the exact figures for March and April are lost, the other ten months together saw 13,346 offences, of which less than 700 were agrarian. The real number of offences was even greater, as the Inspector General of the RIC (Royal Irish Constabulary) acknowledged in August 1920: 'Nor can the figures from the Southern and Western provinces be relied upon, as wide areas are now without police, and many persons prefer to suffer in silence rather than incur the additional hostility of Sinn Féin by making a complaint.' The level of lawlessness continued to grow in 1921 with 12,666 offences recorded in the six months before the Truce.[5]

To explore the geographical distribution of these operations we look at the spread of the most important types of offences and the casualties which they caused.[6] Initially, most of the offences were acts of defiance of a non-violent nature. However, besides being a tool for the public expression of political opposition to British rule, the Volunteers were also intended to be used as a possible military force in the struggle for independence. There was a pressing shortage of good rifles and revolvers in all units, and before such a struggle could develop they had to arm themselves.

According to the police, the organisation had possessed a total of 2,534 rifles prior to 1916, but many of them were lost in the Rising. In February

5 Quote, IG MR August 1920.
6 For the distribution of different types of IRA activities and the resulting casualties I am indebted to Peter Hart who has unselfishly provided me with the results of his work. Without his painstaking accumulation of statistics, an important part of the factual basis of this study would have been missing.

1917, the police again catalogued the arms of the Irish Volunteers. They came to a total of 2,371 arms throughout the country. There were, how-ever, only 902 rifles among these arms, of which just a few hundred were of modern design. Although some arms were obtained in 1918, the growth in membership outstripped the increase in armaments considerably, and only a small proportion of the Volunteers could be provided with a weapon. The available arms were also unequally distributed amongst the units. Munster and Ulster Volunteers were best prepared to initiate hostili-ties, as they possessed a large proportion of the rifles. Connacht Volunteers had comparatively few rifles and only a limited supply of shotguns and small arms. In Leinster, the men had little of anything, totalling 39 rifles, 27 shotguns and 88 small arms in the entire province. This dearth was at least partly a result of the losses incurred during the Rising.[7]

To determine to what extent the differences in armaments caused dif-ferent levels of illegal activities and violence, we look at the distribution of Volunteer operations in each province. In 1917 and 1918 most of the offences were expressions of public defiance. The number of illegal drill exercises, which became prominent during 1917, indicated the willingness of local Volunteers to stand up to the police. Illegal drilling was for the first time separately enumerated in October 1917, when 140 cases were reported. In the next six months drilling became extremely popular, reach-ing a crescendo during the Conscription Crisis when 507 cases were re-corded. Stronger measures of the government then put a stop to it and few cases were reported during the summer. Many Volunteers nevertheless continued their exercises outside the scope of police observation. The willingness of Volunteers to drill openly differed sharply between areas. Out of 334 cases reported in November 1917 81% took place in Munster, with counties Clare and Cork clearly the most affected. In March 1918 the share of Munster Volunteers decreased to 58 per cent, while Connacht saw the largest increase.[8]

The first signs of an intention to use force against the authorities were attempts to take weapons from members of the Crown Forces. Between 1917 and 1919 a total of 49 seizures of arms from policemen and soldiers were recorded, 38 of them in Munster. Seven seizures occurred throughout Leinster, and two in Connacht and Ulster each.

Further proof of the varying levels of commitment to the cause in the

7   The police recorded 262 magazine rifles, 355 single load rifles and 285 other rifles. They also listed 727 shotguns and 742 pistols and revolvers, 'Arms and Ammunition. Returns of Arms in possession of Irish, National and Ulster Volunteers, 1917', PRO, CO904/29/2. In the same file it is stated that 1.017 rifles and 552 shotguns had been surrendered to the Dublin police after the Rising and 1.244 rifles and 1.262 shotguns to the RIC.
8   Distribution of cases of illegal drilling, IG MRs October 1917-May 1918.

four provinces comes from government records. Several types of outrages attributed to the Sinn Féin movement were enumerated by the authorities for the period 1 May 1916 to 31 December 1919. These can be separated into acts of defiance, including the use of some physical violence and attempts to shoot members of the Crown Forces. According to the authorities the number of robberies, burglaries and thefts of arms from the Crown Forces numbered 87, nearly twice as many as direct seizures. They were, however, similarly distributed: 50 of them took place in Munster, 26 in Leinster, 6 in Ulster and 5 in Connacht. The measure of preparation for violent conflict can be read from the raids for arms on private houses, while attempts of the Volunteers to assert themselves as leaders of the community can be read from assaults on and threats to civilians and policemen. The authorities were aware of a total of 502 arms taken from civilians, of 180 threatening letters sent and of 46 assaults on policemen and 17 on civilians. On average the total measure of commitment, military preparation and assertion show a similar distribution as that for arms seizures, but assaults on the police were prevalent in Leinster while threatening letters were relatively common in Connacht.

Table 1: Outrages between 1 May 1916 to 31 December 1919[9]

	Total	Arms seized	Arms taken from:			Assaults on:		Threatening letters
			Police	Military	Civilians	Police	Civilians	
Ulster	134	2	1	5	40	3	5	9
Leinster	429	7	6	20	127	33	4	30
Connacht	205	2	0	5	60	4	1	36
Munster	761	38	13	37	275	6	7	105

A consequence of all these activities was that some units, particularly those in the Southwest, were well equipped to start military operations. However, only a few Volunteers were determined enough to do so. As an indication of this we look at the number of incidents in which firearms were used; these were recorded for each year until 1919. Such incidents numbered 56 in 1915, and grew slowly from 90 in 1918 to 176 in 1919. Of all cases between May 1916 and December 1919, only a small part was attributed to the Volunteers. Fifty of these concerned firing at policemen, while British soldiers were shot at 13 times and civilians 14. The first ambush on policemen resulting in death took place in Tipperary in January 1919, and most other Crown Force casualties between 1917 and 1919 also occurred during

9 Figures on seizures of arms, Peter Hart (1992), Addendum to Chapter 'The Dynamics of Violence'. The 'Return of Outrages Attributed to the Sinn Féin Movement', was compiled by the Chief Secretary's Office, NAD, CBS/Box 24.

1919. The distribution of losses among Crown Forces in this period copies the pattern observed in the growth of other operations. The authorities recorded the murder of 18 state officials in the entire period, 11 in Munster, 6 in Leinster and 1 in Connacht. The police and military suffered a total of 67 casualties between 1917 and 1919 either killed or seriously wounded by Volunteer gunfire or explosives; 44 of these fell in Munster and 12 in Dublin City.

Table 2: Measure of Violence Against Crown Forces, 1916-1919[10]

	Murder of State Officials	Crown Force Casualties	Firing at Police	Firing at Military	Firing at Civilians
Ulster	0	5	1	0	2
Leinster	6	14	15	4	2
Connacht	1	4	5	2	3
Munster	11	44	29	7	7

Before 1920, military activity was largely confined to Munster, and particularly to Co. Cork. Connacht Volunteers were apparently willing to defy the police, but rarely engaged in violence. In Leinster drilling was limited, but there were comparatively many undercover operations which were, however, largely concentrated in Dublin City, while in Ulster activity of all kinds was small.

As shown, conflict escalated in 1920. In line with the increase in offences, a large increase in casualties was recorded from the end of 1919 onwards, confirming the spread of operations described above. Almost one-third of the 1,545 members of the Crown Forces who were killed or seriously wounded by the IRA between January 1920 and the Truce occurred in Co. Cork. Other violent spots were Dublin City and the other Munster counties except Waterford, each having between 84 and 163 casualties. Most Connacht counties follow with around 40 losses each. The Ulster counties noted around 15 each, and outside Dublin City the Leinster counties recorded the lowest level of violence with between 2 and 14 losses among the Crown Forces. The distribution of the 548 IRA casualties in the same period reflects this pattern, with only small deviations.[11]

10 Number of state employees killed and fired at between May 1916 and December 1919, 'Return of Outrages Attributed to the Sinn Féin Movement', NAD, CBS/Box 24. Casualties among the Crown Forces as a result of the use of guns or explosives by Volunteers between 1917 and 1919, Peter Hart (1992), Addendum to Chapter 'The Dynamics of Violence'. Firing outrages per year, 'Intelligence Notes 1919', PRO, CO903/19.
11 Casualties among the Crown Forces, Peter Hart (1992), Addendum to Chapter 'The Dynamics of Violence'. In a yet unpublished article, *The Geography of Revolution in Ireland, 1916-23*, Hart has amended these figures slightly, but no exact figures are provided.

To compare the relative level of conflict, the number of casualties in each county, including those among the Crown Forces, the IRA and civilians, is related to the number of inhabitants. This somewhat alters the above picture. Although Cork still stands out, its lead is less pronounced. It recorded 26 casualties per 10,000 citizens. Tipperary and Clare follow with 16 casualties, Dublin City and Kerry with 15, and Limerick and Belfast City with 14 each. Other comparatively violent counties were Longford, Roscommon and Westmeath in the Midwest with 13, 10 and 7 casualties per 10,000 inhabitants, and Monaghan and Derry in the North with 8 and 7. Particularly unaffected counties were located in Ulster and the Southeast.

From the figures presented above, it is clear that after 1916 the Volunteers were able to stage a serious challenge to British authority. Despite having only a limited number of arms the Volunteers managed to initiate some military style operations during 1919. Republican activity was unevenly spread throughout Ireland, and was particularly strong in the Southwest and Dublin City. Connacht Volunteers were active drillers, but they did not fully engage in the campaign of violence. At the end of 1919 the number of offences spiralled and began to involve more direct violence, which was reflected in the steep rise in casualties. The early activity of Volunteers in the Southwest and Dublin City ensured that these regions bore the brunt of this, while a second area of unrest emerged in the midwest. The comparatively high level of turmoil in Belfast City and Derry was mainly a result of sectarian riots sparked off by the hostilities.

Of course the increasing willingness to use force and its differentiated development have been studied previously. In their local studies of the IRA in the south-western counties of Clare and Cork, David Fitzpatrick and Peter Hart have treated this radicalisation (the increasing willingness to use violence) as an unintended result of local polarisation which was fuelled by the Volunteers' attempts to obtain arms and of a government policy which vacillated between punitive severity and cautious conciliation. Fitzpatrick has emphasised the overwhelming importance of local initiative in the development towards violent conflict: 'The great mass of provincial Volunteers had drifted imperturbably towards revolution, oblivious to the whistling of their leaders, governed by the logic of local experience.' Hart cites the existence of a revenge mentality on both sides as the main cause for the escalation. In his view, the revolution's violence 'can be broken down in a myriad of interlocking tit-for-tat cycles of reprisals', and he states that it was the self-appointed vanguard of revolutionary republicans who prevailed in 1919, and whose actions 'pushed and pulled' their organisation into revolution.[12]

12 Quote on 'drift towards revolution', David Fitzpatrick (1977), 216. Quote on 'tit-for-tat', Peter Hart (1992), Chapter 'The Dynamics of Violence', 107. See also David Fitzpatrick (1989), 249-50; Charles Townshend (1983) 334-7.

Although Hart's tit-for-tat cycles of violence induced by personal feelings of revenge can account for escalation among the revolutionary vanguard in the most active parts of the country, they do not allow for differentiation (the variety in attitudes and levels of violence emerging in different areas) and are unable to account for the less violent developments in other areas. Furthermore, his dependence on those who were willing to act ruthlessly reverts to the old argument that it was bellicose leadership which accounts for the differentiation in violence. This argument has already been refuted by Fitzpatrick in 1978. He emphasised that the absence of violence was due not so much to an insufficient supply of bellicose leaders but to the insufficient demand for their leadership. Hart's explanation for the differentiated development does not extend beyond a recognition of the existence of a pattern of core and periphery in Ireland similar to that within Co. Cork, with different areas conforming to different rhythms. Revenge as the overriding cause for escalating violence also fails to account for the existence of cycles of violence dying out and springing up in different districts at various times, which Hart also observed in Cork. Within the tit-for-tat cycles of violence, he discerned certain geographical correlations. Violence seemed to thrive in more urbanised areas with better land and seemed to be hampered by poverty and physical isolation.[13]

A small number of explanations have been offered for the different levels of violence by various authors. The traditional partisan view that these differences can be ascribed to the presence or absence of strong-willed and bellicose leaders is shown in older works such as Dorothy Macardle's *The Irish Republic*. One of the earliest attempts at a more comprehensive interpretation came from Erhard Rumpf in 1959, who on the basis of statistical analysis discerned an inverse relation between the level of revolutionary violence in each district and the power of interests tending to turn the people against revolution. He argued that an economic connection with Britain and the absence of violence as a generally accepted means of achieving nationalist ends are such 'interests' which explain the relative calm in the provinces of Leinster and Ulster. Lesser economic ties and a strong tradition of violent agitation therefore account for Munster's predisposition to violence.[14]

However, Rumpf can not explain the fact that similar conditions in Connacht resulted in inactivity. To resolve this, he introduced the absence of a prosperous middle class in Connacht, and the hostility of national revolutionary leadership towards 'the demands of its land-hungry labourers and uneconomic holders'. In 1978, David Fitzpatrick challenged the figures used in Rumpf's analysis and showed that the suggested factors were unable

---

13 Peter Hart (1992), Chapter 'The Dynamics of Violence', passim. Refuting importance of bellicose leadership, David Fitzpatrick (1978), 117-18.

14 Dorothy Macardle (1937). The treatment of this aspect in an established more general history, J.C. Beckett (1966), 441-8. Erhard Rumpf (1959), Chapter 2.

to explain fully the distribution of violence. In his detailed study of Clare he had already refuted Rumpf's explanation for the inactivity in the West.[15]

In his analysis of the spatial patterns of resistance against British rule between 1800 and 1921, Herman van der Wusten has also been unable to account for the different levels of violence in Munster and Connacht. He identified a strong correlation between the levels of mobilisation in different areas during the various expressions of nationalist action in the period of his research, notably between the Land League of the late nineteenth century and the republican movement after 1916. However, the absence of violence in Connacht and the local emphasis on political struggle do not bear out this correlation. He suggests that the more differentiated nature of agrarian social structures in Munster (large diversity in size of agrarian holdings and more farm labourers) might have led to a wider use of physical violence in society, which could also be directed at external threats. In line with Rumpf's suggestion, he considers the tradition of violent action in rural parts of central Munster stemming from the beginning of the nineteenth century as a possible supporting argument for this. As an alternative he proposes that the wider presence of modern organisational structures in Munster, such as agrarian cooperatives, provided a basis for organising fighting groups which were lacking in Connacht.[16]

In his critique of Rumpf's work, David Fitzpatrick has not provided a comprehensive explanation for differentiation either. He suggests that greater police efficiency in the years after the 1916 Rising in Connacht might have contained revolutionary violence in 1920-21, but he acknowledges that this does little more than emphasise the links between the efficiency of passive resisters in disrupting police work in 1918-19 and active revolution in 1920-21, and leaves differentiation itself unexplained. In his recent study of Cork, Peter Hart presents far more accurate figures on the distribution of violence in Ireland, which differ significantly from those used by Rumpf. These show that there is no conclusive evidence for the existence of such an inverse relationship between IRA activity and RIC performance. Fitzpatrick has pointed out some other factors which may have contributed to Munster's predisposition towards violence. These include the early organisation of Irish Volunteers in that province, aided perhaps by the existence of a robust tradition of nationalist heterodoxy. Fitzpatrick also follows Rumpf's suggestion that the appeal of republicanism to the rural poor, who were predominant in Connacht, diminished as the movement's dependence on middle-class funds increased. The influence of these factors put forward by Fitzpatrick has yet to be assessed.[17]

15 Challenging Rumpf, David Fitzpatrick (1978), 117-20. See also Charles Townshend (1983), 368-71. Study of Co. Clare, David Fitzpatrick (1977).
16 H. van der Wusten (1977), 288-9.
17 David Fitzpatrick (1978), 116-22. Peter Hart (1992), Chapter 'The Dynamics of Violence', 85-6. Charles Townshend (1979), 322.

Based on Rumpf's inadequate figures, Tom Garvin has offered some further interesting correlations between IRA activity and local characteristics. He reiterates Van der Wusten's pattern in IRA activity which reflects traditions of agrarian inspired violence. A concentration of IRA violence in central Munster and one on the Ulster border corresponds with the distribution of violence during the Land War in the later part of the nineteenth century. Apart from the inactive West, the IRA was more violent where the distance to the two main urban areas of Dublin and Belfast increased. He explains the inactivity of the West by the presence of an economic threshold; below a certain material level no IRA activity could be sustained. The centre of social gravity of the movement lay, in his opinion, among the small-town and rural lower middle classes. However, in order to explain diversity fully, he is forced to introduce a large number of other factors within this general framework. The actual performance of units was affected by: the geographical properties of the area, the ability to capture arms and the ensuing shortage of arms and ammunition in some areas, the quality of officers, the level of local unity, the number of locals consorting with their enemy, and the level of participation in the IRA which was largely affected by emigration. However, no indication is given how to relate the overall scheme to all these factors.[18]

On the basis of research done on other nationalist revolutionary movements, Garvin has recently refined his argument to explain the extremely high level of IRA activity in Cork. He asserts that revolutionary sentiment in nineteenth century Europe was strongest among artisans and a peasantry who were threatened by capitalist change. The areas in which nationalist movements originated tended to be compact, unindustrialised and developmentally intermediate. Substantial small-scale production existed which was geared to the local market. These zones were usually fertile, and agricultural production had exceeded subsistence level but had not yet developed into true large-scale capitalist farming. These core areas of resistance, of which Cork was a classic example, were affected by industrialisation but did not themselves participate in it; capitalism was sufficiently developed to generate problems but not enough to offer solutions. In his view, radical nationalism was a 'disease of development', reaching its peak at an intermediate stage of development in time and space. Although possibly explaining the propensity to violence in Cork and the lack thereof in certain other areas, it cannot provide a common denominator for variation.[19]

In a yet unpublished article Peter Hart has statistically tested several possible explanations. Correlating casualty figures with various socio-economic indicators, he has come to the conclusion that explanations based on wealth,

18 Tom Garvin (1981), 123-6.
19 Tom Garvin (1987), 6-8. In his recent comprehensive account of Irish history Roy Foster has integrated the above arguments, and is similarly unable to explain the quiescence of the West in military terms, Roy Foster (1988), 494-501.

class, occupation or rurality do not hold. The only positive correlations he found were those with the percentage of boys in each county being taught by the notoriously nationalistic Christian Brothers and to a lesser extent with the efficiency of the police and court system in dealing with the movement in 1917-19. However, neither of these correlations on their own is able to account for the variation in the increasing willingness to use violence.[20]

It is clear that a convincing explanation for the differentiated development of violence in Ireland in the 1916-21 period has not yet been provided. As Hart indicates, radicalisation was not a straightforward process. His innovative description of radicalisation provides us with an excellent account of its most extreme form, but does not represent the experiences of most Volunteers in Ireland at this time. Both Hart and Fitzpatrick have based their assessments on the study of one, particularly active, county. The experience of Volunteers in different counties has never been compared, nor has a study been made of how the particular elements which are suggested by these authors to be at play in the process of radicalisation affected local Volunteers throughout Ireland.

To come to a better understanding of the actual workings of this process, and to make a valid assessment of the value of the different causes for variation in the resulting violence which have so far been presented, it is imperative to look at a large range of manifestations of radicalisation. For this reason, I have studied the way in which the nation-wide development towards increased confrontation took place at local level in different areas. This study thus compares the varying experience of Volunteers in the same area, as well as the experience of Volunteers in different areas. The central object is to distinguish general trends within the various forms of radicalisation which occurred among the members of the Irish Volunteers.

To describe the differing experience among the ranks of the IRA, five areas have been chosen for an in-depth analysis. The events in these areas are used to construct a composite image of radicalisation, thereby outlining the possible reasons for the choices that were made by different Volunteers. Although the study of differing circumstances is also used to explain regional variation, the actual events in these areas remain secondary to the attempt to understand the process of radicalisation itself. This work thus has two aims: firstly, to ascertain what regional comparisons can teach us about the process of radicalisation and the circumstances in which it is most likely to take place, and secondly to determine what can be said about the causes of the regional variations in mobilisation and activity in Ireland during the War of Independence.

The Volunteer units singled out for this research were chosen on the basis of differences in the known level of activity; their involvement in the

20 Peter Hart, *The Geography of Revolution in Ireland, 1916-23* (forthcoming).

Easter Rising; the presence of Gaelic as a spoken language, be it native or acquired; socio-economic stratification; distribution of religious denominations; presence of urban areas; existing research; and the availability of archive material and personal contacts. On the basis of these criteria five brigades and one northern county, which only had disparate units, were selected. The combined experience of Volunteers in all these counties reflects a wide spectrum of possible backgrounds, environments and reactions which hopefully provides a representative picture of the lives of the different members of the IRA.

The South or Third Tipperary Brigade was chosen as one of the most active units in Munster outside Cork, whose exceptionally industrious Volunteers have already been researched by Peter Hart. This brigade was situated in a comparatively rich agricultural area with a high degree of urbanisation. Like all other counties, Tipperary had only one brigade at the time of the Easter Rising, but when brigades were reorganised in 1918 it was divided into three separate units. The South Tipperary Brigade initially had three battalions, but this soon increased to six and later to eight. At the time of the Truce these eight battalions, with centres in Fethard, Cashel, Kilnamagh, Tipperary Town, Clonmel, Cahir, Drangan and Carrick-on-Suir, comprised fifty-six companies.

Wexford represents the inactive Leinster counties which had strong ties with Britain. The Wexford Brigade was one of the two provincial brigades that fought in 1916. In this research the emphasis lies on the South Wexford Brigade, which was part of the single brigade this county had until September 1920, when it was divided into a North and South Wexford Brigade. In 1921 the latter comprised four battalions, with centres in New Ross, Campile, Bridgetown and Wexford, incorporating twenty-four companies.

The Volunteers in Co. Derry[21] situated in the province of Ulster were confronted with a large Protestant population, and operated both in rural areas and a large city. There was no brigade organisation here until 1921, but three independent battalions existed, one in the city and two in the southern part of the county centred around Magherafelt and Maghera. There was little contact between the city and the southern battalions. The city battalion was orientated to the west, and temporarily became part of the North-East Donegal Brigade in 1920. The absence of a unit in the northern half of the county can be explained by the dominance of Protestants there.

Two brigades in Mayo represent the poor, predominantly rural and partly Gaelic-speaking province of Connacht. In June 1919 Mayo still had one brigade with nine battalions and thirty-seven companies. At the end of

21 The use of the term Derry for the county and city, which are also known as Londonderry, is not an expression of any bias on the part of the author but a consequence of the basis of analysis: describing events from inside the Irish Volunteers.

1920 it was divided into four brigades. The contact with the only living brigade commander was an important consideration in selecting the South Mayo Brigade, while there was much useful documentary evidence available for the West Mayo Brigade. The South Mayo Brigade had four battalions with centres in Cross, Ballinrobe, Claremorris and Balla. The West Mayo Brigade also had four battalions with thirty-one companies and centres in Castlebar, Newport, Westport and Louisburgh.

The Dublin City Brigade was the internationally most visible stage of IRA operations. Co. Dublin was originally also covered by a single brigade, but in 1918 north Co. Dublin formed an independent brigade, and shortly before the Truce south Co. Dublin separated from the city and formed the South Dublin Brigade together with north Co. Wicklow. Besides four city battalions which formed the core of the original county brigade, there was a battalion of engineers without a fixed territory. After 1916 the area south of the city was divided between two city battalions, but at the end of 1920 a separate Sixth and in 1921 a Seventh Battalion were introduced there. The Sixth Battalion formed the basis of the South Dublin Brigade. The four city battalions comprised thirty-eight companies at the time of the Truce. Although police records relating to the city have unfortunately not survived, the majority of all other available sources relate to events in this brigade.

The indicators presented in Table 3 are taken from the 1911 census and present us with a first impression of the character of these counties. Overall, Tipperary Volunteers came from a highly urbanised county with a large number of young males. It is assumed that males who were between five and thirty years of age in 1911 were most likely to join the Volunteers between 1916 and 1921. In Wexford the Volunteers were operating in a somewhat less prosperous and less urbanised area with relatively few young males and a strong British influence. The large number of Protestants dominate the scene in Derry. In all aspects, membership in Mayo operated in the poorest and least anglicised area with a large surplus of young men, while Dublin represented a large urban area with a strong British presence.

Table 3: Indicators of County Differences

	Population	Catholic	Urbanised	Irish Speaking	Male 5-30
Mayo	192,177	97.9%	13.7%	46.0%	24.7%
Tipperary	89,552	94.6%	27.8%	7.7%	23.5%
Wexford	102,273	92.3%	22.1%	2.8%	20.0%
Derry County	99,845	41.8%	10.5%	}2.9%	21.0%
City	40,780	56.2%	100%		23.0%
Dublin County	172,394	71.0%	57.8%	3.4%	22.1%
City	304,802	83.1%	100%	3.9%	23.5%

This book is divided into two parts. In the first part I take a look at radical organisation prior to 1916, and at the changing activities which members of the IRA engaged in between 1916 and 1921. This chronological account is principally based on developments in the five counties. In this way I account for the differentiated development and give some insight into what it was like to be a Volunteer – what membership entailed to men with varying levels of involvement. The main emphasis, however, lies on determining the pressures under which the transition from public defiance to a full-blown guerrilla was made, and to what extent this transition was completed in different areas. The various reactions of Volunteers are shown by discussing the radicalisation of a small section of the organisation, the rejection of violence by another part and the hesitancy of most members caught in between.

In the second part a closer look is taken at the interaction between Volunteers and their environment. In Chapters 5 and 6 I look at the way in which the attitudes of Volunteers and Crown Forces changed and resulted in an increasing willingness of large groups of ordinary civilians to kill policemen. In Chapters 7-9 I discuss the movement's ability to mobilise public support and justify its campaign of violence, and assess how the measure of its success influenced the level of IRA violence. Based on the various characteristics of the individual areas, some general conclusions concerning the process of radicalisation and a new explanation for the differences in activity and violence are provided in the final section of this book.

Donegal

Londonderry

Antrim

NORTHERN IRELAND

Tyrone

ULSTER

Leitrim   Fermanagh   Armagh   Down

Monaghan

Sligo

Cavan

Louth

Mayo

Roscommon

Longford

Meath

CONNACHT

Westmeath

Dublin

Galway

King's   Kildare

LEINSTER

Queen's   Wicklow

Clare

Tipperary   Carlow

Kilkenny   Wexford

Limerick

MUNSTER

Waterford

Kerry

Cork

- - -   Brigade boundary

....   Battalion boundary

Map 1: General Map of Ireland with Brigade and Battalion Boundaries

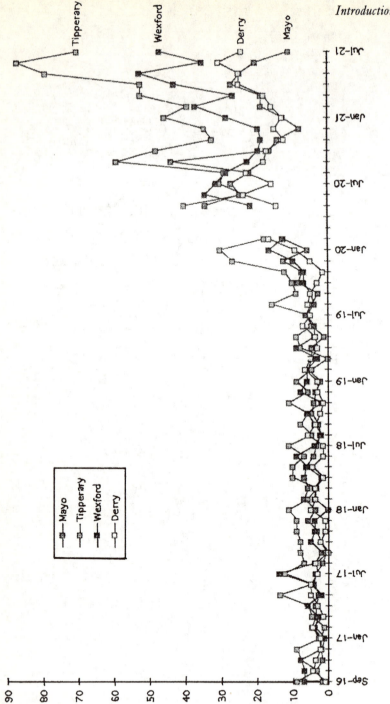

Graph 2: *Criminal Offences per 100,000 inhabitants*

PART I: CHRONOLOGY

THE NATURE OF VOLUNTEERING

CHAPTER I

Organisation, 1900-1916

A question frequently asked regarding the origins of revolutionary movements is whether they emerge spontaneously, or are a result of careful planning by established radicals. Was the Irish Revolution a consequence of a
rising tide of radicalism before the foundation of the Volunteers, or did
extreme nationalism develop suddenly in the favourable circumstances which
arose first in 1913 and again after the 1916 Rising? To answer this question
this chapter explores the mobilisation of Irishmen in extreme nationalist
organisations in the five chosen areas prior to 1916.

The influence of the IRB (Irish Republican Brotherhood)[1] on the emergence of the Irish Volunteers is widely recognised. Garvin claims that there
was nothing spontaneous about the Irish Revolution, but that it was
brought about by the efforts of many activists over two generations. This
image of long-term involvement is largely confirmed for the leadership on a
national level; but the responses on local level are unknown. Garvin ascribes
a particular influence to the Gaelic League, which he sees as a major factor
in the development of the revolutionary elite and often functioned as a
vehicle of anti-British sentiment. The league gained many new members in
the first decade of the twentieth century, particularly in Munster. However,
the existence of personal connections between local radical organisations at
the beginning of the century and the Volunteers of the War of Independence has not previously been investigated.[2]

PREPARATION IN MAYO

The development of radical organisations in the early part of the century is
best documented for west Mayo. Before the formation of the Volunteers, a
trend towards organisation was noticeable amongst radicals in the towns of

---

1 The Irish Republican Brotherhood was a secret society dating back to 1858,
   which had one main objective: to establish an independent Irish Republic.
2 Spontaneity of revolution, Tom Garvin (1987), 5. Role of Gaelic League, ibid.,
   Chapter 5, passim.

west and central Mayo.[3] A small number of men with contacts in Dublin became involved. In Castlebar, Dr Anthony MacBride, a brother of Major John MacBride, was a central figure. In 1905 the MacBride brothers had established one of the first provincial branches of Sinn Féin, the most radical political movement of that period. Dick Walsh, an uncle of the MacBrides, living in Balla, John MacDonagh[4] and another MacBride brother, Joseph, living in Westport, were other leading radical nationalists of this period who continued to play a role in militant politics. The efforts of these men brought together several radical young men into one organisation and established direct contacts with Dublin. However, it took until 1911 before a concerted effort was made after the reorganisation of the IRB in Belfast and Dublin had revitalised the brotherhood and provided local organisers with a common purpose.[5]

Ned Moane, later adjutant of the West Mayo Brigade, remembers weekly meetings with John MacDonagh talking national issues. After these talks had been going on for a couple of years MacDonagh swore him into the IRB in 1911. Joining this secret organisation made a profound impression. He vividly remembers the bimonthly IRB meetings in Westport: '[Joe] MacBride gave us lectures on military subjects and historical items and we had discussions on various subjects.' Through such recruits the organisation slowly expanded. Some years afterwards, Moane took into the IRB Tom Heavey, a young neighbour who frequently sought his company and later became one of the most committed members of the local Volunteers.[6]

Besides this ever-widening circle of IRB men, there were others with a radical nationalist inclination unaware of the IRB's existence who had independently become convinced of the need to use force to obtain freedom. These men had joined different organisations in which they hoped to realise this objective. Initially, the Board of Erin faction of the AOH was the most favoured choice, this traditionally northern organisation had recently extended its activities to the South. Later they were attracted by a radical breakaway group within the AOH, the Irish American Alliance, which already begun training its own volunteers in 1910, long before the start of the Irish Volunteers.[7]

---

3   John MacBride was a former major in Irish Brigade which fought the English during the Boer War. He became heavily involved in the IRB thereafter and was one of the men executed after the 1916 Rising.
4   Brother to one of the signatories of the 1916 declaration of the Irish Republic, Thomas MacDonagh.
5   Start of Sinn Féin in Castlebar, James Chambers, 'Statement'.
6   Quote, Ned Moane, 'Statement'. See also Thomas Heavey, 'Statement'.
7   Training in Irish American Alliance, Ned Maughan (this is the same man as Ned Moane), O'MN, P17b109. The willingness to force things to a fight among the Kilmeena branch of the Irish American Alliance, Jack Feehan, O'MN, P17b113. In Newport, Michael Moran, 'With Michael Kilroy'.

These young radicals became prime targets for IRB recruitment in the years after 1910. In the towns, where the IRB was strong, this was successful. However, in most rural parts of west and south Mayo the organisation had few contacts, and little was done. Bringing all these radicals into the IRB would take until after 1916. In the future South Mayo Brigade area there were only a few IRB men in the northern part under Dick Walsh. There were none in the southern part where Tom Maguire, the future commandant of that brigade, lived.[8]

An example of the exploits of these young men is found in Newport. In 1910 Michael Kilroy and other young men in the parish, dissatisfied with the Junior League of the United Irish League, had joined the Board of Erin faction. Disappointed with its moderate stance, he and the more radical members changed allegiance to the rival Irish American Alliance group in 1911. They extended this organisation to some rural parts of west Mayo, notably Kilmeena, a traditional stronghold of radical nationalists. The Alliance branch there, which soon numbered fifty, believed in physical force and was anxious to initiate a confrontation.[9]

Another branch was set up in Aughagower, a village with strong personal ties to radical nationalists in nearby Westport. The local branch of the United Irish League, an organisation which fought for the rights of small tenants and was traditionally associated with the Irish Party, had been extremely active. Owen Hughes, one of its leaders, was the local symbol of radicalism. His brother Charles was the local IRB 'Centre'[10] in Westport, and in 1914 Owen became the first captain of the local Volunteers. His sons and cousins, most of whom would later become active Irish Volunteers, were among the most energetic members.[11]

It is clear that in Mayo, from early in the century, there were men with more radical views than those held by the Irish Party. Under the influence of extreme nationalists from Dublin these men came together in the IRB. In many places, however, radicals had no contacts with this organisation and were forced to join other political groups, which they then tried to influence towards taking a more radical course. Failing this, they eventually broke away from these traditional organisations and started branches of

8 Situation in South Mayo, Tom Maguire, Interview.
9 Newport, Michael Kilroy, 'The Awakening'. Kilmeena, Jack Feehan, O'MN, P17b113.
10 The IRB was organised in parish circles with a Centre as its leader. Centres from one county together chose a County or Head Centre. The organisation was headed by a Supreme Council with a representative of each province, one each from north and south England and one from Scotland, supplemented by four co-opted members. After 1916 all Irish provinces were divided in two, each with its own representative on the Supreme Council, thus accounting for fifteen members.
11 Aughagower, Charles Hughes, Interview.

more extreme ones, often joined by other members who had been radicalised in recent years.

One of the first signs of this had been the founding of the Irish
American Alliance, a group within the AOH set up in opposition to the
more traditional Board of Erin. After 1910, the recent recruits of the IRB
started to take in the most eager of these radicals and over the years bound
them together into one organisation. This centred round the towns, where
larger groups of young men were more easily found and representatives of
the IRB had their contacts. The main exceptions to this in rural west Mayo
were Kilmeena and Aughagower. The first, situated on the road between
Westport and Newport, had strong ties with the old IRB, remnants of which
still existed. The latter had strong personal ties with activists in Westport. In
most rural areas, however, radicals were scarce and had been unable to organise themselves.

PREPARATION ELSEWHERE

In other counties a similar pattern is discernible. In south Tipperary there
was an equally small number of activists of local and regional importance.
The principal men with contacts in Dublin were: Pierce McCan, a big
Catholic landowner, who, unlike most other representatives of his class
(including his own family) had become involved in radical politics through
his interest in the Irish language; and Eamon O'Dwyer, a farmer with a
high standing in his locality, who was involved in nearly every nationalist
organisation. Through his association with the Gaelic League McCan knew
many people in Dublin; O'Dwyer combined a similar involvement in the
language movement with some agencies for Dublin businesses.[12]

O'Dwyer's interest had been awakened early in the century by the small
Irish lessons in the *Weekly Freeman's Journal*, a widely read newspaper of
that period. Through a locally organised Irish class he became acquainted
with a group of political activists. Soon the discussions with these men led to
action, and in 1908 they started a Sinn Féin Club in the parish. Their activity combined anti-British issues with farmers' interests in the Anti-Enlisting
campaign and the Anti-Ranch struggle. O'Dwyer was sworn into the IRB
around 1911 and became its local Centre; he set out to strengthen the IRB
by encouraging local Sinn Féin and Gaelic League members to join.[13]

12 On family background Pierce McCan, Frank McCan, private conversation.
   Pierce McCan later became the Commandant of the Tipperary Brigade and MP
   for East Tipperary in 1918. He died of the flu while on hunger strike in prison
   in 1919. Eamon O'Dwyer became quartermaster of the Tipperary Brigade and
   following its formation, assistant-quartermaster of the South Tipperary Brigade.
   He also served for a while as IRB Head Centre for Tipperary.
13 Eamon O'Dwyer, 'Statement'.

Besides these leading figures, there were other younger men who had become independently involved in radical politics. The groups around Seán Treacy, later vice-commandant of the South Tipperary Brigade, and Frank Drohan, later commandant of the Clonmel Battalion, are two of the more influential examples of this. Treacy had been an IRB member since 1911 and was president of the local Gaelic League branch. The Gaelic League was an important means of bringing radical nationalists together in Tipperary. This has already been suggested by Tom Garvin; however, contrary to his belief, radicals were most numerous in rural areas. For the time being the activities of these groups mainly had a local focus with few wider implications. Gradually many of their members joined the IRB, which became a binding factor between these groups, although it had not yet initiated any joined action.[14]

In Derry City many future leaders of the Irish Volunteers were also involved in radical organisations early in the century. One local Volunteer remembers some of his officers being active in 'Eire Óg' an organisation which ran a voluntary Sunday school, combining the teaching of Irish history with drill instruction and communal prayers! The drill instructor in this school later became the company captain of the Irish Volunteers; while its lecturer on Irish history became one of its main officers. Apart from Mayo, Derry was the only other county of the five with a branch of the Irish American Alliance faction of the AOH, which provided an early platform for militant nationalists.[15]

In the rural areas of Derry remnants of the old IRB formed the main expression of radical politics. Despite an early reorganisation of the IRB in south Derry and east Tyrone by Thomas Clarke,[16] not much appears to have been done since. A revitalisation also took place here after 1910, when young men again joined the IRB. However, no revolution being immanent, and failing organisational success, they did little for the cause apart from their opposition to the strong constitutional nationalists. According to an IRB organiser in south Derry in 1915: 'The only thing that the I.R.B. did there was to keep alive a feeling of dislike and distrust of the Hibernians [the AOH] and of the parliamentary movement, and to cause a few young people to read "Sinn Féin" or "Irish Freedom".' Radicals remained a tiny minority of the Catholic population in Co. Derry and any activity by them was bound to encounter strong opposition from the highly organised con-

14 On 'Seán Treacy', D. Ryan (1945), 16-18.
15 Background officers in Derry City, Liam A. Brady, *Derry Journal*, 1 May 1953. Presence of Irish American Alliance, CI Derry MRs 1915-16.
16 Thomas Clarke had a long association with the Fenian movement and had been involved in the bombing campaign in England during the 1880s. He was also one of the seven signatories of the proclamation of the Republic in 1916 and was subsequently executed.

stitutionalists. Consequently the AOH functioned as an obstacle, rather than as a vehicle of organisation, as it did in Mayo. The small number of revolutionary nationalists and the resulting secrecy made the banding of radicals into one body much more difficult in Ulster than in the South.[17]

In Wexford, as in Mayo, organisation of radicals started in the towns. Unlike Mayo but similar to Tipperary, the Gaelic League was the main agent. This was centred in two places, Wexford town and Enniscorthy, the former in south and the latter in north Wexford. In Wexford town the Gaelic League was organised in 1890 by Robert Brennan. Like Eamon O'Dwyer in Tipperary, he had become involved in the language movement by accident. Having learned some Irish at the local Christian Brothers School, he was one of the few who were able to sing a song in Irish at a commemoration of the 1798 Rising; some people, anxious to learn the language, then came to him for tuition. He subsequently asked Douglas Hyde, president of the Gaelic League, down from Dublin to organise a branch of the League in Wexford. Hyde agreed and Brennan became one of its most prominent local figures.[18]

As a result of their involvement in the Gaelic League, a radical nationalism developed among Brennan and his associates, which resulted in the founding of a branch of Sinn Féin. This branch attempted to organise branches throughout Wexford. At about the same time they heard rumours that the IRB still existed, and that some members of the local GAA (Gaelic Athletic Association) executive were active in it. After discreet inquiries nine of Brennan's group were sworn into the IRB by Sean T. O'Kelly on a visit from Dublin, and when in 1913 the Volunteers were formed all joined up. Getting people in the Wexford countryside to join radical nationalist organisations was difficult. As in Derry, this was due to the strength of the AOH. Complaints of strong opposition to radical nationalism were voiced by several Volunteers in Wexford.[19]

Dublin was the centre of radical nationalist activity around the turn of the century. Again, most men who became leaders in the Irish Volunteers were

17 Tom Clarke's involvement in reorganising the IRB, W.J. Kelly Sr, 'Statement', Fr O'Kane Papers, AARC. Quote, Ernest Blythe, 'Statement', 17, UCD AD, P24/1783. *Sinn Féin* and *Irish Freedom* were radical newspapers.

18 Robert Brennan (1950), 1–6.

19 Robert Brennan (1950), 9–10 + 31. The importance of the Gaelic League as a meeting point for advanced nationalists is also mentioned by Sean Moylan in Cork, NLI, ms. 27,731. Strength of AOH in Wexford, Mark Killilea, O'MN, P17109; Andy Roe, Interview. Similar opposition to the Volunteers by the AOH in the early stages is reported from Cavan town, Sean Lynch, 'History of Anglo-Irish Conflict 1913–21', NLI, P914 A0152.

already involved in various radical organisations. Several young activists had joined the IRB and, together with men from Belfast, began to reorganise it around 1909. They considered violence a real option; some of them started military drill exercises. The recently established Fianna Éireann, a youth organisation of radical nationalists, was their main vehicle in mobilising further support. One member recalls Con Colbert visiting schools lecturing and attempting to recruit boys; despite active opposition by local priests, he met with some success.[20]

When boys joined the Fianna, they were openly instructed on the revolutionary goals of the organisation. The Fianna 'Constitution and Rules' stated that the object of the organisation was to re-establish the independence of Ireland. For this purpose the youth of Ireland would receive mental and physical training, including scouting, military exercises, Irish history and the Irish language. Each member had to promise to work for the independence of Ireland, refuse to join England's armed forces, and obey his superior officers.[21]

Some IRB men attempted to organise the Fianna in areas outside Dublin. The most active of these was Liam Mellows, who features prominently in the memories of many local Volunteer leaders. Besides this involvement in the Fianna, some Dublin radicals were active in Sinn Féin and the Irish-Ireland movement. Others participated in the founding of Cumann na mBan, the women's organisation, which became particularly strong in Dublin.[22]

The Gaelic League and to some extent the GAA, were channels through which new members were sought and found. Although both organisations were nominally a-political and continued to operate as such, they functioned as rallying points for radical nationalists. Ernest Blythe, who featured prominently in extending the IRB in the country in later years, started his involvement in radical politics by joining the Gaelic League shortly after moving to Dublin in 1905, before becoming a member of the IRB by the end of the decade. Other men came in contact with radical politics through the GAA. One Volunteer claimed that thirty-three members of his GAA club participated in the 1916 Rising.[23]

20 The future commandant of the Squad joined the IRB in 1907. He was also among the first to start drilling, Patrick O'Daly, 'Statement', NLI, P4548. Recruiting in Fianna, Alfie White, O'MN, P17b110. A similar use of the Fianna was made in Limerick, Michael Brennan (1980), 7.
21 Copy of Fianna Éireann 'Constitution and Rules', Lt. R.D. Jeune Papers, IWM, 76/172/1.
22 Visits of Liam Mellows: In Tipperary, Eamon O'Dwyer, 'Statement'; Paul Mulcahy, 'Statement'; P.C. Power (1989), 202. In Mayo, Tom Maguire, in U. MacEoin (1987), 278; Brodie Malone, O'MN, P17b109. In Co. Dublin, Billy Rowe, O'MN, P17b110.
23 Ernest Blythe, 'Statement', 1, UCD AD, P24/1783. On the GAA, Sean O'Duffy, NLI, ms. 21,658.

IMPACT OF CULTURAL NATIONALISM

The radical nationalist cultural organisations which emerged at the end of the nineteenth century, such as the Gaelic League and the GAA, were important vehicles of mobilisation and are therefore often seen as the breeding ground for the republicanism of the early twentieth century. According this view, the growth of cultural nationalism paved the way for the emergence of radical political nationalism. To test this assertion we look at the relationship between the success of these organisations and the strength of the republican movement at local level.

Gaelic culture had largely disappeared during the nineteenth century. From being a predominantly Irish speaking nation in 1800, Ireland had become largely English speaking in 1900, with just 14.4 per cent still having some command of the language and only 0.5 per cent monoglot Irish speakers. With the exception of a few remote areas, the Irish language was only actively used in the western and southern fringes of the country. However, in the late nineteenth century the Gaelic League had begun to change the picture of steady and irreversible decline. Under pressure from the language movement, the teaching of Irish during school hours was permitted by the British Government in 1900, but attendance was optional and subject to State approval. Although this government decision had little immediate effect, a quarter of primary school pupils and two-thirds of secondary school pupils in Ireland were nevertheless taught Irish in 1921; this was primarily a result of the introduction in 1913 of a pass in Irish as a requirement to enter the National University.[24]

The success of attempts to revive the use of the Irish language in the chosen areas prior to 1913 measures the validity of the relationship between cultural nationalism and republicanism. Reg Hindley has indicated that the ability to speak Irish among older age groups in 1911 must be considered a remnant of native speech, while a strong showing in younger age groups at this time largely represents the result of the activity of the Gaelic League. Not the number but the age of Irish speakers is thus the most important indicator of the success of cultural nationalism.

However, in areas where Irish was still the native tongue the value of this assessment is limited. The only county with a significant number of monoglot Irish speakers in 1911 was Mayo. Most of these 1,518 people indeed constituted remnants of the original Irish speaking population. Almost 61 per cent of them were aged sixty or over, and another 16 per cent were aged between forty and sixty. There were clearly fewer monoglot Irish speakers in the age classes below forty. Remarkably, however, 12.9 per cent of them were under ten. As a percentage of their age group, they were

---

24 For a discussion of the decline and the attempts to revive the Irish language, Reg Hindley (1990), passim.

more than three and a half times as predominant as among those between ten and thirty. The fact that the number of Irish speakers among those under six was more than double those between six and nine indicates that Irish was spoken in many homes, but that most of these children would learn English at school. They would then be represented in the group of those who spoke Irish as well as English. This is confirmed by the high number of young people who spoke Irish and English in Mayo. The age of monoglot Irish speakers thus gives no direct clue concerning the impact of cultural nationalism in Mayo. The age of those who spoke Irish as well as English could shed more light on this.[25]

In all five counties a relatively high number of those who spoke Irish as well as English were between ten and thirty years of age. Outside Mayo this indicates recent successes of the Irish-Ireland movement. This success was particularly strong in Wexford, where 57 per cent of Irish speakers were between ten and twenty years old, but also in Dublin where 40 per cent of them were in this age group. The next largest group of Irish speakers in both these counties was aged between twenty-one and twenty-nine. The absence in these two counties of a significant number of elderly people who spoke Irish proves that this ability was acquired outside the home. This is confirmed by the fact that south-east Wexford and Dublin City were among the few areas in southern Ireland where Irish was already extinct in 1800.[26]

In Derry and Tipperary, however, the largest group of English and Irish speakers in 1911 was actually aged over sixty, indicating that an indigenous Irish speaking population was still present. That the Irish-Ireland movement had nevertheless also been successful in these counties is indicated by the fact that the second largest group was invariably between ten and twenty years old, while Irish speakers aged below ten were far less numerous. These figures show that Irish was mainly acquired outside the home.

Table 4: Percentages of those speaking Irish and English in six age groups

	0-9	10-20	21-29	30-39	40-59	60+
Mayo: Irish only	13	3	2	5	16	61
Irish + English	5	19	10	12	24	30
South Tipperary	3	25	10	10	21	32
Wexford	9	57	15	9	7	3
Derry	5	24	16	12	17	28
Dublin City	5	40	24	15	12	5
County	5	45	21	13	11	5

25 Assessment of monoglot Irish speaking in older age groups as a remnant of native Irish, Reg Hindley (1990), 27.
26 Irish speakers in 1800, Reg Hindley (1990), 9.

The nationwide revival of the Irish language appears to have been most actively pursued in Wexford and Dublin City, although these counties had overall only a small number of Irish speakers (see Table 3). The relatively large presence of indigenous Irish speakers in the other three counties makes it impossible to assess the exact influence of the movement. In Derry, however, a small percentage of Irish speakers was combined with a high number of elderly speakers, which indicates a marginal impact of cultural nationalism. It is nevertheless obvious that in all other counties the language movement had made headway.

Confirmation of the above distribution of active Irish-Irelanders comes from the membership of the Gaelic League and the GAA as recorded by the local police. Although the figures are not always entirely accurate, they do provide a picture of general strength. In 1914 Irish-Irelanders were best organised in Wexford, where 1 per cent of Catholic males were mobilised in the Gaelic League and 2.5 per cent in the GAA. In Mayo this was 0.5 per cent and 1.3 per cent and in Tipperary 0.2 per cent and 0.7 per cent respectively. In Derry the first Irish class since the beginning of the Great War was only organised in the month of the Easter Rising, while no GAA club was recorded at all.[27]

It is clear that Wexford had a strong nationalist cultural organisation despite the high level of anglicisation, while Tipperary was a good second. Despite Mayo's high number of Irish speakers cultural organisations were weakly represented, while despite the absence of the Gaelic League the less political GAA was surprisingly well organised among Catholics in Derry. Although there does seem to be a connection between the vibrancy of the cultural and the republican organisations, there is none to the level of violence in the War of Independence.

Although radical nationalism remained a marginal phenomenon, interest in it was growing among young men in the early years of the century. The emergence of branches of Sinn Féin and the Irish American Alliance faction of the AOH, and the growth in organised expressions of the Irish-Ireland movement, demonstrate this. In most areas personality and charisma were crucial factors in the development of radicalism. Locally the lead was taken by activists with a flair for organisation, who were often given the role of decision makers. In the War of Independence they would often dominate the officers' corps of the Volunteers. Most of these initial activists were financially and socially independent. A group of people who

---

27 Although a few women were members of these organisations, the total of Catholic males is used to enable a comparison of the level of mobilisation in these groups to that in the Volunteers in Table 3. Membership figures of the Gaelic League and the GAA per county: CIs Mayo, South Tipperary, Wexford and Derry MRs 1916-21.

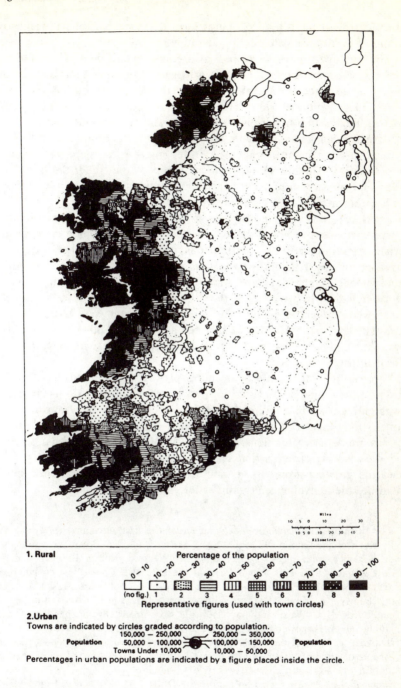

1. Rural

Percentage of the population

0 – 10   10 – 20   20 – 30   30 – 40   40 – 50   50 – 60   60 – 70   70 – 80   80 – 90   90 – 100

(no fig.)   1   2   3   4   5   6   7   8   9

Representative figures (used with town circles)

2.Urban

Towns are indicated by circles graded according to population.

	150,000 – 250,000	250,000 – 350,000	
Population	50,000 – 100,000	100,000 – 150,000	**Population**
	Towns Under 10,000	10,000 – 50,000	

Percentages in urban populations are indicated by a figure placed inside the circle.

Map 2: Irish Speakers by District Electorial Divisions in 1911

gathered around these leading figures formed the nucleus of political activity and of the future Volunteer organisation.[28]

The language movement, and to a lesser extent Sinn Féin and the GAA, were important first vehicles of organisation and radicalisation, but there was no direct relationship between the local strength of the Irish-Ireland movement and violent republicanism. The fact that within many types of organisation nationalists radicalised, and consequently tried to radicalise that organisation, accounts for this. Failing this, they left and joined or founded other organisations, where they might meet more men of similar persuasion. The history of the two factions of the AOH, the traditional Board of Erin section and the smaller but radical Irish American Alliance in Derry and Mayo, are examples of this.

From 1910 onwards, the IRB began to function as a coordinating body between activists in these organisations. Contacts with Dublin were an important stimulus for local leaders to link these groups together. The reorganisation of the IRB in 1910 was thus extended to the country, aided by men sent out to renew contacts with surviving members. Although most of the latter had little drive left in them, they provided useful local contacts. Those who had become local activators of radicalism were taken into the IRB, and their main efforts were directed at recruiting other locals into the organisation. The Fianna and the Irish American Alliance were the first objects of their attention.

As a result of these efforts an increasingly well-organised underground movement of republicans existed in most counties, particularly in provincial towns and cities. They were supplemented by a growing group of radicalised young men who had often had some military training in the Fianna or other militant organisations. Although the IRB had not planned or initiated the growing radicalisation of Irish nationalists, its revitalisation provided the growing group of militant nationalists with a framework which would be able to exploit opportunities for expansion.[29]

28 The financial and economic independence of the first activators: In Tipperary, Pierce McCan, Eamon O'Dwyer, Seán Treacy and Dan Breen were independent farmers whose fathers were dead. In Wexford, Robert Brennan had his own business. In Derry, Hugh Gribbin the local IRB Centre was an independent farmer and the Larkins were from a well-to-do and politically active farming family. In Mayo, Michael Kilroy was a blacksmith with a number of employees. Dick Walsh and Joe MacBride were financially independent. Owen Hughes in Aughagower was a farmer and his brother Charles in Westport was a shopkeeper. None of the other higher officers ever mentions any dependence on parents or attempts at control by them. This also applies to the leading men in Dublin who were all well over twenty.

29 Some of these young men who admitted to their lack of ideological interest: In Derry, Liam Brady, *Derry Journal*, 1 May 1953; and Interview. In Dublin, C.S. Andrews (1979), passim; 'Narrative of Edward O'Connor', NLI, ms. 17,506.

FOUNDATION

Central to determining the role of revolutionary nationalists in the establishment of the Volunteers are three questions. How was this radical militia organised; who were the people that took the initiative; in what way did the local population react? The foundation of the Irish National Volunteers in the Rotunda in Dublin on 25 November 1913 gave radical nationalists throughout Ireland a rallying point. Many had long been waiting for an opportunity to do something concrete to free Ireland: 'I read a lot and my father used to read all the Irish papers and passed them to me and I was really hoping for something like this so I joined the first night in the Rotunda.' From the moment the movement was launched radicals everywhere actively participated in its organisation. Many of the founding members in Dublin and throughout the country were IRB men, often initiating the local unit. However, the sprinkling of IRB circles throughout the country, mainly centred in the towns, meant that the start of the Volunteer organisation was slow and erratic.[30]

These radical connotations of the first organisers and the initial refusal of John Redmond, the leader of the Irish Party, to endorse the organisation scared off many nationalists. After getting several of his own men on the Volunteer Executive in June 1914, Redmond finally approved of the organisation, which then received a huge boost throughout Ireland. Nationalists of all hues joined, including constitutionalists, who outnumbered the revolutionists. Growth was so rapid that within a few months membership reached 160,000. This enthusiasm was to a large extent a response to the apparent refusal of the British Government to act against the Ulster Volunteers Force, who were threatening to resist the introduction of Home Rule. The strong growth of the Irish National Volunteers in Ulster in 1914 indicates this.[31]

The first major incident bringing home the risks involved in joining a militia was the Howth gun-running on 26 July 1914. The shooting of thirty-five civilians of whom three were killed, when the army tried to stop the importation of arms at Bachelors Walk in Dublin, caused anger and fear throughout the country. In Kerry Ernest Blythe found that: 'Mothers and fathers urged their sons not to have anything to do with a

30 Start of Irish Volunteers, Sean T. O'Kelly, 'Statement', NLI, ms. 27,711. Quote, 'Conversation with Lt. General Peadar MacMahon', UCD AD, P7D3. This also discusses the poor state of the IRB organisation in the country. In Limerick City where the public was hostile to the IRB, the organisation induced unsuspecting persons to set up the Volunteers branch in 1913 to attract constitutional nationalists, but made sure to have most of their own members elected on the leading committee, Michael Brennan (1980), 8.

31 The size of Irish National Volunteer membership, IG MR July 1914.

movement which looked more like being dangerous than it had hereto-
fore appeared.' After rumours had circulated locally that Volunteers would
be evicted, half of his eighty-strong company refrained from showing up
for parade the following Sunday. Contrary to Blythe's experience, Volunteers elsewhere record a sudden increase in the number of recruits
after this event. A Belfast man remembers a rush: 'The shooting in
Dublin seemed to have a great effect for the good of the Volunteers in
Belfast, as men here seemed to think after it that the position was becoming serious and that the purpose of the Volunteers was not mainly
playacting.'[32]

However, the late acceptance of the Volunteer force by the mainstream
nationalist party highlighted differences which soon split the organisation.
The founders of the organisation had been mainly radical nationalists and
members of the IRB who wanted to create an independent Irish Army. In
contrast to this, Redmond saw the organisation solely as an instrument for
exerting political pressure. Differences between these two strains became
apparent at the outbreak of the First World War. The Executive of the
Irish National Volunteers failed to agree on the policy regarding the British
war effort. When Redmond called upon all Volunteers to join the British
Army in defence of small nations in his Woodenbridge speech of 20
September 1914, only part of the Volunteer Executive could assent to this,
and the organisation split from top to bottom.

The largest group of Irish National Volunteers supported Redmond and
left the organisation to form the National Volunteers. This organisation
became practically defunct shortly after many of its active members joined
the British Army in response to Redmond's call. The much smaller and
more radical group, which included many of the original founders of the
organisation, remained in what was now known as the Irish Volunteers.
Events after 1912 had fuelled their discontent with the political activities of
their fathers' generation so strongly that they were unwilling to follow
Redmond in his support of the British. To them the mere promise of
Home Rule was insufficient reward to warrant any cooperation with 'the
oppressor'. The most radical part of their Executive saw the involvement of
England in the First World War as an ideal opportunity for an attempt to
gain complete independence for Ireland by force of arms and began to prepare a rebellion. However, only 10,000 to 15,000 at most of the original
160,000 members of the Irish National Volunteers supported the Irish
Volunteers, and many of these potential members were left outside the
organisation in the confusion that followed the Split. Most recent informa-

32 Quote from Kerry, Ernest Blythe, 'Statement', 11, UCD AD, P24/1783. Quote
   from Belfast, Rory Haskins, 'Statement', Fr O'Kane Papers, AARC. Similar events
   in Tipperary, Fr Michael Maher, Diary 1914, St Patrick's College, Thurles.

tion indicates that the remaining membership may have been as low as 2,000 to 3,000.[33]

DERRY AFTER THE SPLIT

The Volunteer Split of 1914 had a devastating effect on the organisation in Derry. In the city most members of the Irish National Volunteers joined the British Army or the constitutional National Volunteers. In many rural parts of Derry the radical Irish Volunteers disappeared completely. The strong response to the founding of the Irish National Volunteers in Ulster had become apparent in May 1914 when the police recorded 3,393 members in Co. Derry, and further growth had followed the endorsement by Redmond. The disastrous consequences of the Split were shown in August 1915 when the Irish Volunteers were left with 111 men, while the National Volunteers still had 4,605.[34]

Apart from their role in establishing the original Volunteers, IRB men from Dublin and Belfast took an active part in rebuilding the organisation in Ulster in 1915. As well as organising the Volunteers in Belfast, men from the city were sent out to establish units throughout the province. At the same time Ernest Blythe was appointed organiser for Ulster by the Dublin IRB. As they did after 1910, these organisers visited existing IRB circles which again served as local contacts for information about 'the fall of the people'. Acting on this information, they again took young men into the IRB. In some cases they also attempted to start a Volunteer company,

33 The consequences of the Split in various counties: Ernest Blythe, 'Statement', 18, UCD AD, P24/1783. In Ballylanders, Co. Limerick, Liam Manohan, 'Statement', UCD AD, P17a149. In East Tyrone, W.J. Kelly Sr, 'Statement', Fr O'Kane Papers, AARC; Rev. James O'Daly, 'Statement', Ibidem. In Letterkenny, Dr J.P. McGinley, 'Statement', Ibidem. In Carrickmore, west Tyrone, W. Loughran, NLI, ms. 17,506. In Belfast only men who had joined after the Howth gun-running remained with them. The followers of Redmond for whom they had had to open regular recruiting offices early in 1914 almost all left, Rory Haskins, 'Statement', Fr O'Kane Papers, AARC; Denis McCullough, 'Statement', NLI, ms. 27,729. In Newmarket, Co. Cork only 8 Volunteers out of 200 were left after the Split, Sean Moylan, 'Statement', NLI, ms. 27,731. Similarly the Volunteers in Naas and Kill dwindled to only 10 men after the Split, James Dunne, NLI, P4548. In Co. Sligo they were reduced to 4 small units, Frank Carty, NLI, P913 A0178. The police put Irish Volunteers strength after the Split at 10,000, and shortly before the Rising at 15,063, PRO, CO904/13. Traditional estimates of membership of the Irish Volunteers after the Split, Dorothy Macardle (1937), 115. Latest figures, Charles Townshend (1983), 279.

34 Men leaving the Irish Volunteers after the Split in Derry City, Liam A. Brady, *Derry Journal*, 1 May 1953; Lt. M. Sheerin, NLI, P921 No.66. Volunteer membership in Derry, CI Derry MRs 1914-16.

but mostly they left this to the local men. In this sense the IRB functioned as a marker of activity by using the existing circles for information, and as an initiator of new activity when promising young men were taken in and encouraged to start a Volunteer company. The important role of outside men in establishing the organisation is evident.[35]

Most attention in 1915 was thus concentrated on reorganising the leadership at local level. Although a disproportionately high number of the original officers had remained with the Irish Volunteers after the Split, there was not a full organisation left. The high percentage of radical officers throughout the country was an indication of the strong involvement of the IRB in the initial organisation, when its members had been ordered to stand as candidates in elections for officers and to vote 'en bloc' for their own men. However, a full officer staff in Derry in 1915, including brigade, battalion and company officers, would encompass almost the entire membership known to the police. The activities of the organisers had some marginal success only at the end of 1915, as testified by the increase from 111 to 194 members detected by the police in January 1916.[36]

Ernest Blythe, the IRB organiser, experienced serious difficulties in finding willing men in Ulster. He had little information on local radicals, and without their support it was practically impossible to start anything. His attempt at organising Derry in 1915 is a case in point. He started in Magherafelt, where he visited Louis Smith, a well-known member of the old IRB. He in turn introduced Blythe to a young cousin of his, Tom Larkin from Belagherty, whom Blythe swore into the IRB. This young man started to organise the movement locally; he soon became captain of the local company and would later head the battalion.

In neighbouring Newbridge Blythe found a group of eager young men

35 Sending out organisers in Ulster, Ernest Blythe, 'Statement', 17, UCD AD, P24/1783; Paddy Larkin, Interview; W.J. Kelly Sr, 'Statement', Fr O'Kane Papers, AARC. Visits of prominent men from Dublin and Belfast, like Roger Casement, Eoin MacNeill, Chief of Staff of the Irish Volunteers and Denis McCullough president of the Supreme Council of the IRB, giving speeches, assistance and encouragement to the organisation on many occasions, are mentioned by, Rev. Canon James O'Daly, 'Statement', Fr O'Kane Papers, AARC. Visiting old IRB men, Ernest Blythe, 'Statement', 17-18, UCD AD, P24/1783. Among these local contacts were a number of radical priests, Rev. James O'Daly, 'Statement', Fr O'Kane Papers, AARC; Denis McCullough, 'Statement', NLI, ms. 27,729.

36 Successful reorganisation was recorded in Tyrone, Rev. Cannon James O'Daly, 'Statement', Fr O'Kane Papers, AARC; W. Loughran, NLI, ms. 17,506. In other areas 'there was nothing doing', Dr J.P. McGinley, 'Statement', Fr O'Kane Papers, AARC. In Castlebar, Co. Mayo most men joined the National Volunteers but the leaders remained with the Irish Volunteers, James Chambers, 'Statement'. Membership Derry, CI Derry MRs August 1915 and January 1916.

around Hugh Gribbin, an active local IRB Centre. From this group came the officers' corps and most active members of the Volunteers around Newbridge. A couple of miles away in Gulladuff Blythe met and took into the IRB Hugh McGurk. After thus completing his activities in this area, he went on to Derry City ignoring the Protestant-dominated northern half of the county. While helping the ailing company of Volunteers in the city, a letter from McGurk asked him to address a meeting. He agreed and went back to Gulladuff: 'We held the meeting in the dead of night in the middle of a bog. There seemed to me to be forty or fifty present, and we actually discussed the possibilities of coming out in the open with the formation of a Volunteer Company.' Following this meeting a company was indeed started, which tried to instigate activity in neighbouring areas by military displays. These three units formed in 1915 would form the backbone of Volunteer activity in south Derry during the War of Independence.[37]

DEVELOPMENTS ELSEWHERE

In the other areas covered by this book developments proceeded along similar lines. Although information about the Volunteers in Wexford in this period is scant, the evolution of the movement there was comparable. Branches of the Irish National Volunteers were started in the towns by existing activists and were later extended to the countryside. The same influx into the Volunteers after the Howth gun-running and Redmond's endorsement was seen. Strong growth in the number of branches had brought in 43 units in July 1914, but a big fall-off followed the Split, when the Irish Volunteers had only 40 men left in the entire county. By August 1915 membership had risen to 178 in four branches. At the end of 1915 a somewhat larger increase than in Derry took place, to 319 in seven units.[38]

In Tipperary, the movement was begun with a visit from Sean MacDermot one of the leading men from Dublin soon after the start of the Volunteers. The initiative was then taken up by local IRB members. In Ballagh

37 Ernest Blythe, 'Statement', 20, UCD AD, P24/1783. The visit of an organiser to south Derry before the existence of a Volunteer company is confirmed by, James Harkin, Fr O'Kane Papers, Tape A9, AARC. The authorities considered Ernest Blythe, together with Denis McCullough, Herbert Pim and Liam Mellows, as the most effective agents of the Irish Volunteers, and ordered them to leave the country on 10 July 1915, NAD, CBS/Box 24.

38 Membership, 'Chronology' compiled for the Bureau of Military History, Dublin; CI Wexford MRs 1914-16. See also Robert Brennan (1950), 31-60; 'Military Service Pension Board Statement in support of the Enniscorthy Volunteers', T.D. Sinnott Papers, Wexford County Library.

Eamon O'Dwyer, active in many organisations in the three parishes around his home, called a meeting and a company was started. Soon afterwards this company began to assist others to organise units in surrounding areas. Through the Gaelic League, O'Dwyer had already met Seán Treacy who had started to organise the Volunteers around Tipperary town some ten miles away. They and a few other local organisers then became involved in expanding the Volunteers further and linking existing branches. In May 1914 the Irish National Volunteers had 2,000 members in south Tipperary.[39]

The Bachelors Walk shootings in Dublin led to an increase in membership, while the Split left only a few men in the Irish Volunteers. In the words of a local curate involved in the Irish National Volunteers: 'I am pleased to record that not many were led away by them and when the matter came to a crisis the anti-Redmondites were routed and Thurles declared for Mr. Redmond and the Irish Party.' According to Eamon O'Dwyer, only two companies remained with the Irish Volunteers.[40]

Some time after this an attempt to establish new units was made on the ruins of the Irish National Volunteers' organisation. As a result, some form of battalion organisation was again evident around O'Dwyer's home in 1915, and he was aware of the presence of similarly loosely organised battalions in other parts of Tipperary. Pierce McCan headed one of these; he had been the only other leader able to hold together the company under his command mainly consisting of men working on his estate after the Split. These local leaders were occasionally visited by men from Dublin. Under their instruction a county brigade was formed in 1915 and McCan was appointed commandant. Although there was some limited contact with other centres in the county, their efforts did no more than sustain the organisation for most of 1914 and 1915.[41]

The police indeed failed to detect any evidence of the existence of Irish

---

39 A visit by Sean MacDermot to Tipperary Town in November 1913 is mentioned as the start of the movement, Sean Fitzpatrick, UCD AD, P7D109; P.C. Power (1989), 201. The police put the start of an Irish National Volunteer branch in Tipperary Town in April 1914. They claim the movement started in Fethard and around Cashel where Pat O'Mahony, the IRB Head-Centre for Tipperary, was considered to be the prime mover, CI South Tipperary MRs 1913-14. For events around Ballagh, Eamon O'Dwyer, 'Statement'; D. Ryan (1945), 18-21.

40 Quote, Fr Michael Maher, Diary 1914, St Patrick's College Thurles. See also CI South Tipperary MRs July-September 1914.

41 Units remaining with Irish Volunteers, D. Ryan (1945), 18-20; Eamon O'Dwyer, 'Statement'. On Pierce McCan's company and visits of national leaders, Paul Mulcahy, 'Statement'. O'Dwyer mentions a visit of the same Ernest Blythe who was active in Ulster to Tipperary in 1915, Eamon O'Dwyer, 'Statement'. In Nenagh, north Tipperary some men were willing, but there was no Irish Volunteers organisation after the Split, Sean Gaynor, 'Statement'.

Volunteers in southern Tipperary until the end of 1915. By January 1916 the RIC and the same Thurles curate had become aware of 380 Irish Volunteers in five units under the leadership of the men previously mentioned. These were: one in Ballagh under Eamon O'Dwyer, one under Pierce McCan around Cashel, one in Fethard, one in Clonmel under Frank Drohan and one near Tipperary town under Seán Treacy.[42]

The initially poor response to the Irish Volunteers was largely a consequence of the hostile environment in which they had to operate. In a time when so many Irishmen were fighting in the Great War, most people considered the anti-British campaign of the Volunteers as a form of treason, particularly in the towns of south Tipperary where many soldiers were stationed. In addition, it was felt that the activities of the Volunteers would jeopardise the introduction of Home Rule. This hostility was experienced at close quarters when, at a parade of Volunteers from all over the South-west held in Limerick in May 1915, the local population pelted the men with refuse.[43]

In Mayo the first Volunteer units were started in February 1914 at meetings in Castlebar and Newport. Colonel Maurice Moore, an organiser from Dublin with Mayo roots and a former colonel in the British Army who had become heavily involved in the Volunteer movement, arrived to supervise proceedings. Soon after this companies were formed in towns throughout the county. The group of radicals that had emerged previously took the lead again, starting the Volunteers by enlisting their own family and friends. Old IRB members like Michael MacEvilly from Castlebar enlisted his three sons. In Westport the IRB ordered its members to join the Volunteers immediately and take control of the organisation. In practice this meant that the IRB men actually started the Volunteers there.[44]

When the Split came most Volunteers sided with Redmond and joined the National Volunteers. The few units that remained with the Irish Volunteers were often directed to do so by their officers. In Westport the local branch was reviewed and addressed by Major MacBride shortly after Redmond's Woodenbridge speech. The majority stayed with the Irish Volunteers; no branch of the National Volunteers was even set

42 The five branches of Volunteers at the end of 1915, CI South Tipperary MR January 1916; Fr Michael Maher, Diary 1915, St Patrick's College Thurles.

43 Opposition of constitutionalists to the Volunteers was reported by the police in Clonmel, when the efforts of the younger members of the AOH to start a branch of the Volunteers were frustrated by the older members, CI South Tipperary MR May 1914. Parading in Limerick, Dan Breen (1981), 30; Michael Brennan (1980), 11.

44 Maurice Moore in Mayo, CI Mayo MRs 1914. In Newport, Michael Kilroy, 'The Awakening'. Volunteers in Westport initiated by the IRB, Ned Moane, 'Statement'.

up. Some of the active men in Newport had refused to join the Irish
National Volunteers in 1913; considering the people involved not radical
enough, they remained with the Irish American Alliance. Only after the
1914 Split did they decide to enrol, and some were then invited to join
the IRB.[45]

The few remaining units attempted to rebuild the organisation mainly
by approaching relatives of members living in neighbouring areas. The
Cumann na mBan used similar tactics. A branch of this organisation was
started in Newport when the wife of Michael Kilroy, the local Volunteer
captain, was visited by the sister of Ned Moane, one of the principal men
in Westport. Nevertheless a wider bond, transcending these kinship groups,
began to develop during 1915. In the search for recruits, attention shifted
towards taking in malleable youngsters.[46]

Despite the survival of the Irish Volunteers' company, the Fianna
became the principal agent of radicalism in Westport after the Split. At the
inception of the Fianna branch in 1915, their commanding officer told the
members they were to become soldiers for Ireland. Accordingly, they were
put through intense training, parading and a lecture scheme which included
Morse code, first aid and military drill exercises. Many of the 1921 fighting
men of the West Mayo Brigade came from Westport, and got their first
training in this Fianna branch. Some had been active in the AOH before,
and many of its officers had been or were taken into the IRB. In Castlebar,
where the first branch of the Volunteers in Mayo had been organised, some
of the most radical youngsters actually transferred from the Volunteers to
the Fianna following the Split.[47]

To promote the movement, Mayo was visited by several leaders of the
Irish Volunteers during 1915. Under their auspices a county brigade was
formed in Castlebar in August or September, led by Anthony MacBride
and Dick Walsh, who had both been previously involved in Sinn Féin and
the IRB. In May 1915 the ties with Dublin were reinforced when the
Castlebar branch of the Fianna attended the funeral of O'Donovan Rossa,

45 Reaction to Split in Westport, Ned Moane, 'Statement'. Events in Newport,
   Michael Kilroy, 'The Awakening'. The police report the forming of two
   branches of the AOH Irish American Alliance, one in Newport and one in
   Glenisland, and one branch of the rival Board of Erin in March 1914, CI Mayo
   MR March 1914. The fact that the radical faction of the AOH seemed more
   successful than the Volunteers might be a result of the initial refusal of radicals
   to join the Volunteers.
46 Women's organisation, 'Statement of Michael Kilroy's wife'. In Derry City the
   Cumann na mBan were led by the wife of the company captain, Liam A. Brady,
   Derry Journal, 4 May 1953. Many young Volunteers in several areas stated they
   had joined simply because they were taken along by friends or family.
47 Fianna in Westport, Brodie Malone, O'MN, P17b109, and Moane/Malone,
   Tape. Fianna in Castlebar, James Chambers, 'Statement'.

an old Fenian leader. In the countryside there were still few Volunteer companies, Aughagower, with its strong personal ties to Westport, being one of the few exceptions. During the rest of this year the few active Volunteers occupied themselves mainly by attending small training camps and lectures.[48]

According to police reports a rapid growth followed Colonel Moore's visit to Mayo. Irish National Volunteers branches numbered fourteen in May and forty-six in July 1914. After Redmond's endorsement the County Inspector of the RIC remarked that the organisation became rather chaotic, with all shades of nationalist politics joining. After the Split, the police never bothered to register the Irish Volunteers separately, simply stating that most National Volunteers branches were following Redmond. In December 1915 the reorganisation attempts had been successful and four branches of the Irish Volunteers with a stronghold in Westport were identified by the authorities. In the same month the National Volunteers decreased from sixty-two to fifty-five branches. In 1916 the Irish Volunteers started with four units, lost one in February and then gained two in March, the five units had 121 men known to the police in the month of the Rising. This extremely small number compared to the Volunteers elsewhere may be explained by the fact that in the same month the radical Irish American Alliance faction of the AOH grew from three branches, with a hundred members, to six branches with 317 members.[49]

In Dublin, the centre of radical politics, the Volunteers were also seriously depleted by the Split. One of the main officers remembers that the Dublin Brigade had nevertheless 350 men left. Despite the decline at the end of 1914, the numbers grew quite rapidly to about 1,500 by the end of 1915. The experience of Liam Tammin, a Volunteer in the Donnybrook Company under Eamon de Valéra, is typical of the few activists who remained with the Irish Volunteers after the Split:

> The majority weren't present the night of the split. [There were] speeches by both sides, and we divided. DeV [Eamon de Valéra] had a majority of 2 or 3 and as [the] AOH owned the Hall, we had to get out. About 50 on our side [...] mostly young and our fathers and

48 Visits national leaders, Ned Moane, 'Statement'. Visit Castlebar Fianna to funeral in Dublin, James Chambers, 'Statement'. Some Volunteers from Ballinalee, Co. Cork went as well, 'History of Sinn Féin Movement in West Cork, 1915-1918', NLI, ms. 15,344. One officer states that Westport, Castlebar, Newport, Kilmeena and Aughagower were the only existing companies in the beginning of 1915, Ned Moane, Moane/Malone, Tape. Activities in 1915, Michael Kilroy, 'The Awakening'.
49 Membership of Volunteers, CI Mayo MRs 1914-16.

mothers advised [us] to keep away. The next parade [we had] 25 till it reached 7. At a field opposite Donnybrook Church DeV solemnly made us form fours. DeV told each of us to be a recruiting sergeant. The remnants of the Dundrum Company came in. [...] We became about 40. [...] I was elected O.C. gazetted in the Irish Volunteer as Company Commander and I had the Company then until Easter Week [it] grew to 68.

Unlike the Donnybrook Company, many companies of the Irish National Volunteers in Dublin that had not been under such radical leadership disappeared completely after the Split. Other companies that had remained with the Irish Volunteers lost steam, leaving them with few members and no clear objective. In one case a company petered out after its secretary joined the British Army. The Dublin organisation nevertheless became strong enough to resist the Crown Forces for almost a week during the 1916 Rising.[50]

CONCLUSION

Since the turn of the century small groups of radical nationalists were continuously active in promoting their ideas and attempting to organise others behind their ideals. An important step in their successful mobilisation of the population after 1916 was the reinvigorating of the IRB in 1910. This secret society united radicals throughout the country in one organisation and provided them with a common direction. Although their number grew and they were increasingly successful in enlisting new members, it took a set of favourable circumstances for these few radicals – who can probably be found in most societies in any era – to have an impact on the political scene.

When the Volunteers were founded these dedicated men and women, with a long history of involvement in radical politics, took the lead in setting up branches, often with the support of men sent from Dublin. Under instruction they tried, often successfully, to get elected as officers supported by an IRB bloc-vote. After the Split in the Irish National Volunteers few stayed with the radical faction, although a relatively large portion of the officers, especially in Dublin, remained. The continuation

50 Number of Dublin Volunteers in 1915, UCD AD, LA 9. Quote, Liam Tammin, O'MN, P17b91. Pat MacCrea claims that 90 per cent of his 'B' Company 2nd Battalion sided with Pearse, Pat MacCrea, O'MN, P17b110. See also Seamus Fox, O'MN, P17b106. Secretary joining British Army, Jack Plunkett, 'Statement', NLI, ms. 11,981.

of Irish Volunteers' units largely depended on the leadership of these local officers. In the provincial areas Irish Volunteers were so scarce that only nuclei of activists were left. After an interlude in the doldrums, they began serious reorganisation with the aid of organisers from Dublin towards the end of 1915.[51]

After the few remaining units, mainly concentrated in the towns, had been revitalised they tried to encourage neighbouring areas to start units by approaching relatives. Recruits outside the circle of friends and family were originally attracted by the public displays of drilling and parading. New Volunteers brought in their own men, and were asked who they thought suitable for admission. Large-scale meetings, which were held by the movement to mobilise political support, were also an opportunity for recruitment. National figures, enjoying an even higher level of respect than the original activators, were its main attraction. These meetings, a highlight in village social life, attracted everyone in the area regardless of their convictions. Despite all these efforts the organisation remained extremely localised and its strength varied widely throughout the country, being most successful in Dublin, rural Tipperary and several provincial towns elsewhere. By the outbreak of the rebellion in Easter 1916 membership was still no more than the originally estimated maximum of 15,000 supporters.

In all organising efforts from 1900 to 1916 the role of outside organisers was of crucial importance, on a local as well as on a national level. Despite the presence of radicals in most communities, few units started spontaneously. It was almost impossible for such radicals to organise and activate local people in a Volunteer company without outside assistance. The number of dedicated radical nationalists was extremely limited, and even after forming a company it was difficult to get the few willing youths to follow their command. One of the organisers described this same problem in 1919: 'The men were raw and did not know anything about military work, their officers had not been "blooded", did not know more than their men and hence, as knowledge begets confidence, they were utterly incapable of handling them.' The outside organisers, often well-educated men, possessed a natural authority partly by their membership of the somewhat mythical IRB organisation and partly just by the sheer fact that they were not members of the local community with its petty antagonisms. This enabled them

---

51 The absence of units of the Irish Volunteers in many other country areas after the Split, C. Browne (n. d.), 1; Liam Haugh, 'History of the West Clare Brigade', NLI, P915 A0363; Frank Carty, 'Statement', NLI, P913 A0178. Re-emergence of companies in other than the selected areas: In Macroom, Co. Cork, C. Browne (n. d.), 1. In Glenmore, Co. Kilkenny, John Power, Mrs Gassin, and Peter Mernagh, NLI, ms. 22,116. Other example of Volunteer units organised at the end of 1915 by men from Dublin, Liam Haugh, 'History of the West Clare Brigade', NLI, P915 A0363.

to initiate a company where locals had failed, while their endorsement provided the local officers with some authority.[52]

The Easter Rising itself was a dramatic gesture with little military impact. Due to poor coordination, only units from Wexford and Galway and the Dublin men participated in the hostilities. This was largely a result of the confusion which followed a countermanding order issued by Eoin MacNeill, the more moderate chief of staff, a day before the uprising. He had only become aware of what was about to happen less than a week before. After five days of heavy fighting in Dublin, all rebels surrendered and subsequently thousands of radical nationalists were arrested throughout the country.

52 Quote, C.K.H. O'Malley (1989), 7.

CHAPTER 2

Public Defiance, 1916-1918

The Volunteer organisation was practically obliterated by the Rising. Fifteen of its leaders were executed, many core members in the country were convicted to long terms of imprisonment, and almost 2,000 men and five women, many of them with no connection to the Volunteers, were interned in large camps. There was no centre of organisation and all public activity was banned.[1]

However, the mood of the population had changed considerably. After the executions of the principal leaders of the rebellion a wave of sympathy swept the country, putting republicans in a much more favourable position. A number of Volunteers were convinced that the Rising had not been the end but only the beginning of the road to freedom. They were not deterred, but rather inspired by the reaction of the British Government.

FIRST EXPRESSIONS

Although open Volunteer activity was impossible immediately after the Rising, minor gestures of public disobedience were made. The flying of the tricolour, the newly adopted flag and symbol of the Irish Republic, was a popular way of doing so. Already on 19 June 1916 republican flags were carried in Dublin to a Mass for the executed leaders, and police attempts to seize the flags led to serious clashes with the public. Although no organised Volunteer activity is recorded, many people showed their admiration by attending the many fund-raising functions held to aid the dependants of the dead and imprisoned.[2]

In the final months of 1916 the only noticeable activity of radical nationalists in most counties was organised by the GAA and the Gaelic League. Many football matches were held at which occasional expressions

1 Intelligence Notes 1916 PRO, CO903/19.
2 Flags seized in Dublin, Larry Nugent, O'MN, P17b88. See also C.S. Andrews (1979), 90. In other areas the flying of the tricolour was observed as well: In Derry, Liam Brady, Oral History Project, Tape 24B, Heritage Library, Derry City. In Tipperary, Ned Prendergast, Interview; Ned O'Reilly, O'MN, P17b126.

of sympathy with the movement were voiced. In the winter months, the Gaelic League became more active in organising Irish classes led by men connected with Sinn Féin. The proceedings of these organisations attracted more interest than in previous years, and the police followed this with apprehension:

> A discontented and rebellious spirit is wide spread, and though to a great extent suppressed, it frequently comes to the surface at Gaelic Athletic Association Tournaments when large numbers of young men of military age are assembled together. On such occasions the Irish Republican badge is conspicuously worn, and seditious songs and cries of 'Up the Rebels', 'to Hell with England', etc. are indulged in.[3]

Wexford was particularly active. In northern Wexford, where the Volunteers had staged a serious fight during the Rising, feelings of dissent were observed by the police in the autumn of 1916. A number of threatening letters were sent to people who had opposed the Rising. Some men were charged with singing seditious songs, and others for defacing a recruitment poster. The local police attributed this restlessness to the recent release of some internees. In November two Manchester Martyrs meetings were held, with 300 people attending in Enniscorthy and thirty to forty and a band in New Ross. Most other counties also saw some attempts at mobilising support for republicans, but in Mayo no activity was reported. No public meetings were noted and even the annual Manchester Martyrs commemoration went unobserved. This absence of Gaelic League and GAA activity in Mayo in 1916 is consistent with the absence of these organisations as meeting points for radical nationalists in the founding period.[4]

REORGANISATION

Despite the forceful measures of the authorities, tentative attempts to reorganise Volunteer units were made within a couple of months of the Rising. The success of these efforts strongly depended on local conditions. Different counties had been diversely affected by the arrests. Areas that had shown somewhat more activity during the Rising, such as Wexford, were almost

---

3   Sinn Féin connection with Irish classes, IG MRs 1916. Quote, IG MR September 1916.
4   For events in various counties, CIs Wexford, Mayo, South Tipperary and Derry MRs 1916. The Manchester Martyrs meetings commemorated the execution of three Irishmen in Manchester in 1867. They were accused of involvement in an attempt to rescue some Fenian prisoners in which a policeman was killed.

completely stripped of their active membership. In most counties, however, only a few officers had been arrested and nuclei of organisation remained. Nevertheless, police control was tight, and only some determined men came together to discuss the (re-)start of local branches. Those involved lacked direction and were uncertain about which step to take next. In Dublin, some attempts to reorganise units and a national executive were made in August 1916 by those who had evaded arrest.[5]

The majority of the interned men and women were released during the summer of 1916, but when the remaining 569 Volunteers were let go at Christmas serious reorganisation became possible. Local units were revived and a provisional executive was appointed. Despite the initial feelings of despair following the Easter debacle, most of the internees returned home in fighting sprit. Their time spent in camps with many other radical nationalists had had a galvanising effect and cemented a shared conviction that they should try again and improve on their previous attempt. Strong personal bonds had been forged during internment which served as a basis for the continuation of the organisation, and they had been allowed to discuss tactics, train and follow lectures on the 'art of warfare'. It was this experience which gave the main internment camp in Frongoch, Wales, the nickname 'University of Revolution'. The failure of most country units to take part in the Rising gave many Volunteers the feeling that they had let their comrades down, and they were now looking for a second chance. This feeling was exacerbated by British military who teased the returned Volunteers in Tipperary with their version of the 'Soldiers' Song': 'Soldiers are we, who nearly fought for Ireland.'[6]

The indiscriminate arrests in 1916 substantially eased reorganisation. They had associated men from all over the country with the movement and had made soldiers of nationalists armed solely with enthusiasm. Having fought in or being arrested following the Rising also gave these men much respect and admiration, particularly among the young men eager to earn their share of glory. They were the natural choice when local officers were sought. Seamus Robinson, who had fought in the Rising in Dublin, was invited by the principal men in south Tipperary early in 1917 to come down as an organiser. His dedication had impressed them during their shared internment. When a brigade was formed there in 1918 he became its commander. On a national level Eamon de Valéra experienced a similar effect. As the only surviving commandant of the Dublin Rising, he was elected president of both the Irish

5 Reorganising efforts in Dublin, Joe O'Connor, O'MN, P17b105.
6 Releases, Intelligence Notes 1916 PRO, CO903/19. Establishing provisional executive, T. Bowden (1973), 14; Joe O'Connor, O'MN, P17b105; Michael Lynch, 'Statement', NLI, ms. 22,117/1, and NLI, P913 A0130. 'Teasing by soldiers', Seamus Robinson, 'Statement', NLI, ms. 21,265.

Volunteers and Sinn Féin in October 1917 at their first conventions since the Rising.[7]

However, having been arrested after the Rising was no guarantee of one's willingness to act. A Volunteer in Wellington Bridge, Co. Wexford blamed the lack of activity in an adjoining area on the local leader: 'He was no use in the world, but he had been accidentally arrested and that is how he got his name.' Among the Volunteers in Wexford it became extremely important who had and who had not been 'out in 1916'. The antagonism which sprang from this created internal tensions that soon paralysed the organisation. This was first experienced by Robert Brennan when he selected a man without experience in the Rising to become his vice-commandant; a mutiny of junior officers who had been out and felt passed over followed.[8]

Although reorganisation still largely depended on local initiative, the IRB was again the main instrument by which the loose threads of the organisation were pulled together. The existing IRB circles often formed the core for Volunteer companies. Veterans recall the first attempts at reorganisation, when the known activists from a considerable area were called together by the principal organisers. The experience of Patrick Ryan in the eastern part of south Tipperary may be indicative of this:

> On a night in the early summer of 1917 I attended a meeting which was held in a place called Downey's Barn at Cramps Castle, Fethard. This meeting was called for the purpose of organising an Irish Volunteer company in Fethard and district, and, if I mistake not, the late Paddy Hogan of Cashel, afterwards Commandant of the 2nd Battalion, was one of those principally concerned in arranging the

---

7   On increased standing of prisoners, Tommy Ryan, 'Statement'. Experience of Seamus Robinson, Eamon O'Dwyer, 'Statement'; 'Conversation with Lt. Col. Tom Ryan, 7th August 1963', UCD AD, P7D1080, Seamus Robinson, 'Statement', Appendix XI, NLI, ms. 21,265; D. Ryan (1945), 48. In Derry City interned men took control of the organisation, Liam A. Brady, *Derry Journal*, 6 May 1953, and Oral History Project, Tape 24B, Heritage Library, Derry City; Lt. M. Sheerin, NLI, P913 A0153. For those interned in Frongoch, Sean O Mahony (1987), Appendix 1.

8   Quote, Mark Killilea, O'MN, P17b109. See also Frank Henderson, O'MN, P17b99. Mutiny in Wexford, Robert Brennan (1950), 156. In west Cork internal disputes between men who had and who had not surrendered their arms after the Rising led to the virtual disappearance of a local company, 'History of Sinn Féin Movement in West Cork', 9, NLI, ms. 15,344. In Limerick, the same problems led to the founding of a rival company, which was set up because the two groups refused to drill together, Michael Brennan (1980), 21. Some interned men felt forced to renew their activities because employers refused to take them on, C.S. Andrews (1979), 102-3; Larry Nugent, O'MN, P17b88; 'History of Sinn Féin Movement in West Cork, 1915-1918', NLI, ms. 15,344; Liam Brady, Oral History Project, Tape 24A, Heritage Library, Derry City.

meeting. He was certainly present that night and was, as far as I can now remember, the principal speaker. The meeting itself was a small one, as for obvious reasons only a selected number of men were invited to attend. I should say, however, that there were about 20 men present, all of whom agreed to become members of the Volunteer organisation. In the election of officers which followed I was elected as Captain of the company.[9]

Simultaneously men in inactive areas who were thought to be willing and able to start a company were approached. The obvious starting point, both locally when initiating a company and regionally when setting up a battalion, was often a relative. The experience of Thomas Ryan from south Tipperary provides a prime example of this tendency. He had always been involved in organising all kinds of activity and was a natural leader in his community. In 1914, he had been the captain of the local Irish National Volunteers company, but the organisation disappeared after the Split because there was nobody around his area willing to join the Irish Volunteers. As a result, he was not involved in the movement in 1916. However, being related to Seán Treacy by marriage made him an obvious choice when Treacy was looking for a local contact to set up the Volunteers in his district in 1917:

Some time about April, 1917, Seán Treacy made a few trips to the locality and suggested the organising of a Volunteer unit there. On his second visit to us, he gave us an outline of the organisation and generally encouraged us, pointing out what should be done and how to do it. Treacy came to Ned McGrath of Cahir who afterwards became Battalion Commandant of the 6th Battalion, and he spent two days between McGrath's place and mine trying to organise that Battalion.

As a result of Treacy's visit, the Battalion was formed with Ned McGrath as the Battalion Commandant. I was Vice-Commandant; [...] This was really the beginning of my career in the Volunteer Movement.

9 There were 350 IRB circles in 1917, L. Ó Broin (1976), 178. Quote, Patrick Ryan, 'Statement'. The methods of setting up new branches is also mentioned by a close associate of Seán Treacy, Paul Merrigan, Interview. A similar call to the known activists to reorganise went out in west Mayo, Michael Kilroy, 'The Awakening'. In Dublin veterans were ordered to reorganise in December 1916, Michael Lynch, 'Statement', NLI, ms. 22,117/1; B. Whelan, MA, A0159; Jimmy Murray (The Turk), O'MN, P17b106.

10 Quote, Tommy Ryan, 'Statement'. Other examples of the use of relatives are found in the extension of the IRB movement in south Derry mentioned before; The relation between the Hughes brothers and their sons and nephews in Westport and Aughagower in Co Mayo; The blood ties between Dublin leaders and the original leading men in Mayo discussed before; In Tipperary, Paul Mulcahy, 'Statement'.

> Following Treacy's instructions, we set to work from then on to
> organise Companies in the surrounding parishes, to appoint officers
> for these and to direct their training.[10]

Besides this externally led organisation, companies were started independently by small groups of men with radical leanings who had been inspired
by the Rising. Tom Maguire from Cross, Co. Mayo was one of them: 'The
Easter insurrection came to me like a bolt from the blue. I will never forget
my exhilaration, it was a turning point in my life. To think that Irishmen,
were fighting England on the streets of Dublin: I thanked God for seeing
such a day.' He subsequently began to visit Sinn Féin and Volunteer meetings as far afield as Galway, and when he got a small group of like-minded
people together in his own parish they started small drilling exercises on
Sundays after Mass. This attracted other young men who came up to them
to ask whether they could join. After having started a company in this way
in his home village, Maguire started organising adjoining areas, approaching
men he had met at the radical nationalist meetings. From this involvement,
he became the first commandant of the local battalion, and later of the
South Mayo Brigade.[11]

Ideally the local unit was to consist of a company of 100 men, and all
companies in a certain county were to be grouped together into battalions
and a brigade. The membership at each level was to elect its own officers.
However, as a result of the dependency on local initiative the organisation
had little formal structure in most counties. Until late 1917 most companies
remained isolated. They consisted of small groups of activists who occasionally came together and called themselves Volunteer companies. The men
who had taken the initiative formed the officer corps. However, slowly the
main organisational structure was restored as a result of the need for local
coordination and by men sent out from Dublin.

The area covered by a company was usually based on the parish or
church area as the main unit of social life in the country. As the Volunteer
leadership put it to the brigade commandants in September 1919: 'While
other factors may determine for you a Company area, the fall of the people
in most country districts is determined by the Church areas and the parish
(or Chapel area, where two or more churches exist in a parish) usually
forms a suitable Company area.' The church and the principal Mass were
often used as a starting point for Sunday parades and consequently for
recruiting. This practical argument also made the parish the natural basis
for organisation in the cities. In practice there were many reasons for
departing from this rule, ranging from working or attending Mass in another
parish, to personal antipathies. Battalion and later brigade boundaries were

11 Quote, Tom Maguire, in U. MacEoin (1980), 278. See also Tom Maguire, Interview. A similar start on veterans' own initiative in Dublin, UCD AD, LA 9.

based on the ability of officers to keep in close touch with their units. They were therefore often determined by natural features, like rivers and mountain ridges, and not church or county boundaries.[12]

Despite the greatly increased sympathy for the Volunteers, organising companies could be extremely difficult. A large section of the population still supported the Irish Party and objected to the Irish Volunteers. The fact that many Irishmen served in the British Army also caused much bad feeling: 'There were still thousands of Irishmen fighting in France and if you said you had been out in Easter Week one of their family was liable to shoot you.' In Wexford and in the many towns and cities of Tipperary which depended economically on the presence of the military this opposition to the Volunteers was particularly strong. As a result the size of companies in this period was extremely small. Areas where in the days of the Irish National Volunteers companies of 100 to 150 men had been formed, only five to ten willing men could be found who were forced to operate on the margins of community life.[13]

In recruiting preference was given to people who knew someone in the Volunteers for security reasons. A prospective recruit was required to find two Volunteers willing to act as referee, after which the captain would have an interview with him. This restrictive attitude to recruitment contrasts with the accessibility to a larger group of people and the ideological demands made on recruits which had been laid down in the original Scheme of Organisation drawn up by the Volunteers before the Rising:

> All Irishmen who subscribe to the following objects:
> 1) To secure and maintain the rights and liberties common to all the people of Ireland.
> 2) To train, discipline, and equip for this purpose an Irish Volunteer Force.
> 3) To unite, in the service of Ireland, Irishmen of every creed and of every party and class,
> are eligible for membership of the Irish Volunteers, and all Irishmen having signed this Declaration:
> I, the undersigned, desire to be enrolled for service in Ireland as a member of the Irish Volunteer Force. I subscribe to the constitution of the Irish Volunteers, and pledge my willing obedience to my supe-

---

12 Quote, NLI, ms. 11,410. See also NLI, P921 No.66. Natural features used as boundaries, e.g. UCD AD P7A19/101 + 116.

13 Quote, K. Griffith and T. O'Grady (1982), 98. In Wexford town the AOH was particularly active against the Volunteers. Mark Killilea remembered how 'they had, during Easter Week, formed the strongest form of Special Constables for services against the Irish Volunteers', Mark Killilea, O'MN, P17b109. For the different size of companies see for instance, Tommy Ryan, 'Statement'.

rior officers. I declare that in joining the Irish Volunteer Force I set before myself the stated objects of the Irish Volunteers and no others. Shall be members of the I.V.F. [14]

After the reorganisation of small Volunteer units secret training was started in many village and city halls. The instruction mainly involved simple drill exercises and physical training but when possible some rifle practice was added. This was, however, handicapped by lack of ammunition. One Dublin Volunteer described training in 1917: 'Some of us enjoyed the drilling and marching and the very rare occasion when we had what was rather grandiloquently known as musketry practice with our .22 rifle for which we never had enough ammunition to give any individual more than 3 shots at the target.'[15]

Drilling was a welcome change for young men and became increasingly common during the summer of 1917. The willingness of Volunteers to parade openly was enhanced by the successful bye-election campaigns of 1917 – in South Roscommon in February and in Longford in May. In the East Clare bye-election of 10 July 1917, Volunteers from many parts of the country participated in the campaign, during which illegal displays of tricolours and drilling with hurling sticks were rampant. The victory was celebrated with a large parade reviewed by the winning candidate, Eamon de Valéra. Despite some arrests after these celebrations, the sheer number of people involved made it impossible to suppress them.[16]

Volunteers everywhere were inspired by the election successes. During the celebrations in Mayo after the Clare bye-election, the Volunteers suc-

14 Recruitment instructions in January 1919, NLI, ms. 900/13. Original recruitment requirements in 'Scheme of Organisation', NLI, P912 A0032. Personal experience of recruiting after the Rising, C.S. Andrews (1979), 95-6; Andy Cooney, O'MN, P17b107; Charles Dalton (1929), 46-50.
15 Quote, C.S. Andrews (1979), 98. See also B. Whelan, MA, A0159. Although drilling by Irish Volunteers from Limerick is reported by him in November, the Inspector General stated in December that no attempt to assemble in public had been made, IG MRs November-December 1916.
16 Dorothy Macardle (1968), 209-15. Visiting Volunteer officers often used their time to organise new units and link the isolated companies into large battalions, 'Talk with Mr. M.V. Sugrue', UCD AD, P7D94. Involvement in East Clare bye-election: From Dublin, Jack Plunkett, 'Statement', NLI, ms. 11,981; From Mayo, Michael Kilroy, 'The Awakening'; Thomas Kettrick, 'Statement'. Volunteers going to bye-elections in other areas: From Tipperary to Waterford, Seán Gaynor, 'Statement'. From Dublin to Armagh, Andy Cooney, O'MN, P17b107; Alfred Rutherford, O'MN, P17b122; Michael Noigh, O'MN, P17b128; J.V. Lawless, 'Recollections of the War of Independence', 239, UCD AD, P7D148; 'Talk with Mr. M.V. Sugrue', UCD AD, P7D94; Joe O'Connor, O'MN, P17b105. From Dublin to Longford, UCD AD, LA9. From Wexford to Waterford, Edward Roe, 'Statement'; 'Activities of A-Company New Ross'.

cessfully defied the police: 'We had a torch light procession and carried the tricolour in Newport. This was looked upon as a big achievement at the time because of the craze the RIC had for pulling down the national flag. They did not interfere on this occasion.' In other areas this victory was celebrated with bonfires.[17]

The police recognised the importance of this new development: 'It is, however, evident from the numerous cases of drilling reported since the Clare Election, and from the growing tendency to use every Gaelic sports and similar public gatherings as an opportunity for marching in military formation, that they intend to resume military training and organisation if they can do so with impunity.' As a result a military order was issued in July banning drilling and subsequently some active Volunteers were arrested. Nevertheless, many noticed the government's hesitancy to act and grew increasingly willing to express their disrespect for the law, but this was mainly restricted to parts of Tipperary and Dublin City.[18]

Despite all this activity no significant growth in Volunteer membership was recorded by the police in any county until November 1917. Sinn Féin was the main beneficiary of the growing support for the ideals of the Easter Rising. Although it had up to then been striving for autonomy under a dual monarchy, it was the only political party publicly identified with total independence and as a result was commonly seen as having inspired the rebellion. Widespread support for the party became apparent after May 1917 when many Sinn Féin Clubs were formed in the wake of the first bye-election success. In July, there were already 166 branches in existence with an estimated membership of 11,000. In December, there were about 1,000 clubs with 66,000 members, and rapid growth continued in the months thereafter.[19]

TACTICS

The convicted Volunteer leaders were released in July 1917 as a gesture of goodwill at the opening of the Irish Convention, set up to find a solution to the problems of political autonomy for Ireland. This provided the re-emerging Volunteer organisation with a national leadership. The subsequent Volunteer Convention of October 1917 was the public confirmation of its continued existence and vitality. The Volunteers asserted that 390 companies were affiliated at this time, while the police estimated that 162

---

17 Quote, Michael Kilroy, 'The Awakening'. Celebrations in Derry after the Clare election victory, John James McGee, Interview; Paddy Larkin, Interview.
18 Quote, IG MR July 1917. Military order in July 1917, Peter Hart (1992), Chapter 'The Dynamics of Violence', 12-3.
19 Membership figures, IG MRs 1917. See also Michael Laffan (1971).

Volunteer branches existed. Delegates elected a new executive and specialised departments were set up. The organisation left no doubt about its intentions. Although, the failure of the 1916 Rising had proven that the British Army could not be defeated in a direct confrontation, no clear alternative was present. As a result future conflict was again defined along the lines of open insurrection. In accordance with a statement of the temporary Volunteer executive set up in the beginning of 1917 the Convention considered it its principal duty: 'To carry on the reorganisation of the Irish Volunteers throughout the country, and put them in a position to complete by force of arms the work begun by the men of Easter Week.' To allay fears of renewed defeat the Executive guaranteed that it would not order to take the field until they considered it possible to wage war with a reasonable hope of success. In the meantime, violence would only be resorted to if Britain tried to disarm them or attempted to enforce conscription in Ireland.[20]

Despite the Convention's statements there were clear differences of opinion concerning the future role and tactics of the Volunteers. Not all Volunteers were convinced that another military confrontation was necessary. In the coinciding convention of Sinn Féin, a programme to attain independence by political means was adopted, and many members of its executive were also members of the Volunteer Executive. Leading Volunteers, who felt that total independence could only be attained by military force, were also divided about the form this should take. Despite these differences, all felt it was imperative to have the Volunteer Force far more numerous and evenly spread over the country than before 1916 and to arm them.

As a consequence of these divisions in policy, military preparation by the movement was haphazard and followed two separate lines. On the one hand, the majority who wanted to use the threat of force by the Volunteers only as a political weapon did prepare for a confrontation, but remained largely on the right side of the law. On the other hand some maintained that although open insurrection was impossible at this moment, all means available were justified to obtain arms. The uncertainty about future tactics meant that the Volunteers were largely reorganised along the lines of a regular army. Due to the experience of some leading Volunteers and the availability of its training manuals, they largely mirrored themselves on the British Army.

The divided approach would characterise the organisation until the Truce. In the development of structure and policy the largely unintended transition from possible open insurrection by a standing army to guerrilla warfare by small mobile units caused many problems. The regular army structure of the original Irish Volunteers described in the Scheme of Organisation had been reaffirmed at the convention, and instructions like those for

20 Quote and attitude of Provisional Executive, NLI, ms. 31,190. Police figures for membership of the Volunteers, IG MRs 1918.

setting up field kitchens were still published in the second issue of the Volunteer paper *An tÓglach*[21] in September 1918. The extensive training in traditional military skills and the emphasis on cycling units were other indications of the preparations for open warfare. The 2nd Battalion of the Dublin Brigade nevertheless clearly stated guerrilla fighting as its central policy in October 1918. However, even in 1920 when such tactics had been generally accepted in the organisation, some leading men still regarded it as a transitional phase to open warfare. They made plans to occupy towns and cities as the next stage to total military victory. The realisation that the moral effect of a guerrilla campaign could defeat a government which depended on public support only gradually dawned.[22]

RISING CONFIDENCE 1917-1918

The death on hunger strike in September 1917 of Thomas Ashe, a recently imprisoned Volunteer leader, marked the start of a more concerted display of regained strength. After his funeral open parading ordered by the Volunteer Executive commenced throughout the country, and drilling became common, particularly in southern and western counties. The large attendance at the burial also forced the Dublin Volunteers to found a coordinating body to oversee the proceedings. Up to then they had been organised on battalion level only, but now a Dublin Brigade staff was formed. This event was also a stimulus for many young men to join the Volunteers.[23]

The uncertain police response to this open defiance made Volunteers more eager to expose their new-found strength, often making a point of parading in the direct view of the RIC. In November 1917 all companies were ordered to drill in the second week of December. Uniforms when

21 *An tÓglach* was the official organ of the Irish Volunteers set up to inform the Volunteer on the practical aspects of organisation and warfare. The first issue was published on 15 August 1918. It was originally published twice monthly but became a weekly in April 1921. The paper was not published between May and November 1919 when the editor was arrested, Seán T. O'Kelly, NLI, ms. 27,711; Charles Townshend (1979), 336.
22 A treatment of the development of the IRA as a guerrilla organisation, Charles Townshend (1979). For a Volunteers' assessment of this development, C.S. Andrews (1979), 98 + 114-15. Policy statement 2nd Battalion, NLI, ms. 901/56. Plans for a 'spectacular' rising among Cork's IRA leadership, Peter Hart (1992), Chapter 'The Dynamics of Violence', 107-9.
23 In October 1917, 140 cases of illegal drilling were reported almost entirely confined to Munster, mainly in the counties Cork and Clare. Out of the 334 cases reported in November, 272 took place in Munster, with Co. Clare clearly the most affected. Open drilling became more widespread in Connacht in early 1918, IG MRs September 1917-March 1918. Stimulus of Ashe's funeral, K. Griffith and T. O'Grady (1982), 111.

available were to be worn, but no arms were to be carried; 288 of these parades were recorded; most took a simple form:

> A party of about 150 Sinn Féiners assembled [in] the Market Square at Kiltimagh about 9 p.m. on 5th inst. and were put through drill movements there by John Walsh of Kiltimagh, who put them through the formation of fours and marched them in fours through the town and back to the Market Square where he dismissed them.

To give their drill exercises an air of realism, many Volunteers used sticks or made wooden rifles. The men involved made no secret of their involvement. The most dedicated, like Sean Treacy in Tipperary, were proud to display their membership by wearing home-made symbols of 'the Irish Army': 'John Treacy wore the following articles of military equipment – haversack, belt, puttees, and cap, blew a whistle and immediately 70 men and boys fell in in 2 ranks. [...] Maurice Crowe, Shop assistant, Tipperary in uniform of an officer of Irish Volunteers, dark green frock, trousers and cap with waist belt took charge of 44 men.'[24]

Most company officers had only limited military experience, and the inability of some to inspire their men was observed by the police: 'If Rogers continues as instructor he will probably break up the drilling as, apart from his bad word of command – a guttural, hoarse, consumptive – he is very abusive. I saw John Barlow, [...] break away, apparently disgusted.' To improve their skills the Tipperary officers then attended training classes.[25]

REACTION OF THE AUTHORITIES

The authorities were uncertain as to what the most appropriate reaction was to stop these large-scale displays of defiance. Initially they believed all Volunteer activity could be stopped if they singled out and discouraged the few 'bad apples'. The continuous arrest of leading Volunteers for small offences and their imprisonment for a couple of months at a time was a direct consequence of this. However, the prosecution of men leading drilling before local magistrates instituted in July only presented the republicans with occasions for inflammatory speeches and popular demonstrations, and required police reinforcements to keep the peace even in small villages. The short sentences meted out to these men were also inadequate to prevent drilling.

Although the police were seriously worried by this, the Inspector General of the RIC stated that the military commander in Ireland considered

24 These quotes and many other reports on cases of illegal drilling in this week, PRO, CO904/122.
25 Quote, PRO, CO904/122. Training classes in drilling, Patrick Ryan, 'Statement'.

drilling of insufficient military value to render trial by court martial desirable. In January 1918 he reported to the government that the County Inspectors opposed dispersing any massed parades of Volunteers, as it might stir up more trouble than local police could handle. Consequently the government decided to stop prosecuting men leading parades, but rather to keep a close eye on the proceedings. Policemen were instructed to observe every parade or drilling exercise they encountered and to note the names of those involved.[26]

However, the growing defiance soon became intolerable for the authorities and the police were eventually forced to act. Men leading parades were again singled out for arrest. Anyone flying the republican flag, singing seditious songs, giving orders, wearing a uniform or even carrying a wooden gun was liable for prosecution. Later, arrests were limited to those carrying weapons or wearing uniforms. Despite ingenious ploys to avoid arrest, many were prosecuted: 'It was illegal to drill or to give words of command and each man would take it in his turn to step out to take charge of the men.'[27]

OPEN DEFIANCE

Those arrested became increasingly defiant. In keeping with the movement's policy, many of them refused to recognise the courts' right to try them. As a result of this refusal, every breach of the law on their part led to a prison sentence. In jail these men went on hunger strikes to support their often successful demand for 'political prisoner' status. The impending death of their prisoners and the uproar this created among the population disconcerted the authorities. After Ashe's death while force-fed they were particularly careful not to have another dead martyr on their hands. The release of many hunger strikers in November 1917 had left the police feeling powerless: 'As it is now evident to the parties concerned that they have only to hunger-strike for a couple of days in order to get them out of gaol, whether convicted or untried, it is really very little use arresting them.' [28]

This sense of strength and the admiration that released prisoners experienced resulted in a situation in which some prominent Volunteers began to invite arrest:

> The first job we had was an arrest in Whitehall when the Company was out on manoeuvres under Simon Donnelly and Captain Paddy

26 Developments regarding drilling, IG MRs September 1917-January 1918.
27 Limitation of causes for arrest, PRO, CO904/122/2. Quote, Pat Fallon, O'MN, P17b109. A similar effect is described in north Tipperary, Seán Gaynor, 'Statement'.
28 Quote, Military Intelligence Report dated November 1917, Charles Townshend (1975), 5. See also IG MR February 1917

Flanagan. They had outposts out and about 50 DMP [Dublin Metropolitan Police] got in on them without the outposts reporting their presence. Simon ordered those who had arms to get away and those who had not to stand fast. Then Paddy Flanagan stepped out, and he told all to stand fast and he stood fast, which we did. We were ordered to go in two ranks under arrest to Rathmines Road. [...] But after a 12 day hunger and thirst strike we were released.

The police interference with training exercises inevitably led to clashes. Units confronted by numerically smaller parties of police occasionally resisted attempts to arrest their leaders. Some RIC men were disarmed and tied up.[29]

As a result of this open defiance organisation became more open at the end of 1917 and many new members were attracted. The police monitored many of the attempts to organise companies. The leading activists were observed travelling the country, addressing local people and taking small groups through drill exercises. One of these meetings to induce young men to join the movement took place at Drummin, Co. Mayo on 9 December 1917. The local drum band played at a meeting where 400 were present. The police recorded the speakers' attempts to arouse their audience with remarks like: 'We are out for a free and unfettered nation and we mean to die or get it. [...] The men of Easter Week saved Ireland from Conscription and many a young Irishman from a grave in Flanders or France.' And: 'I'm no speechmaker I believe in nothing but the rifle and the sword.' Afterwards, forty-two men were recorded drilling. The assistance of these outsiders was essential for activating local men, and their support continued to be demanded.[30]

Most eager youngsters found drilling an exhilarating experience. Humour and entertainment were ingredients that attracted many of them to training. Drilling in rural communities was often combined with other leisure activities, such as football. Training in Dublin was supplemented by some field exercises held in the hills surrounding the city, and involving several units. Some of the pre-1916 members, however, soon became disillusioned with the proceedings and the limited prospect of action, and stopped attending parades.[31]

29 Quote, Alfred Rutherford, O'MN, P17b122. See also Joe O'Connor, O'MN, P17b105; Peter Hart (1992), Chapter 'The Dynamics of Violence'.
30 Speeches by organisers, PRO, CO904/122.
31 The different attitude of old and new members particularly in Dublin, Charles Dalton (1929), 49-51; C.S. Andrews (1979), 95-8; Alfred Rutherford, O'MN, P17b122; James Henry, Interview. Many older IRB men did not join the Volunteers after the Rising: In Derry, Paddy Larkin, Interview; Frank Himphey, Fr O'Kane Papers, Tape 50a, AARC. In Aughagower, Co. Mayo, Charlie Hughes, Interview. The membership list shows that a number of the older officers, including the captain, Charlie's father, left after 1916, CBHC. For the role of humour and enjoyment, Michael Kilroy, 'The Awakening'. Drilling combined with football, Brodie Malone and Ned Moane, O'MN, P17b120.

Most recruits coming into the organisation now were of a much less ideological type than the original men. They were young, not more than twenty years old, and joined in groups. They had gone to the same school, had played football and hurling together or met each other regularly after work. They were mainly interested in action and had little time for politics or cultural activities. Most of these young recruits were not attracted to the Gaelic League like many of the pre-1916 men had been. Some of them even considered its members to be 'queer fellows'. Many were attracted to the Volunteers because of their interest in drill and parade. In their activities they followed the example given by a local leader. When Volunteer organisers visited the area to form a company, these groups went to the meeting and, following the local trend-setter, they joined. As one Wexford Volunteer put it: 'I went to school with him [the captain] sure. That's the thing, you see, I went to school with most of them that were drilling. They took up this, and then you would follow them.' This is confirmed elsewhere: 'The captain, because of him, if he would join up you would join up too.'[32]

The initiative for Volunteer activity in towns often came from men who had recently come from the countryside, looking for work. One could attribute this to the lack of social restraint and economic independence, making it easier to join even if it might endanger their family. The import-

---

32 This generalisation of the way in which the Volunteers organised in Wexford is based on oral testimonies by a number of rank and file from south Wexford, Peter Wall; Willy Parle; John Quinn; Andy Roe; 'Statement of the Activities of Thomas Stafford 1916 to 1923'. Quote on Gaelic League members, Peter Wall, Interview. One man who moved to Dublin and became a member of the Gaelic League states: 'For the purely academic Gaelic student the Volunteer leaders or the rank-and-file had little time and some of the Ard Craobh [his GL club] big shots were regarded in this light. It was the social side of the League's activities that attracted us young people most.', J. Matthews, 'Statement', in F.S. Bourke Papers, NLI, ms. 9,873. Another Volunteer dismissed them: 'The Gaelic crowd who were not good with one or two exceptions', Andy Cooney, O'MN, P17b107. Quote on 'school', Ned Colfer, Interview. Similar groups are described: In Tipperary, Jack Gardiner, Interview. In Duneen close to New-bridge, Co. Derry, John Duffy, Fr O'Kane Papers, Tape A20, AARC. Quote on 'following the captain', Willy Parle, Interview. Recruitment in Dublin after 1916, Mick O'Hanlon, O'MN, P17b106; Ben Doyle, O'MN, P17b101; Andy Cooney, O'MN, P17b107. Young men eager to join because of military displays: In Derry, Liam A. Brady, *Derry Journal*, 1 May 1953; Edward O'Connor from Carrickmore, Co. Tyrone, NLI, ms. 17,506. Thomas Costelloe, in Limerick City, NLI, P919 A0173. In Mayo, Michael Kilroy, 'The Awakening'; Tom Maguire, in U. MacEoin (1987), 278, and Interview. J. Matthews in Drogheda, F.S. Bourke Papers, NLI, ms. 9,873.

ance of the socialising aspect of joining the Volunteers should not be underestimated for this group either.[33]

REGION AL VARIATION 1917-1918

Volunteer activity varied widely throughout Ireland. The inactivity of the end of 1916 was in several counties replaced by a myriad of organised action, but offences remained few. In 1917 drilling had been largely concentrated in Munster, but at the beginning of 1918 a shift took place towards Connacht. In Mayo and Tipperary drilling was now widespread and some public meetings were held where violent and seditious language was used. In south Tipperary a Sinn Féin concert raised £45, and a large raid for arms was carried out by eighteen masked men. In the West the activities of the Volunteers were combined with expressions of agricultural strife, such as cattle-driving and the breaking up of grassland for tillage. The latter was encouraged by Sinn Féin as part of their policy to ensure a sufficient food supply to Ireland.[34]

Meanwhile in places like Wexford and Derry Volunteer activity went practically unnoticed by the police. Although companies did exist, few Volunteers were willing to challenge the police, and no drilling was reported in either county. Two small route-marches were observed around Wexford town in February, but the rebellious spirit was confined to the safer public meetings of Sinn Féin and the Gaelic League. Other demonstration of support for the movement followed the visits of national figures. For the time being most Volunteers limited themselves to indoor drilling. Eager young members found further entertainment by attending recruitment meetings for the British Army with the sole intention of asking awkward questions and causing disruption. Particularly in Derry, many of the other attendants objected to this: 'There was many a scuffle and the Volunteers had to make many a hasty retreat.' Although enthusiasm was increased, the object of all of this activity was unclear.[35]

Even in active counties the number of Volunteers and their sympathisers was still marginal in many districts. The organisation relied heavily on

33 Men from the country among the activists: In New Ross, Ned Colfer, Interview. In Monasterevin, Co. Kildare, Ned Prendergast, Interview. In Magherafelt and Draperstown, Co. Derry, Major Morris, 'Typescript of Interview', Fr O'Kane Papers, AARC; Thomas Toner, Tape A13, Ibidem. Also in the composition of the Flying Columns in Belfast and Derry City, see the Derry experience discussed later.
34 IG and CIs South Tipperary, Mayo MRs June 1917-March 1918.
35 Quote, Liam Brady, *Derry Journal*, 8 May 1953. Similar activities are reported in Dublin, C.S. Andrews (1979), 91. Activities in Wexford, CI Wexford MRs 1918.

a few dedicated men. Besides leading the displays of Volunteer strength, secret organising was their main activity. Ned Moane was the principal organising officer of the Westport Battalion in Mayo:

> All this year [1917] we kept the pressure up as far as organising was concerned. The work had to be done altogether at night. [...] We wanted our organising to be done without any great fuss or bother. This was very important. [...] It was common among our fellows – Brodie Malone, Joe Ring, John Gibbons, Charlie Gavan and six or seven of us who were on this work – for two of us to go together. [...] We had the Volunteers out on manoeuvres so that they all would get to know the district thoroughly and that the people would be aware of the fact that the Volunteers were becoming more active every day.[36]

This cautious attitude was prompted by the continuous arrests of these men. Since the Rising the same cadre of activists were imprisoned two or three times. Ned Moane, for instance, was apprehended early in 1917 for singing a seditious song at a fund-raising concert held in Carrowkennedy school. After his release he continued his Volunteer work and, following the general parade ordered in December 1917, was rearrested for wearing a uniform.[37]

The organising work of the original activists only slowly led to a growth in membership. Volunteers in Mayo had been least organised at the end of 1916 when only 164 members were known to the police; even in heavily Protestant Derry more members were noted, 188. The 367 Volunteers present in south Tipperary at that time made it the best organised county followed by Wexford with 324. However, Volunteer membership in these counties clearly developed differently until the Truce. In November 1917, the Volunteers in Mayo were the first to record any significant growth, joined by the Volunteers in Wexford in January 1918. As a result, membership in Mayo more than tripled during 1917, while in Wexford it nearly doubled. According to the police, Tipperary and Derry had actually lost a few members in that same year.

ARMING 1917-1918

Not only was the size of Volunteer membership variable in these counties; their armaments also widely differed. According to police assessments the

36 One area in Tipperary had only one Volunteer within a twelve mile radius in 1918, Ned Prendergast, Interview. Quote, Ned Moane, Moane/Malone, Tape. Moane's arrest, Ned Moane, 'Statement'; Thomas Kettrick, 'Statement'.
37 On continuous rearrest of the same cadre of activists, Peter Hart (1992), Chapter 'The Dynamics of Violence', 19.

Derry Volunteers of 1917 were relatively the best armed of all the units covered in this book. However, although more than half of them could be provided with a weapon, they had only 17 rifles. The 78 rifles possessed by the men in Tipperary meant that despite the fact that only one in four were armed they did possess the means for violent activity. Wexford and Mayo Volunteers both held 21 rifles, but despite the larger number of shotguns and small arms only one in nine Volunteers in Wexford could be armed, while one in 6.5 of the few Mayo Volunteers could be provided with a weapon. No arms were reported available to the Dublin Volunteers in 1917 at all. This was obviously an inaccurate assessment, probably attributable to the assumption that all arms had been confiscated after the Rising. The possession of ammunition was even less widespread. The police were only aware of 8,000 rounds of rifle ammunition, all in the possession of the Tipperary Volunteers.[38]

Besides drilling, the gathering of arms was therefore the main military activity of the Volunteers. Some were bought on the marketplace, but most were gathered locally. Many shotguns were donated by friendly locals; in addition, random raids were made on private houses. Arms were mainly sought in one's own community. In Derry Nationalists rather than Unionists were visited. The local gentry were only subjected to arms raids when the Volunteers had gained more confidence. When the arms gathered in this way proved to be insufficient, soldiers and policemen became targets. Soldiers home on furlough were an easy prey. Other soldiers eager to earn a bit of money on the side sold their arms to Volunteers. Besides this, raids on military posts, ships and docks were attempted in Dublin. Some Volunteers travelled to England to obtain arms there. A small group from a Dublin company sailed to Liverpool in 1918 and raided a Territorial Army hall, procuring thirteen rifles.[39]

To buy arms funds were raised by holding concerts, dances and raffles and making collections. Some, mainly revolvers, could be bought through the battalion from headquarters in Dublin. However, the number of arms obtained never amounted to much. Most companies possessed only a few

38 'Arms and Ammunition. Returns of Arms in possession of Irish, National and Ulster Volunteers, 1917', PRO, CO904 Box 29/2.

39 A total of 311 arms raids were reported in 1918 throughout Ireland, David Fitzpatrick (1977), 214. Raids for arms: In Dublin, Pat MacCrea, P17b110; Patrick O'Daly, 'Statement', NLI, P4548. In Derry, James Harkin, Fr O'Kane Papers, Tape A9, AARC; Liam Brady, *Derry Journal*, 6 & 13 May 1953. Buying arms from Crown Forces in Dublin, UCD AD, LA9; Alfred Rutherford, O'MN, P17b122. In Derry City, Liam Brady, *Derry Journal*, 1 May 1953. Soldiers who wanted to desert were given civilian clothes in exchange for their rifle and uniform, Jimmy Murray (The Turk), O'MN, P17b106; Joseph A. Cripps, NLI, ms. 22,117(1). Other targets for raids in Dublin, Joseph A. Cripps, Ibid. Raid in Liverpool, Hugh Early, O'MN, P17b110. See also Ernie Noonan, O'MN, P17b94.

shotguns and the odd revolver. To militarily orientated Volunteers collecting arms became their main preoccupation. In the provincial areas rifles were particularly difficult to obtain. Soldiers and policemen were far less numerous and less able to sell their arms undetected. Any opportunity to obtain a rifle was therefore seized by the eager but inexperienced Volunteers. Before the end of 1916 one had already been taken from a soldier in Tipperary, and this practice spread to other areas. The use of force was new and was used hesitantly even by these activists:

> In October 1917 this soldier got off the train at Goold's Cross on furlough. [...] We got in touch with Seamus Robinson who was in Kilshenane with Eamon O'Dwyer: and I located this soldier. Eamon Dwyer was at home from gaol, so the two Keefe's and I went on with 3 lads from Knockaville to Kilshenane and they wanted to put on a disguise on their faces. [...] Eamon Dwyer was inclined to tell us that it was too dangerous. [...] Seamus went with us. We 4 went into the house. We had a sort of an old .32 and 1 round of ammunition. Con Keefe had a .300 and he had a strange round of ammunition as he should put a paper around it when he was putting the round into the magazine. Seamus Robinson had a .22 Smith and automatic. This soldier got married and he was more or less on his honeymoon. They were all gone to bed. [...] I went to 1 room. There were 4 huge bloody men in 2 beds. I took a squint but I couldn't see any sign of a rifle but I heard Con's voice 'It's here Jack,' he said. [...] I handled the rifle and the other two fellows were very aggressive by this [...]. I had to tell these fellows that I'd have to blow out their brains, and I said we were soldiers of the Irish Republic doing our duty. [...] Seamus was delighted and we came out on the road. Seamus Robinson fired [the rifle], and when he had the gun in his hand I thought it would make an awful report to frighten them, but all it did was to make a ping.

The chance to force rifles from soldiers on furlough passed in January 1918 when the government forbade military to take rifles home.[40]

40 Arms bought from GHQ: In Mayo, Tom Maguire, O'MN, P17b100; Johnny Duffy, O'MN, P17b109; P.J. Kelly, 'One of the Men of the West'. In Derry, Thomas Morris, 'Typescript of Interview', Fr O'Kane Papers, AARC. Scarcity of arms in Tipperary, Patrick Ryan, 'Statement'. Collecting money for arms in companies in Dublin, NLI, ms. 1,413. Quote, Ned O'Reilly, O'MN, P17b126. See also Paul Merrigan, Interview. On taking arms from soldiers in Mayo, Thomas Kettrick, 'Statement'; Brodie Malone, O'MN, P17b109. See also CIs MRs 1916-18. Government measure, IG MR January 1918.

Most officers, however, saw the Volunteers as a political instrument and failed to see the necessity to arm oneself at such costs; to them using its military potential was only a remote option. Eamon O'Dwyer, a leading organiser in Tipperary, made this clear in a short speech in November 1917. He stated that the Volunteers' objective was to make England's rule in Ireland impossible, and he believed they would achieve this without firing a shot. He added, however, that if necessary they would adopt a policy of active resistance.[41]

TOUGHENING STANCES 1918

The rivalry and struggle for dominance between the Volunteers and the police which developed from the commencement of public parading inevitably led to confrontation. The police efforts to keep track of the main people involved often led to further clashes, as the Volunteers were increasingly prepared to engage the police directly. The arrests and trials which followed were occasions when large-scale engagements between police and the public were likely to take place. During Ned Moane's trial in January 1918 riots broke out in Westport. The victory celebrations when bye-elections were won also led to conflict.[42]

The police increasingly reverted to the use of the baton to disperse radical nationalist crowds. Volunteers reacted to this by arming themselves with batons as well. These engagements polarised relations between police, populace and Volunteers. The police, often outnumbered by protesters, had to resort to using firearms when in serious distress. Eventually this led the Volunteers to doing the same. As a result of the confrontations in Westport a bomb was thrown into the RIC barracks in March 1918. The diminishing acceptance of the Crown Forces as the legitimate authority justified this in the eyes of the population.[43]

The accelerated pace of organisation and more overt display of Volunteer activity led to a sharp increase in lawlessness. The successful use of hunger strikes as a political weapon gave rise to contempt for the law and to the belief that it could be disregarded with impunity. To deal with this new regulations were introduced in March under the Temporary Discharges Act, also known as the 'Cat-and-Mouse' Act. Force-feeding was abandoned, weakened men were released and rearrested when in better health, thus compelling all convicted Volunteers to complete their sentences or avoid

41 Speech Eamon O'Dwyer, PRO, CO904/122. Initial hesitancy, Ned O'Reilly, O'MN, P17b126.
42 Clashes after trial of Ned Moane, Brodie Malone, O'MN, P17b109; Thomas Kettrick, 'Statement'. The trial of these men led to further clashes in Castlebar, James Chambers, 'Statement'.
43 Use of batons by Volunteers in Mayo, Michael Kilroy, 'The Awakening'. In Tipperary, Peter Morrissey, 'Memoirs'. Bomb in Westport, CI Mayo March 1918.

arrest. As a result the police felt more able to act and many people were arrested. In Mayo alone thirty-three men from twenty-two different localities were charged with at least one case of illegal drilling in March 1918. Agrarian agitation, in particular, subsided after the introduction of these measures and many active Volunteers became more cautious.[44]

CONSCRIPTION CRISIS, SPRING 1918

This situation, in which a few groups of increasingly confident Volunteers in a limited number of areas were looking for confrontation, was radically altered by the threatened introduction of conscription in March. The entire nationalist population reacted against this with a widespread determination to resist. A pledge was taken by the majority of Catholic men in Ireland promising to resist conscription by every means available. Although all nationalist parties resisted, Sinn Féin was soon identified as the leading force. Sinn Féin membership grew from 66,000 in December 1917 to 100,000 in April 1918, and similar strong growth is recorded for the Volunteers.[45]

The Volunteer leadership ordered all prisoners to take bail and prepare for military resistance. At public meetings men spoke of shooting policemen, attacking their barracks and blowing up bridges. An inventory of all kinds of goods and skills was ordered in each company area in preparation for taking to the field. In many areas women were baking large supplies of breadcakes and other foodstuffs which were gathered in dumps. Open drilling was ordered to stop, as the leadership wanted to protect officers from rearrest. This policy was adhered to in Munster, but in Connacht orders were largely ignored. In some localities radical Volunteers refused to attend anti-conscription meetings or to take the pledge because they interpreted this as passive resistance.[46]

Looming military confrontation emphasised the necessity of arming, training and coordination. Every company in Ireland was asked to provide details on the state of their area to Dublin. This included information on the introduction of special services, the police presence, the number of cars, bicycles, arms and ammunition at the command of the Volunteers, and the amount of food that could be commandeered in case of conflict. Many companies started to improve their situation by raiding houses and stealing explo-

---

44 CI Mayo MR March 1918.
45 Police figures for membership of Sinn Féin and the Volunteers, IG MRs 1917-18.
46 Inventory by sending men and Query forms, UCD AD, P30/3-4; Fintan Murphy, O'MN, P17b107. Despite the ban on drilling, 507 cases were reported in April 1918, which was the highest recorded figure since the Rising, IG MR April 1918.

sives despite an order from Sinn Féin forbidding this. The lack of arms in
rural areas also led to the casting of pikes in many places. To improve military skills, classes were set up in signalling, engineering, first aid and
armoury at company level. Training in Engineering was the first to be coordinated, and every company was to have approximately six men specialised
in it. In Dublin this was attempted, but in the rest of the country most
Volunteers failed to appreciate the need for engineering skills at this stage.
Cycling units were organised to maintain communication. Particularly in
Dublin, the organisational structure was more rigorously implemented, and
officer meetings started to be held regularly at all levels.[47]

It was apparent that for a new confrontation the civil structure of organisation would not suffice, and it was set on a more military footing. In
March a GHQ (Volunteers General Headquarters) and more specialised
departments were introduced who gave direct advice to country officers.
The Chief of Staff, then Cathal Brugha, became the most important man
in the Volunteer organisation. He was supported by the Adjutant General,
the Quartermaster General, the O.C. Chemicals, and the Directors of
Intelligence, Organisation, Engineering, Finance, Publicity and Training.
Nominally GHQ remained under control of the General Executive, but in
practice it commanded the Volunteers from then on. Although an impro-
vised Volunteer Convention was held in secret in October 1918, the civil
structure of the Volunteers could not be used anymore due to the growing
risk of arrest.[48]

°Differences between Dublin, Tipperary and Mayo on the one hand, and
Wexford and Derry on the other, again show up in the Conscription Crisis.
While some military preparations took place in all counties, the Volunteers

47 Request to every company from Dublin, UCD AD, P30/2-3. The ban on raid-
    ing private houses was instituted by Sinn Féin on 25 February 1918, NLI, ms.
    11,410(11); NLI, P3269. Improvement of structure and training during
    Conscription Crisis, UCD AD, LA9; Frank Henderson, O'MN, P17b99; UCD
    AD, P30/4; NLI, ms. 17,880; Papers of the Engineering Department, NLI, ms.
    11,410(1-8); Jack Plunkett, 'Statement', NLI, ms. 11,981. Casting of pikes is
    reported from most areas: in Mayo, P.J. Kelly, 'One of the Men from the
    West'.
48 On the General Executive and GHQ, 'Notes on the Gerard Costelloe Papers',
    and Risteard Mulcahy, 'The Origins of the IRA and its Achievements during
    the War of Independence', UCD AD, P7D96; Oscar Traynor O'MN, P17b98;
    'Notes from Beasley's Michael Collins', NLI, P913 A0139. In September 1918
    the annual convention was called off, UCD AD, P7b172/24. According to the
    police this Convention was held secretly, IG MR October 1918. This is con-
    firmed in a history of A-Company, 1st Battalion, Dublin Brigade, UCD AD,
    LA9. Delegates for the 1920 national convention were appointed by the differ-
    ent brigade conventions in November 1919, but the General Executive again
    deferred it in June 1920, NLI, ms. 901/7; Communication from GHQ to F.
    O'Donoghue dated 12 June 1920, NLI, ms. 31,194.

in the first category did not hesitate to show this, while those in the other two counties largely restricted themselves to political demonstrations. In Tipperary the strength of its Volunteers was displayed by a full mobilisation of all companies with arms and equipment. To meet the new demands made on the organisation, the battalions were systematically reorganised and all units were instructed to elect new officers. Anti-conscription meetings were held and money was raised through raffles and dances. A contribution of one penny a week was also asked from all Volunteers. In April the police found the county 'full of parties drilling and gathering in bands and showing a united front to oppose the law.'[49]

Police in Mayo also observed frequent drilling and many arms raids. The Volunteers prepared seriously for military confrontation:

> We made caves in the mountains and there we hid food during Conscription. The food was potatoes particularly, oat-bread made and prepared by the Cumann na mBan. We went to the caves in the mountains, which were really fox dens. We brought them in there by night. There was a jumble of rock and earth thrown over it. There was a section there every night to do that. We made dumps for arms under ground: for shotguns etc. We used large drain pipes which were built into the side of a sandy bank.

The attention paid to gathering food and arms was supplemented by the organising of first aid posts by Cumann na mBan.[50]

In Wexford and Derry the Volunteers attracted very few new recruits and acted with far more restraint. In Wexford there was no separate Volunteer action recorded in March. One large Sinn Féin meeting was held in New Ross where two Volunteers in uniform and forty with caps showed themselves. In April more than fifty anti-conscription meetings were held; but only four cases of drilling were reported. Some companies had, however, started secret preparations, including raiding for arms and the making of buckshot to fill shotgun cartridges, but the emphasis remained on public dissent.[51]

A similar development took place in Derry. Many political gatherings were held but there was no sign of open Volunteer activity. Meetings were well attended and emotions ran high. Nevertheless, most speakers advocated passive resistance; the question of active protest was only raised in Maghera, where some speakers suggested blowing up bridges and railway lines. Sinn Féin met with considerably more enthusiasm than the military

49 Raising money and election of new officers, Paul Mulcahy, 'Statement'; Matt Morrissey, Interview. Mobilisation Order, O'MN, P17b127. Police reaction, CI South Tipperary MR April 1918.
50 Quote, Jack Connolly, O'MN, P17b120. See also James Chambers, 'Statement'.
51 Activities in Wexford, CI Wexford MRs March-April 1918. Making buckshot, 'Activities of A-Company New Ross'.

wing, and grew rapidly everywhere during this period. As in Wexford, the Volunteers did, nevertheless, secretly prepare for a military engagement and arms were vigorously collected. One Volunteer reported that his IRB unit was all set: 'We had collected every arm we could lay our hand on. We were instructed that in the event the Act was passed that we were immediately to leave home and take to the country and join our unit.'[52]

Table 5: Points of significant growth in Volunteer and Sinn Féin membership

	Irish Volunteers			Sinn Féin		
	Sept. 1916	January 1918	April 1918	June 1917	January 1918	May 1918
Mayo	164	581	1,081	433	3,328	5,563
Tipperary	367	361	653	280	2,544	3,991
Wexford	324	608	603	278	1,919	2,451
Derry	190	188	188	154	425	802

END TO OPEN DEFIANCE, SUMMER 1918

After the Conscription Crisis the authorities took a tougher stance. The leaders of drilling parties were again actively prosecuted and in May most Volunteer leaders were arrested accused of conspiring with Germany. This resulted in a substantial reduction of Volunteer activity. Aided by the ban from GHQ, open drilling was almost completely stopped. In July Sinn Féin, Cumann na mBan and the Gaelic League were proclaimed dangerous associations, which prevented alternative manifestations of republican sympathy. The County Inspector of south Tipperary was satisfied with the effect: 'The proclamation of Sinn Féin has brought about a more settled feeling and there has not been nearly as much activity among suspects and clubs recently.' The almost total end to drilling was attributed to prompt arrest and prosecution of the leading members of drilling parties, while further drilling was successfully prevented by a system of police and military patrolling in the more disaffected areas. In September he felt confident enough to remark: 'Many young country fellows who were noticed as drilling were glad when the practice was stopped, the orders began to get irksome and they saw no sense in it.'[53]

52 Quote, William John Himphey, Fr O'Kane Papers, Tape A23, AARC. Activities in Derry City, Liam Brady, *Derry Journal*, 8 May 1953. See also CI Derry MRs March-April 1918.
53 Quotes, CI South Tipperary MRs July & September 1918. Figures on drilling, IG MRs 1918.

Ambivalence about the future direction led GHQ to opt for a cautious approach. During the Conscription Crisis the authorities had been so disturbed by the drilling activities in Tipperary and Limerick that they issued a warning: unless drilling stopped, these counties would be declared special military areas; a mild form of martial law. Although GHQ instructed the Volunteers to continue their training, it was to be done in secret, using scouts to avoid detection. This was immediately noticed by the police in Mayo: 'Illegal drilling is not so prevalent as it was. This is partly due to clerical advice and partly to the fact that drilling is now carried out by night or in out of the way places with a view to escape police observation and the prosecution of leaders.' A company report in south Tipperary reveals that despite the new policy the police still followed drill exercises during the summer without interfering with them. Some day-long training exercises led by GHQ organisers were also held at that time.[54]

Large parades, extensive manoeuvres and route-marches were thus abandoned in favour of small-scale secret training. The lack of excitement provided by this combined with the lack of ammunition that made rifle practice almost non-existent, soon bored rank-and-file Volunteers. During the second half of 1918 the military side of the movement clearly lost momentum. An order on the content of company training issued by the 2nd Battalion of the Dublin Brigade on 5 October, acknowledged the problematic situation: 'Training must be interesting to the men. The failure in this respect is undoubtedly responsible for the small parades.' As a consequence of this waning enthusiasm some companies fell into disorganisation.[55]

This Dublin Brigade training order instructed officers extensively on how to maintain Volunteer interest: Training was to be practical, have a definite objective, and be progressive. No time should be wasted in repetition. The men were to be grouped according to their capabilities and acquirements, and at each parade something new was to be introduced. Although the importance of close order drill, which was often the only activity of Volunteer companies, was recognised ten minutes were considered quite sufficient. The most important branch of Volunteer training was stated to be marksmanship. However, the instructions clearly show the lack of armament: all recruits were to be thoroughly instructed in sighting and aiming without firing. Firing was to be practised indoors with air guns as much as possible, while hand-grenade throwing was to be practised with dummies.

---

54 Quote, CI Mayo MR April 1918. The order by GHQ to drill secretly, UCD AD, P7b172/27. Report on drill in south Tipperary dated 24 July 1918, NLI, ms. 8,413. Large scale manoeuvres 8 May 1918, MA, Lot 1.

55 Training Order 2nd Battalion Dublin Brigade, NLI, ms. 901/56. Similar orders, NLI, ms. 902/172. A disorganised unit in Dublin, NLI, ms. 902/168.

The half-hearted tactical change from large-scale military operations to guerrilla warfare also become apparent. On the one hand the men had to learn to make barricades and obstruct roads. On the other special attention was to be given to night operations, as it was considered certain that a large amount of work in action would be done at night. Furthermore, mobility and physical endurance, two main requirements of a guerrilla force, were to be strengthened. (The assessment was that the current physique of the men would endure little hardship.) Lastly, in order to make successful operations possible, each unit's area was to be thoroughly studied.

The divided approach also showed up in the further development of the organisation. The importance of a large Volunteer army continued to be emphasised over the need for small secret units, and consequently Volunteer membership continued to grow in the remainder of 1918. In Mayo and Tipperary extremely strong growth was recorded. In November Mayo membership had increased by 50 per cent from April to 1,592 and Tipperary Volunteers had nearly doubled in number to 1,135. Wexford's organisational efforts, however, had almost come to a standstill adding only 56 members, while in Derry the first 22 new recruits since the Rising were recorded. Wexford's involvement in the Rising had ensured an early growth, but paralysed the organisation in 1918.

The extension of the organisation to all parts of the country was a slow process. The first and one of the most successful organisational efforts of GHQ was the regularisation of brigade areas throughout the South at the end of 1918. However, a full complement of battalions and companies within this brigade structure was still lacking. Even in the best organised brigades there were areas without a unit, and companies that had not joined a battalion or were left without any direct control. The latter could be situated between two brigades or on the fringes of the brigade areas.[56]

TOWARDS CONFRONTATION, WINTER 1918

The apathy permeating the Volunteer organisation in 1918 did not, however, apply to every member. Those who had become most intimately absorbed by Volunteer activity could not (and often did not want to) distance themselves from their involvement. Unattached young men with no serious responsibilities were most likely to get caught up in this way. Those

---

56 Regularisation of brigades, Charles Townshend (1983), 332–3. A loose company in Cork Brigade, letter GHQ to Commandant Cork Brigade dated 19 November 1918, NLI, ms. 31,191. Inch between the South and Mid Tipperary Brigades was described as: 'a sort of no mans land where a small unit of about eight willing and able men formed a unit under no one's control', Ned O'Reilly, O'MN, P17b126.

who had gone through the cycle of arrest, hunger strike and release became more personally involved and reluctant to return to prison. To protect these men they were ordered not to attend parades or any other public Volunteer or national activity. A simple choice was presented to them: either leave the Volunteers or evade and resist arrest. The first possibility became increasingly difficult the longer they remained with the Volunteers, as they became known to and wanted by the authorities. The latter choice was therefore almost forced upon them, inevitably leading to more violent confrontation with the police and military.[57]

Despite the measures taken by the government, this small group of activists slowly stepped up their operations. After the conscription scare had died down their first priority remained the procurement of arms. Despite the official ban, arms raids continued to be popular. The ambivalent attitude of GHQ towards violence became apparent when a group of young enthusiastic Volunteers from Derry City raided a local estate. After being court-martialled by their captain, the leader of the group appealed to GHQ, emphasising that arms were easily obtained in the vicinity of the city. GHQ was strongly divided on the subject.[58]

The more politically-orientated leaders had initiated the ban as they were afraid to lose public support, while the militarily-minded men realised the necessity of raids if they wished to become a serious threat to the government. Consequently the Derry Volunteers were allowed to continue raiding. The general attitude taken by GHQ was summed up by another Volunteer: 'Now raids at that time [spring 1919] were more or less forbidden officially by our headquarters staff. If you got away with it you got a pat on the back, and if you didn't get away with it you were disowned.'[59]

Reported attempts to obtain arms by raid, burglary or larceny increased in some areas during 1918. In Mayo a few raids for arms and one larceny of explosives took place in the entire year, while in Tipperary a couple of raids were reported each month. Drilling had continued in both counties on a small scale and now occurred in Wexford and south Derry also. However, in neither of the latter two counties were any arms raids reported. In Wexford the political strength of the movement was, nevertheless, formidable. Unlike Mayo or Tipperary, large protest meetings against the arrest of the national leaders took place in May, with 500 attending in Wexford and 3,000 in Enniscorthy. In September the funeral of, James Rafter, one of Wexford's 1916 leaders attracted 3,000 people, while 600

57 Examples of men getting wrapped up in their involvement, Andy Cooney, O'MN, P17b107; C.S. Andrews (1979), passim; Alfred Rutherford, O'MN, P17b122. Order to activists to stay away from public meetings, J.V. Lawless, 'Recollections of the War of Independence 1916-1921', UCD AD, P7D148.
58 Enthusiastic Volunteers in Derry, Liam Brady, *Derry Journal*, 6 May 1953.
59 Quote, K. Griffith and T. O'Grady (1982), 187.

Volunteers marched in military formation. Rafter died of burns he received while experimenting with explosives. Five of the marchers were later arrested and prosecuted for wearing uniforms. The start of drilling in Derry also gave a boost to its political organisation. It was the only county in which Sinn Féin showed significant growth between the Conscription Crisis and 1919.[60]

The leadership also continued attempts to improve armaments and training. Production of home-made grenades and ammunition which had started during the Conscription Crisis was stepped up. In Dublin small munitions-workshops were set up where complete grenades were manufactured, including the casting of shells, and by the end of 1918 the first of these were ready. In the meantime the Department of Training ordered some men to write handbooks for the different tasks with which the Volunteers were confronted.[61]

Besides these manuals, special lectures on military subjects were organised every Saturday for the officers of the Dublin Brigade and for any other officer who happened to be in the city. These lectures started in 1918 and continued to be held well into 1920. At the same time the Engineering Staff organised lectures to both officers and men on high explosives, chemicals, explosive fuses, small arms, raiding and on obtaining information.[62]

However, open activity was made even more difficult by the conclusion of the First World War in November 1918: many expected that Home Rule would soon be introduced, and feared that Britain would come down hard on the Volunteers, now that its continental wartime commitments were over. The attention of most Volunteers turned to securing the return of Sinn Féin candidates in the General Election of December 1918. Votes had to be registered and active canvassing took place. In Mayo, where poverty was widespread, this included the collection of food and its distribution to the needy to encourage them to vote Sinn Féin. Even dependants of British soldiers were thus approached. The election-campaign was again marked by minor expressions of defiance, ranging from singing rebellious songs to burning the Union Jack; but apart from a few small incidents, no serious violence took place. The main exceptions were the wounding of a British corporal by a Volunteer in Westport in the heat of the campaign, and the

60 Events recorded by the police, CIs South Tipperary, Mayo, Wexford and Derry MRs 1918. Other accidental deaths due to a lack of experience with arms in 1917, C. Browne (n. d.), 11; Liam Haugh, 'History of the West Clare Brigade', NLI, P915 A0363.
61 Making bombs in Dublin, J.V. Lawless, 'Recollections of the War of Independence', UCD AD, P7D148; Pat McHugh, O'MN, P17b110.
62 Improved training, Leo Henderson, O'MN, P17b105; Joseph A. Cripps, NLI, ms. 22,117(1).

development of some tension in Derry City after a man was injured by a revolver shot fired from a Sinn Féin crowd.[63]

Election-day was the first opportunity for many units to appear in public. Rural units that had only been active in secret drilling and marching paraded openly and were prepared for a possible clash with the police:

> First public appearance was when we marched from Rosegreen to Cashel dressed out with haversack and bandoleer. By marching openly, we were giving away our identity to the peelers [slang for policemen], which put us on the lists of wanted men. We carried no guns, except for a good heavy baton concealed inside our coats, which were to be used if the RIC made an attempt to arrest us, or prevented us from marching.[64]

Many Volunteers were involved in the elections. Their tasks prescribed by GHQ included: giving protection for public and private meetings, acting as peace patrols at all times, guarding polling booths and escorting ballot boxes to counting centres. Often this involvement went beyond the call of duty: 'Also we did duty on ballot boxes in the Election. The Drummin people were to have come in, but only a few of them came, so we voted for them. There was a peeler who said to me there are dead men voting here today.' Although this election rigging was observed by the police, most constables were too frightened to interfere. The extremely large support Sinn Féin had gained in the previous year was demonstrated by the election victory. The party took 73 out of 105 seats. The elected Sinn Féin MPs formed their own Irish parliament, Dáil Éireann, in January 1919. They constituted a republican government which hoped to gain independence for Ireland at the Versailles Peace Conference.[65]

CONCLUSION

Open activity after the Rising was practically impossible. Individual radical nationalists were hesitant to express their feelings, as the least show of rebelliousness was confronted by the police. Nevertheless, some die-hards publicly sang seditious songs or shouted rebellious slogans. Until the

63 Consequences of the end of the War, Michael Brennan (1980), 36; Paddy Gallagher, 'Looking West', Tape B620, RTE Radio Archives. Attention to electioneering in Tipperary, Paul Mulcahy, 'Statement'; Ned Prendergast, Interview. On distributing food in Mayo, Patrick Owen Mugan, Interview. Violence and campaigns for election, CIs MRs November-December 1918.
64 Quote, Peter Morrissey, 'Memoirs'.
65 GHQ orders, NLI, ms. 31,191. Quote on 'dead men voting', Johnny Duffy, O'MN, P17b109.

Volunteer organisation grew sufficiently in strength, most radicals expressed their allegiance through organisations like the GAA and the Gaelic League. Their meetings were well-attended in many counties as they were one of the few safe ways to express one's sympathy for the ideals of the Easter Rising. In areas where the GAA and the Gaelic League were poorly represented, such as Mayo, no nationalist activity was reported in 1916.

The release of the internees was of extreme importance for reorganisation in all areas. Their involvement in radical politics had often been the main reason for their arrest, and most of them returned more determined than ever to further the cause of Irish freedom. The suffering they endured earned them much respect and admiration and gave them authority, which enabled them to re-establish and extend the Volunteer organisation. Local centres were restarted, often via contacts in the IRB which were concentrated in the towns. From here, men went out to rural districts to initiate new units. The visit of an outsider often gave the necessary impetus to local men who had been inspired by the Rising. Recruits outside the circle of friends and neighbours of the first activists were originally attracted by the public displays of drilling and parading. In this way the organisation was slowly enlarged and condensed.

Immediately after the reorganisation some secret drilling and training started. Volunteers only came out in the open during large-scale events like bye-elections and big funerals, in which one could disappear into the crowd. The experience and successes gained on these occasions slowly diminished the reluctance to identify as a Volunteer. After the display of Volunteer strength and public support during the funeral of Thomas Ashe in September 1917, open defiance became a general policy of the Volunteer Executive. The main expression of this was the order to each unit to drill openly during the second week of December 1917.

The emergence of open drilling was largely confined to the southern and western counties. The inability of the police and the hesitancy of the authorities to deal with this meant that drilling became a regular feature of life in several districts. Nevertheless, the Volunteers remained a relatively small and inactive organisation in most counties, with only limited public support. Companies met irregularly for drill exercises and only the most ardent members engaged in secret operations such as arms raids.

The police tried to limit Volunteer activity by prosecuting leading activists for minor offences, for which they received short sentences. However, on their return from prison their fear of the authorities and prison in general was lessened, while public admiration for them had grown. The resulting sense of strength was increased by the government's inability to deal with their hunger strikes. These had forced the government to grant imprisoned Volunteers a status equal to political prisoner, and to release many before completing their sentence. This led to a situation in which determined men could show their dedication to the cause by publicly defying the authorities and inviting arrest without fear of significant punishment. To deal with this increasingly embarrassing situation, the Cat-and-Mouse Act was introduced early in 1918, which allowed the release and rearrest of these men.

The Conscription Crisis that followed the introduction of this act made Volunteer membership and public displays of disregard for the law widely accepted and established Sinn Féin as the main representative of popular opinion. Many people associated resistance to conscription with support for the Volunteers. However, as open conflict was now considered probable, the Volunteers Executive ordered its men to go underground to minimise the risk of arrest. The large-scale demonstrations associated with opposition to conscription were the main reason for the government to suppress all open displays of a military nature when the crisis had subsided. The arrest of many Volunteer officers and most national leaders in May 1918 marked a tougher line by the government. This made most ordinary Volunteers who had joined as an expression of their refusal to join the British Army rather than as a willingness to fight, hesitant to show their involvement, and inclined them to limit themselves to political activities like preparing for the general elections and unarmed protests.

However, some of the militarily minded men refused to believe in the ultimate success of the political process, and slowly began to engage the police in their attempts to obtain arms. They were radicalised after having been imprisoned frequently during 1917 and 1918, and were determined to resist further arrest by force. The Conscription Crisis thus changed the challenge to the authorities from open defiance of large groups of Volunteers led by men who often invited arrest, to secret preparation for military conflict by a small circle of dedicated Volunteers.

From the summer of 1918 the organisation was characterised by falling interest and membership on the one hand, and on the other hand by radicalisation of a small number of Volunteers who evaded arrest. Although some members of GHQ supported the growing violence associated with this, there was no official sanction for operations against the Crown Forces. The presence of militants was largely confined to the areas that had engaged in open drilling most fervently before the Conscription Crisis. The professionalisation of a small part of the Volunteers and the differentiation in activity can thus already be detected from the moment the Volunteers reorganised in 1917.

At the end of 1918 the most radicalised members, worried by the falling interest in the Volunteers, tried to force the large group of inactive members to join them by stepping up military operations. Their attacks on policemen were generally unpopular. The militant Volunteers came under attack from the police as well as the population and even from within the movement itself. However, as a result the situation was polarised, and more and more Volunteers were forced to make a choice: get involved in military activity, leave the organisation or do nothing. The developments between 1916 and 1918 had opened the way to more serious confrontation. A decreasing fear of the authorities and a growing determination to avoid and resist arrest among a number of men were combined with the possession of at least some weaponry.

Several aspects influenced the further development of the struggle. First, action of any kind was a strong impetus to further activity, both to the men involved and to others inspired by what took place. The reaction of the authorities to this was often an equally strong stimulus. This process in which activity stimulated more activity led to a separation between the active and the cautious, thus limiting involvement to a small group. Second, the diverse experience of action led to an increasing differentiation between areas. Combined with the first aspect, this became a self-sustaining process, leading to ever-growing differences in levels of activity. Third, the dominance of those among the leaders who saw the Volunteers as a political instrument, over those who felt a military conflict was necessary, meant that military operations were not led from above, but were largely dependent on the activities of the most dedicated and radical members. The official non-violent policy of GHQ therefore facilitated the development of ever-growing differences in activity between the various counties.

The importance of the IRB clearly diminished in this period. After its initial involvement in reforming the Volunteers, the need for a secret society working for Irish independence became unclear. Most members still refused to see the Volunteers as an Irish Army, and had little affinity with the violent intentions of the IRB, but many militarily minded members considered the IRB to be largely superfluous as well now that the Volunteers had become the agent of resistance. The restraints that older IRB-men put on some younger members – who were quite willing to go a lot further than parading and simply defying the police – turned some of them away. In 1918, after Seán Treacy had been arrested for the third time since the Rising, some of his IRB comrades wanted to kidnap the police sergeant responsible for this in order to initiate a trade-off. This was prevented by the local IRB-centre: 'The IRB he stated stood for something higher than the capture of "a bloody old policeman".' The result was that many of the Tipperary town officers severed their connection with the IRB and the local circle of the brotherhood never met again. Eamon O'Dwyer, who had become the Head-Centre of the IRB in the county, also felt that the time for a secret society had long gone. He and his officers decided to let the IRB die a silent death. Some of the national leaders like Eamon De Valéra, the President of the Irish Volunteers and Sinn Féin, felt the same way and left the IRB at this time. The traditional rejection of secret societies by the Catholic Church also played an important role in this decision. The IRB nevertheless continued to exist, and would play an important role again in the acceptance of the Treaty in January 1922.[66]

66 Reaction of IRB to plan, 'Notes on the IRB and the South Tipperary Brigade', UCD AD, P7b181(97). This is confirmed by Mick Fitzpatrick, O'MN, P17b114. Letting IRB die, Eamon O'Dwyer, 'Statement'.

CHAPTER 3

Transformation 1919–1920

The slow militarisation described in the previous chapter applied mainly to the active ringleaders who had begun to use violence without sanction from GHQ. Most ordinary Volunteers preferred to protect their livelihood, on which a whole family might rely, to active participation, which had become increasingly dangerous. Among those without prison experience, only some were willing to do more than occasionally engage in secret drilling exercises, while many lost interest altogether. In areas where many activists had been involved in acts of public defiance and more had consequently been arrested, it was most likely that a development towards increased violence would take place. This sometimes involved some of the less experienced but willing young members. In this way small regional differences which had established themselves in 1917 and 1918 were amplified. Between 1918 and 1920, a much larger proportion of Volunteers became engaged in open conflict. This development towards violent confrontation was most apparent in Tipperary and Dublin, where public defiance had been widespread up to 1919, but did not emerge in Mayo although it had been equally defiant.

FIRST BLOODSHED, EARLY 1919

After the displays of defiance were curtailed in the spring of 1918, confrontation between police and Volunteers became increasingly confined to the few attempts to disarm constables at gun point. Despite several earlier incidents of this kind, the shooting of two policemen at Soloheadbeg, Co. Tipperary on 21 January 1919, coinciding with the first public meeting of the alternative Irish Parliament, Dáil Éireann, came as a shock. These were the first policemen in Ireland to be killed by the Volunteers since the Easter Rising. As a result, the police in Tipperary panicked and began to see threats all around: 'Everywhere it is pervaded with young men who show hostility to any form of control. Imbued with Sinn Féin propaganda and possessed of arms and ammunition they are a danger to the community.' Similar acts of violence took place elsewhere. In the same month a bomb was thrown into the prison in Derry City. In March the Resident

Magistrate in Westport, Co. Mayo, W. Milling, was shot, and in Dublin a raid on a military post at Collinstown Aerodrome was highly successful.[1]

Although these operations roughly coincided, they did not signal the start of a military campaign. As with other Volunteer operations in this period, the sole object of the ambushers at Soloheadbeg had been the explosives the police were guarding in transit. The attack in Derry was enacted to test a home-made grenade and the raid on the aerodrome in Dublin was merely an exceptionally large arms raid. The shooting of the magistrate in Westport, Co. Mayo, however, was an example of a different approach. It was probably a direct result of the magistrate's action in sentencing Volunteers, and therefore an attempt to intimidate the authorities. Although the remainder of the year was fairly unsettled in some areas, few other engagements between the police and Volunteers took place. The militarists in the movement were possibly held back by a GHQ order explicitly forbidding military style operations without prior permission.[2]

As stated, only a tiny minority of Volunteers was engaged in these unauthorised attacks. Among them were the main brigade officers in Tipperary who had carried out the Soloheadbeg ambush. The national leaders of the Volunteers were, however, still unwilling to face the implications that this attack presented. Their initial reaction was to advise the men involved to leave the country; this traditionally had been the result of any engagement in which representatives of the British Government were killed for political reasons. It had been done during the campaign of the 'Invincibles', a group within the IRB which tried to assassinate British officials in the 1880s, and more recently when Michael O'Callaghan shot two policemen in Tipperary when they tried to arrest him shortly after the Rising. However, the dedicated men from Tipperary declined to follow this advice, which if taken up by all such activists would have prevented the development of guerrilla warfare.[3]

Despite their refusal to leave, these men had no intention of starting a violent campaign yet and did not initiate any further confrontation. Nevertheless, when one of their close associates, Sean Hogan, was arrested a few months later they did not hesitate to try to rescue him. On 13 May, the train transporting him to Cork prison stopped in Knocklong, Co. Limerick, where the police-escort was attacked by several Volunteers. In the ensuing fight two policemen were killed and one of the successful res-

---

1   Quote, CI South Tipperary MR January 1919.
2   Attack in Derry, Lt. M. Sheerin, NLI, P915 A0394; CI Derry MR January 1919. Reason for shooting of magistrate in Mayo, Thomas Heavey, 'Statement'; CI Mayo MR March 1919. Raid on aerodrome, Pat MacCrea, O'MN, P17b110. GHQ order to ask permission for serious operations, NLI, P919 A0525.
3   Experience of Tipperary officers, Dan Breen (1981), 54. Seamus Robinson, 'Statement', NLI, ms. 21,265.

cuing party, Dan Breen as well as the prisoner were seriously wounded. To avoid persecution and to recover from their wounds, the Volunteers involved in the attack, who were among the most violent Volunteers in south Tipperary, left the county and went to Cork. The two wounded men and the two other main brigade officers, after travelling through Limerick, Kerry, and Clare, ended up in Dublin, only to return to Tipperary in the spring of 1920. Their absence meant that most operations were suspended. Likewise, many of the few militarists in other counties were arrested or restrained from taking violent action during this period.[4]

During much of 1919 militant Volunteers diverted their attention to attempts to substitute British rule with a republican alternative. To finance their rival administration, the self-proclaimed Irish parliament had issued a kind of government bond which was to be sold all over the country under the Dáil Loan. Activists were also active in arbitration courts introduced to replace the local assizes, particularly in Mayo. As an alternative to the RIC, Volunteers sometimes acted as a police force at public meetings and fair days. This was supported by a boycott of the RIC, which had begun during the Conscription Crisis and was resumed by local activists in 1919. A police boycott was called by Volunteers in August 1919, while a nation-wide ban on dealing with the RIC was instituted in June 1920. The hostile environment in Derry meant that local Volunteers were directing their energy somewhat differently. Particular attention was paid to the registration of voters, but no attempt to sell Dáil Bonds is mentioned in police reports. Although all these activities implied a direct challenge to the authorities, they did not involve any direct engagement with the Crown Forces.[5]

GENERAL INACTIVITY 1919

The growing dangers involved in being a Volunteer had led to a decline in activity and participation, aggravated by the lack of opportunity and excitement that Volunteer work presented to ordinary members who

4 See note 3; D. Ryan (1945), 100-10.
5 Involvement in political activities in Mayo, 'Activities of Owenwee Company'; John Joe Philben, 'Statement'; Jack Feehan, O'MN, P17b113; Ned Moane, 'Statement', and Moane/Malone, Tape. Volunteer police activity, Ned Moane, 'Statement'; Thomas Kettrick, 'Statement'. Police boycott in Conscription Crisis, Charles Townshend (1979), 321; Peter Hart (1992), Chapter 'The Dynamics of Violence', 22. Boycott in April 1919 in Clare, David Fitzpatrick (1977), 10. Boycott in Tipperary in 1919, Seamus Robinson, 'Statement', NLI, ms. 21,265. National boycott June 1920, NLI, ms. 739. Activities in Derry, Wm. John Himphey, Fr O'Kane Papers, Tape A20 & A23, AARC; CI Derry MRs 1919.

were unwilling to engage in violence. To avoid losing members, a concerted effort was made in 1919 to improve attendance at secret drilling,
which remained the main occupation of most Volunteers. Everywhere
Volunteers managed to find places where they could safely exercise: 'We
had several raids by the military but they could never surprise us as the
hall where we drilled was about 80 yards from the main road and the
back of it led into a field we had our scouts posted in such a way [that]
before they got to within 600 yards of it we would be about 6 fields
away when they arrived.' Some rural companies had more problems
avoiding police attention: 'If you drilled you had to land in some place
that no one would see you. You might go to some field at night.' In
Leenane, Co. Mayo it was described as follows: 'In 1919, we used to
mobilise the Volunteers and do a small bit of drill, dodging the RIC
who were intent on getting the names of those who were drilling, or trying to accuse them of some other offence.' Drilling was supplemented
with some special service training: 'There was flags and all that thing
going on, from hill to hill, what you should do and how you should
transfer information. [...] We were taught all that and how to take cover
and fall into marching.'[6]

The drilling exercises were, however, unable to maintain the interest
of less dedicated Volunteers. In December 1919, one organiser reported a
general malaise in the Volunteers: 'The men are sick of doing the same
"form fours" all the time and the officers are not very willing either.'
Inspecting officers who were sent to companies in Dublin during the last
months of 1919 reported that most sections in the companies had only
roughly half their strength on parade, and that the state of training in
special services (i.e. first aid and signalling) was, with a few exceptions,
poor. Some moderate Volunteers who had never envisioned engaging in
actual fighting, now left or were pushed into the political wing. Several
resigned with the excuse that they did not have the time necessary for
the job. Such lack of commitment also became apparent among many
others. The commandant of the 2nd Battalion in Dublin felt forced to
suspend his adjutant in September: 'You have failed to report for the last
fortnight or to reply to or even acknowledge receipt of my letters and
orders during that period or to attend Brigade Adjutant meetings during
the same period.' The man apologised but his sole excuse was lack of
time. Apparently he saw his involvement in the Volunteers mainly as a
leisure activity. Some officers were so inactive that their own men, who

6 Attention to parade strength in 1919, David Fitzpatrick (1977), 200–1. Quotes:
   'Safe places', Laurence Casey, NLI, ms. 10,723(2). 'In fields at night', Patrick
   Owen Mugan, Interview. In Leenane, P.J. Kelly, 'One of the Men of the
   West'. 'Special service training', Patrick Owen Mugan, Interview.

found they had failed to fulfil their duties to the company, urged their resignation.[7]

As a result leading Volunteers were forced to spend most of their time travelling around to keep units alive and to instil some activity. The inexperience of most low-ranking officers demanded constant attention from superior officers. In their attempts to initiate activity in local companies the latter replaced many inactive company officers. The new men were often more enthusiastic than their predecessors, but even more inexperienced in exercising command. The involvement of higher officers also heightened the inability of officers to act on their own. This inexperience and the constant attention needed for organisation made it even more difficult to mount operations. Some activists realised that only the Crown Forces could spur locals into action. Seán Treacy is reported to have observed this in 1918: 'If this is the state of affairs, we'll have to kill somebody, and make the bloody enemy organise us.' Whether he said it or not, he did indeed act upon it, but in most areas nobody was willing to do so.[8]

The lack of drive in most country officers was particularly disheartening to GHQ organisers, who spent all their time and energy to getting the organisation on its feet. An organiser in Co. Louth wrote to Michael Collins in September 1919 after a meeting of all brigade officers he called had only brought out four men: 'I will write you when I get home. That is if I am in a better frame of mind. Do you know Mick there is absolutely no use in my holding on to this job; it's only a farce, in this damned County.' Ernie O'Malley, one of the first full-time organisers, described the half-hearted attitude of most officers in this period:

> The brigadier and his staff, the battalion staffs, lived at home and attended to I.R.A. routine as it suited them or as their conscience dictated. [...] The brigade staff (1918-20) seldom or ever visited battalion councils, were satisfied with issuing odd orders and transmitting an odd report, for the greater part untrue, to General Headquarters. Brigade staffs actually could not tell the names of the companies in the brigade. [...] Here and there one met men eager to work. I generally endeavoured to pull a member of the brigade and battalion staff round with me, to show them what the area was like

7 Quote from organisers report dated 5 December 1919, UCD AD, P7a158. Visits by inspecting officers, NLI, ms. 1,413. Resignations in Dublin, NLI, ms. 901/96-7 + 104-5. Quote on suspension and excuse, NLI, ms. 901/60-1. Officers called upon to resign, NLI, ms. 901/88. Some Volunteers in Mayo left for England and Scotland, after some operations had led to raids and arrests in the area. Others were so disappointed with the lack of activity that they went to Liverpool, only to return when a Flying Column was set up in 1921, John Joe Philben, 'Statement'; Jim O'Donnell, 'Recollections'; Paddy Duffy, O'MN, P17b138.

8 Quote from Seán Treacy, K. Griffith and T. O'Grady (1982), 131.

and to make them get in touch with the men, but often as General Headquarters was far away, and they knew I would not complain they gave me a dog's life.[9]

SHORTAGE OF ARMS

The general lack of arms was a factor which severely limited activity by the more eager members. Possession of a weapon was of vital importance to these Volunteers, who were not taken seriously without one. The ownership of a gun was often a prerequisite for participation in operations. In the country this applied mainly to rifles, while in the city, the possession of any type of revolver was greatly admired: 'As a Company, we were very poorly armed. If a fellow had a bloody old .45 at that time he was something like Napoleon.' As a result obtaining arms was an ongoing obsession. Those who had acquired a weapon at the beginning were most likely to be involved in arms raiding and were most likely to become part of the minority of fighting men.[10]

In Tipperary and Dublin the early activity of the Volunteers had ensured a somewhat better supply, but the raids for arms mainly brought in shotguns which had limited military value. Some rifles and revolvers could be bought from GHQ, but they asked up to £5 each, a considerable sum at the time. Fund-raising therefore became a major necessity for local Volunteers. In many places this was done very successfully, but GHQ's ability to procure arms was highly overestimated. Funds available to the country units soon far exceeded the value of the arms on offer, and GHQ sent most war-material to the active units in the South. To ensure that some arms were allocated to one's own area, frequent visits to Dublin were necessary. The Westport Battalion in Mayo was one of the western units most seriously involved in this. They sent their quartermaster to Dublin several times to negotiate purchases. It was a slow process, but about twelve rifles came through in the end. The general difficulties in obtaining arms is evidenced from the fact that these rifles made Westport the best armed battalion in the county for the entire War of Independence.[11]

9 Quote, Report from Drogheda dated 7 August 1919, NLI, P911. Quote from Ernie O'Malley, C.K.H. O'Malley (1989), 10-11.
10 Quote, Gus Connolly, O'MN, P17b91. See also Charlie Dalton (1929), 56-7.
11 Fund-raising in Mayo, Thomas Kettrick, 'Statement'; Ned Moane, 'Statement'. In Tipperary, Ned Glendon, O'MN, P17b103. In south Derry, Thomas Morris, Fr O'Kane Papers, Tape A13, AARC. Activities QM of West Mayo Brigade, Thomas Kettrick, 'Statement'. The GHQ policy of sending arms to the active South, Staff memo 'The War as a Whole', dated 24 March 1921, UCD AD, P7A47. Reported arms raids went down considerably in 1919, from 311 raids in 1918 to 191, David Fitzpatrick (1977), 214-24.

SLOW BUILD UP OF CONFLICT

Violence remained extremely limited during 1919. One of the most active counties was Tipperary, where a few activists were already involved full-time in Volunteering and a total of eight RIC men were killed or seriously wounded in 1919. Due to their participation in previous attacks they were permanently on the run from the police. The leading officers of the South Tipperary Brigade had left the county after the Knocklong rescue and fewer than ten raids for arms and five cases of drilling were reported in the brigade area throughout the year. It is, however, safe to assume that more occurred. Drilling was done in secret and most raids for arms went unreported because weapons were handed over voluntarily or because those who were raided were afraid to inform the police. After a reported incident in January 1920 the police admitted that they had to uncover the extent of the raiding themselves. They were well aware that only genuinely loyal people would report to them. Despite the small number of reported raids, it had already become an accepted occurrence. In November 1919 the police casually recorded: 'Two raids for arms, with the usual accompaniments of masks & revolvers.'[12]

In the other counties raids for arms were rarer; none were recorded in Mayo, some in Wexford at the end of 1919, and in Derry one was registered in October and November. Some Volunteers recall a general raid for arms in September 1919, but despite a small increase in raiding, they probably confused this with the general raid ordered in September 1920. The somewhat higher level of recorded activity in Wexford and Derry compared to Mayo can be explained by the much larger proportion of people opposing Sinn Féin. Supporters of the Parliamentary Party and the Unionists were more likely to report the Volunteer raids to the police than the Volunteer-friendly population in Mayo. A particularly resistant section of Parliamentary Party supporters lived in Wexford town, where clashes between followers of the two parties took place as late as 1920. The total recorded activity in Mayo in 1919 consisted of two cases of illegal drilling, one in August and one in December, and one raid on the mail in December.[13]

The different environments in which the Volunteers in these counties had to operate are reflected in the way raids were organised. In Mayo many shotguns were given up voluntarily, while few put up any resistance: 'Anybody in the area who had shotguns or small guns and who did not

12 In 1919 7 men were reported to be on the run in the South Tipperary Brigade, Seamus Robinson, 'Statement', NLI, ms. 21,265. Quote, CI South Tipperary MR November 1919. See also the reports for rest of 1919 and January 1920.
13 General raid in September 1919 reported in Derry, Wm. John Himphey, Fr O'Kane Papers, Tape A23, AARC. In Mayo, Ned Moane, 'Statement'. Activity level and support for Sinn Féin, CIs Derry, Mayo, Wexford MRs 1919-20.

offer them to the Volunteers had their houses raided and those arms commandeered. They were given receipts.' In Derry the men mainly raided Catholic farmers, but hostility meant that the fear of recognition was high, and most raids took place in localities outside their company areas. Protestant farmers, who possessed most of the arms, were rarely visited. Local Volunteers claim that this was because the Protestants were too strong and they lacked sufficient information about them. For good rifles they visited the Big Houses. The first of these raids in south Derry took place in November 1919 on Springhill House some distance away from the homes of the Volunteers involved.[14]

There are no surviving police records for Dublin City, but some company activity-lists show that the main events were comparable to the rest of the country. Despite initial hesitance raids became casual affairs to the ordinary Volunteers in Dublin in 1919: 'Within a few months we were going into every house in the Company area that we thought might have arms of any kind. At that stage we went into twos and threes, knocking at the doors and politely enquiring if we might look around for arms and were never refused.' In the occasional larger operation in 1919, such as the raid on Collinstown Aerodrome, active members from several units were involved. Some of these men who became increasingly involved, were taken into the Squad in August. This was a special unit of about ten full-time members set up both for the protection of leading Volunteers and for the shooting of police detectives. Despite their professional approach, the activities of this unit were also haphazardly organised. Often neither the top officers nor the participating men had prior knowledge of what was about to happen, and most of those involved were drawn from Volunteers who happened to be available.[15]

In the most serious operation in Dublin since 1916, the assassination attempt on Lord Lieutenant French in December 1919, active Volunteers who were visiting from other parts of Ireland were invited to join. Among them were the four officers from Tipperary who had come to Dublin after being wounded in the Knocklong rescue. As a result of their involvement, it was seriously considered whether they should become full-time members of the Squad. This was rejected by one of the Dublin leaders who felt it reflected poorly on his own men. All operations of the

14 Quote from Mayo, Jim O'Donnell, 'Recollections'. Experience with Protestants in Derry, Paddy Larkin, Interview; James Harkin, Fr O'Kane Papers, Tape A9, AARC; John Duffy, Tape A20, Ibidem. For a vivid report of a similar raid on Moyola House in 1920, Wm. John Himphey, Fr O'Kane Papers, Tape A23, AARC.

15 Quote, C.S. Andrews (1979), 116-17. Squad, George White, O'MN, P17b105; Patrick O'Daly, 'Statement', NLI, P4548. Poor preparations by the Squad leading to danger, Jim Slattery, O'MN, P17b109; Michael Lynch, 'Statement', NLI, ms. 22,117(1).

Dublin Volunteers together led to twelve casualties among the Crown Forces prior to 1920.[16]

Ordinary Volunteers everywhere were extremely reluctant to get involved in violence. The few military operations in different parts of the country, including some attacks on police barracks, resulted in many police raids and searches in which a good deal of arms, ammunition and seditious documents were confiscated. Men found in possession of these items were jailed. Particularly in areas where the police was well-informed about the republican movement, this seriously affected operational strength. However, the few military style operations and the subsequent arrests resulted in a slow but steady increase in the number of radicalised Volunteers willing to do more.

INCREASING ACTIVITY, EARLY 1920

Sinn Féin's attempts to secure Ireland's independence at the Peace Conference faltered during the summer of 1919 and in September the Dáil was suppressed. This apparent failure of political means gave the militarists in the movement a free hand. In January 1920 the Volunteer Executive finally endorsed open attacks on the Crown Forces. However, it realised that the British Army could never be beaten militarily. In an internal memo GHQ stated that although they considered themselves capable of conquering 75 per cent of the country by destroying most police barracks they could not hope to keep it under control for long and ultimate defeat was likely: 'All our training, lectures etc. drive us to the one conclusion, namely that no matter what strategy we may adopt we will eventually be beaten in a military sense.' An active defence strategy was recommended in which the main consideration was to cause as much damage to the enemy and least to oneself. Consequently, they proclaimed the smashing of all government communication as the main priority. This included attacks on telegraph wires, post offices, police barracks and military posts. In the following months attacks on police barracks became particularly widespread in the South, with the acquisition of rifles as its main objective.[17]

Coinciding with the return of the main brigade officers from Dublin, violent activity flared up in south Tipperary. Fully recovered from their wounds and with more fighting experience, they were determined to start

16 Objections to Tipperary men in Squad, Michael Lynch, 'Statement', NLI, ms. 22,117(1).
17 Sanction by GHQ, Peter Hart (1992), Chapter 'The Dynamics of Violence', 43. Internal memo, IG MR February 1920. Smashing communications, O'MN, P17b127.

direct attacks on the Crown Forces. An outbreak of arms raiding and involvement in two attacks on barracks in January was followed in February by the first shots fired at the military. Three men, including the brigade adjutant, were arrested. In the following months many large-scale assaults on barracks were reported. In some cases the police were forced to surrender and the barracks destroyed. In most other counties the men were not ready to take this step, and only a few politically motivated minor offences were reported. All other activity was immediately nipped in the bud by the police, who were particularly vigilant in Derry. Some raids for arms by Volunteers in the southern part of that county were immediately answered with extensive police raids in which a few people were arrested for possession of arms and seditious documents.[18]

The violence that developed in places like Tipperary had serious consequences. As a result of some successful attacks on police barracks in the Southwest, up to 500 isolated indefensible police posts were evacuated throughout the country. This enabled Sinn Féin and the Volunteers, often one and the same outside Dublin, to take over civil control in these areas. The effect of this on inactive areas is particularly noticeable in Mayo. Despite the inability of Mayo Volunteers to initiate any serious attacks, the police, intimidated by events in other areas, evacuated many outlying posts. Several of these were burned during the year; twenty-one in July and August alone. With the disappearance of close police control, open drilling was resumed in many rural areas. The lack of any large military engagement in Mayo was substituted by a large number of small operations which could now be enacted with little chance of detection. A similar development took place in parts of Wexford and Derry.[19]

Mass burning of courthouses and evacuated barracks, and raiding of tax offices, was ordered by GHQ for Easter 1920. This was a big occasion for the Volunteers, involving a large proportion of men everywhere. For most units this was their first operation and many were still afraid to get involved in such direct contravention of the law. One of the first burnings in west Mayo took place at Aughagower. Of all the local Volunteers summoned only three showed up. The local 1st lieutenant was never again seen on company work. A similar small number of Volunteers turned up in

---

18 Activities of Volunteers, CIs South Tipperary, Derry, Mayo, Wexford, MRs January-February 1920.

19 In Co. Cork alone 10 barracks were stormed during the first three months of 1920 of which two successfully, Peter Hart (1992), Chapter 'The Dynamics of Violence', 43. According to official figures 12 occupied barracks were destroyed and another 24 damaged between 1 January 1919 and 1 July 1920, Charles Townshend (1975), Appendix V. According to Townshend's own figures, however, 16 occupied barracks were destroyed and 29 damaged in the first six months of 1920, Ibid., 65. Burnings in Mayo, CI Mayo MRs 1920.

Castlebar for burning the barracks on Easter Saturday and raiding the local income tax office on Easter Monday.[20]

The burnings and growing number of raids for arms and raids on the mail for intelligence purposes meant more exciting involvement for the rank and file without exposing them to too much danger. Participation in these operations instilled activity in many local companies which had been practically dormant during 1919. In these operations renewed differentiation became apparent as some rank and filers showed themselves to be more willing and daring than others. These men were most likely to be chosen for further operations. By the process of initiation the active were separated from the cautious and it became increasingly difficult for men who joined later or had not been around at the right time to be involved in operations. Although most Volunteers were intimidated by the fighting, the experience of action and danger made some others extremely eager.

In 1920, military operations became dominated by these small groups of activists. This was largely a result of the tendency to rely on men with experience. If someone showed himself to be reliable in action in the early stages of the fight, officers preferred to use him again over someone with no experience. The importance of experience also accounts for the high number of ex-soldiers among the IRA fighting forces. The Dublin Brigade Adjutant claims that his brigade had a total strength of about 1,550 men in 1920, but qualifies this as follows: 'This was paper strength. If a man was a good and steady man, it was piled on to him so as not to risk training another man.' Frank Henderson, another senior officer in the Dublin Brigade, concurred and added: 'If a man got accustomed to a gun, it helped to have him use it again. So when you found a good man you continued to feed work to him.'[21]

In the provincial areas active men from different companies who had gained some experience started to call on each other when planning bigger operations, thus enhancing the concentration of activity. The local company men, many of whom were scared away by the growing violence, were then only used occasionally as auxiliary troops. The lack of arms reinforced this

20 According to official sources a total of 447 vacated barracks and 30 courthouses were damaged or destroyed between 1 January 1919 and 1 July 1920, Charles Townshend (1975), Appendix V. According to Townshend's own figures, 424 abandoned barracks (of which 298 at Easter) and 47 courthouses were destroyed in the first 6 months of 1920, Ibid., 65. Burning in Aughagower, Charles Hughes, Interview. In Castlebar, James Chambers, 'Statement'.

21 Quote by Dublin Brigade Adjutant, Harry Colley, O'MN, P7b97. Quote by Frank Henderson, O'MN, P17b99. Another assessment puts paper strength at 3,500, but only 1,000 of these were armed, and not more than 15 per cent were free to take part in action, Charles Dalton (1929), 35. The O.C. of the Dublin Brigade puts fighting strength at 1,200-1,500 in 1920-21, Oscar Traynor, O'MN, P17b96.

tendency, as only a few men could operate at any one time. Although some companies in Dublin later devised systems to rotate the use of arms, serious activity was left in the hands of a few experienced Volunteers.[22]

This concentration of activity can be witnessed at company level throughout the country. The New Ross Company in Wexford, 101 Volunteers strong, engaged in 25 different activities in the period 1916-21. These ranged from a general parade in 1918 to transfer of arms and participation in ambushes. Only 26 of the men were active in more than 8 of these activities and only 12 of these 26 participated in more than 10. In the Bray Company of south Co. Dublin the same tendency is seen. Besides its routine work, this company was involved in 22 operations. Of the 39 Volunteers, only 5 participated in 10 or more of these, another 8 took part in 4 to 9 actions and the other 26 did not participate in more than 3.[23]

The growing radicalisation of Volunteers was exacerbated by a government policy which vacillated from coercion to conciliation. Initially it answered the outbreak of activity in January with widespread internment, arresting many active Volunteers. However, the violence from both sides that erupted during the spring shocked public opinion to such an extent that the government decided to try a more positive approach and released all prisoners. Instead of dealing effectively with the emerging violence, this only involved more Volunteers in the fighting, who had been radicalised by their prison experience. Nevertheless even the most active men continued to exercise caution and preferred safe jobs. The step towards open engagement with the Crown Forces was taken with extreme hesitancy by only a handful of Volunteers. Cautiousness remained the predominant characteristic.

IMPROVING STRUCTURE AND TRAINING 1920

With increased activity the company organisation that had disintegrated somewhat during 1919 was given more attention. In order to oversee the extent of mobilisation, GHQ began to collect exact information about battalion and brigade boundaries, and the name and strength of all companies. A directive was sent out to each brigade commandant on 30 September 1919, stressing the importance of clearly defined company

22 A good description of the concentration of activity in the hands of a few men from different companies and battalions around Fethard, Co. Tipperary, Patrick Ryan, 'Statement'. In Mayo, the younger brother of a Volunteer claimed that local Volunteers were not called on at all during the Tan War, Luke Gilligan, Interview. System of rotating arms, Joe O'Connor, O'MN, P17b105.

23 Figures for New Ross, Activities list of New Ross Company. Figures for Dublin unit, James MacSweeney, 'The Fight in the Bray Area', in *Dublin's Fighting Story*. 1916-21 (n. d.) Similar concentration confirmed by, Michael O'Reilly, O'MN, P17b115.

areas of workable size. The commandants were further ordered to leave no ground in the brigade area uncovered. To facilitate this a new unit was introduced for areas where supporters of the Volunteers were scarce. Small groups of men would constitute an 'Outpost' and in due time form the nucleus of a company. To stimulate the development of units of workable size on all levels, GHQ sent organisers to the different country areas. They extended and adjusted boundaries, and reassigned areas to different units.[24]

The first of these organisers were appointed on a full-time basis in 1918. Up to August 1920 no more than six travelled the country at any one time, dealing with at least fifty independent brigades and countless smaller units. The main task of these men was to implement the Scheme of Organisation and instruct the men on military skills. GHQ relied heavily upon them in its attempts to obtain more control over the provincial units. The effectiveness of these organisers differed considerably and largely depended on their capabilities and the willingness of local Volunteers. The lack of enthusiasm among officers and men in most country units meant that organisers needed to pay a lot of attention to a single unit before anything was done. The subsequent strong involvement of organisers in the day-to-day running of some units made many local men entirely dependent on these outsiders. Funding sufficient good organisers and having brigades make good use of them continued to be a serious problem for GHQ.[25]

To improve the availability of organisers the Department of Organisation recruited another six whole-time organisers in August 1920. They had to be: 'Competent Officers capable of organising Volunteer Activities in any part of Ireland and with a sufficient knowledge of training to instruct Section Commanders and Company Officers in their duties and work. They must also be men imbued with the "imperturbable offensive spirit".' After an intense training course of a week by established organisers and

---

24 The importance of companies of workable size, NLI, ms. 11,410(11). GHQ request for information on boundaries dated 24 May 1919, NLI, ms. 739. The introduction of Outposts, circular of 30 September 1919 re 'formation of Outposts': 'The survey should cover the whole area of your Brigade, and in respect of Parishes and other areas without either a Company or outpost man the "Remarks" column should be made indicate what is being done to form outposts there.', O'MN, P17b127. See also NLI, ms. 11,410(11). Sending down organisers, Michael Chadwick, 'With the Sixth Battalion 1916-1921', in Dublin's Fighting Story (1949), 184-5; C.K.H. O'Malley (1989), 6-7. Despite these efforts many companies still had no clearly defined boundaries in 1921, notebook of Ernie O'Malley, MA, LOT 1.

25 Ernie O'Malley started as organiser in 1918, C.K.H. O'Malley (1989), 6-7. Other GHQ Organisers in 1918: In Derry, Lt. M. Sheerin, NLI, P921 No66; In Cork, NLI, ms. 31,181(8-10, 17 + 31). Number of organisers in 1920, Letter from Director of Organisation dated 10 March 1921, UCD AD, P7A17/97-8.

GHQ staff they were sent down the country. Despite this preparation, those chosen were poorly equipped for the job. The men set off with scanty instructions, and a poor impression of GHQ's ability to keep in touch with the local units.[26]

Poorly qualified and inadequately instructed, it was no surprise that some of these organisers failed to live up to the duties they were expected to perform. They were often unable to improve the state of organisation and mobilise more locals into the Volunteers. It was extremely difficult for the organisers to stimulate the frequently reluctant men into action. On one occasion an organiser was nearly assaulted when he called the men out for exercises after a hard day's work in the fields. Instead of wasting their energy on improving the organisation of unwilling Volunteers, many of them concentrated on working with the small number of dedicated men who were present in the more active areas. GHQ lost its grip on many of these organisers, who rarely visited Dublin and often identified with the local activists they worked with. Most of the latter viewed GHQ's attempts at control as interference which needlessly impaired activity.[27]

Apart from organisers GHQ attempted to assert its control over country units through written communications. This became an ever growing aspect of volunteering much to the dislike of most provincial officers. The collection of exact information on all units in September 1919 was one of their first concerted efforts since the Conscription Crisis, followed by an attempt to regulate the intelligence that was to be obtained by companies and outposts in November. A more serious bid to create a unified code of conduct and to enhance GHQ control on Volunteer activity was made in 1920. On 19 May a new series of general orders were started, of which twenty-eight were issued before the Truce. Brigade officers were responsible for the systematic conveyance of these instructions to their officers and men and for ensuring that they were acted upon. To complement the general orders, several further rather elaborate forms of standard instructions were introduced. Operational Memos were issued from 19 July giving instructions on conduct during operations. Organisational Memos gave directions on matters of structure. Weekly Memos were introduced to give the brigades up-to-date information and instructions concerning new developments.

26 Quote, Mick O'Hanlon, O'MN, P17b106. For the experience of organisers with their own training and with the country units, Jerry Davis, O'MN, P17b106; Andy Cooney, O'MN, P17b107; Billy Rowe O'MN, P17b110. Requirements for Organisers, NLI, ms. 11,410(11). New Organisers were told to leave their employment, letter dated 8 January 1921, NLI, ms. 901/74.

27 Assessment of Inspecting Officer on organisers, UCD AD, P7A48. Anger of local men with organiser, Ned O'Reilly, O'MN, P17b126. See also Tom Barry, in K. Griffith and T. O'Grady (1982), 144-5; Seamus Robinson, 'Statement', NLI, ms. 21,265. A vivid description of the experience of the early organisers can be found in, C.K.H. O'Malley (1989).

Training Memos were issued in 1921. Lastly, the Engineering Department issued circulars in 1921 giving detailed advice on how to trench and mine roads, how to tap phones, demobilise trains and railways, etc.[28]

To monitor the results of all these instructions the brigades were directed to keep a monthly diary of operations carried out or attempted. From December 1920 onwards some brigades indeed started to record their activities. However, for many it took until April 1921 before their first report was submitted, while a few apparently never sent in any. Looking at the content of these orders, one can say that in general GHQ did not initiate policy but reacted to questions and demands from local units. Before a general order or memo was issued, one can frequently find a query from a local unit about the official policy concerning the issue treated in that order. This happened for instance after questions about: women spies, the police boycott, the levy put on civilians, the duties of outposts and with the introduction of the division in 1921.[29]

The lack of personal contact between GHQ and the provincial units led to complaints about a lack of empathy with the problems encountered by the Volunteers there. GHQ's overemphasis on administration was one of the main complaints, particularly familiar to the Dublin Brigade: 'He [Richard Mulcahy, IRA Chief of Staff] was always terribly impressed by reports. He once showed me reports from Owen O'Duffy. He showed me 6 pages of an operation report. Isn't that a magnificent report, he asked? It was all 1.2.3.4. a.b.c.d. Now what strikes me about that man, I said, is that he must have plenty of time on [his] hands.' The distant country brigades were even less impressed with GHQ's attempts at control. When GHQ criticised the actions of the West Mayo Brigade in one of their few successful ambushes they reacted angrily:

> 'To hell with Dick Mulcahy and his operation reports and his attempts at centralised command!' Such was the way and the direction in which our thoughts and expressions ran. Of course there was no such thing as centralised command. The very nature of the struggle was against control by a GHQ. Lines of communication linking

28 Collection of intelligence in November 1919, NLI, ms. 31,199. This was apparently a reaction to questions raised by the South Roscommon Brigade concerning the function of intelligence officers which were introduced earlier that month, NLI, P915 A0365. Several of these different orders and memos can be found in, O'MN, P17b127; UCD AD, P7A50; NLI, ms. 739, and ms. 22,121.

29 Order on monthly diary dated 24 November 1920, NLI, ms. 739. The Mulcahy Papers in UCD contain hundreds of these reports. Also specialised forms to report attacks can be found in, MA, A0837, and A0838. Some maps of attacks, mostly from Dublin, can be found in, UCD AD, P7A38. Inquiries predating general order: On the levy, Seamus Robinson, 'Statement', NLI, ms. 21,265. On the duty of outposts, NLI, ms. 31,199, and P915 A0363.

brigades in the country with GHQ in Dublin were flimsy affairs generally, however reliable their operations were. It follows, therefore, that GHQ had no controlling influence, or, in fact, any influence over a particular engagement.[30]

To bring military skills in line with the demands of the type of warfare in which the Volunteers were now engaged in, GHQ ordered officers to be appointed to supervise training in each special service. In 1919 there were Special Service Officers in Dublin for cycling, first aid and bombing. From 23 January 1920, a battalion Captain of Intelligence was added, and by the end of June captains for musketry, signalling, armoury and probably transport were introduced. In 1920 groups of special services officers from provincial units were occasionally called to Dublin to receive training. A course in the making of munitions was given and one in engineering was planned for the autumn. However, only in a few of the most active brigades were these men appointed and were attempts made to pass on these skills.[31]

Signalling and first aid were the first two disciplines in which selected Volunteers were trained. The relative simplicity of these specialities meant that most units in Dublin and elsewhere took them up and continued to do so until the Truce. Training in cycling, which was less suitable for guerrilla fighting but continued right into 1921, and bomb throwing was mainly confined to the Dublin Brigade. The gathering of information was extremely haphazard in the provincial units. With the development of conflict the importance of detailed intelligence became increasingly pressing. Already on 1 November 1919 instructions were sent out by GHQ to organise and supervise information services. The brigade commandants were to appoint a brigade captain and battalion lieutenants of intelligence. The company

---

30 Quote on Mulcahy's love for detail, Oscar Traynor, O'MN, P7b98. The O.C. of the South Tipperary Brigade complains that GHQ Officers never came to the country, that they were completely dependent on reports from their Organisers and that the training manuals were not suitable for guerrilla warfare, Seamus Robinson, 'Statement', NLI, ms. 21,265. Quote on GHQ from West Mayo Brigade, Thomas Heavey, 'Statement'.

31 Details on training in special services in Dublin, NLI, ms. 1,413. A good example of the work of intelligence officers in Dublin is given by: John Neary, O'MN, P17b122. Outside Dublin and the South few of these officers were appointed. In Tipperary, Tom Smyth, O'MN, P17b103. On the Munitions Department and the training of country officers, Pat McHugh, O'MN, P17b110; Tony Woods, O'MN, P17b96; Michael Lynch, 'Statement', NLI, ms. 22,117(2). The engineering department found it particularly hard to find men willing to take up engineering owing to its technical nature, Papers of the Engineering Department, NLI, ms. 11,410(1-8); Jack Plunkett, 'Statement', NLI, ms. 11,981; Jimmy Ryan, O'MN, P17b92; Liam O'Doherty, O'MN, P17b91.

captains had to appoint a Volunteer to coordinate the company information for him and the same applied to outposts. Despite the order it is questionable to what extent it was implemented. To facilitate the increased activity of the Volunteers the introduction of special transport sections was ordered in each company in February 1920.[32]

The state of training in special services is hard to assess for most units, but was generally poor. In Dublin, where organisation was most evolved, it can be deduced from the inspection reports on several companies and the attendance at classes in the 2nd Battalion. In the last four months of 1919 there were some Volunteers specialised in first aid and signalling in all companies of this battalion. Most had a good selection of cyclists and all had some men trained in bomb throwing, but this was apparently not as yet a recognised separate speciality. In the summer of 1920 all companies had men specialised in signalling, first aid and bombing. There were company transport sections and a Battalion Musketry Instructor. There was, however, no mention of cyclists any more. This was probably because the cycling units in each company were abandoned when a separate cycling company was formed in each battalion.[33]

Every company was expected to have about 12 men efficient in first aid and signalling and more than that in bombing. Although some Dublin Volunteers were already competent, many more had to be trained to reach this figure. Attendance at special service classes was recorded in Dublin from September 1919 onwards. First aid was the only one running consistently until July 1920. Between 1 and 3 men attended from each of the smaller companies, and about 5 to 10 from the larger companies. Signalling was also taught throughout the period, but somewhat sporadically. In October 1919 5 of these classes were held, with similar attendance to those in first aid. Besides 2 classes held in January, regular lessons were only recorded again in May 1920. The numbers attending per company then

32 A company of cyclists was intercepted in Dublin in September 1920, PRO, WO35/205. The development of intelligence services, NLI, ms. 11,410(11). Charles Townshend erroneously states that orders to this effect were not issued before December 1920, Charles Townshend (1979), 326. The formation of transport sections and arrangements for musketry and bombing instructions, NLI, ms. 901/12.

33 Inspection reports and class attendance in 2nd Battalion, NLI, ms. 901/90, ms. 902/126-7, and ms. 1,413. A completely separate organisational structure of cyclist companies under the Dublin Brigade Staff was started on 8 June 1920, NLI, ms. 900/14. On 2 June members of B-Company of the 2nd Battalion were called to volunteer for the 'Mounted Infantry Company': 'Volunteers for this Company have been asked from all Companies of the Battalion and a response in accordance with the customary loyalty of the men is expected. The organisation and highly specialised training of this Company is vital to the continued success of the fight in which the Irish Volunteers are engaged', NLI, ms. 901/90.

varied somewhat erratically between 1 and 11. Cyclist classes were only given during September and October 1919. A total of just 4 bomb-throwing classes were held, evenly spread throughout this period. Musketry classes were introduced in May 1920 and were well attended each week by 1 or 2 members from each company. Despite these efforts, the inspection reports in the summer of 1920 show that most companies still needed more training to make enough men proficient.[34]

The attention given to the company training and the prospect of exciting operations caused a resurgence of interest in Volunteer work, particularly in Dublin. This is clearly shown by the Baldoyle Company – a particularly small rural unit of the Dublin Brigade. After a period of inactivity, it experienced a rapid development between the end of 1919 and April 1920. Eight former members rejoined the company together with two new recruits, bringing membership to eighteen, of whom fourteen were considered active. Average attendance at company parades rose from four to eight, while frequency went up from once to twice weekly.[35]

The activities of the company grew in accordance with this. In January 1920 learning Morse code was the only work engaged in. From 21 February men went to Howth every alternate Saturday for instructions in special subjects. In March training in wall-climbing was added and shooting-practice with a miniature rifle was introduced. Possible involvement in military activity was impeded by the lack of arms. In this month the entire company armaments consisted of two .45s with forty rounds of ammunition, two .32s both in need of slight repair, one miniature rifle with 200 rounds, three bayonets and 100 rounds of Morris tube ammunition. During the remainder of the struggle the company continued to grow, reaching twenty-seven by the spring of 1921.

The tasks of the officers at different levels within the organisation grew in step with the growing activity. In Tipperary and Dublin battalion staff-meetings were ordered to be held every week, during which a programme was to be mapped out for each officer. All officers were forbidden to leave their area without first informing their O.C. where they were going and when they expected to return. In the 2nd Dublin Battalion the 'weekly' battalion council was held thirty-four times between September 1919 and October 1920. At these meetings the battalion staff, the company captains and the battalion officers of Special Services were present. They were well

34 These figures from, NLI, ms. 1,413, and ms. 901/65-71.
35 From September 1919 until April 1920, the average attendance at company parades for the 2nd Battalion of the Dublin Brigade as a whole was about 230. After April 1920, the average increased steadily to 379 in November. During inspections in the summer of 1920, 357 out of 560 men on the roll attended parade, while only 44 of the 203 absentees had excused themselves, NLI, ms. 1,413. See also NLI, ms. 901/90; ms. 902/126. Reports from Baldoyle Company, NLI, ms. 902/165-7.

attended; occasionally an officer was excused due to illness or for some other reason, but most were then replaced by their assistants. If one was arrested, a temporary replacement took over. From 2 May 1920 fortnightly Battalion Officer Meetings were introduced, at which the battalion staff, the captain and the lieutenants of all companies were expected to be present. However, although most officers attended, only seven of these meetings were recorded, the last in September 1920.[36]

The growing conflict and the introduction of special service officers at every level increased the demand for suitable officers during a period in which involvement had become dangerous. Although a full complement of special service officers was present in the Dublin Brigade in 1921, many country units found it impossible to fulfil all these vacancies. As a result, some brigades had to ask GHQ whether there was any objection to officers holding dual positions. The problem was further aggravated in December 1920, when it was decided that due to increasing risk of arrest every officer should have an understudy. It was impossible for the officers, most of whom had a full-time job, to execute all these duties satisfactorily. The fact that many officers were forced to go on the run during 1920 saved the Volunteers from falling into disarray, as it made many available on a full-time basis.[37]

IMPROVING QUALITY OF OFFICERS

To a large extent the effectiveness of the organisation depended on the quality of its officers. From the foundation of the Irish National Volunteers in 1913 officers had always been elected by the members, and this practice continued unaltered after the Rising. However, as Charles Townshend has remarked: 'Election, where used, tended to produce popular, easy-going, ineffective officers, who frequently "kept their areas quiet" and out of the conflict.' A poor capability and reluctance to act affected the entire unit under their command. It was therefore extremely important to GHQ to replace such officers. The right of ratification was the main instrument at the hands of the leadership to prevent inefficient officers from being appointed. According to the Scheme of Organisation, officers could also be

36 Stepping up officer activities, General Orders no. 4 and 5, Tipperary no 3 Brigade, O'MN, P17b127. In Dublin, NLI, ms. 902/127. Attendance at officer councils in Dublin, NLI, ms. 1,413.

37 On dual positions, NLI, ms. 22,118. Demand for understudy, NLI, ms. 31,201. List of all officers in 1921 in Dublin Brigade, NLI, ms. 902/174. When the IRA Chief of Staff lost his briefcase containing lists of country officers in a police raid, many were arrested. In Wexford, the arrests of officers were so frequent that one company had to appoint six captains over a period of six months, *Life of Mick Radford* (n. d.), 11-12.

stripped of their rank on a motion from GHQ or on the requisition of the majority of the company, but they rarely exercised this right.[38]

It was extremely difficult for higher officers to go against the choice of local units. In the rural brigades in particular, most of the Volunteers felt that the man elected represented them personally. Consequently, they were unwilling to dispose of him, even if he was a total failure at his job. In many country areas the elections had been a foregone conclusion, with only one candidate put forward. In active districts the man most likely to be elected company captain during the reorganisation of 1917 was the one who had tried to get the Volunteers organised in the first place. Often no election took place as everybody automatically accepted him as their leader. This way of getting officers at least ensured some enthusiasm. In less active areas, however, the most popular or powerful local man was often chosen. Volunteers tended to elect their 'own man' irrespective of his leadership qualities. Even GHQ organisers could not always do much about this situation:

> My instructions were to make the area efficient and to organise it, to raise companies, form them into battalions, call a Brigade Council and elect officers. The latter were always elected, some being absolute 'duds' even though all officers present knew the calibre of the men, but had not the moral courage to forward a second name for nomination.[39]

The strong personal loyalties in the country units were less common or were more divided in the companies of the Dublin Brigade. In elections for officers in the 2nd Battalion between December 1919 and January 1921, there is ample proof of choice. At twelve different elections, one for battalion commander, one for captain and several for lieutenants, between three and six candidates were put forward. In contrast with the countryside, it was not always the candidate with the highest rank who was chosen, and more than one round of polling was often necessary to come to a decision.

---

38 Election procedures, communication from GHQ to commandant South Tipperary Brigade dated 5 July 1920, O'MN, P17b127. Quote Charles Townshend (1979), 321. In 1975, Townshend inaccurately stated that officers could not be replaced from above, Charles Townshend (1975), 18. For official rules see, 'Scheme of Organisation', NLI, P912 A0032. An election taking place in 1917 was recorded by the police in Soloheadbeg, Co. Tipperary, PRO, CO904-/122. Only one case in which company men availed of their right to request the dismissal of their officers is known to me: B-Company of the 2nd Battalion Dublin Brigade made such a request on 27 January 1920, NLI, ms. 901/88.

39 In one company in Mayo the only man proposed as captain was selected by a sort of Company Committee, Patrick Owen Mugan, Interview. Quote, C.K.H. O'Malley (1989), 8.

Popularity was, however, also an indication of one's chances of being elected in the city. Even in Dublin, where GHQ had most direct influence, the most common reason for an election was still arrest or resignation of the officer involved. Resignations sometimes followed pressure from the men or from superiors but were seldom a consequence of a sacking.[40]

A direct repercussion of the intricate relationship between officers and their men was the problem many officers had in establishing their authority. The officers' dependency on the rank and file created a democratic attitude unsuitable for warfare. The frequent reminders by GHQ passed on by the brigades to company captains that they alone were responsible for all activity, together with the warning not to discuss any of the orders with the rank and file, were a direct result of this.[41]

The existing loyalties did save inefficient officers from dismissal or caused local Volunteers to ignore GHQ instructions to that effect. In Wexford a local battalion commander had been dismissed under instructions by GHQ in March 1920 after discussing operational plans in a public house. Although he was declared ineligible for commissioned rank for a year, it was reported to the Adjutant General that the local Volunteers would re-elect him. The Adjutant General openly questioned their wisdom, but felt unable to enforce his judgement without the local men's cooperation. Nevertheless, most of the few sacking of officers by GHQ were, although sometimes grudgingly, accepted by local units.[42]

---

40 Elections in Dublin, NLI, ms. 901/87-106, and ms. 902/116-19, 125 + 152-4. See also the changing composition of the leadership of A-company 1st Battalion, UCD AD, LA9. Letters of resignation of 1st and 2nd Lieutenants of B-Company, 2nd Battalion, because of dissatisfied Volunteers dated 30 December 1920 and 1 January 1921, NLI, ms. 901/96-7.

41 GHQ instructions, Order of the 2nd Battalion Dublin Brigade dated 11 May 1921, NLI, ms. 902/150; Letter to the Wexford Brigade, UCD AD, P7A17/62-9.

42 Situation in Wexford, NLI, P916 A0478 & A0479. Officers of Kerry No.1 Brigade refused to obey any commands from GHQ after their commander had been dismissed, Andy Cooney, O'MN, P17b107; Charles Townshend (1979), 335. In the Waterford No.1 Brigade lower officers dismissed their own O.C. in contravention of the rules in May 1921. They felt he was unsuitable, while GHQ considered him the only real fighting men in the brigade, UCD AD, P7A19/103-13. Despite these cases of disobedience, Townshend and Fitzpatrick overemphasise the strength of local independence and the lack of effective control by GHQ. Their own examples of ready acceptance of dismissals contradict their assessment (see the early dismissal of Michael Brennan, an extremely warlike officer from East Clare, which they both mention). They seem to expect a regular army like discipline and tend to turn the exception into the rule, Charles Townshend (1979), 334-5; David Fitzpatrick (1977), 207-8. Although GHQ did indeed tread lightly in this area, its ultimate control over appointments and dismissals was generally accepted. The experience of its organisers and its own increasingly forceful instructions in this regard testify to this.

The fact that officers with a lack of leadership qualities often remained in their positions caused irritation among more determined men. In November 1919 the Second Battalion officers of the Dublin Brigade brought a motion to the Brigade Convention asking 'that the present system of electing Company officers be revised to prevent incompetent unpopular men from being appointed.' GHQ was unable to dispense with the election of officers, but it tried to increase its influence on the process. New procedures were introduced allowing for appointments as well as elections. In July 1920 the Director of Organisation issued standard forms to the brigades on which vacancies among commissioned officers were to be reported:

> If you are of the opinion that any position would be more readily filled by nomination than by election, you should instruct your adjutant, to strike out the word 'election' and to fill in the name, rank and place of residence of the person whom you consider best fitted for the position. [...] On receipt of form, I will, as I may decide (a) order an election to be held when the form will be returned to your adjutant for completion of the position marked 'O' and return, or (b) submit your nomination for ratification to the Chief of Staff.

From then on it became standard practice to dismiss and appoint officers. Nevertheless, until the Truce, officers continued to be elected. In June 1921 both the appointment and the election of battalion officers occurred simultaneously in Derry City. Appointment had often become a substitute for election, because organising elections on all levels had become dangerous. Large gatherings of important officers involved grave risks to the survival of the organisation and normal company work was already minimised.[43]

When fighting erupted the efficiency of the different officers became increasingly important, and consequently replacement of inefficient officers became more common. The ultimate means to dispose of such officers was court martial for neglect of duty, which was increasingly resorted to. In April 1920 the Brigade Commandant of Kerry No.1 Brigade expressed his hesitation about the dismissal of certain particularly passive officers. In his reply the Adjutant General assured him that he was not exceeding his duties and was definitely justified in having them removed, but he proceeded to instruct him on how to approach the dismissal: 'The procedure should be regular and in accordance with the Constitution, so you should act as follows: – "An Officer who has not been working is guilty of neglect of duty. He should be suspended pending Court Martial. In the meantime, you should select the

43 Motion of Dublin Brigade dated 9 November 1919, NLI, ms. 901/7. Quote from Director of Organisation dated 5 July 1920, O'MN, P17b127. Appointment and election in Derry, UCD AD, P7A20/56. On one occasion GHQ sent down an officer to dismiss the brigade commander of the North Tipperary Brigade personally, Seán Gaynor, 'Statement'.

most efficient man to carry on as Acting O.C. pending an election. The
Court Martial must sentence any officer guilty of negligence to reduction to
the ranks".' The Adjutant General expressed his hope that the newly
appointed officer would live up to his new position and consequently be
elected commandant. Although the organisation was non-compulsory and
based on friendship, the increased danger, especially for the higher officers,
made this tougher stance necessary.[44]

DIVERGING ROADS, MID 1920

Distinctly different types of conflict established themselves in 1920 in various
parts of the country. The most violent form developed in Tipperary. Initially,
isolated RIC barracks and later the patrols of police and military, well supplied
with rifles and revolvers, were the main targets of the Volunteers. Several barracks within and outside the brigade area were attacked by members of the
South Tipperary Brigade in the spring of 1920; one taking place on 28 April
1920 in Ballylanders, followed by Hollyford Barracks on 10 May, Kilmallock
on 27 May and Drangan Barracks, one of the few successful attempts in
Tipperary in which the police surrendered, on 3 June.

A pattern in these attacks was soon established. The main brigade officers together with the local battalion commandant and Ernie O'Malley, a
GHQ organiser, stood at the centre of its organisation and execution.
These men, who were engaged on a full-time basis in Volunteer work, were
aided by the most active Volunteers of surrounding battalions. Some local
companies were involved in manning blockades on the roads leading to the
barracks and in dispatch riding. Those involved in the attack took up positions around the barracks, while the main assault was centred on the roof
in an attempt to set the barracks alight:

> It was arranged that all the roads leading into Drangan would be
> blockaded, patrolled and the telegraph wires cut – the village would
> be completely isolated. The men occupied a house which was
> attached to one of the gables of the barracks. This house was left
> unguarded by the police. Seán Treacy, Dan Breen and Tommy

44 Letter to Brigade Commandant Kerry No.1 dated 22 April 1920, NLI, P916
A0494. Guidelines for court martial, NLI, ms. 11,406(2); Scheme of Organ-isa-
tion, NLI, P912 A0032. Examples of court martials: A case of Volunteers not
turning up for an operation in Tipperary early in 1920, NLI, P917 A0499.
Neglect of duty and giving away plans both in Wexford in March 1920, NLI,
P916 A0478 & A0479. The misappropriation of funds in Mid Limerick, NLI,
ms. 11,406(2 + 6). The failure to execute orders by officers in Dublin, in May
and October 1920, NLI, ms. 902/115 + 135. One officer in Dublin was court-
martialled for indiscreet talking, NLI, ms. 901/27.

Donovan made 'mud-bombs' which consisted of yellow clay moulded around sticks of gelignite, to which a fuse and detonator were attached. It was planned to break through the roof of the barracks with these mud bombs and then pump paraffin through the holes in the roof, throw grenades in and set the building ablaze.[45]

These attacks involved a large number of Volunteers. Local men called upon to participate felt appreciated and some were inspired to do even more. To most of them, however, ordinary life continued to take precedence. Daily routine was not broken even for a barracks attack: 'You're to be in Hollyford this evening at six o'clock. What's up? We're burning the barracks at Rea tonight. I said to Jim, will ye be able to finish before the cows? Ah, we will, said he.' Although their involvement remained part-time, many were forced to take safety precautions and sleep away from home at night. Some officers overestimated the risk and ordered all involved in the attack to do this, leading to a shortage of 'safe' places: 'Tim Dwyer sent me word not to sleep at home. I found that the toughest part of the whole thing – going around looking for lodgings. I slept at Mulcahy's for weeks. 'T would be as easy for the Tans to get me there as at my own house, but I had to obey orders.'[46]

Not all Volunteers and officers in Tipperary were willing to get more closely involved in fighting; nor had they the necessary knowledge or ability. Many refused to engage in any fighting. Some officers were court-martialled for this and lost their rank. Even many of the most willing Volunteers were scared when under fire for the first time. The commandant of the North Tipperary Brigade describes their first attack on a barrack: 'We were a bit nervous in the beginning. In fact, I had to threaten some of the lads with my gun to force them to take the first bottles [with petrol to burn the roof].' The local men who became involved in these engagements could not always withstand the strains under which they were forced to operate and as a result many ambushes failed:

We were up there at 6 o'clock in the morning we had about 150 men, of the 7th Battalion at this side. Some of the 8th Company Cloneen at the Drangan side. We stayed there all day expecting a lorry to pass, that didn't happen but a cycling party of military came from Mullinahone and we were at the back of the rocks, and one fellow behind me got up, he got kind of nervous or something, and said, 'I'll fire at them'. The Commandant Nick C. of this Battalion said get down and stay there until you get orders. They were going

45 Quote, 'Drangan Barracks attack', Killenaule Community Project – Team Work (Local History).
46 Quotes, Bryan Ryan (1969), 5-6 + 9. See also Jack Gardiner, Interview.

to let them up in the ambush site. However, in a minute he fired and the military took cover down along the side of the road. They all fired at them, but they got away anyway. Then the whole area was cleared and the crowds went to their own places.[47]

The half-hearted approach of most Tipperary Volunteers and the increasing danger resulting from the emergence of violent conflict actually led to a decline in Volunteer membership during 1920 from 1,293 to 958. As a result, operations relied increasingly on the active men of several battalions and even from different brigades. Large-scale operations, in particular, attracted all activists from miles around. Similar to the main brigade officers some of these men were now forced to abandon their homes altogether. In the attack on Rearcross Barracks Volunteers from the North and South Tipperary Brigades and from East Limerick worked in close cooperation. This was not always harmonious. The commandant in charge tended to give the important jobs to his own men, disappointing experienced men from other areas. The enthusiasm of overzealous Volunteers caused some to attack barracks in other brigade areas without the approval of the local brigade commandant, in contravention of general orders.[48]

Tipperary Volunteers were among the first in the country to concentrate on the destruction of barracks. In most other areas Volunteers were less willing to risk their lives in such direct attacks. Primary reasons for this were the general lack of arms necessary to make such assaults successful and the absence of active officers to take the lead. Unlike the Tipperary officers, few of these local leaders were wanted men who were permanently on the run and involved full-time in Volunteer operations. Men on the run, free of the constraints put on them by their community, were more willing to attack the Crown Forces. The part-time attitude of officers in other areas well into 1920 was epitomised by the commandant of the West Mayo Brigade, who only visited the brigade area at weekends when he called on his parents; during the week he worked as a teacher outside the area![49]

47 Unwilling officers court-martialled, Paul Merrigan, Interview, and O'MN, P17b126. Quote on 'bottles', Seán Gaynor, 'Statement'. Quote on 'losing nerves', Jack Gardiner, Interview. See also CI South Tipperary MR December 1920; Bryan Ryan (1969), 6-8; Ned O'Reilly, O'MN, P17b126.

48 Membership figures CI South Tipperary MRs 1920. In a report of the South Tipperary Brigade dated 4 August 1920 an ambush by 55 men was described, which was executed by 1st Battalion men together with eight men of different battalions who were on the run, NLI, P919 A0509. Joining in attacks elsewhere with and without permission, Ned O'Reilly, O'MN, P17b125, P17b126; Dan Breen (1981), 122 + 128. Less than harmonious cooperation, Bryan Ryan (1969), 18.

49 The positive influence of constraints which the local population put on the Volunteers was observed by the police in Mayo in October 1920, CI Mayo MR October 1920.

Officers in Castlebar refused to allow any violence, afraid of the consequences. They failed to take the responsibility for arms raids and left it to
local Volunteers with more initiative to do so:

> In Castlebar, I found only traces of a movement [in August 1920].
> Old Johnny Hoban was in charge, but he was not anxious to get any-
> thing done. [...] Only when he got out did we succeed in getting
> Castlebar going, for we had to build up a movement in spite of him
> and outside of him. [...] We were stopped each time on our way in to
> attack by senior officers who didn't want us to make an attack in the
> town.[50]

The commandant in Castlebar even handed over the gelignite in his possession to subordinates. The military inactivity of Mayo disappointed
some local activists, many of whom left the area, as well as the Volunteer
leadership in Dublin. They expressed their disappointment over the failure of the West Mayo Brigade to use the rifles they had received from
GHQ to the brigade quartermaster: 'Gearoid O'Sullivan said "what the
hell are you losers doing": and Collins said "why the hell don't you use
the arms".'[51]

Volunteers from the South Mayo Brigade remember some attempts to
attack barracks, but these went unrecorded by the police. The most carefully
planned attack which had GHQ sanction took place in Cross when two
Volunteers in uniforms of the British Army tried to take the barracks by
surprise. This failed because they were afraid to act when they had the
opportunity. In an unprepared attempt in nearby Cong the brigade commandant simply knocked at the barracks door at night, hoping to rush the
guard. Although he heard someone inside, nobody responded.[52]

In west Mayo the idea of taking a barracks was only considered on a few
occasions. One attempt was called off by hesitant battalion officers, despite
the promise of inside aid. Another took place in Louisburgh on 1 July 1920
while a fair was being held. The Volunteers were patrolling the town that

50 Quote on situation in Castlebar, Mark Killilea, O'MN, P7b109. Many com-
plaints were made afterwards about the original activators from Castlebar and
Balla, Co. Mayo, John Madden, O'MN, P17b113; James Chambers, 'Statement'; Michael Hughes, 'Statement'; Jimmy Swift, O'MN, P17b136; Liam
Langley, O'MN, P17b101; Pat Fallon, O'MN, P17b109; Tom Maguire, O'MN,
P17b100, and in U. MacEoin (1980), 279.
51 Actions of Castlebar officers, Mark Killilea, O'MN, P17b109; Michael Hughes,
'Statement'. Officers leaving, Joe Baker (1988), 29; Patrick Owen Mugan,
Interview. Quote, Tom Kettrick, O'MN, P17b136.
52 Barracks attacks in South Mayo Brigade, Tom Maguire, in U. MacEoin (1987),
279-81. Similar attempt in Newry in 1920, Pat Casey, 'Idle thoughts of an officer of the Irish Volunteers', Fr O'Kane Papers, AARC.

day as part of their attempt to replace the police force. When a quarrel occurred the RIC intervened and dragged a man to the barracks. To justify their presence the Volunteers had to act as well. They moved in, grabbed the policemen and relieved them of their revolvers. The local Volunteer commandant then considered the possibility of taking the barracks:

> The thought flashed into my mind as to whether we should go the whole hog and take possession of the barracks; which was an easy job, as there were only three other policemen there at the time, and the front door was open. However we had no permission from our Headquarters to start operations such as that, but later we regretted that we didn't take the chance, because from that day, all of us who were identified had to go 'on the run' as a result of this episode. Some of the IRA men were arrested in their beds. The RIC garrison in the barracks was strongly reinforced by men from the other barracks and also by some Black and Tans.[53]

Despite this absence of barracks attacks, the evacuations by the police facilitated a major increase in Volunteer activity in Mayo in the spring of 1920. The number of offences rose from eleven in January to sixty-six in May. In July the County Inspector stated:

> As repeatedly pointed out the closing of Police Stations has proved a most disastrous and dangerous expedient, whilst the lack of men, of transport, and of effective military co-operation have only added to the mess. Sinn Féin given a free hand has grown more and more active and aggressive and intimidation is much more general and effective.

As a result Volunteer membership continued to increase rapidly in Mayo during 1920 from 2,362 to 6,608, making it the by far best organised county in this research. A similar continuous growth took place among Sinn Féin clubs in this county. The list of offences shows the different aspects of Volunteer work. Besides illegal drilling and minor attacks on the Crown Forces and their supplies, most offences involved the civil population. Threatening notices and letters backed up by intimidation were used to force the people to boycott the British institutions and use republican alternatives instead.[54]

Apart from a failed large-scale attack on Clonroche barracks in April 1920,

53 Attempt in west Mayo, Jack Feehan, O'MN, P17b113. Quote, P.J. Kelly, 'One of the men of the West'.
54 Quote, CI Mayo MR July 1920. Membership figures, CI Mayo MRs 1920.

set up in similar fashion to such attempts in Tipperary, Wexford Volunteers were somewhat slower than their counterparts in Mayo in stepping up activity. Offences were of a comparable nature, mainly consisting of minor assaults on Crown Forces and their supplies, and intimidation of the population. In line with a general order to raid for arms, a large increase in reported cases is noted in August. As the County Inspector rightly asserted, the Volunteer order was a direct result of the interception by the IRA of a government circular ordering the confiscation of all privately held arms.[55]

A clear shift in activity from the northern to the southern part of the county became evident during the summer. The northern part had so far been the centre of activity; but apparently the Volunteers there were adequately dealt with by the police while the southern men became more inspired to act. In August, twenty-two of the twenty-nine offences were committed in the southern New Ross and Wexford districts. The movement continued to pay relatively much attention to the political side, as witnessed by a number of meetings and concerts held in this period. However, the police and military attended these and nothing illegal was permitted. The relative low-profile of the movement in Wexford coincided with an absence of recruits for the Volunteers.[56]

Officers in Derry City took a similar attitude as those in Castlebar. Their vulnerability to police reaction made them reluctant to become involved in serious operations. The same hesitancy applied to many rank and filers, who would endanger people near to them if they became active. Most of the sparse activists in Derry City had no immediate family living in the city. Many of them were young and had come to the city looking for work. Half of the twelve men sent out as a Flying Column from Derry City in December 1920 were from other counties. However, the presence of such men was strongly related to the amount of work available. As a result, IRA activity suffered in the post-War depression, which started to be felt at the end of 1920, and many of these active Volunteers returned home. The remainder was not particularly enthusiastic about drilling or other Volunteer duties. Some had to be forced to attend parades under threat or even arrest. However, the riots between Catholics and Protestants which erupted in the City during the summer of 1920 – resulting in three days of sectarian warfare, causing nineteen deaths and thirty wounded, ending only when

55 Attack on Clonroche barracks, *People* (Wexford), 28 April 1920. Activities in Wexford, CI Wexford MRs 1920. Arms raiding had clearly increased in 1920, but was extremely prominent in September. The number of raids for Ireland per quarter in 1920 were: 204, 159, 2,307 and 132, David Fitzpatrick (1977), 224.
56 Activities in Wexford, CI Wexford MRs 1920.

the military intervened – led to strong growth in the number of Volunteers from 240 to 305.[57]

Similar problems are observed in south Derry. One way of dealing with the fear of adverse consequences through fighting in one's home area was to operate outside it. In Derry a strong tendency to act exclusively in neighbouring areas existed. During the entire period leading activists of several south Derry companies took part in taking the mail from two trains in Co. Antrim and in an attack on the barracks in Cookstown, Co. Tyrone. The height of activity in their own area was the burning of the empty barracks in Ballyronan. The Flying Columns sent out from Derry City and Belfast to more Volunteer-friendly country in Donegal and Cavan in 1921 further underlines this. Due to the small number of Volunteers in Co. Derry, this hesitancy made cooperation between the few willing Volunteers of different units even more essential to sustain activity.[58]

Some effort was made to broaden the experience of the local Volunteers. Thomas Morris, a former major in the British Army, who had joined the IRA after his demobilisation in 1919, was appointed organiser for south Derry by GHQ early in 1920. To train the men in the area in the use of arms, secluded places like the Sperrin mountains and the Lough shores were used as instruction grounds. Explosives were made in Maghera and buckshot filled into shotgun cartridges was produced. Gelignite and other explosives were also obtained from quarries, but only used twice in 1921 to blow up a bridge. Training was supplemented by first aid classes given by a local doctor. As a result a small increase in activity took place. In June 1920 a few evacuated barracks were burned and some minor incidents, including raids for arms, took place. However, a comparatively low level of activity continued during the rest of the summer months.[59]

Even in Dublin most Volunteers did little in 1920. Professionalisation was limited to a few men concentrated in the Squad, rendering most companies militarily inactive. The entire work of an average Dublin company during the year consisted of three arms raids. Most Volunteers limited their

---

57 Attitude of local officers, Lt. M. Sheerin, NLI, P921; Peadar O'Donnell, O'MN, P17b98. Consequences of economic depression, CI Derry MR December 1920; Lt. M. Sheerin, NLI, P915 A0394 & P913 A0153. Membership figures, CI Derry MRs 1920; Lt. M. Sheerin, NLI, P913 A0153; Liam A. Brady, *Derry Journal*, 20 May 1953. Similarly the IRA in Belfast and Lisburn grew strongly after the pogroms that took place there during 1920, T. Gunne, MA, A0148.

58 Activities south Derry Volunteers, Wm. John Himphey, Fr O'Kane Papers, Tape A23, AARC; Thomas Morris, 'Typescript of Interview', Ibid.; Paddy Larkin, Interview.

59 Training in south Derry, John McQuillan, Fr O'Kane Papers, Tape A9, AARC; Thomas Morris, 'Typescript of Interview', Ibid.

involvement to turning out for drilling exercises, while a few members of these inactive companies sometimes gathered intelligence. It took until September before the first accidental engagement with the military was recorded. When two Volunteers were called to the city centre for a job, they found all the bridges crossing the canals around the centre guarded by military. Out of frustration with their inability to get to the meeting, one fired a shot and ran off as quickly as possible. They were anxious as to whether they had taken the right course of action and were afraid to report it to their superiors. However, GHQ had become more open to military action, and to their surprise the following week's edition of *An tÓglach* reported it as a 'splendid example of initiative', being the first attack at British military in Dublin since the Easter Rising. In a similar way, the first grenade was used against a British lorry by Paddy Flanagan that same month. This bellicose Volunteer was soon thereafter appointed commander of the Dublin ASU (Active Service Unit).[60]

The members of the Squad were the first to take a professional approach to Volunteering in the city. Their task lay mainly in counter-intelligence: tracing and eliminating enemy agents. Initially, much of their time was spent hanging around observing, but slowly their activities opened the way for other Volunteers to act: 'April/May of 1920 we were ready for fighting. We had warned off the minor police spies. They were taken down lane ways, beaten up and told to leave things alone or worse would happen to them.'[61]

Strong ties existed between the Squad and the units from which they were recruited. Some members continued to operate as company officers in their spare time, and if arms were captured they tried to save some for their own battalion. If they needed back-up in an operation, they called on their old unit. The Squad also had a following among young members of the Fianna, the republican boy scouts; one of them is reported to have used a particular boy who always accompanied him, to dump his revolver after an operation. Some of these boys, who were too young to join the Volunteers and were forbidden to mix in any fighting were, nevertheless, taken along when British intelligence officers were shot on Bloody Sunday. Although there were only a few engagements in Dublin in 1920, the operations of the few activists thus caused an increased involvement of ordinary Volunteers similar to Tipperary.[62]

---

60 Company activity consisting of three arms raids, Captain J.M. Nolan, NLI, P916 A0473. Gathering intelligence by 4 or 5 out of 46 members, Michael O'Reilly, O'MN, P17b115. First shooting on military, Charlie Dalton (1929), 76-81.

61 Quote, Frank Henderson, O'MN, P17b99.

62 Squad in operation, Patrick O'Daly, 'Statement', NLI, P4548; Jim Slattery, O'MN, P17b109. On use youngsters, Liam Langley, O'MN, P17b101; Patrick O'Daly, 'Statement', NLI, P4548; Martin Bell, private conversation.

TOWARDS GUERRILLA CONFLICT

A successful barracks attack became less and less feasible in the course of 1920. Indefensible posts had been abandoned and protection of most other barracks was reinforced. In Tipperary no serious attack was reported after the summer. To provide the newly activated Volunteers with action and to protect the men on the run, a general onslaught on lines of communication was initiated in Tipperary in August 1920. The police reported a systematic attack on trains, mails, postmen, telegraph wires and telephone apparatus. The most violent activists developed a new type of engagement, of a small hit-and-run nature. The men blooded in barracks attacks began to seize other opportunities, including assaults on police and military:

> The late Senator William Quirke was then a member of my company. In a hotel in Fethard he overheard four strange R.I.C. men talking. They had a motor car outside and Quirke learned from their conversation that they were going to Mullinahone. He came to me at once and suggested that we go to Downey's Cross and hold them up there. I was slow to consent as I thought we should consult the Battalion Commander first. Quirke was impetuous and in his brisk manner said, 'Come on, we will do it'. So having sent word to Tommy Lee to come to Downey's Cross as soon as possible, I went with him.

The result of this unplanned ambush was the capture of a motor car and four revolvers. The policemen were locked in a shed and put under guard. In the middle of the night the door of the shed was unlocked and the guard slipped away. It consequently became impossible for the Volunteers involved, most of whom still had regular work, to remain in their home area and they went on the run. Here they enjoyed the companionship of men from other units in similar situations. Together they engaged in several similar small skirmishes with the police during 1920, and most joined the Flying Column when they were set up in October.[63]

To quell the upsurge in violence which had become common in parts of the country in the summer of 1920, the British Government introduced the Restoration of Order in Ireland Act. This act, passed on 9 August 1920, allowed for internment and court martial of civilians. This led to the arrests of a large number of IRA-officers, particularly in Mayo. In October, twelve Mayo officers were arrested; in November eighty-two followed and another twelve were taken in December. This contrasts sharply with the

---

63 The attack on communications, CI South Tipperary MR August 1920. Quote, Patrick Ryan, 'Statement'. This incident probably relates to a case in June 1920, CI South Tipperary MR June 1920.

other counties, including Tipperary, where comparatively few arrests were recorded in this period.[64]

The higher level of organisation and visibility of the Volunteers in Mayo provides an explanation for this difference. As a result GHQ ordered all officers everywhere to sleep away from home and to appoint deputies to replace them in case of their arrest. Most officers and active men who were not yet on the run now joined the small number of activists who had already left home. This made the transition to the next phase in the conflict, involving the emergence of Flying Columns engaging in hit-and-run operations, also feasible in Mayo and some other areas where the Volunteers had so far been relatively inactive.

In Wexford the end of the year was also characterised by increased raiding by the Crown Forces, leading to some arrests. Initially the number of offences dropped as some local suspects went on the run. However, the consequence of an increased number of Volunteers on the run became apparent in the second half of December when an outbreak of IRA violence followed. An unsuccessful barracks attack took place and an attempt to blow up another was made. According to the police, the Foulks Mills Barracks was attacked by 200 to 300 Volunteers. They claim that when the nine policemen inside counter-attacked through a special door with grenades the assailants fled, leaving behind a motor car, forty-four bombs, petrol, a shotgun and a pistol. However, the IRA itself claims that the attack was called off after the local Parish Priest had intervened. The attempted bombing of the barracks in Carrick-on-Bannow in the same month was stopped after a shopkeeper was killed when he resisted an attempt to place a bomb in his shop which adjoined the barracks. The first policeman in Wexford was killed in the same month when he approached three suspicious-looking men in a public house.[66]

However, this upsurge in violence was only temporary. Wexford lacked a sufficiently large group of men on the run to initiate independent action. The police raids had only led to sporadic arrests and few considered it necessary to leave home altogether. As a result, a Flying Column was never formed in south Wexford. This was also a consequence of the reluctance of Wexford Volunteers to get involved in violence. When someone was to be shot, men from Dublin were brought in. This was the case with the shooting of Captain Lee Wilson in 1920 and the same applied to the assassination of Captain Harvey in Wexford town and an ambush on the road to

---

64 Arrests in Mayo, CI Mayo MRs August-December 1920. A large increase in court martials can be detected from August 1920 onwards. In 1917, 137 persons were court-martialled, in 1918 202, in 1919 138 and in 1920 94 took place prior to August. In the following five months 23, 111, 295, 160 and 220 persons were court-martialled respectively, Charles Townshend (1975), Appendix X.

66 Police report, CI Wexford MR December 1920. IRA version, BMH Chronology.

Courtown in 1921. Only combat experience could generate a mentality whereby one was willing to shoot members of the Crown Forces at sight. The interference from outside had stopped direct fighting from taking place, and prevented the emergence of such a mentality among the Wexford Volunteers. The inability to engage in violence continued to characterise Wexford in 1921.[67]

The increase in police operations also led to the arrest of some activists in south Derry. This included Thomas Morris, the local GHQ organiser, who was arrested on an arms raid in September 1920 together with three Volunteers from Co. Tyrone. These arrests seriously depleted the strength of the small local companies. The three arrested men were among the few active members of the Belagherty Company in south Derry, which had already lost its captain, who had left the country while on temporary release following a hunger strike. There were not enough Volunteers in the companies aspiring to take the place of the arrested men. As a result there was little activity in south Derry thereafter. In the last few months of 1920 the police recorded some raids for arms, the holding up of one rural postman and the flying of a tricolour. The increase in Volunteer activity that had followed the heightened activity of the police in other areas therefore did not take place in south Derry.[68]

In Derry City a similar fall-off in recorded felonies occurred at the end of 1920. Nevertheless, the IRA made its first active use of arms in an attack on police men in November. A police sergeant and constable were wounded when Volunteers attacked the guards at the Custom House. The main objective of this attack was the acquisition of arms, and although the attackers got away with a carbine it did not lead to more violence in the city. In December the few local activists were sent out as a Flying Column to Donegal.[69]

Dramatic changes took place in Dublin at the end of 1920. The authorities had also increased their operations against the IRA in the autumn. British military intelligence officers replaced the G-Division of the police, and the new Restoration of Order Act made raids and searches by the military a constant feature in the city. As in the rest of the country, many men went on the run and even active rank and filers had to exercise greater caution but their lives were not greatly affected:

At that time the British had not devised any method of picking IRA

---

67 Involvement Dublin Volunteers in Wexford, B. Owens, NLI, ms. 10,723(2); Patrick O'Daly, 'Statement', NLI, P4548. Captain Lee-Wilson was shot in Gorey for his activities during the 1916 Rising, Leon O Broin (1980), 19. Although a Flying Column was observed by the British in south Wexford in June 1921, the local brigade never reported one.

68 Arrests in Derry, *Derry People and Donegal News,* 30 October 1920.

69 PRONI, FIN 18/1/154; CI Derry MR November 1920

activists up of the streets; they had no police force, the DMP having
been neutralised. They did not usually raid houses except after dark
so that, apart from sleeping away from home, it was possible even
for a known IRA man to lead a normal life.

Going on the run, nevertheless, changed the attitude of the men involved.
The Volunteer who had fired the first shot at the military in Dublin in
September was on the run for several weeks afterwards, looking for a different place to sleep each night. Finally, he and other Volunteers in a similar predicament found a permanent hide-out through a friend. As a result,
these activists mingled exclusively with other extreme nationalists: 'I only
spoke to or passed the time of day with people whom I knew to be sympathetic to the Movement.'[70]

This meant that they were rarely confronted with any dissenting opinions. As a result, the parameters of acceptable behaviour were slowly broad-
ened to include attempts at taking life. The few open confrontations with
the Crown Forces often resulted in a chain of violent events. The killing of
twelve British officers on Bloody Sunday, 21 November 1920, and the
ensuing police reaction further polarised the situation in the city. Armament had improved to such a level that it facilitated military activities
involving ordinary Volunteers. A new approach exceeding the mere objective of individual survival was now feasible and was needed to maintain the
movement.[71]

In order to occupy the men on the run and to counteract the renewed
arresting policy of the authorities, men were recruited for a new unit in
December 1920. An ASU of about 100 men was drawn from members of
all the battalions of the Dublin Brigade. They were ordered to engage the
British on the streets of the city. This coincided with the implementation
of a new company policy. An order was issued to every company to conduct weekly armed patrols within their area. They were to attack all hostile
forces they encountered, using grenades and revolvers. The introduction of
the ASU and these patrols heralded the final phase of violent engagement
in Dublin.[72]

The development towards guerrilla warfare was still precarious. The
small groups of fighting men on the run were extremely vulnerable. Their
success could make or break the activity of the Volunteers in a particular

---

70 Quotes, C.S. Andrews (1979), 146 + 158. Experience of man who shot military,
   Charlie Dalton (1929), 98. The same occurred in Tipperary where the men on
   the run spent all their time with each other, Patrick Ryan, 'Statement'. See also
   Brighid Lyons, in K. Griffith and T. O'Grady (1982), 41.
71 Improved armaments, Pat MacCrea, O'MN, P17b110.
72 Start of ASU and company patrol, UCD AD, LA9; Oscar Traynor, O'MN,
   P17b96; Patrick O'Daly, 'Statement', NLI, P4548.

district; losing them often meant the end of operations. This occurred in the eastern part of the South Tipperary Brigade. Tom Donovan, the local battalion commandant, was ordered by GHQ to shoot an 'infamous' army lieutenant stationed in Killenaule. Donovan instructed the small group of men on the run that if the opportunity ever came their way they were to shoot the lieutenant on sight. They patrolled the village several times at night and tried to draw the man out. On 31 October 1920 they again went into the village, where they met what appeared to be two drunk British soldiers: 'When the two soldiers were about two yards from us they shed all signs of intoxication and fired point blank at us with revolvers which they had in their hands.' Donovan was killed and another Volunteer was badly wounded. As a result of this shooting, most military operations of the IRA ceased in this area. The County Inspector came close to the truth when after the shooting of Donovan he stated: 'It is hoped that the disappearance of this young ruffian from the countryside will have a salutary effect.' Few operations were recorded thereafter, and almost no Volunteer from this area joined the Flying Columns.[73]

CONCLUSION

The development towards guerrilla warfare depended on an extremely small segment of Volunteers concentrated in the Southwest. After a brief outburst of violence in the beginning of 1919 most members in all counties remained inactive, and confined themselves mainly to attending an occasional drilling exercise. Restrained from engaging in violence by GHQ, most of the few activists concentrated on political activity in the Dáil Loan and Dáil Courts. However, the sporadic and unsanctioned attempts of some activists to procure arms led to growing confrontation with the police towards the end of 1919. As a result of their activities and police pursuit some of these men were forced to go on the run and become involved full-time in Volunteer work, often determined to resist further arrest. This represented an obvious shift in attitude from 1917-18, when their public defiance had invited arrest. Overall, the number of men on the run remained extremely small and varied widely from area to area, thus facilitating the development of differentiation in activity. It was particularly apparent in Tipperary, where some activists were already wanted by the police for their involvement in the Soloheadbeg ambush in January 1919.

A small nation-wide increase in Volunteer activity followed the outlawing of the Dáil and the founding of the Squad in Dublin. The leadership of the movement, which had hitherto relied on political means to attain

73 Death of Tom Donovan, Patrick Ryan, 'Statement'; CI South Tipperary MR October 1920.

independence, considered the banning of the Dáil and their failure to get a hearing at the Versailles Peace Conference as a sign that other methods were necessary. As a result, attacks on the Crown Forces were finally officially sanctioned by GHQ in January 1920. This resulted in a large increase in military operations, particularly in the Southwest. Initially, most of these involved attacks on isolated barracks in an attempt to obtain more arms.

A growing number of Volunteers were radicalised by their involvement in these operations and were increasingly prepared to attack the Crown Forces openly. This was exacerbated by the large-scale arrests of Volunteer activists at the beginning of 1920 and their subsequent release in May. More and more of these men then had to leave home to avoid further arrest. The evacuation of outlying police posts and the improved defence of other barracks made barracks attacks increasingly difficult in the summer of 1920. Full-time Volunteers in active areas then turned their attention to the patrols of police and military to supplement their still sparse stocks of arms.

This development was again largely confined to the Southwest. In most other areas the Volunteers still hesitated to engage in direct violence. Some were anxious to follow the example set elsewhere, but were restrained from acting by fearful officers. Some of these young men then left for Dublin or England. However, this situation was altered by the Restoration of Order in Ireland Act, which was introduced in an attempt to curb the growing violence. The resulting increase in arrests throughout the country forced many Volunteers, including these inactive officers, to leave their homes – not only in active counties like Tipperary, but also in places like Mayo and even in totally inactive areas in the North. Fear of arrest was exacerbated by the aggressive behaviour of the new auxiliary police forces during raids and searches. The increased number of Volunteers on the run led to an escalation of violence in many parts of Ireland. Reluctant officers were now pushed aside and militants returned to service or came to the fore.

Within the development of larger operations in 1920, the rank and file had become increasingly involved in violence. The military operations in Tipperary and Dublin had introduced several previously inactive men to the fighting, thus extending the potential group of activists. Some of them became full-time involved in Volunteering. The appearance of large groups of men who attempted to avoid arrest heralded a new phase in the fighting, which further increased the gap between active and inactive men that had been prevalent in 1919.

The change from barracks attacks to ambushing, causing many more fatalities on both sides, made the conflict more vicious and hardened attitudes. Most Volunteers who still lived at home refused to engage in these attacks due to the fear of losing their family and livelihood. Outside Dublin and Tipperary the inability to stage serious attacks during the summer of 1920 had impeded this development. Nevertheless, the renewed vigilance of the Crown Forces generally in the final months of 1920 caused many militarily inactive Volunteers known to the police to go on the run as well, thus creating similar conditions in which violence was likely to develop.

In the period from 1919 until the autumn of 1920 the differentiation in the level of activity between areas and between Volunteers became much more pronounced. In a self-sustaining process active Volunteers became ever more active, taking along some willing men but leaving behind a large part of the Volunteers who were inhibited from further participation by a lack of opportunity, fear, disinterest, a restraining environment and by moral hesitance to go along with a militarisation of the conflict.

Nevertheless, activity increased everywhere during 1920. This was caused by the influence of operations elsewhere, and the effects of government policy. The high-profile operations of Volunteers in the active areas stimulated Volunteers everywhere to follow their example and share in their glory. The precautionary evacuation of police posts throughout the country, in reaction to the limited violence in a few areas, had left the IRA in control of large parts of the countryside. Most damaging in this respect were the large-scale arrests at the end of 1920, which forced many IRA officers from their homes, almost predisposing them to violent activity. At the same time GHQ had become convinced that a full military campaign was needed to attain independence. Although often hesitantly, it became increasingly involved in professionalising the Volunteers.

CHAPTER 4

Guerrilla Warfare

Government policy towards IRA violence, which had been somewhat conciliatory since May 1920, radically changed under pressure of the growing lawlessness. The introduction of the Restoration of Order in Ireland Act in August signalled this new approach. The employment of auxiliary police forces during the summer of 1920 made the new policy possible. These forces known as Auxiliaries and Black & Tans, were mainly unemployed ex-soldiers recruited in England. Arriving in Ireland from March 1920, the full deployment both of these forces and of the powers under the new Act took until the end of the year to take full effect. The introduction by the IRA of Flying Columns was a reaction to the growing conflict, and led to the emergence of the type of small-scale operations by mobile units – the classic form of guerrilla warfare.

ORIGINS OF THE FLYING COLUMN

The first columns developed spontaneously in active areas during the spring of 1920. They consisted of Volunteers who had been forced to go on the run due to their participation in barracks and other attacks. These men had started to group together for reasons of security and comradeship. As Michael Brennan from Clare explains, this happened 'partly for company, but mainly because the "safe areas" were now fewer and we usually met in them.' Some of these groups then began to engage in joint operations. However, many simply lay low and their numbers in the Southwest became a heavy burden on the people and on local Volunteer companies, who were relied on for food and protection. At a GHQ meeting in June 1920 this problem was discussed and the idea of a Flying Column was developed.

> Dick Mulcahy was not too keen on the idea, but Michael Collins was very keen on it: 'We'll have to get these bloody fellows doing something' said Collins referring to the men on the run. (At that time and for some time later, they were a bloody nuisance, for they lounged

around, slept late, ate peoples food and did no work for the Company or Battalion in which they happened to be.)[1]

Working on this proposal, some more or less fluid battalion ASUs (Active Service Units) were set up in areas like south Tipperary by battalions who had sufficient men on the run. Although these units were meant to initiate operations, they merely formalised the existing situation. Restricted to their own battalion area and without a clear objective, these ASUs remained an inadequate solution.[2]

The stronger measures of the government in the autumn forced GHQ to rethink its strategy. To give the ASUs greater scope for action, an order to all brigades to start a Flying Column which was to operate throughout the brigade area was issued in October 1920: the terms ASU and Flying Column then became interchangeable. The Flying Column's larger size and greater freedom to act made successful operations more likely and provided an opportunity for the increasing number of men who were on the run. However, the initial reasons for establishing the Flying Column did not apply to all areas. Many brigades had been insufficiently active to drive enough men on the run and no columns were formed.[3]

The Organisational Memo describing the shape of the Flying Column, issued by GHQ on 4 October, clearly stated the reason for the introduction of this new unit:

> At the present time a large number of both of our men and officers are on the run in different parts of the country. The most effective way of utilising these officers and men would seem to be by organising them as Flying Columns. In this way – instead of being compelled to a haphazard and aimless course of action – they would

1 Quote, Michael Brennan (1980), 70. Quote on GHQ meeting, Artie Barlow, O'MN, P17b114. The comment between brackets is from Ernie O'Malley who was the original interviewer and himself an IRA organiser.
2 In the Cashel, Cahir, Tipperary and Kilnamanagh battalions of South Tipperary such a unit was set up, Paul Mulcahy, 'Statement'; Mossy McGrath, O'MN, P17b127; Michael Fitzpatrick, O'MN, P17b114; Paul Merrigan, O'MN, P17b126.
3 In south Tipperary many Volunteers report the formation of small fighting groups of between four to fifteen men in the summer and autumn of 1920, Mossy McGrath, O'MN, P17b127; Mick Fitzpatrick, O'MN, P17b114, Seán Withero, O'MN, P17b114; Paul Mulcahy, 'Statement'. One officer from Tipperary remembers a meeting with a number of top officers in June 1920 discussing the forming of units for those on the run, Artie Barlow, O'MN, P17b114. Some writers report an order to form Flying Columns in mid-August, Charles Townshend (1975), 113-14; David Fitzpatrick (1977), 217. This cannot be confirmed, but the actual general order was dated 4 October 1920, O'MN, P17b127.

become available as standing troops of a well trained and thoroughly reliable stamp, and their actions could be far more systematic and effective. Permanent troops of this kind would afford an exceedingly valuable auxiliary arm to the remainder of the Republican Army which is in great measure only a part-time serve militia.

The official Flying Column was to consist of twenty-six men divided in four squads. Most of the men taken on in these columns were to be officers. They were to function as an auxiliary force for local enterprises of individual battalions but had to instigate independent action as well. When a neighbouring brigade offered an opportunity for action this was only allowed by definite arrangement with the brigade commandant concerned. The appointed Flying Column Commander received clear instructions:

1) To gain experience for himself and his men by planning and then carrying out simple actual operations as outlined in operation orders No's 1 to 7.
2) By harassing smaller and quieter military & police stations.
3) By interrupting and pillaging stores belonging to the enemy.
4) By interrupting all communication.
5) By covering towns threatened by reprisal parties.[4]

The operational orders referred to in point one relate to attacks on buildings; disarming police patrols, guards and escorts and the interruption of their dispatches; cutting lines of communication of police and military posts; respond to reprisal parties; and shooting all Black & Tans and the most 'vicious' RIC men.

INTRODUCTION OF FLYING COLUMNS IN TIPPERARY

The majority of column men in Tipperary came from the group of first activists around the original instigators of activity, who had often led the turn to violence. Their high profile in the previous period had marked them for police attention and thus forced them to go on the run. Immediately after the official order men from the 3rd and 4th Battalions in the western part of south Tipperary established a joint column. The relatively large clusters of active men around Tipperary town and from the Hollyford area had evolved around Seán Treacy and Eamon O'Dwyer and formed the core of this Flying Column.

4 For the exact features of the official Flying Column, Organisational Memo, O'MN, P17b127. Instructions to the column commander, Operational Memo, O'MN, P17b127.

A commander of the column was elected and a small training camp was held in a remote area: 'We had a fine farmhouse, an empty house. There were mattresses and bedclothes there and the whole column could stay in it, but they'd have to forage around for food.' After some training they went out to engage the Crown Forces. However, after their first ambush a disagreement developed between the Volunteers from the 3rd and 4th Battalion. The leader of the 3rd Battalion men was accused of cowardice after he had allegedly failed to use his grenade. As a result of this charge, all Volunteers from the 3rd Battalion went home. The 4th Battalion men were then supplemented by activists from other battalions in the end numbering almost sixty men. Shortly after the introduction of this column a clear increase in the number of ambushes is recorded in south Tipperary.[5]

In other parts of this brigade some battalion ASUs continued to exist but activity remained low. The group of active men in the eastern part of south Tipperary had practically ceased operations after the death of the Battalion Commander, Tom Donovan, in October. In the central area no ASU was formed at all. In the southern part of the county little happened until a second brigade column emerged from the existing battalion ASUs in March 1921. Men from the Cahir Battalion formed the core of this column, later supplemented by members of the Clonmel and the Carrick-on-Suir battalions. The column vice-commandant was unable to find sufficient men willing to fill its ranks. Nevertheless, the second Tipperary column finally numbered 38 men, drawing 22 men from Cahir Battalion, 11 from Clonmel Battalion, 2 from Carrick-on-Suir Battalion and a staff of 3.[6]

INTRODUCTION OF FLYING COLUMNS IN MAYO

A similar development occurred in other areas. In Mayo most active Volunteers had remained at home during 1920. The lack of serious outrages made the likelihood of arrest minimal. However, the concerted effort by police and military to arrest officers of the IRA at the end of 1920 changed that, forcing many of them on the run and resulted in a general order for Volunteer officers to leave their homes. In Westport this coincided with the arrival of some Auxiliaries, whose fame had preceded them. The announcement of their coming alone, sent on to the IRA by a friendly

5 Quote, Ned O'Reilly, O'MN, P17b126. On disagreement, Michael Fitzpatrick, O'MNs, P17b126 and P17b114; Ned O'Reilly, O'MN, P17b126. Taking in more men, Ned Glendon, O'MN, P17b103; Michael Fitzpatrick, O'MN, P17b114. Increase in ambushes, CI South Tipperary MR December 1920.
6 Difficulties recruiting, 'Conversation with Lt. Col. Tom Ryan', UCD AD, P7b179(21). See also UCD AD, P7D108. Despite this criticism, he had stated himself that he did not want to join the column until he had to, Tommy Ryan, 'Statement'. See also Mossy McGrath, O'MN, P17b127.

policeman, made some of the men flee their homes instantly. Several Volunteers from this battalion gathered on a nearby hill-top waiting in vain for instructions from the brigade officers. These anxious hours spent in extremely poor weather was a disheartening experience, and as a result most men returned home the next morning. When the Auxiliaries finally arrived they did not live up to expectations:

> This murder gang consisted of 3 plain's clothed [sic] men, for we had expected armoured cars and lorries, but actually only the 3 men came then. It was a kind of a bombastic show-off around the town. They were swinging guns. They brought the military from the Quay. The 3 of them raided with the military then: and there were quite a number of raids. Their attitude in Westport was to kind of make us look foolish. But these 3 were not violent. It was really a bit of swash-buckling more than anything else.[7]

The initial result of the increased police vigilance was a marked decrease in Volunteer activity. However, after a while the men on the run with nothing else on hand began to act, often in reaction to police violence aimed at their families and overt sympathisers. Some of the more eager men initiated their own actions. One of them stripped two British soldiers on the road from Castlebar to Westport, and later tried to shoot the local District Inspector in a hotel in Westport.[8]

So far the men on the run in Mayo had not taken the risk of openly taking to the field by forming a Flying Column. However, inspired by the successful ambushes of columns in other parts of the country and stimulated by GHQ, the first serious attempts to ambush Crown Forces were recorded in February 1921: 'Several cases of anticipated ambushes where rebels were seen lying-in-wait, were reported during the month, and the places were immediately visited by the Crown Forces, but nothing was discovered. [...] Sinn Féin agents were reported visiting the County to ferment trouble, and organise parties for ambushes.' All these attempts resulted in two ambushes in March. These were the first direct engagements in south and west Mayo in which members of the Crown Forces were shot in direct combat.[9]

In south Mayo about twenty men started a Flying Column after having been involved in the Partry ambush on 7 March. In the Westport Battalion in west Mayo, men from the Westport and Aughagower companies had

7 Quote, Thomas Heavey, O'MN, P17b120. One of the men on the hill that did return home, Charlie Hughes, Interview. The police observed known Volunteers leaving home, CI Mayo MR November 1920.
8 Starting to act, Brodie Malone and Ned Moane, O'MN, P17b120; Thomas Heavey, 'Statement', and O'MN, P17b120.
9 Quote and Volunteer operations, CI Mayo MRs February-March 1921.

mobilised on 16 March to ambush a lorry on the road to Louisburgh. Although the lorry failed to show up, most men involved decided to stay out and form a column. In its diary of operations for March, the West Mayo Brigade reported to GHQ that the Westport Battalion had formed a column and that two other battalions were organising their own. The 4th Battalion was said to be too low on 'fighting men', the battalion staff and one captain were the only active Volunteers.[10]

Those already on the run formed the majority of members of these small units, incorporating the brigade and battalion staffs and some company officers mainly from the towns, the original centres of the four battalions where police presence was strongest. The active Westport Battalion had sufficient members on the run to form a small ASU, but in the other battalions men had to be recruited from the companies. In the Newport Battalion this was no problem:

> Each Company was mobilised on its own ground. The organiser lectured us on the formation of the column. He said that a Volunteer who agreed to join had nothing to gain from it but an early death, and that anyone who did not feel he could see it through would be thought none the worse of it if he stood down. [...] The organiser asked that anyone willing to serve should cross a given line which he made. [...] Total 16 plus officers. [...] People got a haversack to pack to be ready if they were called on. [...] Michael [Kilroy] picked a certain number of men from each Company and gave them the arms on hand. [...] Causing a little disappointment or jealousy among those who were not picked.

In the Castlebar Battalion men were recruited in a similar fashion. The active men, who had so far been frustrated by their officers in their attempts to attack the enemy, finally got their chance. Subsequently the commander of the battalion, who had always blocked activity for fear of reprisals and who was considered too old for active service, left for England.[11]

---

10 Mobilisation in south Mayo, Tom Maguire, O'MN, P17b100. Mobilisation in west Mayo, Michael Kilroy, O'MN, P17b101; Joe Baker (1988), 19-20; West Mayo Brigade report March 1921, UCD AD, P7A38.

11 Origins of West Mayo Flying Column, List of Flying Column members, CBHC; Dan Sammon, Interview; Moane/Malone, Tape. In this column the Duffy brothers from Aughagower were some of the few rural members, partly due to their family connections in Westport. Quote, Jim O'Donnell, 'Recollections'. Mobilisation in Castlebar Battalion, Michael Hughes, 'Statement'; Mark Killilea, O'MN, P17b109; Paddy Cannon, O'MN, P17b136.

MILITARISATION ELSEWHERE

In Wexford a relative calm had set in after the introduction of the Restoration of Order in Ireland Act. Although some men were arrested, few went on the run. The handful of activists in south Wexford continued to operate as part of their original units. As we have seen, the initial calm was broken during the Christmas period when two barracks were attacked and a constable was shot. However, tranquillity was re-established in south Wexford at the beginning of 1921, interrupted only by some non-violent Volunteer activity. December was apparently a common period for increased crime, and the temporary activity could also have been initiated by active Volunteers returning home for Christmas from elsewhere. A few attacks on the police also occurred in the northern part of the county, where a Flying Column had been in existence for a short while at the end of 1920. Despite the low level of activity, martial law was proclaimed in the county in January 1921 mainly to prevent active Volunteers from neighbouring counties from moving into Wexford.[12]

To provide inactive areas like Wexford with men experienced in all aspects of fighting a special arrangement was made in 1921. To give the local officers some experience Officer Training Camps were held often led by a representative of GHQ. After a week of intensive training involving lectures, drill, parades and rifle practise, the men involved constituted an ASU, which was roughly similar in design to a Flying Column. After having engaged in some operations against the enemy, they were to return to their units. A new group of officers, NCOs and later the best of the rank and file were then to be trained in a similar manner. It was hoped these men would initiate more action upon their return. Some of these groups remained together after their first operations and constituted a small Flying Column. However, in Wexford this never occurred.[13]

In Derry after the arrests of the autumn of 1920, most active Volunteers were in custody or had decided they were safer elsewhere. The remaining men were unable or unwilling to build up or even sustain the level of activity of the summer months that Volunteers in other parts of Ireland had

12 IRA activities, CI Wexford MRs 1920–1921.
13 Officer Training Camps, Training Memo No.2, NLI, ms. 739. For activities in these camps, UCD AD, P7A17/114; NLI, P921 No.66. In Offaly No.2 Brigade, 10 officers and men from the 1st Battalion and 14 from the 2nd were mobilised for an OTC and to act as an ASU in April 1921, UCD AD, P7A17/270. In the North Tipperary Brigade two OTCs were held in May 1921 each taking in half of all brigade, battalion and company officers, NLI, P921 No.66; UCD AD, P7A17/114 + 307; Seán Gaynor, 'Statement'. In the spring of 1921 GHQ merged the Officer Training Camp with the Flying Column, probably dated March 1921, UCD AD, P7A17/119-25. In an annexed note there were slight adjustments made to this scheme.

done. In the first few months of 1921 the only recorded IRA activity was in the southern part of the county. It consisted of a few arms raids, two attempts to hold up a train and the burning of a couple of houses thought to be intended for use by the police.[14]

In Derry City little occurred at the end of 1920 and the beginning of 1921. One of the main reasons for this was the attitude of the officers who wanted to keep the city quiet. Nevertheless, there were sufficient arms in the city to provide a column. In December, twelve of the most active and wanted men in the city were sent to Co. Donegal as a Flying Column. However, the unwillingness of local men to get involved was testified by the fact that only half of them came from Derry. The other half consisted of temporary workers from other counties, two each from Cork and Donegal, one from Armagh and one from Tipperary. As a result, even less was done by the men remaining in the city. The only reported activity in January 1921 was a raid by twelve masked and armed men, possibly the flying column, on a railway carriage containing military goods, who overlooked a much-prized Lewis machine-gun.[15]

A second column of eight men was sent out from the city in May 1921, further depleting the ranks of activists: 'The City was now left without any Volunteers of more than one year's service.' The experience of the columns with local men in Donegal was discouraging. In June the Divisional Staff sent half of the 2nd Derry Column, consisting of four men, to south Donegal to initiate some activity there. Although they had some engagements with the Crown Forces and captured some arms, they were unable to inspire the local men: 'For a month before the Truce we were carrying two rifles and a revolver each together with ammunition. We could not get men to carry or use the surplus.' [16]

The dramatic increase in Crown Force operations at the end of 1920 changed conditions in Dublin as well. Up to then the use of violence had been confined to an extremely small group of active Volunteers who only engaged those pursuing them. Most other Volunteers had occupied themselves with drilling and parading. Now a situation evolved in which a great number of them attacked the Crown Forces indiscriminately. This develop-

---

14 File on Londonderry dated 23 June 1921, PRONI, FIN18/1/729; CI Derry MRs 1921.

15 Founding of 1st column in Derry, Lt. M. Sheerin, NLI, P921 No.66. Background column men in Derry City, Liam A. Brady, *Derry Journal*, 25 May 1953. Raid on railway carriage, CI Derry MR January 1921.

16 Availability of arms, Peadar O'Donnell, O'MN, P17b98. Founding of 2nd column in Derry, Lt. M. Sheerin, NLI, P921 No.66; Liam Brady, *Derry Journal*, 25 May-3 June 1953; Charlie MacGuinness (1934), 120-50. The police reported that they found papers of the Chief of Staff with plans to start Flying Columns in Derry and Belfast, PRO, WO35/90, Appendix A. Both quotes, Lt. M. Sheerin, NLI, P921 No.66.

ment was speeded up by the successful targeting of the government's intel-ligence-services. The unarmed DMP had long been sidelined by the activ-ity of the IRA and their own reluctance to endanger their lives. The effect-iveness of the DMP's G-Division, consisting of detectives who targeted political organisations, had diminished sharply after some of them were shot, and by IRA infiltration. Military intelligence that had replaced them was seriously affected by the events of Bloody Sunday. As a direct result of the killings of British officers, the remnants of the G-Division and most of the military intelligence men left their lodgings and sought safety in bar-racks.[17]

The IRA now knew most of its intelligence adversaries, while the author-ities lost track of many active Volunteers. As a result the police and military had to operate largely in the dark. In countering the IRA the authorities had to rely on random searches and raids by the military and Auxiliaries. Although it resulted in many arrests, these were mainly Volunteers of little importance whose names were found in captured roll-books. These searches and raids became an important factor in the trans-ition to a guerrilla war, by forcing more Volunteers to go on the run. The comparative anonymity provided by the city enabled most Volunteers to continue working, although many could not sleep at home. The most want-ed men, many of whom had lost their jobs, were facilitated by the start of the ASU, whose members received a wage. The lesser-known Volunteers were involved in operations by the introduction of the company patrols operating in the evenings and at weekends. After this, military conflict developed rapidly. The growing availability of arms and grenades in Dublin was crucial to this.[18]

FLYING COLUMN LIFE

Few of all the columns conformed to the organisational and administrative directions given by GHQ. Most were just a band of full-time fighting men. A variety of types emerged, ranging in size from about ten men in less active areas to as many as 100 in Cork. In Tipperary the original 'fluid' ASUs continued to operate in some of the battalions alongside the brigade Flying Columns. In the West Mayo Brigade each battalion had its own reg-ular column, while in South Mayo the single brigade column consisted mainly of men from the Cross Battalion. During operations it was occasion-ally supplemented by Volunteers from the other battalions. In the Tour-

17 IRA spies in police force and Castle, Frank Thornton, O'MN, P17b100; John
   Neary, O'MN, P17b122; Harry Colley, O'MN, P17b97; David Neligan (1960).
18 Military raids in Dublin, PRO, WO35/122. Captured roll books, Harry Colley,
   O'MN, P17b97. Establishing ASU and company patrols, NLI, ms. 901/35-7.

makeady ambush the only successful engagement of this Flying Column, a total of sixty Volunteers cooperated. Forty-two of these were drawn from the Ballinrobe Battalion and the remaining eighteen constituted the column.[19]

A training camp was often the first step taken. After the successful ambush at Partry in south Mayo the column had been officially established and a training camp was started: 'Early in March [1921] we camped out in the woods in felt tarred shelters to keep out the rain, straw beds with bed clothes given to us by the people.' Following a strict programme the camp was intended to prepare the men. Before a second brigade column came into action in south Tipperary one of these camps was held under auspices of a brigade officer:

> Our drill and training was gruelling, our leaders object being to submit each member to the acid-test of his durability and stamina and readiness to endure the hardships and dangers that were yet to follow. Often when after a strenuous day of fatiguing work, during the night we were suddenly called for a 'Stand To'. This meant that every man was to be fully equipped and standing to attention within 3 minutes. The use of lights was strictly forbidden and no noise or floundering was to be overheard. At times we did not know whether this was a genuine 'stand to' at the enemy's approach or just one of the leaders acid-tests. A night route march often followed, so as a result of this fortnight in Glenpatrick the members were hardened into outdoor military life.

Three of the men involved could not bear the heavy exercises and returned to their units. Operations with the column were equally demanding. After having taken a rest in the city the second Derry column went out again in April 1921: 'Two of the remaining eight did not travel as we found that their physical condition was not such as could stand up to the long tramps and poor food.'[20]

The brigade staff were directly involved in the organisation and running of the columns, but officially their commanders had a free hand to act. The training camp in south Tipperary was led by the brigade staff and a GHQ training officer. They left when the column went out to tour the area. Control over the columns' operations was strict but it left room for actions

19 Composition of West and South Mayo Brigade Flying Columns, West Mayo Brigade report dated 4 April 1921, UCD AD, P7A38; Reports on Partry and Tourmakeady ambushes, Ibidem.

20 Quote on training camp in south Mayo, Tom Maguire, O'MN, P7b100. See also Pat Fallon, O'MN, P17b109. Similar training camp was held for the column from Castlebar Battalion in west Mayo, Jimmy Swift, O'MN, P17b136. Quote on training camp in Tipperary, Mossy McGrath, O'MN, P17b127. Quote on Derry, Lt. M. Sheerin, NLI, P921 No.66.

by individual members. Small groups split off now and then for separate jobs. In Tipperary, a democratic attitude was shown by the column council held before each operation.[21]

Most of the columns' time was spent evading the police. The smaller battalion ASUs in Mayo remained in those parts of their battalion area where they felt relatively safe. Travelling from one safe-haven to the other usually at night, they stayed well away from the main roads. On their rambles the columns were guided and guarded by local Volunteers. When moving to another locality word was sent ahead to the local company so that scouts could be put out and houses prepared for the men. Depending on their size the columns then billeted in a set pattern:

> Two men were allocated to each house in a townland. Some townlands were smaller than others and in some instances we would have to occupy two of them. They were usually adjacent to each other and the Brigade Staff and officers always made a point of occupying the houses in the centre of the area, so that we would be able to get in touch with all the men if necessary

A routine developed soon after the columns' inception:

> We rose at a fixed hour, washed, breakfasted, and paraded with arms, did certain drills and training practices and lived much like soldiers in garrison, except that we were on constant guard against surprise. The extent of our security precautions was determined and decided by the nature of the place we were in and its proximity to the enemy posts. At night, guard duty was done by local Volunteers, though again, if we felt that extra precaution was necessary, regular Column men would be detailed to stiffen the guard.

The larger columns in Tipperary were more professional in their organisation than in Mayo. In some places they organised their own sleeping-quarters in derelict houses, and later underground dugouts were made. The large size of the columns in Tipperary necessitated this, as the lack of accommodation meant that the column was often dangerously spread out.[22]

---

21 Staff activity in south Tipperary, Mossy McGrath, O'MN, P17b127. Jobs by small groups, Thomas Heavey, O'MN, P17b120. Column council, 'Conversation with Lt. Col. Tom Ryan', UCD AD, P7b179.

22 Staying in safe areas, Patrick Owen Mugan, Interview; John Madden, O'MN, P17b113; Johnny Duffy, O'MN, P17b109; Ned Moane, 'Statement'; Paddy Duffy, O'MN, P17b138; Mossy McGrath, O'MN, P17b127. Quote on 'billeting', Moane/Malone, Tape. Sleeping quarters in Tipperary, Paul Merrigan, Interview; Mossy McGrath, O'MN, P17b127. Quote on 'routine', Thomas Heavey, 'Statement'. See also Ned Moane, 'Statement'; Michael Kilroy, 'ASU Operations'.

Local people provided the columns with supplies and entertainment in the form of music and dance. Some areas were more hospitable than others, making the column members feel at home:

> There was a great house, Pat Joyce's of Durlis at the back of Croagh Patrick in Drummin, and they'd kill a sheep each the Joyce's and a few ducks whenever we came, for there [were] no women in the house. Kettrick was in bed one morning and he walked to the door 'It's a great house he said you can have a piss from the door'.

The column sometimes bought livestock from local farmers. They were killed and one of the column members then acted as a cook. In Mayo clothing and equipment was contributed by friendly shopkeepers. Providing for the large number of men on the run in Tipperary became a major financial burden. The existence of battalion ASUs and a brigade Flying Column made such demands on the brigade's finances that a levy of ten shillings [50p] per week was imposed on each company in January 1921.[23]

The columns' inclination to stay in only a few safe areas was a heavy burden on the locality. The presence of the column in the neighbourhood implicated local people in its actions, which meant risking the wrath of the Crown Forces. Most Volunteers were aware of this, but at the time there was little they could do in return. A column member in west Mayo who was a qualified doctor was regarded as the only useful member of the column in that respect. To protect both themselves and the population, the importance of secrecy of movement was emphasised, but was difficult to maintain with so many men billeting in one or two hamlets. The men's desire to socialise led to some dangerous situations. To protect the columns from approaching enemies, warning systems using flags, fires and empty bottles were successfully used, particularly in Tipperary.[24]

FLYING COLUMNS IN OPERATION

Despite the full-time involvement of Volunteers in the Flying Columns, the new units never got involved in much fighting. In Tipperary, the first

23 Column entertainment, Mossy McGrath, O'MN, P17b127. Quote, Brodie Malone, O'MN, P17b109. Buying and cooking, Johnny Duffy, O'MN, P17b109. Clothing provided by shopkeepers, Ned Moane, 'Statement'; Ned Maughan [same man as Ned Moane], O'MN, P17b109. Levy on companies, O'MN, P17b127.
24 Doctor, Jimmy Swift, O'MN, P17b136. Warning systems by the IRA: Fires first mentioned in east Clare, UCD AD, P7A17/197. See also CI South Tipperary MR June 1921. Lamp signalling was used in Tipperary, Markham, O'MN, P17b101. Use of bottles, Andy Cooney, O'MN, P17b107.

brigade column initially managed to stage some successful ambushes which alarmed the police: 'In fact it is not too much to say that a state of open rebellion, evidenced by incessant and cowardly guerrilla attacks, is existent in the greater part of the Riding.' However, counter-measures by the Crown Forces were increasingly successful in reducing their activity. The second column introduced in March failed to mount any successful ambushes in its entire existence. The only fighting it was involved in were the result of attempts to arrest them. That casualties nevertheless remained at a high level in 1921 was a result of executions of spies and individual members of the Crown Forces by small groups of activists.[25]

Columns in other areas were equally unsuccessful. In West Mayo the small battalion columns remained in their own area and occasionally attempted an ambush. The almost complete lack of intelligence about where and when they were likely to engage the enemy was shown by their inability to make any contact. The first engagement on 22 March was the result of coincidence. Three brigade officers who were walking on the Oughty Road were approached from the rear by three policemen on bicycles. When the police came close the Volunteers turned around and opened up on them, resulting in the wounding of two, after which the police surrendered. This small victory gave a great boost to ASU morale, but no further engagements took place and the column men grew impatient: 'All our planning, debating, marching and counter-marching had seemed so much waste of time.' Keen to start a fight, some Westport column men urged their officers to go into town to attack the police or military in the daytime: 'Some of the officers [were] not in favour of this idea as they thought it flavoured too much of Dublin tactics.' Despite this refusal, some column members went into town. Although they failed to engage they were court-martialled, but no punishment was meted out.[26]

A month after the brush with the policemen on bicycles, another accidental meeting took place with some police lorries in the night of 22 April. In May their luck changed for the better, although initially with poor results. An attempted ambush near Islandeady ended in disaster when a military raiding party from Castlebar turned around prematurely. They surprised some local Volunteers who were digging a trench to prevent reinforcements

25 Quote, CI South Tipperary MR January 1921. For activity of the second column in Tipperary, Mossy McGrath, O'MN, P17b127; Tommy Ryan, 'Statement'. Peter Hart has shown that the majority of casualties in Co. Cork in 1921 were victims of murder attempts by a few hard men and did not fall in combat between columns and Crown Forces, Peter Hart (1992), Chapter 'The killing of Sergeant O'Donoghue', 29.
26 Small victory in West Mayo, Michael Kilroy, 'ASU Operations'; Joe Baker (1988), 21. Quote on 'bad luck', Michael Kilroy, 'ASU Operations'. See also Moane/Malone, Tape. Quote on 'Dublin tactics', Thomas Kettrick, 'Statement'. Going into town, Thomas Heavey, 'Statement'.

coming from Castlebar. In the ensuing shooting two local Volunteers were killed. Success came with an attack in Westport by three impatient column members who had finally been allowed to go into town. From the railway bridge they threw two grenades onto a police patrol, wounding six.[27]

This inability of the battalion columns in west Mayo to engage Crown Forces was comparable to the experience of the battalion ASUs in Tipperary in the summer of 1920. To deal with this problem the Mayo men came up with a similar solution. The three battalion columns were merged into one large brigade column, and also included the few fighting men from the 4th battalion. In order to provoke a fight, Volunteers were sent into the towns of Westport and Newport to shoot a policeman, while the main body took up position between the two towns at Kilmeena, hoping to ambush reinforcements sent from one town to another.

The men sent to Newport were successful and shot a local RIC sergeant. However, when the anticipated reinforcements from Westport reached the ambush site some of the column men had fallen asleep. All were tired from a long night's march and had waited in position since early morning. The results were disastrous; five Volunteers were killed and six more arrested, five of them being wounded. The whole ambush was badly planned and executed and some Volunteers had fled as soon as the fight had started.[28]

Hiding from their pursuers, the column was again surprised a few days later, another Volunteer being killed. To prevent a recurrence of the panic that had overcome the men in the ambush, sections were set up with one man in charge of every six members. Finally, a successful ambush took place at Carrowkennedy on 3 June, in which seven policemen, including the local District Inspector, were killed. Furthermore, two police lorries were burned, and a machine-gun, several rifles, revolvers and a great deal of ammunition were captured. The strong reaction of the authorities that followed this ambush ensured that this was the last operation of the Flying Column in west Mayo.[29]

A similar lack of real fighting occurred in south Mayo and Derry. The south Mayo column had equally bad luck, and several ambushes were called off; because the men either refused to stay out in bad weather or there was insufficient ammunition. Their first successful engagement since March took place at Tourmakeady in May. However, while fleeing from the site of the attack the brigade adjutant was killed and the brigade commandant was seriously wounded. The first Derry City column established in December 1920

27 A veteran of Islandeady ambush, Patrick Owen Mugan, Interview. Railway bridge ambush, Moane/Malone, Tape.

28 Failed ambush, Jimmy Swift, O'MN, P17b136; Michael Kilroy, 'ASU Operations'; Ned Moane and Brodie Malone, O'MN, P17b120; Johnny Duffy, O'MN, P17b109; Paddy Duffy, O'MN P17b113; Thomas Heavey 'Statement'.

29 Changes to organisation column, Tom Kettrick, O'MN, P17b136; Joe Baker (1988), 23. Both ambushes are described by several Mayo Volunteers. See also CI Mayo MRs May-June 1921.

fought only one unsuccessful battle, after which no further attempt at fighting was made. The second column, sent out to Donegal in May 1921, was unable to do much either. It was immediately caught up in a military round-up and after a narrow escape they returned to Derry. Their presence in the city coincided with a day of violence in which some of them were possibly involved, after which they returned to Donegal.[30]

END OF THE FLYING COLUMN

The fighting that flared up during 1921 made the position of most Flying Columns in the country untenable. The counter-measures of the military, combined with the lengthening days, made their existence increasingly dangerous and military successes increasingly unlikely. In Mayo, the South Mayo Brigade column avoided all activity after Tourmakeady. The West Mayo Brigade column was also forced to break up early in June, after their first successful ambush had resulted in pursuit by a massive military force. Unable to meet such a challenge the brigade leaders decided to disband the column. The men dumped their arms and tried to escape from the military in small groups. Surprisingly, none of them were caught when passing through the military cordon that was thrown around the area. As a result of this, there was no Flying Column in operation either in West or South Mayo from early June 1921.[31]

The columns in south Tipperary had been active for a considerable longer time than in Mayo. Nevertheless, they had had only limited success in 1921. All told, six policemen, eight military and ten Volunteers were killed in combat. In the spring the columns experienced the same problems as those in Mayo. The stronger measures by the authorities forced them to avoid the military instead of engaging them. As a result the existence of the columns became a burden which had no military return for the organisation. The newly appointed IRA division commandant overseeing Tipperary acknowledged this situation and suggested GHQ to disband at least two of the three columns he had found in this brigade. He reported that the existence of these three groups was exhausting Volunteer resources, while they

30 Experiences in south Mayo, Tom Maguire, in U. MacEoin (1987), 283-8, and O'MN, P17b100; Pat Fallon, O'MN, P17b109; Report Tourmakeady ambush, UCD AD, P17A38. Column in Derry City, C.J. MacGuinness (1934), passim; Lt. M. Sheerin, NLI, P921 No.66.
31 Disbanding of brigade columns: In East limerick Brigade, NLI, ms. 17,880; In Galway, NLI, ms. 21,288; In West Mayo, Ned Moane, 'Statement'; In Tipperary, Seán Fitzpatrick. UCD AD, P7D109; Seamus Robinson, 'Statement', NLI, ms. 21,265. Inactive Flying Column in South Mayo, Tom Maguire, in U. MacEoin (1981), 185-9 + 288; Pat Fallon, O'MN, P17b109. West Mayo Column, Joe Baker (1988), 37; Michael Kilroy, O'MN, P17b101, and 'ASU Operations'.

had little to show for. The men of the Flying Columns and the areas where they operated, were fed up. There were not enough mines to attack successfully and intelligence was poor. The Chief of Staff agreed to this on 22 April, and early in May the men were sent back to their original units to engage in small operations with the Volunteers there. Most then joined the battalion ASUs. These were, however, fairly inactive and did not travel the area in large numbers. The Tipperary police, nevertheless, remained unable to perform its tasks in the countryside as the continued presence of many armed Volunteers meant they could only go out in large numbers.[32]

ACTIVE SERVICE IN DUBLIN CITY

The Dublin ASU was formed in December 1920 with a target strength of 100 men, but it is doubtful whether this was ever reached. Its main task was to combat the Auxiliaries, who had become a serious threat to the survival of the movement. The ASU was recruited from the four city battalions and divided into four units, which shared a barrack, a dump and an office. All the men involved had their own lodgings and reported every morning at the office for instructions. Most of the men were extremely young and had no social commitments. Some were so young that the British did not even consider them potential Volunteers. The ASU received no special training before starting operations, but most of its members had already gained some fighting experience before joining the unit. As information on enemy movements was scarce, most of their time was spent wandering around their battalion area looking for an opportunity. These men carried their own small arms, while grenades, ammunition and rifles were kept in the ASU dump.[33]

Operations consisted of street ambushes and sniping at military and Auxiliary patrols. As a general instruction they were to concentrate on the highest British officers and on 'Igoe's Gang'. The latter was a unit of about

32 Forming battalion columns, Ned Glendon, O'MN, P17b103; Kennedy, O'MN, P17b114; Paul Merrigan, O'MN, P17b127. Report from Divisional Commandant dated 14 April 1921, UCD AD, P7A17/231-3. To show the confusion between Flying Columns and ASUs the Tipperary Volunteers always speak of the existence of two Flying Columns only. The third one discovered by the Divisional Commandant was probably a battalion ASU. The inability of the RIC to police the countryside in Tipperary, CI South Tipperary MR June 1921.

33 This description of the experience of the Dublin ASU is based on, Oscar Traynor, O'MN, P17b96; Harry Colley, O'MN, P17b97; George White, O'MN, P17b105; Paddy Rigney, O'MN, P17b105, P17b90; Joe McHenry, O'MN, P17b95. Contrary to the country units the Dublin ASU members were paid at 4 pounds 10 shillings a week, Patrick O'Daly, 'Statement', NLI, P4548; Risteard Mulcahy, 'The Origins of the IRA and its Achievements during the War of Independence', UCD AD, P7D96. Member who was too young to be considered a Volunteer, Paddy Rigney, O'MN, P17b105.

twelve hardened provincial policemen who were called to Dublin at the end of 1920 to identify visiting IRA officers. However, the ASU never managed to hit either target:

> For a long time we concentrated on General Tudor and on General Macready. Dozens of times we tried to get them, and we lay in wait for them, but they always changed plans at the last moment. [...] We could have got Igoe's gang, but GHQ were afraid of casualties amongst the people, for the gang always patrolled in a crowded thoroughfare.[34]

With the introduction of the ASU the role of the Squad changed. The ASU became the new unit of action, while the Squad started to function more as a bodyguard for top officers, particularly Michael Collins. Although there was a division into units similar to the country areas, there was not such a strict division of labour in Dublin. The ASU cooperated with any Volunteer who happened to be available at the time. Especially on larger operations, such as train ambushes, the ASU and the Squad joined forces. Other Volunteers who mixed with the ASU socially were also likely to be asked for these larger operations. One ASU member claims that the Squad refused to carry grenades and that if they had to be used they insisted on having the ASU with them. The ASU did indeed practise in bomb-throwing and shooting: 'We had revolver-practise in the Green Hills once a month from the time the unit started. We'd fire 6 rounds a man at an old civilian coat which was hung up on a tree at 25 yards range.' The Dublin ASU was increasingly active during the first months of 1921, laying several successful ambushes and inflicting many casualties. However, after sustaining heavy loses in its attack on the Custom House the Dublin ASU was merged with the GHQ Squad into the Dublin Guards.[35]

FEAR, ENTERTAINMENT AND ITS CONSEQUENCES

Involvement in the fighting deeply affected the members of the ASUs and columns. The fear that overcame the men in their first fights manifested itself in various ways. Many inexperienced members were paralysed:

> Jimmy Brennan once told me that a friend of his Keogh who later went Free State, went out on a Castle job. They went out into a pub

34 Quote, George White, O'MN, P17b105. See also Jack Corneer, O'MN, P17b103.
35 Quote, George White, O'MN, P17b105. Involvement through social contacts, Andy Cooney, O'MN, P17b107; Charlie Dalton, O'MN, P17b122, and (1929), passim. Disbanding ASU and Squad in Dublin, Patrick O'Daly, 'Statement', NLI, P4548; George White, O'MN, P17b99.

near the Castle but when they were going in there, Brennan said 'you wait at that door I'll do the other door'. The man collapsed. He wasn't able to face a door and what it meant by himself.

Many fired too early; others forgot to fire and started praying, one swallowed his cigarette in the excitement, while a number refused to execute their orders. Even experienced fighters had such problems; in the heat of battle many forgot to take the arms or to search the men they shot as was ordered. In extreme cases men fled. According to Ernie O'Malley, this happened three times in fights of the west Mayo column. Only the strong bonds of friendship that evolved in the columns prevented their court-martial.[36]

The violence often unnerved the men. Most active Volunteers vividly remember their first shooting. One of the future members of the Dublin ASU was greatly affected by the killings during Bloody Sunday: 'Charlie Dalton was very nervous. We went into the Capitol [a cinema] to ease his mind. [...] Charlie Dalton couldn't sleep that night of Bloody Sunday. He thought he could hear the gurgling of the Officer's blood and he kept awake in fright until we told him a tap was running somewhere.'[37]

Nevertheless, most of the men who were fully committed to the cause soon grew accustomed to this, and took the dangers and fears that were obviously connected with active service in their stride. The strong bond which had developed between the members of the columns and ASUs pulled them through. Most of them were in awe of their direct leaders who took responsibility for their operations. In Dublin, a strong loyalty to Collins developed among members of the Squad and ASU. He closely associated himself with any large operation and often met the men involved before and afterwards, to give encouragement and show his appreciation.

There were several ways to deal with fear. In the Carrowkennedy fight the only truly successful ambush by the west Mayo column, the men sang: 'Kelly the boy from Killane', in order to overcome their nerves. It was common to resort to alcohol before and after going into action:

> I was told to pick twelve men for a raid on Castlebar. [...] We arrived at Mickey Walsh's pub on the Newport Road and in we went. I ordered 13 pints of stout although I had no money to pay for them. He understood who we were. I said to the men that we

36 Quote on 'Brennan', Frank Henderson, O'MN, P17b99. Fear affecting men's behaviour in Dublin, Charlie Dalton, O'MN, P17b122, and (1929), 102-10; Andy Cooney, O'MN, P17b107; Paddy Rigney, O'MN, P17b105. Men deserting in Mayo, Ned Moane and Brodie Malone, O'MN, P17b120; Paddy Duffy, O'MN, P17b113; Johnny Duffy, O'MN, P17b109. In Tipperary and Clare column men also deserted, Paul Merrigan, Interview; Sean Gaynor, 'Statement'; Liam Haugh, 'History of the West Clare Brigade', NLI, P915 A0363.
37 Fear of Charlie Dalton, Matty MacDonald, O'MN, P17b105.

might never be together again and to enjoy a drink. Most of these lads never put a glass to their lips before but on this occasion each man drank his pint.

Drinking became a habit, and indeed a serious problem, for many active Volunteers. Many members in Dublin, especially those who were paid, drank excessively. Leading republicans involved in the different departments and units in Dublin met each other socially in hotels and bars at night. Some of them, including Michael Collins, became heavy drinkers. Due to the psychological strain of his work, one of the leaders of the Squad drank so heavily that he had to be replaced. Alcohol abuse seriously endangered Volunteers on many occasions. The commandant of the Dublin Brigade recalls an incident involving a GHQ officer:

> My brother came across a man lying in the gutter, very drunk. Another man was trying to help him to get on his feet. He has IRA papers on him the man said and my brother did not know whether the man who was helping Price was then in the IRA. My brother brought Price to Killarney Parade for it was just before curfew. Price's pockets were filled with papers.[38]

This situation conflicted strongly with the official line of the movement which emphasised the dangers of drinking: 'Drinking was frowned upon by the Volunteers and generally anyone who drank even mildly was regarded as untrustworthy and of no use to any self-respecting revolutionary movement.' This attitude was particularly prevalent among activists in the first part of the struggle. The contrast with Irish revolutionary organisations in the past was remarked on by a British intelligence officer in December 1917: 'Drunkenness is almost unknown amongst those deeply implicated, and is apparently severely dealt with. This is [...] foreign to the usual state of things in such movements.'[39]

38 Singing in Mayo, Michael Kilroy, 'ASU Operations'. Quote on 'pints', Michael Hughes, 'Statement'. Drinking by Collins and other activist in Dublin, Alfie White, O'MN, P17b110; Robert Briscoe, O'MN, P17b97; George White, O'MN, P17b105; Frank Henderson, O'MN, P17b105; Garry Houlihan, O'MN, P17b105; Harry Colley, O'MN, P17b97; Eamon Martin, O'MN, P17b105; Bob Brennan, O'MN, P17b108; Alfred Rutherford, O'MN, P17b122; Jim Slattery, O'MN, P17b109; Patrick O'Daly, 'Statement', NLI, P4548. Quote on '[Bob] Price', Oscar Traynor, O'MN, P17b98.

39 Quote on drinking in movement, Patrick Casey, 'Idle thoughts', Fr O'Kane Papers, AARC. The old IRB was particularly renowned for their drinking and were often referred to as 'the whiskey drinking Fenians', Alfie White, P17b110. Quote from military intelligence officer in 1917, Charles Townshend (1975), 7. The strong discipline among column men is emphasised by, David Fitzpatrick (1977), 219.

Apart from this, the Pioneer total abstinence movement was strong and many young men had taken its oath. As a result, the alcohol abuse that developed under strain of the fighting led to tensions within the organisation. The less serious attitude of some irritated the more ardent officers. Some accused Collins of abusing drink and funds to buy people's loyalty. This accusation got them into serious trouble. In turn Collins made fun of the overzealous attitude of these men. Provincial officers had equally strong feelings: 'Michael Kilroy had an antipathy towards us Westport fellows. We were a bit too tough, Rabelaisian and irreverent for Michael's puritanical mind. In fact, some of them even drank, and in Kilroy's sight nothing could be expected from a drinker.' Some men used this irritation to get into favour with zealous officers. Before visiting the Director of Organisation, who had strong views on drinking, many men pinned on a Pioneer badge. The commandant of the Dublin Brigade was aware of the true nature of these men: 'He was being codded all over the place for these men who honoured the pin [the badge] would drink out of an old boot.'[40]

Despite the antipathy towards drinking among many higher officers, they were unable to prevent it. Although some dismissals were a direct result of drinking, it had no lasting effect. In Wexford drinking had led to the removal of a battalion commandant and the brigade commander in 1920, and of another battalion commandant in May 1921. The feelings of Michael Kilroy were not sufficient to enforce a ban on drinking in the west Mayo Flying Column. It took an incident, afterwards named 'the night of the long bottles', in which alcohol abuse seriously endangered their lives, before he could do this. Although all column men then took the pledge, their hearts were not in it: 'Someone asked what was to be done with the whiskey now that all had the pledge, when in a fierce whisper from Kettrick came the words: "Give me that bloody bottle".'[41]

Many Volunteers were diverted from their tasks by a strong interest in socialising, which included meeting the opposite sex. Although a lot of information was obtained through relationships with young women working in various establishments, this could also endanger the organisation. There were numerous examples of courting taking precedence over Volunteer activities. In attempts to impress the ladies, Volunteers sometimes jeopardised their own safety. Many members of the opposite sex did not shy away from the attentions of the Volunteers either. Young men in uniform with zeal, determination and authority attracted young females, who often

40 Men challenging Collins, Eamon Martin, O'MN, P17b105; Alfie White, O'MN, P17b110; Garry Houlihan, O'MN, P17b105. Collins making fun of zealous attitude, Pat MacCrea, O'MN, P17b110. Quote on Kilroy's 'feelings', Thomas Heavey, 'Statement'. Quote on 'Pioneer pin', Oscar Traynor, O'MN, P17b98.

41 Results of drinking in Wexford, UCD AD, P7A17/62-3. Ban on drinking after incident in west Mayo, Thomas Heavey, O'MN, P17b120. Quote on 'bottle', Thomas Heavey, 'Statement'.

were already (or about to become) involved in the national struggle themselves.[42]

At times the courting stage was transcended, and some unconfirmed reports of illegitimate children springing from these liaisons come from secondary sources. Volunteers themselves do not openly confirm this, although an interest in women was clearly present: 'When I was in a good billet with a good looking girl Mick Sheehan would say to me: "You're tired: you'd best go to bed early".' Acknowledging that this interest affected Volunteer operations, the commandant of the second Flying Column in Tipperary who himself had been arrested in 1919 on a late night rendezvous with a girl, stated that: 'Ireland will never be free until she can produce a Robert Emmet who doesn't give a damn about women.'[43]

LACK OF WEAPONRY AND ITS CONSEQUENCES

Another problem common to Volunteers in all areas was the lack of arms and ammunition. After the Flying Columns had started, bringing with them the constant likelihood of open conflict, the lack of ammunition became particularly acute. Units that had been less active in procuring this early in the struggle were most affected. The South Mayo Brigade was, like many rural units of the IRA, soon paralysed by this need and the inability to supplement the shortages. Their frustration spills over in a report to GHQ in April 1921:

> Regarding operations generally I would like to say that we have material here, from a man-power point of view good enough to make the place as hot as H--- Everywhere the Companies are working well and the men are eager to get going. In addition a Flying Column of 25 has been formed, of men I believe as good as any in Ireland. But we have absolutely no stuff. G.H.Q. never gave us anything but 5 Mauser rifles with 50 rounds in all, and 100 rounds revolver ammunition. For these rifles there are only a few rounds each left. When that is expended they are useless to us. If you can't send stuff we

42 Effect of courting, Liam Tammin. O'MN, P17b91; Andy Cooney, O'MN, P17b107.
43 Many relatives of veterans hinted or were explicit about illegitimate children of Volunteers, May Moclair, Interview; Nicholas Furlong, private conversation; P.C. Power, private conversation. Quote on 'girl in billet', Ned Glendon, O'MN, P17b103. Quote on 'Emmet', Seamus Robinson, 'Statement', NLI, ms. 21,265. Robert Emmet was the leader of a rebellion in 1803, who was apprehended in similar fashion. The arrest of this Volunteer in 1919 led to the rescue operation from the train in Knocklong in which two men were seriously wounded and which caused the departure of the brigade officers from Tipperary.

would send them back. With all we can pick up, we will work immediately. In the area there are some splendid roads for mining, but we have no mines. There are 3 police Barracks in the area which might be attacked with every hope of success but we have no explosives. We have no bombs. We have little shotgun ammunition. Since last November a sum of £300 has been deposited to our credit at GHQ for which we have got nothing to speak of. Also there is a large sum of money in the hands of our Quartermaster. Under the circumstances how can G.H.Q. expect big results here.

Despite being slightly better armed, the West Mayo Flying Column had similar problems. They were forced to ensure that every operation returned an amount of ammunition at least equal to that expended. The lack of success of the west Mayo columns in this regard caused serious problems in their last ambush. They were forced to fire slowly and some even stated they threw stones as an alternative; resistance was nevertheless overcome.[44]

Even in Dublin every round had to be paid for and consequently every round that was expended had to be accounted for. If used for any other purpose than in direct combat, the Volunteers were reprimanded. The shortage of arms and ammunition limited all military operations by most provincial units to a few ambushes. In Dublin this dearth predisposed the men to hit-and-run tactics centred on the use of home-made grenades.[45]

Shortages led to disputes over arms. Since only those with arms were likely to be considered for a job, the possession of some kind of weapon was crucial. In Mayo one unit refused to hand over arms which were intended for another. In south Tipperary arms and ammunition were stolen from other Volunteers on such a scale that the brigade commander considered it necessary to issue an order against this on 29 October 1920, in which he described this as a disgraceful, mean and cowardly act. Each Volunteer was ordered to return at once all arms over which he had no legitimate control. This order was to be read out at three consecutive parades.[46]

Another serious consequence of the lack of arms was an almost complete absence of firing experience among men involved in operations. The shortage of ammunition limited shooting practice everywhere. To deal with the inexperience of the Volunteers in Dublin, a staff of instructors was set up, teaching the technique, theory and care of small arms. Events during a

44 Quote in south Mayo, Report dated 28 April 1921, UCD AD, P7A38. See also West Mayo Brigade report dated 4 April 1921, UCD AD, P7A38. Using stones, Tom Kettrick, O'MN, P17b136.

45 Justifying use of ammunition, Joe O'Connor, O'MN, P17b105; Tony Woods, O'MN, P17b96.

46 Problems over arms in Mayo, Thomas Kettrick, 'Statement'; Ned Moane and Brodie Malone, O'MN, P17b120; Ned Maughan, O'MN, P17b109. Order against stealing in Tipperary, UCD AD, P17b127.

lesson by one of the Fianna instructors made the need for this particularly apparent:

> I ran lectures on bombing, and on small arms. [...] I lectured A3 [A-Company, 3rd Battalion of the Dublin Brigade] on grenades. They were the Dardanelles Company I stripped a grenade for them and it was the first grenade they had ever seen stripped. When [...] I assembled it I missed the detonator. I didn't say anything for I felt that someone had taken it. I got down on the floor on the excuse that I had dropped a pencil and when I got up without saying anything I saw the Company Captain rattling the detonator unit between his teeth.[47]

As a result of this inexperience fatal accidents were no exception. Soon after the formation of the Westport Battalion ASU the captain of a local company was accidentally shot dead while Volunteers were play-acting with a revolver they thought was unloaded. Despite the shock this event gave them, another Volunteer was accidentally shot dead a few days later when this column was billeted in a nearby village. Before they had even engaged the enemy, they had already killed two of their own. Similarly, a member of the Castlebar Column was shot in the toe by a fellow Volunteer while waiting to meet the Newport men for their first operation. As a result he had to spend two months in hospital.[48]

This inexperience also led to the failure of several ambushes. The position of the columns was frequently given away by nervous men who accidentally fired their weapons long before the enemy had come into the ambush site. Some Volunteers did this deliberately to prevent reprisals on their family. An ex-RIC man, who had joined the south Mayo column with a supply of Mills bombs, showed his anxiety during the Partry ambush: 'The ex-R.I.C. man, I could see was busy throwing his little grenades. But he must not have known to remove the pin because they were rolling down the road like pebbles and not exploding.' Although they were meant to be a professional unit, the inexperience of the Dublin ASU also frequently led to failure and accidents.[49]

47 Staff of instructors set up, NLI, ms. 900/8. See also Joseph A. Cripps, NLI, ms. 22,117(1); Tony Woods, O'MN, P17b96; Charlie Dalton (1929), 166; Jack Plunkett, 'Statement', NLI, ms. 11,981. Quote, Billy Rowe, O'MN, P17b110.

48 Accidental shootings, Joe Baker (1988), 24; Thomas Heavey, 'Statement'; Jack Connolly, O'MN, P17b120; West Mayo monthly report May 1921, UCD AD, P7A19/84. The man from Castlebar, Mark Killilea, O'MN, P17b109. Another Volunteer claims Killilea shot himself, Michael Hughes, 'Statement'.

49 Premature firing, Ned O'Reilly, O'MN, P17b126. To prevent this GHQ issued instructions not to have shotguns ready to fire until the enemy was in the ambush site. Quote, Tom Maguire, in U. MacEoin (1987), 284. Accidents in Dublin, George White, O'MN, P17b105; Alfred Rutherford, O'MN, P17b122; Jack Plunkett, 'Statement', NLI, ms. 11,981.

LACK OF WEAPONRY: REMEDIES

The arms that could be bought from GHQ were totally insufficient to equip all willing men. Arms could not be bought openly either, as many restrictions had been put on the sale, importation and ownership of weapons since the beginning of the Great War. In distributing its small supply, GHQ showed a clear preference for the active areas in the Southwest, particularly for Cork. It felt that arms sent to other areas would never be used by the inexperienced and apparently unwilling men there. In order to break the vicious circle where a lack of arms caused a lack of activity which gave GHQ a reason to refuse to sent arms, these units sent representatives to Dublin to obtain whatever was available. GHQ's hesitancy was, however, sometimes justified by the attitude of Volunteers in inactive areas. In Wexford large mines made available by GHQ were never used and some companies buried their weapons when the fighting started. The inability to use GHQ mines was also a result of their large size, necessitating the use of a horse and cart to transport them.[50]

To supplement the shortages, weapons were bought or forced from soldiers and policemen. British soldiers stationed in Ireland for a short period were often willing to sell equipment to supplement their pay. Volunteers tried to take advantage of this, but they were naturally more successful in the early stages of the struggle. Particularly in Dublin, some companies had managed to obtain large quantities of weapons in this way. One company, whose quartermaster worked as a caterer for the military, is recorded to have bought 100 revolvers and 5,000 rounds of ammunition for £90. Several of these revolvers were sold to men in other units, making a £20 profit. Despite this incidental success, most Dublin units were equally unable to arm their own men.[51]

A direct consequence of the successes of some Dublin companies was that GHQ regularly ordered the sale of material to equip the provincial units. After some grumbling, the Dublin battalions provided the requested material. Rifles and .303 ammunition were particularly favoured, as they were unsuitable for use in the city but essential in the country. Around

50 Growing restrictions on possession of arms, David Fitzpatrick (1977), 213. Policy to sent arms to South, Jack Plunkett, 'Statement', NLI, ms. 11,981; Staff Memo dated 24 March 1921: 'The War as a Whole', UCD AD, P7A47. Burying arms in Wexford, Peter Wall, Interview.
51 Examples of Crown Forces selling arms to the Volunteers: In Dublin, Robert Briscoe (1958), 54; Jimmy Murray, O'MN, P17b106; Letter dated 6 August, PRO, WO35/70; Michael Chadwick, 'With the Sixth Battalion', in *Dublin's Fighting Story* (1949), 185. In a private conversation it was reported to me that Dublin prostitutes functioned as go-betweens in the exchange of arms, making a two-way profit. In Tipperary, Patrick Ryan, 'Statement'; Michael Fitzpatrick, O'MN, P17b127. In Mayo, Jimmy Swift, O'MN, P17b136. Particularly successful QMs, Patrick O'Daly, 'Statement', NLI, P4548; Tom Burke, O'MN, P17b98.

September 1920 all rifles in the Dublin Brigade were bought or exchanged and sent down the country. Conversely, special military goods which were known to have been acquired in other units were sometimes bought by GHQ. The continuous demands for arms and ammunition made the Dublin units wary. To protect their own supply, many quartermasters reported only the possession of a small proportion of their actual arms and ammunition.[52]

Another major source of arms and ammunition was found abroad. GHQ as well as some country units sent men to England, the US and even to Germany to obtain weapons. In England, where the IRA had many contacts and even some companies among the many Irish living there, every possible source of arms was tried, from private owners to military who stole them from government stocks. Initially, these arms were smuggled by passengers on the boats between England and Ireland. Soon a regular route was set up, using sailors. Contacts in the Customs Department and a special IRA company made up of dockers provided the necessary assistance.[53]

Many brigades sent their own representatives abroad to buy arms. Volunteers from Mayo, Tipperary, Wexford and Cork visited England in their quest for arms and ammunition. GHQ tried to prevent this, as these missions would spoil the market and increase prices. Although the bulk of material went to GHQ, the IRA in England provided most brigade representatives with something 'on the side'. A special GHQ mission was sent to Germany in 1920 with a large sum of money at its disposal which came directly from supporters in the US. They were ordered to get a whole list of items but nothing bigger than machine guns. The leader of this mission actually went around provincial units taking orders. This man reported that during his tour the commandant of the South Tipperary Brigade tried to get him to work for him exclusively. When he refused this brigade sent their own men to Germany. This was observed by the GHQ mission:

> Seamus Robinson had sent 3 men from Tipperary to Germany about 9 months before the Truce. [...] I was told by Collins to watch these boys, but I was not to interfere with them. They did not then, cut

52 Ammunition for country, Oscar Traynor, O'MN, P17b98; NLI, ms.901/35. Rifles to the country, Harry Colley, O'MN, P17b97; Oscar Traynor, O'MNs, P17b96, and P17b98; Alfred Rutherford, O'MN, P17b122; Tom Burke, O'MN, P17b98. Buying gun-cotton from the Wexford Brigade, NLI, P916 A0478.

53 Buying arms in England, Michael Chadwick, 'With the Sixth Battalion', in *Dublin's Fighting Story* (1949), 183; John McCann (1946), 149-50; Hugh Early, O'MN, P17b110; Dinny Kelleher, O'MN, P17b107; Thomas Kettrick, 'Statement'; John Madden, O'MN, P17b113; Bob Briscoe, O'MN, P17b97. Smuggling on boats, John J. Sherlock, NLI, ms. 9,873; Ernie Noonan, O'MN, P17b94; Tom Duffy, O'MN, P17b105; Pat Fallon, O'MN, P17b109; Fintan Murphy, O'MN, P17b107; Jimmy Murray, O'MN, P17b106.

across my lines of communication. First McGrath, who had evidently never been outside Tipperary, was brought to London for 3 weeks, where he was taught to behave like a gentleman to use a walking stick and to walk properly, but you could pick him out as a country-man a mile away.

The attempts of the Tipperary men never came to anything. The GHQ representatives, however, were more professional. They bought a ship and let it run cargo for a while to divert any suspicion and then tried to smuggle the arms to Ireland. However, all this took such a long time that arms obtained in this way were never used during the War of Independence.[54]

Despite all these efforts, there was always insufficient material to provide all IRA units. Supply of ammunition was so short that many units manufactured it themselves. Most country units made buckshot to fill shotgun cartridges. In Dublin large .303 rifle ammunition was cut down to fit into revolvers, but this often damaged the revolvers. Another tedious job was the reloading of faulty ammunition that was bought from British military. After the authorities discovered that the IRA bought their ammunition they tried to sell them exploding ammunition that ruined the gun when fired. When the IRA found a distinguishing mark, they took the explosives out of the ammunition and replaced it with gunpowder.[55]

Grenades posed another major problem. They were essential for street fighting in Dublin, and were partly bought from and partly provided by the brigade. The first grenade-making workshop was started in the Dublin Brigade in 1918. In the first workshop a small foundry was installed where grenade shells were cast and the complete grenade was assembled. More workshops were set up later; each specialised in a different aspect of grenade-making, and some mechanisation was started. Constant experimentation and adaptation was necessary to create an efficient grenade. It took until 1921 before production reached a satisfactory level. One of the men involved claims that at the end of the struggle about twenty-six people were involved and up to 1,000 grenades were produced each week. Some country units had their own small workshops of this kind. One was started

---

54 Police reported in July 1920 that arms were about to be shipped from Germany, Papers marked S368, NLI, P918 A0413. Quote, Robert Briscoe, O'MN, P17b97. Experience of men going to Germany, Robert Briscoe (1958), 80-96, and O'MN, P17b97; Michael Crimmins, O'MN, P17b98. When GHQ heard of such a trip by men from Mayo, they asked them to hand in the arms bought in England for some operations in Cork. GHQ promised to return the arms if they agreed. The men conceded but the arms were never seen again, Thomas Kettrick, 'Statement'; John Madden, O'MN, P17b113.

55 Cutting down ammunition, Paddy Rigney, O'MN, P17b105. Faulty ammunition, Joe O'Connor, O'MN, P17b105; Tony Woods, O'MN, P17b96; Jack Plunkett, 'Statement', NLI, ms. 11,981.

in Tipperary at an early stage and another was set up in Wexford aided by GHQ. This grenade factory, however, exploded on 12 October 1920 killing nine Volunteers.[56]

Different types of grenades and later even mines were produced. Few of the latter were used due to their size and the danger to civilians. The first grenades made by the Munitions Department of the IRA had little power and exploded only in one direction, limiting their effectiveness. Inexperience of the men involved in making grenades meant that 25 per cent failed to explode. The factories had to provide grenades for Dublin and most other areas. Consequently, production was always under pressure, particularly when one or other of the factories was discovered by the police. Some members of the munitions staff were a little carried away by their interest in experimentation, and developed an incendiary bomb and a grenade thrower. However, due to the increasing stress on production, such experimentation was forbidden by GHQ in June 1921.[57]

DEALING WITH RELUCTANCE TO FIGHT

In addition to a lack of arms the reluctance of many officers to fulfil their Volunteer duties and endanger their lives seriously restricted activity. Despite all attempts at improving organisation and training, the Volunteers never became the envisioned efficient military organisation. In a GHQ Staff Memo of 1921 titled: 'Serious deficiencies in Country Units', a bleak picture of the workings of the brigades is painted. They failed in coordination, in internal brigade organisation and had a lack of good NCOs. The special services were not organised in detail, their officers did not function properly, and no one realised the importance of intelligence gathering. In the battalions the vice-commandant and the quartermaster did not fulfil their functions. There was no agenda, battalion orders were either badly issued or not issued at all and generally a laissez-faire attitude prevailed. In the companies the complaints included: the absence of half-companies, insuffi-

---

56 Grenade making in Dublin, J.V. Lawless, 'Recollections of the War of Independence 1916-1921', UCD AD, P7D148; Pat McHugh, O'MN, P17b110; Jack Plunkett, 'Statement', NLI, ms. 11,981. In Tipperary, Wexford, and Cork a munitions and grenade factory was set up, where shotgun cartridges were filled and a crude type of grenade was made, Sean Fitzpatrick (n. d.), 8; Jack Plunkett, 'Statement', NLI, ms. 11,981; Pat McHugh, O'MN, P17b110.
57 Care taken with mines in Dublin, Michael Crimmins, O'MN, P17b98. Reported failure of grenades in several Dublin reports, UCD AD, P17A19-22. Detailed description of problems, Pat McHugh, O'MN, P17b110. Ineffectiveness of Wexford grenades, John Quinn, Interview. Forbidding experimentation, Oscar Traynor, letter to Director of Munitions dated 6 June 1921, UCD AD, P7A19/60-1. See also Jack Plunkett, 'Statement', NLI, ms. 11,981.

cient rivalry between the sections, officers exercising too little command, junior officers with insufficient responsibilities and battalion orders which were not carried out. The company council was a casual affair, the battalion failed to set sufficient specific tasks, orders were verbal and inexact, notes were never taken and there was no statistical information available.[58]

To deal with the lack of dedication detailed instructions for officers at all levels were drawn up, and inefficient officers were threatened with court martial. However, the punishments provided for in the court martial regulations, temporary suspension, demotion or even dismissal, were ineffective when trying to force men to risk their life against their will: 'Drumming out is no use in such a case – the type of man concerned would only welcome it.' GHQ was reluctant to take stronger measure, which it might not be able to implement, but when confronted with a growing number of desertions in the spring of 1921 it finally realised that strong measures were needed. A Staff Memo on the question was formulated which stated that: 'Unless, disciplinary measures are taken there is a good prospect of large numbers running away in the Western areas. It is absolutely essential to stop this rot.' It was realised that a clear code of conduct was necessary to ensure an intensification of the conflict: 'It is now imperatively necessary to draw up a Code of Disciplinary Regulations to enable glaring military defects to be dealt with in a speedy and comprehensive manner. It is too often the case that serious shortcomings are condoned that condonation is taken for granted by all parties, and that not even an investigation is made.' The suggestion that physical punishment might help was however quickly rejected: 'Flogging has never been done in the case of Irish troops and should not be started now.'[59]

The memo suggested dividing both offence and punishment into two categories, i.e. grave and minor. A sliding scale was considered to be too difficult to implement. Grave offences were to be treason, cowardice and gross neglect of duty. If the situation demanded it, the death penalty should be administered for these offences. Minor offences should be punished by loss of rank, discharge without honour or drumming out. As a long list of minor offences would have a similar effect as uncontrolled desertions, the memo concluded with stating that: 'In general the tendency should be to deal very sternly with serious offences, and not to make too much fuss about minor failings.' This memo was followed up on 2 April

58 Staff Memo, UCD AD, P7A17/169.
59 Detailed instructions for officers, 'Note for Organisers', UCD AD, P7A48. In the Third Tipperary Brigade the Battalion Vice-Commandants got detailed instructions in March 1921 on their responsibilities. Including work on communications, intelligence and drawing up of routine programmes for every department and also for Officers Classes, Council Meetings and Active Service Groups, NLI, ms. 17,880(1); UCD AD, P9/1-4. Staff Memo dated 30 March 1921, UCD AD, P7A17/277.

1921 by a General Order listing offences punishable with death. The extreme penalty could be inflicted for knowingly conveying information to the enemy, disclosing particulars of plans of operations to unauthorised persons, the surrender or destruction of war material and grave insubordination on active duty involving danger to others and to the success of the operation. The death sentence for any member of the IRA was only to be inflicted after written authority from GHQ.[60]

Alternative punishments were also discussed. Although flogging had been rejected by GHQ, it did actually take place when punishing unwilling Volunteers in some areas. In answer to a memo Michael Collins replied on 2 July 1921 that he was absolutely opposed to flogging for any offence under any circumstances, even as a reprisal: 'It has a more degrading effect upon the person or the authority administering it than the person to whom it is administered.' New offences, for which punishment was unclear, also came to light. In July 1921 the O.C. of the 2nd Southern Division asked whether looting could be punished with execution. This request followed several cases of plunder by Volunteers in the Mid and South Tipperary Brigades. Although not agreeing in principal with it, the Assistant Chief of Staff stated: 'If this looting gets started at all it will be hard to stop it, but if a few are shot now for it it will be all right.'[61]

Local officers had a great deal of freedom to act in disciplinary cases. Although they were to work under guidelines from GHQ, they only had to report after they had taken action, except in case of a death sentence. This freedom made it possible to be lenient in cases which involved Volunteers with whom they closely associated. One impetuous member of the Flying Column in the West Mayo Brigade was court-martialled twice for endangering his comrades by acting on his own initiative. His first conviction was confinement to a particular company area. However, during this confinement he accidentally shot a civilian who approached him in the dark, and instead of further disciplinary action his confinement was lifted. When he and some other column members then again acted on their own initiative all were dismissed from the column; but before the day was over the sentence was first reduced to disarmament and finally they were let off with a caution. In the same brigade column men who had fled the scene during a fight were never punished for it.[62]

60 Staff Memo dated 30 March 1921, UCD AD, P7A17/277. General Order no.17, NLI, ms. 739.
61 Quote on 'flogging', UCD, P7A21/10. On 'looting': Request, UCD AD, P7A-21/11. Quote from answer by Chief of Staff, UCD AD, P7A22/14.
62 Guidelines for local officers, General Orders No's. 18 to 27 dating April to May 1921, NLI, ms. 739. The impetuous Volunteer, Thomas Heavey, 'Statement', and O'MN, P17b120. On desertions in West Mayo, Brodie Malone and Ned Moane, O'MN, P17b120; Paddy Duffy, O'MN, P17b113; Johnny Duffy O'MN, P17b109; Thomas Heavey, 'Statement'.

This type of court martial was rarely held due to the lack of control GHQ could exert over the provincial units. A more effective way of dealing with the lack of willingness to get involved in operations was initiating operations themselves by calling upon those who were willing. At the end of 1920 GHQ took on many more organisers for this purpose. Four organisers had been employed in the summer of 1920, but by March 1921 it had thirty-two men going around the country. In some areas this lead to a clear increase in Volunteer activity.[63]

OPERATIONS OF NON-COLUMN VOLUNTEERS: WEXFORD

GHQ's efforts to instil activity in local units was particularly successful in south Wexford. An organiser arrived there early in 1921 and on the basis of his report a plan of operations was drawn up. This contained detailed instructions aimed at making travel and communication impossible for the Crown Forces. All main roads and those between enemy posts in the area were to be trenched, and the Crown Forces were to be constantly harassed with sniping and occasional ambushing.[64]

Although this harassment campaign provided ample opportunity for the more cautious local men, the commandant of the South Wexford Brigade was often frustrated in his attempt to implement these instructions fully by his officers' refusal to act. GHQ now reacted sharply and did not hesitate to threaten dismissal:

> We cannot retain in position of authority at the present time men who do not carry out instructions given to them, more particularly, we cannot retain Officers who do not obey their orders, and where you have any such, who cannot be talked into shouldering their responsibilities and giving strict attention to orders, they should be paraded before their Battalion Council in case of Battalion Officers and before their Companies in the case of Company Officers, and it should be explained to the council or the company, that in consequence of failure to carry out the particular order in question, the safety of the men in the Army and the honour of the Army itself demands that they be removed from Office and someone put in their place; who can be relied on to carry out his duties.

It was further impressed on the brigade commandant that the commander at each level was responsible for giving orders and deciding on operations within his own sphere. The battalion and brigade council existed only to

63 Number of organisers, UCD AD, P7A17/97-8.
64 Instructions to Wexford, UCD AD, P7A17/53-4.

carry out the instructions of the commander concerned, or to assist and advise him when he required their assistance or advice. Under no circumstances were orders to be discussed or criticised by subordinates.[65]

Despite the internal opposition the Volunteers in south Wexford went to work according to the directions given by GHQ. A large increase in small operations, which generally did not involve any physical violence, was reported in the spring of 1921; most of these were executed by small groups of between two and five Volunteers under a company officer. They involved simple and comparatively safe jobs, such as raiding the mail, digging trenches or cutting telegraph wires. The occasional more serious operation, such as a feint barracks attack, involved larger groups of up to twenty, taking in men from different companies. This increase in activity led to an increase in membership of the Volunteers in 1921 from 657 to 888, which was unique to Wexford.[66]

Raiding the mail had started in 1919 and simply entailed holding up the postman and asking him for his bag, then checking the letters for their destination. Those coming from or going to the authorities were confiscated while the rest were generally returned unopened. On a few occasions post offices and mail trains were held up. Blocking roads and cutting telegraph wires to prevent communication and transport by the Crown Forces were new features introduced in areas like Tipperary at the end of 1920 to protect the Flying Columns. Although there was no column in Wexford, this practice was also introduced there in an attempt to involve the rank and file in operations. The digging of trenches had its own dynamics: first, small trenches were dug just over hill-tops or around corners, hoping that military lorries would run into them, damaging their vehicles. After the Crown Forces began to take planks with them to cross these trenches, trees were knocked down and laid across roads to restrict their speed of movement.[67]

The absence of a Flying Column in Wexford meant that sniping attacks were made by company activists. However, apart from the three previously described attacks in 1920, they were not intended to take any barracks. Frequently attacks on barracks were a form of Volunteer entertainment coloured by the fireworks the police used to raise alarm: 'Every week we used to fire at the barracks. We would fire and then you had to lie down and the Very lights went up. [...] Others would rattle slates at the back of barracks to keep them inside.' The six attacks on barracks in May lasted from

65 Communications between GHQ and Wexford, UCD AD, P7A17/53-63.

66 Operations in south Wexford, UCD AD, P7A19/12, and P7A21/1-2; Andy Roe, Interview; Ned Colfer, Interview; John Quinn, Interview. Growth in membership, CI Wexford MRs 1921.

67 Digging trenches, Andy Roe, Interview; Ned Colfer, Interview. Introduction of cutting lines of communication in Tipperary, O'MN, P17b127. Consequences, CI South Tipperary MR August 1920.

ten minutes to a half-hour without causing any casualties. If the police counter-attacked, the Volunteers withdrew quickly.[68]

Active Volunteers in many rural units were limited in their activity by a lack of targets. There were few military and only a small number of police barracks in south Wexford. The closing of the smaller police posts necessitated companies to share the remainder. In the 2nd Battalion area only two barracks remained, shared by seven companies. One of these barracks was alternately sniped at by several companies, also involving some from another battalion. After frequent complaints that they had nothing to attack, F-Company 1st Battalion was permitted to attack Clonroche Police Barracks situated in the North Wexford Brigade. The frequent sniping of the few barracks confined most RIC to their barracks at night. However, the police realised the inability of the Volunteers to stage a serious attack and often did not even bother to answer the shotgun fire of these companies.[69]

Most Volunteer activity in Wexford was of little military significance. The GHQ organiser in Wexford, who practically superseded the local brigade staff, had forbidden large-scale engagements. The few radical Volunteers were frustrated by this; they wanted to lay an ambush or attack a barracks, as the Flying Columns did in the Southwest. Despite the brigade commandants' complaints, GHQ supported the concentration on small targets, stressing that experience had first to be built up. Most junior-officers, who had little desire to get involved in direct fighting, fully agreed. Despite gaining in confidence, even the activists continued to act cautiously. This was observed by the local police: 'This organisation has become more active and more daring. Armed gangs are moving round openly.' However, no willingness to fight was encountered: 'The rebels have, so far, not shown any desire to come to close quarters with the crown forces.'[70]

The concentration on smaller operations along the lines of GHQ's directions is confirmed by the operation reports of this brigade. In May they recounted forty-four actions, including one ambush and five sniping attacks on barracks and one on a patrol. The roads were blocked nine times by cutting trenches or felling trees; telegraph lines were cut six times and the mail was raided eleven times. The remaining nine actions were seizures

---

68 Quote, Peter Wall, Interview. See also John Quinn, Interview; CI Wexford MR April 1921.
69 Lack of targets in Wexford, Report dated 5 May 1921, UCD AD, P7A39; Report for May, UCD AD, P7A19/10-14. Police reaction, CI Wexford MRs 1921.
70 Organiser forbidding attacks and reaction GHQ, UCD AD, P7A17/67-68. Unwilling officers, Report dated 5 May 1921, UCD AD, P7A17/59. Quotes from police, CI Wexford MR May 1921.

of government or Belfast goods.[71] Twelve of these actions were in the eastern (Wexford district) side of the brigade, the remaining thirty-two in the western (New Ross) area. The police reported an almost similar number of offences in this month. They reported nineteen offences in the New Ross district and twenty in the Wexford district. The difference can be explained by the fact that the areas did not entirely coincide; police figures also included a few non-political offences.[72]

The attack on the District Inspector of the RIC in Wexford town in this month is not recorded by the local IRA. It was enacted by two undisguised men in broad daylight which supports the presumption this was an operation of the Dublin Squad. Wexford Volunteers were still very cautious in exposing their membership. Most of them lived at home and the extent of their involvement was yet unknown to the police. As a result most of the few direct attacks in June 1921 were still committed by disguised men. This fear of recognition had by then largely disappeared in active areas. Remarkably, the police reported one more sniping attack on a barracks, three more raids on the mail and two more telegraph wires having been cut than the IRA themselves recorded in May. This could be a result of initiative by local Volunteers who did not bother reporting their actions to their superiors. The emphasis on small operations was even stronger in June. Road cutting and bridge breaking together accounted for twenty-nine out of forty-nine actions in three of the four battalions. The only firing engagement in the brigade in 1921 was the first ambush of a police lorry.[73]

OPERATIONS OF NON-COLUMN VOLUNTEERS: DERRY

The Volunteers in Ulster were generally inactive and largely neglected by GHQ. In April 1921 most northern counties still had no brigade structure, and whole regions, heavily populated with Protestants, had no Volunteers at all. After GHQ had instituted a certain level of authority over the southern units and military pressure on these units began to build up, it also became more involved with the northern units. The first sign of its increased involvement was the improvement of the poor communication lines between the northern areas and Dublin at the end of 1920. In most other areas this had already been done in 1919. After the arrest of the local

---

71 The Belfast Boycott was a reaction on the violence directed against Catholics in Belfast in June 1920. The intention was to stop the sale of all goods produced in Belfast and other northern areas.

72 IRA reports, UCD AD, P7A19/10-14. Police report, CI Wexford MR May 1921.

73 CI Wexford MR June 1921.

organiser, Thomas Morris, a GHQ man was sent to south Derry early in 1921 to initiate operations.[74]

The main expression of GHQ's growing involvement in northern units was the introduction of divisions in the spring of 1921. A unit larger than the brigade had been envisaged by GHQ from the beginning of 1918. However, the necessity of this larger unit was not recognised until the end of 1920 when from the point of view of logistics, decentralisation became desirable. The larger involvement of GHQ in the running of all the brigades was difficult to maintain safely and efficiently. They were endangered by the development of the British espionage system in Dublin, and the more frequent visits by officers to the capital increased the likelihood of detection. Dealing with a small number of divisions would make GHQ's tasks much lighter and less conspicuous.[75]

From their point of view, active brigades felt that good opportunities for effective operations were frequently missed because the operating area of the responsible officer was too circumscribed. Early in 1921 the southern brigades had come under strong pressure from the military who did not limit themselves to IRA brigade areas in their operations. These brigades came to realise that one unified command would be better able to resist the army, and a meeting of their principal officers took place to discuss the idea. Although some disagreement existed about the scope and form of the cooperation, a summary of the proceedings was forwarded to GHQ embodying some recommendations.[76]

Initially GHQ reacted with some hesitancy, but soon the idea to divisionalise the organisation was taken up. In accordance with the assessment of the southern brigades GHQ stated that the principal reason for the

---

74 Improving communication, *Derry People and Donegal News*, 4 December 1920. Role of organiser in south Derry, Thomas Toner, Fr O'Kane Papers, Tape A13, AARC; Wm. John Himphey, Tape A20 & A23, Ibid.; James Harkin, Tape A9, Ibid..

75 First mention of the division, Letter from GHQ in 1918, UCD AD, P7b172(16). The divisional idea was also put forward in November 1918, David Fitzpatrick (1977), 207. Assessment of GHQ's position in a retrospect on the division, probably written by J.J. O'Connell, NLI, P920 A0629. Problems of efficiency and safety, Memo on the 'Divisional Idea', NLI, ms. 31,195; 'Note on the Gerard Costelloe Papers', UCD AD, P7D96.

76 The need for a larger unit was first indicated in May 1920 by the Adjutant of the Cork 2nd Brigade. This can be seen as the seed from which the division idea grew, Letter from Cork 2nd Brigade, NLI, P917 A0499. On the letter of Cork 2nd Brigade GHQ had written it was a good idea and concerned three Cork, three Clare, three Limerick and the Waterford brigades, added were nearly all of Kilkenny and some of the three Tipperary brigades. When the divisions were implemented a different set of brigades were brought together. See also Seamus Robinson, 'Statement', Appendix V & VI, NLI, ms. 21,265. The events in the South, Seamus Robinson, 'Statement', Appendix V & VI, NLI, ms. 21,265.

introduction of the division was: 'A necessity for harmonising the nature and direction of operative activity in adjoining Brigade Areas which are so placed as to influence the Military situation in one another.' The idea to use the divisional command as a type of training institution in the form of a divisional school of Administration and Training was given as a secondary consideration. Another reason was GHQ's lack of desire and ability to deal with incompetence in certain IRA units and border disputes between others. Some more adjacent authority was deemed necessary for dealing with such problems. The many appointments of local men and established organisers as divisional commanders discounts the suggestion that divisionalisation was an attempt by GHQ to obtain more control over the country units. Increasing and coordinating activity must therefore have been the main objective.[77]

Soon after the idea of closer cooperation was suggested to GHQ by the southern brigades, the First and Second Southern Divisions had been formed. The first comprised all brigades in Cork, Kerry and Waterford supplemented with the West Limerick Brigade. The second brought together the East and Mid Limerick Brigades, the Mid and South Tipperary Brigades and the Kilkenny Brigade. By 13 April divisional commanders were appointed to both these divisions. In March, at a conference of all northern officers held in Dublin, Ulster was divided into five divisions by amalgamating existing brigades and battalions. Subsequently, the rest of the country was provisionally divided in divisions at another conference rather as a logical administrative consequence than from military necessity. The only other divisions formed before the Truce were the Third Southern Division which brought the North Tipperary, Leix and two Offaly brigades together, and the 1st Eastern Division embracing four brigades in Meath, and the South Louth, Mullingar, Edenderry, Naas and Fingal brigades. Although a total of nine divisions were thus organised before the Truce, few were fully operative. Few counties in the North were brigaded by the time of the Truce, and most battalions still reported directly to GHQ. Even the commandant of the Second Southern Division, where structures were much more developed, had to instruct his brigade

77 GHQ's position, NLI, P920 A0629; 'Note on the Gerard Costelloe Papers', UCD AD, P7D96. Quote on introduction divisions, UCD AD, P7A17/199 see also 214. GHQ's hesitancy was caused by its fear that country officers were incapable of carrying out their new tasks, UCD AD, P7A17/102; NLI, ms. 31,195. On incompetence in local area (Kerry), UCD AD, P7A17/199. The lack of willingness in GHQ to deal with local problems gains some credibility by the fact that when a divisional commander was appointed the Chief of Staff informed him that he had arranged with the Director of Organisation that a special man be sent to Kerry No.1 to replace the present brigade staff. Further support to this is given by other examples of GHQ's hesitancy to interfere in border disputes.

O.C.s to keep in direct touch with GHQ until less than two weeks before the Truce.[78]

The initial introduction of the divisional structure in the South was thus a way to coordinate activity and communication between brigades. However, the stated intention to introduce divisions only when an area had become fit for it did not apply to the North. In 1920 most northern areas had no IRA organisation at all or had not transcended the battalion level. Nevertheless, the North was the first to be divisionalised after the start of the two southern divisions. The reason for this was almost directly opposite to that applying to the South. The low level of organisation and the hostile surroundings in which the IRA had to operate meant that little had been done in the North, and that keeping contact between northern units and GHQ was extremely difficult. The special problems of the IRA in Ulster were recognised and the early introduction of divisions there was intended to: 'a) enable the local Volunteers to tackle their special problems in a more comprehensive way then formerly, and b) enable G.H.Q. to keep in better touch, by reason of having fewer units to deal with.' In this light the introduction of the division was rather an attempt to obtain control over and initiate some activity in the North, than a way of enabling adjoining brigades to coordinate their activities more effectively. By stepping up activity there, GHQ also hoped to divert attention from the hard-pressed units in the South.[79]

In April 1921 a division covering most of rural Derry and Tyrone was instituted. The recently appointed organiser was made divisional commander, and indeed initiated some activity. As in Wexford, this concentrated on the breaking of enemy communications by cutting telegraph wires, trenching roads and blowing up bridges, and coincided with a similar reluctance to get involved in direct fighting. Even the commander of the most active brigade in neighbouring Donegal was reluctant to kill any one: 'He did not believe in shooting police but in disarming them, for that took more mind courage.'[80]

---

78 Formation of divisions, NLI, P920 A0629, and ms. 22,117(2); UCD AD, P7A-17/199. Conferences on the North held in March, and on the rest of the country, NLI, P920 A0629; UCD AD, P7A17/108, 111 + 318; Seán Gaynor, 'Statement'; Mick O'Hanlon, O'MN, P17b106. Appointment of Divisional Commandant of 1st Southern also referring to the situation in the North and 2nd Southern division, UCD AD, P7A17/199. Report from Second Southern Division, UCD AD, P7A20/53. Instructions from Divisional Commandant in the North, UCD AD, P7A48.

79 Quote, 'Letter to the Secretary Pensions Board', dated 13 August 1936, NLI, P913 A0148. See also NLI, P920 A0629.

80 Role of organiser in south Derry, Thomas Toner, Fr O'Kane Papers, Tape A13, AARC; Wm. John Himphey, Tape A20 & A23, Ibid.; James Harkin, Tape A9, Ibid.. Quote, Peadar O'Donnell, O'MN, P17b98.

The lack of confrontation with the police in the early phases of the conflict had prevented a sufficient radicalisation of these Volunteers. Consequently, Derry was almost free from political crime well into 1921. The police reported only three offences in January, eight in February and two in March. These consisted mainly of raids for arms and attempts to burn houses designated to become police barracks. Due to Volunteer inactivity and the reinforcement of the police with Specials, the RIC's fear of attacks on their posts had sufficiently diminished to start reopening evacuated barracks; seven of them in March alone. The South Derry Brigade also reported two operations in March. One house selected as a police post was destroyed and an attempt to hold up a train failed because the daughter of the signal man opened the gates and put the signal at clear.[81]

Both these operations were carried out by men from the two active Derry companies analysed in the appendix. In the same month three men from south Derry were charged with shooting a 'Special'. This shooting was not recorded by the Derry police, probably as a result of the Ulster Volunteers' tendency to work outside the area. Most Volunteer time in south Derry was taken up by inter-party rivalry. In May, two-thirds of the fifteen political offences consisted of threatening letters between Unionist and Nationalists. This antagonism between Catholics and Protestants and between Volunteers and Hibernians diverted attention from the 'real struggle'.[82]

Inactivity in Derry City was temporarily interrupted when a new Brigade Commander was appointed in April. When he visited the city he ordered immediate action. As a result a day of violence erupted in the city, in which a police sergeant was shot through the head while walking home, two bombs were thrown at a military post and the Lecky Road Police barracks was sniped at, killing one constable. However, the next day the local officers put an end to this and nothing more happened in the city before the Truce. A strong animosity involving the new brigade O.C., the new division O.C., overseeing Donegal and Derry City, and the Derry City Battalion O.C. developed from this, paralysing the organisation. Emotions and distrust were so intense that when the brigade O.C. warned the division O.C. of a coming military raid this was disregarded and the division commander was arrested. Subsequently, the police could safely report that the state of the county was satisfactory, especially in the city.[83]

---

81 Report South Derry Brigade, UCD AD, P7A39. Activities, CI Derry MRs January–March 1921.
82 Volunteers charged with shooting Special, *Coleraine Chronicle*, 26 March 1921. Activities, CI Derry MRs March–May 1921.
83 Day of violence, *Coleraine Chronicle*, 9 April 1921; CI Derry MR April 1921; Liam Brady, *Derry Journal*, 27-9 May 1953. Assessment by new brigade commander, Peadar O'Donnell, O'MN, P17b98. Detailed reports containing allegations, counter-allegations and investigations, UCD AD, P7A18/277-306.

As intended by GHQ, the introduction of divisions eventually led to a build-up of military confrontation. The police recorded this increased IRA activity but were not worried or alarmed. On 5 June the first successful ambush in south Derry took place in Swatragh, resulting in the death of a sergeant and the wounding of two constables. However, as a result of disinterest and fear few local men were involved. The captain of a neighbouring company answered the question whether it was the local Swatragh new who had shot the sergeant: 'Not altogether. Not everybody was fit to handle arms, do you see. It was them who was fit to handle them was fixed for the job.' The perpetrators are unknown, but a man from Derry City was eventually charged. Showing the lack of involvement of the local people, extremely little incriminating evidence was found when the police searched 200 houses in the area. The only arrest was of the man from the city. Nevertheless a semblance of fighting finally erupted in rural districts of Derry. In the first ten days of July another two ambushes took place, three bridges were blown up and a bread van was held up; the cart was burned and the money taken.[84]

OPERATIONS OF NON-COLUMN VOLUNTEERS: MAYO

In Mayo minor activities induced by GHQ were not so prevalent in the beginning of 1921. No organiser was sent down and a directive giving specific instructions to the Volunteers as to which targets to concentrate on was lacking. The only guideline was an order to isolate enemy posts with a systematic road-trenching campaign, issued on 30 March. A marked increase in offences is nevertheless noticeable in 1921. Unlike Wexford and Derry, the thirty-two outrages attributed to Sinn Féin in March were mainly directed at persons and property of representatives and supporters of the British Government. Besides the ambushes and other attacks on police, they consisted of malicious injuries, intimidation, arson, robberies, larcenies, housebreaking, and a raid. Although the number of small 'Sinn Féin outrages' decreased only slightly in the following months, the concentration on ambushing by the members of the Flying Columns was shown during April and May, while in June road cutting and raids on the mail became more prominent.[85]

The involvement of ordinary company men was largely confined to drilling. Despite the possible consequences of arrest, this was continued

84 Ambush, *Coleraine Chronicle*, 11 June 1921; CI Derry MRs June–July 1921. Quote, James Harkin, Fr O'Kane Papers, Tape A9, AARC.
85 Activities, CI Mayo MRs 1921. Guideline from GHQ, UCD AD, P7A38. In May 1921 the West Mayo Brigade reported that they had trenched practically every road in their area, UCD AD, P7A19/88.

throughout the struggle. Providing for the men on the run added some small jobs to the duties of the rank and file, including protection duties and running despatches. The latter had become more important now that the officers and the columns were continuously on the move. Company men were also occasionally involved in the transfer of arms and ammunition from one area to another or from a dump to the Flying Column.[86]

Rank and file involvement in military operations of the Flying Columns in west Mayo was small. One company's total involvement in military affairs in 1921 was limited to bringing ammunition to the column just before the Carrowkennedy Ambush and cutting the road twice in preparation of an ambush by the column. In the South Mayo Brigade, where the Flying Column was much smaller, ordinary Volunteers were called on to participate in ambushes. However, this concerned only a small number of activists who were often on the run locally but had not joined the Flying Column, which was dominated by men from the Cross Battalion. Other Volunteers were often reluctant to participate, as their own work and safety took precedence. This attitude was not liked by the column men, who sometimes showed this. A local guide who refused to do what Michael Kilroy wanted, was given 'three swift kicks' to make him cooperate.[87]

OPERATIONS OF NON-COLUMN VOLUNTEERS: TIPPERARY

The efforts in all these areas to involve the rank and file in direct fighting were extremely minor when compared to efforts by the South Tipperary Brigade. Looking at brigade orders in the final part of 1920, one can observe the IRA's attempts to respond to the military pressure by the authorities with an increased professionalism. As early as August 1920 all battalions were requested to submit plans for attacking barracks and for dealing with enemy reprisal parties. Company captains were to select ambush positions in their areas. In order to prevent detection in case company papers were seized by the enemy, numbers were to be introduced on the company roll instead of names. The appointment of captains of supply, signalling and medical services and the start of a register of those who had taken the Oath of Allegiance to the Dáil are other features of this stream-lining. In September the brigade staff tried to deal with the enemy more thoroughly by introducing the somewhat vague concept of 'The Line', an

86 Drilling in 1921, Peter Hegarty, O'MN, P17b109. Ordinary Volunteers aiding columns, Patrick Owen Mugan, Interview; Ned Moane, 'Statement'; Thomas Kettrick, 'Statement'; Jim O'Donnell, 'Recollections'; Thomas Conroy, Interview; Edward O'Malley (1981), 25-7.
87 Military involvement company, 'Activities list Owenwee Company'. Quote, Thomas Kettrick, 'Statement'. See also Thomas Conroy, Interview; Patrick Owen Mugan Interview.

imaginary front line between Crown Forces and IRA units which did not involve the defence of any military positions.[88]

These attempts to become more professional had, however, little effect on the average Volunteer. In December the brigade complained that in some battalions the 'Weekly Programme' had fallen into abeyance, and that monthly reports had been neglected in others. The Brigade Staff recognised that few Volunteers were wholeheartedly engaged in the fight. In relation to the order dealing with the destruction of main roads, they stated that in some cases it seems not to have been taken seriously. They also admitted that some Volunteers had buried their arms.

In an attempt to deal with this, detailed instructions for operations were issued in cooperation with neighbouring brigades. Each battalion was given an action-programme for the third week of January. During this week all enemy posts were to be sniped at at least once at night and as often as possible during the day. Furthermore, all enemy proclamations were to be torn down whenever and wherever possible, wires were to be cut twice weekly, the worst and most vicious of the RIC and all Black & Tans were to be shot on sight. If possible an ambush on a patrol or lorry was to take place once during the week, and all main roads were to be destroyed at two points at least. In the same month the battalion commandants were ordered to encourage activity by establishing a permanently staffed centre in their area, keeping in constant touch with the standing army groups, and to visit the companies regularly. To make sure that the different brigade officers could be reached, a list of where they would be each day of the following week was provided.

Standing army group was another term for battalion ASU, which consisted of the men who were on the run within their own battalion area but had not joined one of the Flying Columns. They occasionally initiated operations, especially in those battalions where none of the brigade columns originated. To counteract the military round-ups, these units frequently broke up into small parties. This procedure enabled members of these groups who were company officers to look after Volunteer affairs in their company areas. Work such as the collection of levies, Volunteer police work, billeting of brigade columns, blocking and trenching of roads and assisting at Dáil Courts needed constant attention. However, the continued part-time attitude of many officers allowed for participation in an occasional operation; but paper work was far from their minds. The brigade staff again complained that, notwithstanding appeals and promises repeated at every brigade council, reports failed to come in.[89]

---

88 South Tipperary Brigade orders, O'MN, P17b127. Appointment of Special Services Captains, UCD AD, P9/13.
89 Standing Army Groups, Paul Mulcahy, 'Statement'. Complaints by brigade, O'MN, P17b127.

Despite the reluctance of local Volunteers, they supported the Flying Columns. Guard duty at night in particular, demanded some dedication: 'Scouting was our hardest job. Often we envied the column men in their beds when we had our backs to a ditch from dark till dawn. Always at a turn of a road where there was sure to be a fresh breeze.' The growing vigilance of the Crown Forces made attention to the other company duties, such as blocking and trenching the roads, increasingly dangerous. Fearing nightly visits to their families, more and more local Volunteers were forced to sleep away from home, each trying to find his own safe-house.[90]

The policy to destroy barracks one by one, that had characterised Tipperary in the spring and summer of 1920, ended in the autumn of that year. From January 1921 onwards barracks were only sniped at in a way similar to Wexford. Although often done by column men, it was equally intended to confine the police to their barracks and keep them in a state of anxiety. Occasionally sniping was used to draw attention away from another area. A total of eleven feint barracks attacks were recorded in January, and several took place in each of the following months. The measures taken by the Crown Forces and the lack of ammunition meant that few large-scale barracks attacks and ambushes took place in 1921. As in most areas, the first months of this year were characterised by a large number of minor offences. Nevertheless, the number of casualties still grew.[91]

DUBLIN: THE COMPANY PATROL

Involvement of rank and file in the fighting in Dublin was clearly strengthened by the company patrol instituted in January 1921. Some form of patrol existed since 1918, but they had been mostly unarmed and had only intelligence duties. During 1920 these patrols became increasingly important. The military confrontation which regular patrols were likely to generate was essential to sustain the organisation; but the risks attached to carrying arms was growing. As a result, the 2nd Battalion temporarily ordered its patrols to stop carrying arms at the end of 1920. However, the Volunteers were facing wholesale arrest if the daily raids and searches by the Crown Forces, instituted after Bloody Sunday, were not countered. In answer to this dilemma GHQ developed a policy which balanced the risks of carrying arms against the needs of the war.[92]

90 Quote, Bryan Ryan (1969), 5. Dangers of trenching, Mossy McGrath, O'MN, P17b127. Ordinary Volunteers sleeping away from home, Jack Gardiner, Interview; Bryan Ryan (1969), 9; Nonie Kennedy, O'MN, P17b119.
91 Attacks in 1921, CI South Tipperary MRs 1921. Reasons for barracks sniping, Ned Glendon, O'MN, P17b103; Patrick Ryan, 'Statement'.
92 Problems with carrying arms, 'Talk with Major General Paddy Daly', UCD AD, P7D1.

A special memo was issued on 4 November expressing GHQ's policy on carrying arms. Although it acknowledged the obvious military advantages of this, it was stressed that anyone arrested with a gun was either shot immediately or was likely to receive a severe term of imprisonment. Depending on personal and local circumstances, GHQ gave Volunteers the freedom to determine for themselves whether to carry arms. However, in making up their minds, they were to consider the following points. For a known Volunteer it was worthwhile to take the risk attached to the use of firearms and to avoid arrest if he had any kind of chance of success. From a national point of view Volunteers should show they would not tamely submit to capture or arrest. The enemy must be made to know that he was fighting an Army, which would oppose him to the utmost personal effort and sacrifice.[93]

Despite the risks attached to using armed patrols, some had continued to operate. In or about September 1920 one of them had used the first grenade against the military in Dublin. Wanting to build on successes like this, the Dublin Brigade now ordered each company to organise an armed patrol each week. Fear of being caught with arms gradually diminished due to the low arrest rate. Initially most companies only had a patrol out one evening each week, but when confidence increased patrolling gradually intensified. On 11 May 1921, each company in the 2nd Battalion was ordered to have an armed patrol out every night, and if possible by day as well.[94]

These patrols differed in size and tactics depending on the lay-out of the company area and the number of men involved. In some areas the men went around in pairs trying to locate the enemy; but in most companies larger groups of ten to twenty men, led by a section commander or company officer, patrolled together. When frequency increased, special nights were assigned to different patrols or the week was divided between two half-companies. Depending on the company's armaments, most of these patrols were armed with only a couple of revolvers and some grenades. The object was to attack all lorries of military or Auxiliaries. Similar to the raiding by the Crown Forces, Volunteer patrols had little knowledge of troop movements and tried to locate targets at random.[95]

When patrolling in larger groups they went in two files on opposite sides of the streets often confining themselves to the areas where they expected to encounter the enemy. In areas with a large military presence, taking up stationary positions was favoured because of the high risk of detection while moving around. Each company area was clearly defined, outside of which individual patrols were forbidden to operate. Even if another company was in

---

93 Memo, NLI, ms. 900/17.
94 First grenade attack, George White, O'MN, P17b105; Joe O'Connor, O'MN, P17b105. Intensifying patrolling: In January, NLI, ms. 901/35. In May 1921, NLI, ms. 902/147-9.
95 Instructions, Billy Rowe, O'MN, P17b110. Dividing between half-companies, Paddy Farrell, O'MN, P17b115.

trouble, they were not supposed to come to their aid as this meant a stand-up fight which GHQ wanted to avoid. In such a situation, the Crown Forces could quickly cut off the area and move in on them.[96]

In reality the patrols were informally organised; often they depended on a couple of Volunteers who met each other at night, took some grenades and possibly revolvers from the company dump and went out to see what came up. The dumps were usually hidden in stables, in lane ways or in houses; one company used the city sewers. Only a few men in a company knew the location of dumps and they had to ask the quartermaster for permission to get the arms out. The increased patrolling and the shortage of arms forced some companies into elaborate rotating schemes:

> When the Monday night patrol finished, the Tuesday night patrol was waiting there to take the revolvers from the men coming off patrol and their grenades. Each member of the Tuesday night patrol kept his arms that night and he reported armed next evening on parade. We had practically no dumps for such small arms.[97]

The tactics used in attack were of a simple hit-and-run nature: 'The bombers were to open up first, and then the small arms men would open up to allow the bombers to retire, but retiring meant run away where you liked.' One Volunteer from Mayo, who was studying in Dublin in 1921, described his involvement in these ambushes: 'I took part in some small engagements which involved lobbing Mills bombs into British lorries and skipping off as fast as you could.' After leaving the scene of the fight in this hurried manner, the men were to regroup at a certain point where they were to dump arms. Here they were met by a company officer who received their report.[98]

The geography of the city meant that some companies operated in an area where they were much more prone to find targets than others. In

96 Experience of company patrol, Joe O'Connor, O'MN, P17b105; C.S. Andrews (1979), 163-4; Sean Smith, O'MN, P17b122; Paddy Farrell, O'MN, P17b115; Tony Woods, O'MN, P17b96; Tom Duffy, O'MN, P17b105; Jerry Davis, O'MN, P17b106; Joe McHenry, O'MN, P17b95; Gus Connolly, O'MN, P17b91; Billy Rowe, O'MN, P17b110. Not helping each other, Joe O'Connor, O'MN, P17b105; George White, O'MN, P17b105; Alfred Rutherford, O'MN, P17b122.
97 Dumps, Paddy Brennan, O'MN, P17b90; Frank Henderson, O'MN, P17b99. Quote, Joe O'Connor, O'MN, P17b105. Sometimes this rotation system led to unofficial operations.
98 Quote on 'tactics', Billy Rowe, O'MN, P17b110. Quote from Mayo Volunteer, John Joe Philben, 'Statement'. Many Volunteers were transferred from country units to the Dublin Brigade, NLI, ms. 901/155-63. Regrouping and reporting, C.S. Andrews (1979), 163-4; Joe O'Connor, O'MN, P17b105.

some companies where Crown Force lorries frequently travelled the same streets, a few men waited on corners in hall-doors or shops. Other companies seldom had military or police vehicles travelling their area, or were limited in their freedom to attack due to the large number of civilians, or the proximity of a police or military barracks. It took one company two months before a patrol actually engaged the enemy. For many such companies extra effort was needed to force a fight, and they occasionally sent out several patrols on one night. On 14 March 1921, thirty-eight members of B-Company, 3rd Battalion were ordered out in four different patrols with elaborate instructions:

> All enemy to be engaged and if possible wiped out. In the event of a patrol coming in contact with enemy, all patrols to concentrate on that sector of the area to be in the fight, as the men had not been in action before with one or two exceptions. Cyclists to be used as connection links in order to keep in touch, unarmed men to be in advance of patrols as scouts. Patrols to move in files, two men on each side of the street and five paces between each file. First Aid men to move at the rear of each patrol, two First Aid men with each patrol. Bombers to keep on the outside of each file, each bomber to be with a Gunman. Unarmed men [scouts] to fall back with First Aid men in the event of getting in touch with enemy.

The pooling of 'target-rich' areas between different companies was another solution used to deal with this problem.[99]

The effectiveness of these patrols was also limited by the fear and hesitancy of many Volunteers. The unsuitability of many officers who had been good organisers only became apparent under fire:

> Frank O'Grady was O.C. He was mild and weak. [...] He would give you instructions and that is all you would see of him. [...] On the first job I was on. [...] I was placed at the corner across and I was told if you see a car attack it and use your own discretion. [...] Along came a small 10 cut car which had an open back and in the back were 4 Tommies with Rifles, sitting up. I looked at them and I waited for the [officers] to act, but the car went through and nothing happened. And they went for me: 'Why didn't you attack?' I was waiting for a lead, I said, and if I did what you did I'd have beaten you going up Liberty Street, for both of them I had seen hushing away when the car had passed them.

99 Quote, 'Report on the Brunswick Street Action', dated 14 March 1921, UCD AD, P7A39. Proximity of Crown Forces stopping operations, Tom Duffy, O'MN, P17b105. Examples of pooling areas, Joe O'Connor P17b105; Harry Colley, O'MN, P17b97; UCD AD, P7A19/224.

However as shown before, it was virtually impossible to get rid off such officers who did not function to either their men's or their superiors' satisfaction.[100]

Most patrols had nothing to report, but if an engagement had taken place an extensive report was written and forwarded to the brigade. These reports had to contain details on the procedure followed, the disposal of the Volunteers and the enemy, the ammunition expended and the possible casualties on either side. The haphazard organisation and limited military significance of these ambushes is shown by a report which GHQ considered: 'A striking example of the splendid work that can be done by a small patrol.' They sent this report to all battalions to improve the success rate of patrols:

> Procedure: Patrol was instructed to attack any enemy lorry, foot-patrol or convoy they met in the Company's area. The attack was to be opened by bombs, if possible and sustained with revolver fire.
>
> Disposal of men: The patrol was stationed on both sides of Sandford Road, Ranelagh: 3 men including o/c patrol armed with bombs on one side of the road, and 4 men armed with revolvers on opposite side in pairs.
>
> Information about enemy: The enemy were in Convoy; 6 tenders and 1 Ford car. The latter appeared first travelling from city in direction of Dundrum. The attack was opened on the Ford and the following tender. One bomb fell right behind the first tender injuring three of its occupants and damaging the car. Upon the attack being opened, the remaining tenders halted and the occupants started to search the neighbourhood. Another Auxiliary, R.I.C. man was wounded in Hollybank Avenue, when following one of patrol.
>
> Information about own men: The patrol retreated through the houses on the road. One man carrying a .45 Webley was held up and searched by an Auxiliary who was so excited that he failed to discover the weapon and let the man go.
>
> Ammunition expended: 2 bombs, 19 rounds .45 revolver ammunition.
>
> Casualties: There were 4 known enemy casualties. Our men had none.
>
> Remarks: The patrol fought a splendid action.[101]

100 Quote, Billy Rowe, O'MN, P17b110.
101 Patrol report, NLI, ms. 900/27. Many other examples of patrol reports can be found in, UCD AD, P7A19-23 (in particular, P7A19/217-25).

From a study of the large collection of patrol reports available, it is clear that most engagements were the result of coincidence. Major problems were the complete failure of grenades or explosions in the wrong place wounding bystanders. Despite the limited number of successful ambushes by company patrols, finding targets was much easier for a willing Volunteer in Dublin than in the country. The latter often had to lie in an ambush position for days in cold and wet weather without ever encountering anyone.[102]

PARTICIPATION IN OPERATIONS

To measure the involvement of various Volunteers we have to rely on material from Dublin. Personal initiative by rank and file Volunteers in Dublin was greatly stimulated by the introduction of patrols. Even industrious Volunteers had always been apprehensive about engaging in operations without sanction from superiors. Up to 1921 most of their operations, like general raids for arms and the burning of official buildings, were done under direct orders from GHQ. Having become accustomed to fighting in the company patrol, they became more willing to seize other opportunities to do something for the cause. This growing initiative caused a distinct increase in the number of minor operations. These included the seizure and burning of enemy goods, taking the mail and the enforcement of the Belfast Boycott. Some involvement in the gathering of information and enforcing the authority of the Dáil is also reported.[103]

Despite all this activity, the company parade continued to be the best attended aspect of Volunteering. In Dublin City they were held in halls and parks with guards posted to warn in the event of a raid. The attendance records for company parades in the 2nd Battalion from September 1919 to January 1921 show that all companies paraded once a week. Most possessed a hard core of men who attended parades regularly. In December 1920 and January 1921, the size of this core varied from about twenty to almost sixty. The variable attendance above this involved almost half that number again, ranging between ten and twenty-six.[104]

Every company had three officers, most of whom were usually on

102 Wounding innocent bystanders, UCD AD, P17A19/222.
103 One of the biggest coups in Dublin came off after a Volunteer disregarded the need for GHQ's permission and acted on his own. When he set the National Shell factory ablaze, 6 armoured cars, 67 motor cycles and some other cars were destroyed, UCD AD, P7A20/2. Other activities: Closing pubs, George Gilmore, O'MN, P17b106. Raiding offices, Laurence Casey, NLI, ms. 10,723(2). Enforcing Belfast Boycott, Tom Duffy, O'MN, P17b105; Tom Burke, O'MN, P17b98; UCD AD, LA9.
104 Parade reports, NLI, ms. 901/73, ms. 1,413. Numbers on roll, not dated but probably from May 1921, NLI, ms. 901/85.

parade. The number of NCOs varied between the large and small companies, but grew on average from six to twelve between 1919 and 1921. E-Company had only six NCOs until the summer of 1920, while F-Company already had thirteen in October 1919. The total men on the roll in each company was again considerably higher than the best attended company parade. The contrasting level of participation can be read in Table 6, listing the total on roll in 1921, the highest number reported on a parade in December 1920 or January 1921 and the average parade attendance during these two months.

Table 6: Participation in Company Parade in the 2nd Battalion Dublin Brigade

	B	C	D	E	F	Cyclist
On Roll	76	65	78	142	115	41
Highest	44	55	71	83	51	30
Average	39	44	56	72	45	24

Although most activity in 1921 was organised on company basis, some coordinated attacks were arranged by the battalion staff. In a train attack reported by the 2nd Battalion in May, 20 men from B-Company, 10 from C, 5 from D, 11 from E, 12 from F, 10 from the cyclists and 3 from the signalling unit (a total of 71) cooperated. In smaller operations one company sometimes worked as flank-guard for another. Larger operations continued to be initiated by GHQ. Although most of these were executed by the ASU, ordinary Volunteers sometimes assisted. These had either a wider political motive or were a result of promising information; they included the attack on the London and North West Railway Hotel where a military post was based, the preparations to shoot some British agents should Terence MacSwiney die on hunger strike, the planned attack on every uniformed and armed British representative in Dublin on one particular night in June 1921, and the attempted rescue of Sean MacEoin from prison.[105]

The largest of these coordinated operations was the disastrous burning of the Custom House in May 1921. This operation was initiated by President De Valéra to show the world the strength of the revolutionary movement in Ireland. The 2nd Battalion commandant was ordered to organise it. In its execution this battalion was aided by the Squad and the ASU, while other battalions did some covering duty. Although successful in its objective about seventy Volunteers were arrested after this attack, and

105 Coordinated battalion attacks, NLI, ms. 901/83. Companies working together, NLI, ms. 902/133.

many were shot. The ASU and the 2nd Battalion, two of the most active units in Dublin, were particularly badly hit. This had been anticipated by GHQ, but not by the political leadership. Staging the attack despite the misgivings expressed by GHQ demonstrates the continued dominance of those who saw the IRA as a political instrument over those who considered military victory possible.[106]

The increasing confidence of the company patrols in 1921 is shown by the tenfold increase in operations reported by the Dublin Brigade between January and May. These consisted mainly of ambushes and harassing tactics, most of them by company patrols. In April and May roughly a quarter of all operations were ambushes and a fifth were feint attacks on barracks. The remaining actions included the barricading and trenching of roads, raids for arms and mail, and the destruction of goods. The shooting of spies and other foreign agents became prominent in May, five taking place in that month and ten in June. These murders soon became casual affairs to those most intimately wrapped up in Volunteering:

> While out on Intelligence Patrol on Sat. 14/5/21. We saw a man who aroused our suspicions. My companion was lucky in getting into his company. Afterwards we held him up & searched him & found an ex-Soldiers badge in his pocket. We demanded a confession from him which he refused to give. We then took off his belt put it round his neck & proceeded to strangle him & not till he got blue in the face did he admit that he was a Black & Tan on week end leave & promised if we stopped to give us some information. We took him away with us to — and I put my revolver to his head asked him to give us the information or say his prayers. He refused to tell us anything & as it was coming near Curfew I had no other alternative but to fire – he fell & I leant over him and put another round into him. We then made a good retreat.

Having lost many of their full-time activists in the Custom House attack, ambushes by company patrols became even more prominent in June, comprising twenty-seven out of ninety-three operations.[107]

---

106 Custom House attack, Oscar Traynor, O'MN, P17b96; George White, O'MNs, P17b105 and P17b99; Jim Slattery, O'MN, P17b109; Patrick O'Daly, 'Statement', NLI, P4548, and UCD AD, P7D1; NLI, ms. 901/76 + 102, and ms. 902/122; UCD AD, P7A19/186-93, and P7A17/272-5; PRO, WO35/90, and Intelligence Summary week ending 29 May 1921, WO35/91. Afterwards, IRA battalion commanders were asked to intensify their work to camouflage the losses, Harry Colley, O'MN, P17b97; Joe O'Connor, O'MN, P17b105.

107 April report, UCD AD, P7A39. May report, UCD AD, P7A19/186-93. June report, UCD AD, P7A21/98-9. Some detailed reports, UCD AD, P7A19/152-7. Quote, NLI, ms. 901/109.

In Table 7 the number of actions each battalion and specialised unit operating in Dublin engaged in are specified for the spring months of 1921. These show a steady and equal increase in the activity of the city battalions. This was interrupted in the 2nd Battalion in June due to the arrests after the Custom House attack. The inclusion of operations by the 6th Battalion in May distorts the overall picture somewhat. Without them, May showed only a small increase from April. The brigade staff blamed the overall decrease in June on GHQ instructions restricting ambushes in thickly populated streets in the city. There is, however, no decrease in the number of street ambushes; only barracks attacks and raids fell sharply. No explanation for the sudden decrease in activities of the 5th Battalion in May can be offered. The operations of the 6th in June were probably reduced by the formation of the South Dublin Brigade which took in most of its territory. The 7th Battalion was formed in the same month, covering the south-west of the county. The steep reduction in ASU actions was again a result of the casualties from the Custom House attack, but was also caused by the subsequent merging of the ASU and Squad in the Dublin Guards, which led to internal squabbles.[108]

Table 7: Operations of the Dublin units in 1921

	1st	2nd	3rd	4th	5th	6th	7th	ASU	Squad	Guard	Total
April	9	5	9	7	15	0	–	22	0	–	67
May	10	15	11	14	0	31	–	21	1	–	103
June	12	10	16	23	10	8	2	5	0	6	92

Despite the steady increase in operations, many companies remained inactive. Out of 15 operations during May in the 2nd Battalion (which consisted of 10 ambushes, 2 failed attacks on a train, 1 execution of a Black & Tan and 2 seizures of goods) one company 173 was responsible for 6 operations, and the other five were engaged in between 1 and 3 during the entire month. From this limited activity it is obvious that even now only a few Volunteers were willing to risk their lives. The cautious approach of many officers and their tendency to use experienced men led to reports of impatient Volunteers waiting for a chance to act. That companies were more active than the battalion indicated can be discerned from company diaries. Besides the reported

108 The attempts to organise a 7th Battalion in south-west Dublin, Dublin Brigade report April 1921, UCD AD, P7A39. Squabbles after merging ASU and Squad, George White, O'MN, P17b105; Alfred Rutherford, O'MN, P17b122.

operations these note weekly parades, many unsuccessful patrols and ambushes, and some meetings and organisational work.[109]

The small number of casualties suffered by the 2nd Battalion further testify to this restrained fighting. Arrests were by far the biggest drain on the IRA. In April 1921 only one Volunteer was killed and one wounded in action; in May 4 were killed, 6 wounded and 68 taken prisoner, mainly at the Custom House. The organisation of first-aid posts in each company to care for the wounded demonstrates that serious fighting had only begun recently. These were staffed by Cumann na mBan and sometimes by a doctor. Seriously wounded Volunteers were taken in by hospitals and kept out of the view of the authorities. Realising this, the military often raided hospitals immediately after a fight.[110]

It is clear that the rank and file in Dublin were extremely important in keeping the military campaign going. In Tipperary and particularly in Mayo involvement by regular company Volunteers in operations was much smaller due to the monopolisation of activities by the Flying Columns. The absence of a Flying Column in Wexford and south Derry meant that all operations were organised by company members, but this only concerned a few active Volunteers.

The only means of assessing involvement in other counties are the membership figures recorded by the police and the parade attendance reports of the IRA. In June 1921 the RIC estimated that there were 6,608 Volunteers in Mayo, 958 in south Tipperary, 888 in Wexford and 305 in Derry. The measure of mobilisation per county is more accurately presented by relating membership to the number of Catholic males.[111] Mayo was clearly the best organised county with 7 per cent of Catholic males as member of the organisation. In Tipperary Volunteer membership reached a maximum of 2,9 per cent at the end of 1919 before shrinking to 2,2 per cent in the summer of 1920 where it remained until the truce. In Wexford mobilisation was 1.9 per cent and in Derry 1.0 per cent.

The parade reports of the IRA compiled in June and July 1921 show a widespread willingness to publicly expose membership in all counties at the height of the struggle. According to these reports the Derry City Battalion had 160 active members, while the South Derry Brigade recorded 124. This makes a total of 284 activists in June 1921 almost similar to the police assess-

---

109 2nd Battalion diary, NLI, ms. 901/81-2. Company operations for March 1921, NLI, ms. 901/113 + 122.

110 Casualty reports April and May, NLI, ms. 901/75-7. Another undated casualty report mentions 2 killed, 7 wounded and 94 arrested. This is likely to be June 1921. First Aid posts and raids on hospitals, Joe O'Connor, O'MN, P17b105; Alfred Rutherford, O'MN, P17b122.

111 Although some Protestants were member of the Volunteers, the total number was insignificant and their impact can be ignored for this purpose. Some more precise figures for Protestant membership of the Volunteers are presented in the Appendix. Membership figures, LIs south Tipperary, Mayo, Derry and Wexford MRs.

ment of 305 Volunteers. In south Tipperary, the brigade reported 1,117 active members compared to 958 recorded by the RIC. In Wexford, the southern brigade reported 627 members on parade in July, while the northern brigade added another 603. This accounts for 1,230 members in the entire county which compares to 888 recorded by the police. This underestimation can be accounted for by the fact that the police in Wexford and south Tipperary, contrary to the RIC in Derry, had lost track of events in many rural areas due to the evacuation of barracks and the more secretive operation of the Volunteers. Parade reports for Mayo are only available from the South Mayo Brigade. The 890 men reported on parade in this brigade seem scarcely able to account for the 6,608 members recorded by the police for the four Mayo brigades. However, the membership rolls of one of the four battalions of the West Mayo Brigade alone record 773 members in July 1921 making the police figure more likely. Apparently a large part of the male population in Mayo was on the rolls but never participated in potentially dangerous Volunteer activity. The parade reports of the Dublin Brigade for which no police estimates are available record 2,152 Volunteers on parade. It is clear that the willingness to parade was general but this bore no relation to the measure of involvement in other Volunteer operations.[112]

VOLUNTEER PROFILE

Although various assessments of the social background of the Volunteers have been made, an analysis of its nation-wide membership has only recently been made.[113] This analysis by Peter Hart is based on names of

112 Reports on Volunteer strength in June-July 1921, UCD AD, P7A23/215. West Mayo Battalion rolls, CBHC. The South Wexford Brigade reported 6,270 members on parade in July. This is unlikely considering the size of the population and the activity of this brigade. In October, the same brigade reported only 1,210 members. Growth from 627 to 1,210 is more consistent with developments after the Truce than a decrease from 6,270, October reports, UCD AD, P7a18.

113 The rural and youthful aspect of the movement has been emphasised by most historians. In the earliest analysis of membership by David Fitzpatrick concerning Co. Clare, clear differences between officers and rank and file emerged. In the early part of the struggle, officers were predominantly in their twenties while rank and file were younger and older. A larger proportion of officers worked in villages rather than on farms, and they had inherited attributes likely to win them social prestige, such as being an eldest son and coming from the larger farms in the area. The composition of officers in Clare changed when fighting had broken out. The new officers were younger, sons of labourers rather than shopkeepers, and from medium sized rather than larger holdings, David Fitzpatrick (1977), 203-4 + 222-4. Charles Townshend has emphasised the working class background of the rank and file in Dublin City, Charles Townshend (1979), 323. See also Tom Garvin (1981), 120-5. Most recent nation-wide analysis, Peter Hart (1992), Chapter 'Volunteers'.

Volunteers taken from newspaper reports, IRA rolls, and prison, police and military reports. As a result an over-representation of active members – who were more likely to be arrested or mentioned in newspaper reports – is inevitable. Not surprisingly, the membership was 99 per cent Catholic and mainly young. Outside the Dublin District, 70 per cent of rank and file membership was between twenty and twenty-nine years of age, and another 18 per cent was under twenty. Officers were somewhat less youthful, with 73 per cent and 12 per cent in these age groups respectively. Of the entire male population in 1911, only 37 per cent were aged between fifteen and twenty-nine. In general, Hart's figures show that Volunteers were broadly representative of Irish Catholic male society. Their backgrounds were wide ranging, coming from most sectors of the working and middle classes, although rarely from the upper middle or upper classes, and few were unemployed or indigent. Among the numerous Volunteers who were employed as professionals the lower end of the scale was dominant, largely represented by part-time and assistant teachers. Considering previous assessments, the most surprising result of Hart's analysis is the extent to which the membership came from urban areas.

These characteristics applied to both officers and rank and file; but there were also some clear differences. Officers tended to be older, more urban based, and of a higher status – better educated, more skilled and financially better-off. Apart from the urban membership, farmers much more than their labourers were prevalent among officers in Munster and Leinster. In Dublin Hart's figures confirm Townshend's assessment that the majority of officers and men had working-class backgrounds. There are clear changes in the composition of membership between the early period and the period of guerrilla war. They all became younger, but the age gap between officers and rank and file remained. In Munster and Connacht the number of farmers declined strongly, while in Leinster and Ulster the opposite occurred. The rank and file in the most active areas – Dublin, Munster and Connacht – became more working-class and urban. In Leinster and Ulster members from farming families became better represented, and Volunteers thus became less urban based. Outside Leinster (excluding Dublin City), officers became more middle-class. This difference in developments is largely a result of the strongly urban base of Volunteers in Leinster and Ulster in 1917-19. Membership was thus converging towards a more uniform organisation in 1920-21.

In order to get an adequate picture of the social composition of the IRA in the five counties, some demographic characteristics of Volunteer membership are compared to those of the community they lived in. This is done by taking the entire membership of a number of rural companies in each county and contrasting its characteristics to those of the entire population in the company areas. In this way, the proportion of each age group and each occupational group that joined the IRA is established. This approach also makes it possible to look at the effect wealth had on a farmers' willingness to join. Besides the analysis of age, occupation and wealth, the Volunteers' position in the family, the influence of fathers and the presence of kinship-ties between IRA members are established. All these characteristics when taken together provide a more precise answer to the question as to who were particularly attracted by membership of the movement, and what position the IRA had in the various communities. Due to problems which made a complete match between membership lists used for this analysis and the census and valuation records impossible, the outcome of this analysis does not represent absolute figures. Nevertheless, it provides a reasonably accurate indication of the social composition of rural membership in 1921. (The reasons for the much higher mobilisation figures presented here when compared to those in Table 3 are explained in the appendix.)

From the analysis enumerated in the appendix it becomes clear that Volunteers had diverse positions in the various rural areas and Dublin City. In Mayo the two adjoining companies of Aughagower and Owenwee (part of the Westport Battalion, West Mayo Brigade) had many members, and mobilised a particularly large proportion of men in all age groups and occupations. With 48 per cent of the boys between fifteen and twenty years of age, and 34 per cent of Catholic males between fifteen and sixty, the Volunteers had established themselves at the heart of the community and could count on solid support. Due to the socio-economic structure of the area, dominated by small subsistence farmers, the organisation was almost entirely made up of farmers. Members with other occupations were few, but comparatively highly mobilised. Two groups, just below and above the middle-income farmer, were over-represented. Particularly lower and higher income groups, but also the middle-income group, were under-represented. Overall poorer people tended to join at a later stage, while members of richer farming families became more hesitant to do so when fighting escalated. The central position of the IRA in Mayo is underlined by the high percentage of members living with their father, from whom they apparently experienced little opposition. The fact that many Volunteers were first-born sons, who are often supposed to have been dissuaded from joining the IRA, further confirms this.

The two averagely-sized rural companies from Laffansbridge and Moyglass in Tipperary had almost the same level of mobilisation in the different age groups as those in Mayo. However, in the substantial village of Killenaule, with 110 families, significantly fewer men joined. Overall mobilisation reached 13 per cent of males in the community, and was strongest in the age group between twenty and twenty-five. A dominance of farmers was particularly apparent in the two rural companies, with overall labourers, artisans and merchants reaching roughly half the mobilisation level of the farmers, 12-15 per cent compared to 24 per cent. The distribution of wealth among farmers who joined was similar to that in Mayo, with an over-representation of the groups just below and above the average-income farmer. The percentage of first-born sons and of brothers active in the movement supports this level of integration in the community, somewhat less than in Mayo but substantially more than in Wexford. The exceptionally high level of economically independent members in Tipperary, when compared to Wexford, contradicts its more integrated position in rural Tipperary. The high number of labourers in its ranks, who became wage earners at an early age, offers only a partial explanation for this.

In the Wexford companies of Adamstown, Glynn and Crossabeg the profile of Volunteers is less distinct. The companies were small and the level of mobilisation was almost half that in Tipperary, standing at 7 per cent of the male population. The significant difference lay in the type of people it attracted. They were much more concentrated in the age group between twenty and thirty, and disproportionately many members came from the small groups of merchants and others, while tradesmen and farmers were attracted to the IRA in equal measure. Nevertheless most Volunteers were farmers, and mobilisation among them again showed a similar two-peak phenomenon around the middle income group as in Mayo and Tipperary. The comparatively high level of mobilisation among young non-farmers indicates a more peripheral position of the organisation there. The low level of first-born sons and of brothers in the movement confirms this more marginal status. Apparently Volunteers experienced more opposition from constitutional nationalists, which were particularly numerous among older people, many of whom were parents of Volunteers. The high level of members who were economically dependent on their parents contradicts this, but might mainly be a reflection of their younger average age.

The two south Derry companies of Belagherty and Newbridge were small, mobilised only 4 per cent of Catholic males, and were entirely dominated by those aged between twenty and thirty, who came mainly from among the richer farmers. These figures bear out the continued strong support for the AOH among older people in Ulster. The unexpectedly high level of dependent members and of brothers when related to the low level of mobilisation, is probably closer associated with the youthfulness and level of secrecy of operation needed in a hostile environment than with integration in community life. The confinement of Volunteer membership to a small group of families can thus be explained by security reasons, and also by the strong link between membership of a particular family and political allegiance. The fact that Derry Volunteers who were first-born sons were significantly less active than younger sons shows that certain constraints were nevertheless put on them.

In Dublin the IRA was mainly limited to young men from the lower and middle social strata. Unskilled or semi-skilled labourers were particularly over-represented among the rank and file, while white-collar workers in particular dominated the officer class. On the basis of the month of enrolling of

members of two small city companies and the suburban 6th Battalion, it is
apparent that the organisation originated disproportionately from among
skilled labourers, but became more appealing to the lower working classes
and to a lesser extent to white-collar workers when large-scale hostilities
began. Among the officers a distinct and increasing relative dominance of
white-collar workers and professionals is shown, with few unskilled or semi-
skilled labourers reaching high rank. The IRA in Dublin was less integrated
in society. The small number of Volunteers with brothers in the movement,
the youthful membership and the low level of activity until 1920 indicates
that the organisation often functioned as a means of socialising for young
people as well.

To a certain extent the diminishing level of mobilisation from Mayo to
Derry runs parallel with an increasing measure of economic dependency
through export of agricultural products, and to the presence of Crown
Forces. As mentioned in the introduction, Erhard Rumpf has suggested that
such an economic dependency made the development of violent resistance
against British rule less likely. The more people depended on this, the less
support there was for IRA violence. However, we have seen that the levels
of violence in the different counties followed different patterns, being most
prominent in Tipperary.

The characteristics of IRA membership indicate a connection between
mobilisation and the position of the Volunteers in the community. I have
argued here that the organisation that stood at the heart of a community
had a strong mobilisation in all age groups and was strongest in the main
occupation of the area, usually farming. Contrary to the image of the IRA
portrayed by its enemies as 'people with no stake in the country', the IRA
clearly appealed more to people who did have a stake in the country,
although possibly not the largest. My figures confirm Hart's assessment that
few of the richest or poorest members of society joined; additionally they
also indicate a lesser attraction to farmers with a middle income.

Among the other professions teachers and their sons featured strongly;
out of a total in all areas together of eleven six joined, giving a mobilisation
of 54 per cent among teachers. Labourers as a whole were apparently more
concerned with earning a living and were perhaps economically too dependent on the larger farmers to join the IRA until the end of the struggle.
Although the high level of independent Volunteers everywhere leads to the
conclusion that the presence of a father as a figure of authority and control
had a dampening effect on young men's enthusiasm to join the IRA, the
important function of relatives in organising the IRA is underlined by my
figures. It must be concluded that having an active family member was an
important albeit not a deciding factor, in one's reasons for joining the IRA.

Garvin's assertion that membership in the active South emanated from
the lower middle classes in small towns is not born out by the facts.

However, in inactive Mayo and also in south Wexford the organisation did start in the towns where a certain level of wealth was present. The small farmers in the Mayo countryside were rarely involved in the initial stages, thus reinforcing Garvin's idea that below a certain subsistence level no IRA activity could be sustained. Contrary to this, however, the organisation showed exceptional growth in Mayo after the Rising. This supports Fitzpatrick's correlation between the proportion of people living on agrarian holdings and the propensity to join nationalist organisations.[114]

The weight Garvin assigns to Volunteers from small urban areas, which is supported by Peter Hart's figures of the background of active members, may be explained by the effects of operating in urban areas. In the towns and cities, contact with radical politics was more likely in the first two decades of this century, but extreme nationalists could also expect stronger opposition from the garrisons of the Crown Forces and from people who were in some way dependent on that presence. The traditional popularity of the British Army among the urban working class is an example of this. This hostility induced a siege-mentality and drove some urban activists into early radicalisation. After 1918 they were often forced to go on the run, long before radicals in the countryside had to do so. The dominance of Volunteers from the towns in all phases of organisation and operation in west Mayo shows this most clearly. It remains nevertheless remarkable that despite the strong urban background of active membership throughout Ireland, few activists in south Tipperary came from urban areas.[115]

RELATIVE MEASURE OF FIGHTING

The high level of activity in Dublin and south Tipperary in 1920-21 is mirrored in the number of casualties, either killed or seriously wounded. In Dublin City Crown Force losses in this period numbered 163, in Co. Tipperary 114, in Mayo 40, in Derry 15 and in Wexford 10. The IRA casualties were similarly distributed, but the suitability of a large city for guerrilla warfare is proven by the comparatively low level of IRA losses in Dublin City. Dublin City Volunteers nevertheless suffered most casualties, totalling 55; the IRA in Tipperary lost 35 men; in Mayo they lost 22; in Derry 8 and in Wexford 2 men. The spread of casualties among the civilian population indicates that the violence affected them differently. The indiscriminate vio-

114 On dominance of small town and artisan membership, Tom Garvin (1987), 6-8. On not 'sustaining' IRA activity under certain subsistence level, Tom Garvin (1981), 124. Correlation between proportion of people living on agrarian holdings and propensity to join nationalist organisations, David Fitzpatrick (1978), 132.

115 Peter Hart (1992), Chapter 'Volunteers', 22-3. Popularity of British Army in urban areas, Tom Garvin (1981), 120-1.

lence in urban areas is demonstrated by high civilian casualties in Dublin City, totalling 240. This is confirmed in Belfast and Derry City, although most civilian casualties there resulted from large-scale sectarian riots between Catholics and Protestants. A total of 83 civilian casualties occurred in Tipperary, 74 in Derry, 12 in Wexford and only 6 in Mayo.[116]

To trace the development of violence in each county, the casualties per quarter from July 1920 onwards are listed below, supplemented with the totals between January 1920 and the Truce. The intensity of the struggle grew steadily in this period. Casualties among the Crown Forces rose steeply and continuously, while IRA losses stabilised in 1921 at a much lower level. In Tipperary, violence was already quite high in the summer of 1920, reaching a bloody summit in the final quarter of 1920. Casualties among the Crown Forces continued to be high in 1921, but after the disbanding of the Flying Columns the IRA became more successful in avoiding their pursuers. In 1920, Dublin City had a level of Crown Force casualties similar to that of Tipperary. But as a result of the introduction of the ASU and the company patrol, violence continued to escalate during 1921. A particularly high number of losses were incurred by the Crown Forces in 1921. The Volunteers in Mayo were unable to inflict any casualties in the final quarter of 1920, largely due to the intensification of Crown Force activity. However, after the introduction of Flying Columns the Mayo Volunteers made a considerable impact in the second quarter of 1921. No Flying Column was active in south Wexford or Derry, and a consistently low level of violence persisted there throughout the whole War of Independence.

Table 8: Crown Forces and IRA Casualties per Quarter and Total January 1920–July 1921

	Crown Forces					IRA				
	3rd 1920	4th 1920	1st 1921	2nd 1921	1920–1921	3rd 1920	4th 1920	1st 1921	2nd 1921	1920–1921
Mayo	6	0	9	20	40	0	1	1	20	22
Tipperary	13	32	21	29	114	3	16	22	7	51
Wexford	0	1	1	3	10	1	1	0	0	2
Derry	0	5	1	5	15	0	6	1	0	8
Dublin	9	29	54	63	163	3	9	24	19	55
Ireland	187	294	369	452	1,545	62	125	159	157	548

The continually growing ability of the IRA to inflict casualties becomes even more telling if we consider the number of Volunteers arrested. By January

116 Figures on arms seizures and casualties as a result of the use of guns and explosives, Peter Hart (1992), Addendum to Chapter 'The Dynamics of Violence'. See also Charles Townshend (1975), Appendix V.

1921 1,478 Volunteers had been interned, and before the Truce another 3,000 persons were added. Although not all of them were Volunteers, the total included 2,010 officers. Particularly in Dublin, arrests had become frequent after Bloody Sunday; 274 persons were arrested in November, most of them in the last ten days, and another 534 in December. In 1921 about 150 were arrested in Dublin District each month, bringing the total of internees from the Dublin District in May to 1,007.[117]

The commandant of the 3rd Battalion of the Dublin Brigade claims that at the time of the Truce half of his 500 Volunteers were interned. The capture of company rolls had enabled the British to arrest a large proportion of Volunteers in some of the battalions. This, however, affected a disproportionate number of inactive company men who were easier to locate from these lists since most of them were still living at home. Another 1,049 internees in May came from the South, while 389 had been arrested in the North and 889 came from the rest of the country.[118]

Other factors besides arrests impeded activity – the lack of arms, cautiousness and the part-time availability of the men. There was also what was later called the 'Republican Itch', a virulent form of scabies which removed many Volunteers in city and country from active service. Also, not all Crown Forces were seen as legitimate targets; for a long time unarmed British soldiers walking the streets were not attacked. The introduction of curfew in December 1920 in Dublin and some other cities was another factor which made operations more difficult. The large number of workshops and GHQ offices operating behind facades of shops and businesses further restrained activity in Dublin, as actions near them were obstructed by higher officers.[119]

---

117 Arrest figures Dublin District, PRO, WO35/90. In March 1921, 2,079 persons had been interned under the Restoration of Order in Ireland Act and 953 persons were imprisoned or convicted to penal servitude, *Mayoman*, 12 March 1921. Detailed figures for whole Ireland, Charles Townshend (1975), Appendix XII:

Cumulative figures of internment of IRA-members in 1921:

	Brigade	/	Battalion	/	Company /		
	Commandant	/ Staff /	Commandant	/ Staff /	Officer	/ Others /	Total
17 Jan. 1921	11	31	35	80	608	713	1,478
16 July 1921	19	58	93	217	1,623	2,444	4,454

118 Rolls captured, Joe O'Connor, O'MN, P17b105; Frank Henderson, O'MN, P17b99. Internment figures for 5th Division, War Diary December 1920, PRO, WO35/93/2; History of the 5th Division in Ireland November 1919–March 1922, 58 and 86, IWM, 72/82/2.

119 Two Dublin men unable to function due to the 'Republican Itch', Michael O'Reilly, O'MN, P17b115; Frank Henderson, O'MN, P17b99. Operation of offices, etc., Tom Hannigan, O'MN, P17b96; Frank Henderson, O'MN, P17b99; Harry Colley, O'MN, P17b97; Oscar Traynor; O'MN, P17b98.

The lack of arms was exacerbated by the successful uncovering of IRA dumps by the Crown Forces. During 1921 300 rifles, 554 shotguns, 731 pistols and 45,593 rounds of ammunition were captured, and many more had been surrendered to the authorities. In April the Dublin IRA privately admitted that their military capability was severely affected by this. Special measures were taken to reduce these losses; the quantity of war material stored together was limited and the number of people involved in taking arms from the dumps was reduced. The men were also instructed to guard the remaining weapons with their lives.[120]

Considering the type and number of engagements in relation to the number of potential targets, it is clear there was never an all-out war in Ireland. Although targets became more random in 1921, most Volunteers were not prepared to shoot just anybody with connections with the government. Even when they were sure about the danger presented by a particular enemy, most Volunteers only killed if they were ordered to do so. Many among the leadership, the Minister of Defence, Cathal Brugha, and the President in particular, were reluctant to permit such a war. They were afraid that when innocent people were hurt it would cause a loss of support at home and abroad. In their view each death had to serve a direct political or military purpose. According to one of the organisers the Dublin fight was therefore entirely directed in terms of politics, unlike the situation in the country. However, the restrictions on the IRA in Dublin were not liked and were often ignored by the brigade officers who were looking for a military victory; this led to some tension between the Minister of Defence and the Dublin Brigade.[121]

The measures taken by the British Army in 1921 had limited the number of possible targets and increased the risks attached to being arrested for Volunteers everywhere. The frustration that resulted from this was exacerbated by the introduction of the death penalty for those arrested with arms in the martial law area. As a result, activists began to look for other targets. Civilians who were seen as responsible for the arrests of Volunteers were the first victims of this. In Wexford, seven attempts to kill ex-soldiers, who had continued their contact with the Crown Forces, are recorded by the police between January and April. In most of these cases the IRA had notices with them reading: 'Warning to Spies', which they intended to pin to the corpses of their victims.[122]

120 Figures, Charles Townshend (1975), 195. Order to guard arms with their lives, NLI, ms. 900/28.
121 Squad shooting only those enemies they were instructed to shoot, Alfred Rutherford, O'MN, P17b122; Pat MacCrea, O'MN, P17b110; Patrick O'Daly, 'Statement', NLI, P4548. Attitude Minister of Defence and President, and antagonism with Dublin Brigade, Oscar Traynor, O'MN, P17b98; Frank Henderson, O'MN, P17b99.
122 CI Wexford MRs 1921.

A similar increase in attacks on civilians took place in Tipperary and Dublin. Most of the eight civilian victims in Tipperary were again ex-soldiers, but some Protestants were also singled out. In Mayo and Derry, no attempts on the life of civilians were recorded by the police, but intimidation was widespread. Although the percentage of ex-soldiers in Mayo was lower than in Wexford and Tipperary, this was mainly an expression of the greater acceptance of the IRA by society in Mayo. In Derry, the IRA was never sufficiently active or strong to be able or need to enforce such control.[123]

CONCLUSION

In the discussion of the changing activities of the Volunteers, the large degree of differentiation between individual Volunteers and between units was the most striking feature. Only a small number of Volunteers in a few areas were fully professionalised in their involvement. Activity was continuously limited by a lack of arms, courage, and moral and physical willingness. The reliance on a small number of dedicated Volunteers was augmented by frequent arrests and the part-time availability of most Volunteers. That violence nevertheless spread to large parts of the country was largely a consequence of GHQ's growing involvement and the government's policies at the end of 1920. Their indiscriminate approach and exaggerated reaction to the violence radicalised and involved an increasing number of men everywhere.

The start of the Flying Column was the main feature of this escalation. The formation of these small groups, which started spontaneously in places like Tipperary and Clare in the summer of 1920, was soon repeated in other areas often under directions from GHQ. After the introduction of several measures under the Restoration of Order in Ireland Act the leadership had become convinced that a more thorough military approach was necessary if they wished to survive. To improve the state of organisation, more organisers were appointed. These special officers visited units all over the country to improve structures and to instil some activity. Under their direction Flying Columns were set up in many active brigades. In 1921, when the fighting intensified and some southern units became hard pressed, special attention was given by GHQ to activate 'slow' areas to divert military attention. The introduction of divisions in Ulster was part of this attempt to extend the fighting. In places with less direct GHQ involvement but with several willing men, the news of Flying Column operations elsewhere inspired them to do the same.

123 CIs South Tipperary, Mayo and Derry MRs 1921. The relationship between Volunteers and civilians is further explored in Chapter 7 to 9.

A new type of struggle then developed particularly in the South. Ambushes on Crown Force patrols became the main occupation of the Flying Columns. The rank and file were slowly involved in dangerous operations, initially by helping the activists during ambushes and barracks attacks, but later mainly through guiding, protecting and housing the Flying Columns. Local Volunteers started to disrupt transportation and communication lines of the police and military in order to protect the columns. Roads were trenched, mail seized and telegraph wires cut. Areas with the most active Volunteers and the largest columns saw the strongest involvement of local Volunteers. In the spring of 1921 GHQ successfully stepped up this type of activity, which involved less direct danger to the Volunteers, in 'passive' areas such as Wexford and Derry. In Dublin the influence of GHQ on activity is seen most clearly in the founding of the ASU and the start of the armed company patrol. The latter caused large-scale involvement of rank and file into direct combat which was unique to Dublin.[124]

Approaching the Truce most active areas were militarily unable to keep their large Flying Columns in the field. They were disbanded and the men returned to their battalions, where they became involved in small operations. These men were radicalised by their involvement in hostilities and as a result conflict became more vicious, causing many casualties. In areas like Mayo, however, where military activity had only recently been started and was dominated by the Flying Columns, local Volunteers were not yet so much involved in activity, and military operations were consequently almost suspended after the disbanding of the columns. Many inactive areas had only a few officers on the run, most of whom were reluctant to engage in serious operations. Nevertheless, they gave continued attention to cutting communication lines. Preceding the Truce, direct military confrontation had become extremely limited in most areas, but a large number of Volunteers were engaged in minor operations, sometimes involving a lot of violence which prevented the authorities from governing large parts of the countryside.

Several factors determined to what extent one area or other, one Volunteer or other, completed the road to professionalism and violence. Action of any kind was a strong impetus to further activity, both to the men involved and to others inspired and often directly affected by what took place. The reaction of the authorities to this was often an equally strong stimulus. This self-sustaining process, in which activity created more activity, led to a sep-

124 When comparing the two year period from January 1919 to December 1920 with the period before the Truce in 1921, we find an increase in the number of mail raids from 959 to 1,605, raids on coast guard stations or lighthouses from 47 to 50, on rate collectors from 0 to 122. Raids for arms were largely confined to the last three months of 1920, when 2,213 took place compared with 760 in the 21 previous months together and 245 in 1921, Charles Townshend (1979), 342; Ibid. (1975), Appendix V.

aration between the active and the cautious, thus limiting involvement to a small group in a few areas. The cautious approach taken by GHQ until 1920 ensured that this differentiation could develop unchecked.

Inactive units were, nevertheless, inspired by the military successes of Volunteers and the brutality of the Crown Forces elsewhere. In this way activity slowly extended from a small group of dedicated militarists in a limited number of areas to many, more peacefully inclined, members and areas. In the latter part of the conflict GHQ managed to extend new developments from active to inactive areas. Whether they could instil violent conflict in these areas was largely dependent on local circumstances. GHQ was often able to give a first impulse to start activity but mainly of a non-violent nature, which was sometimes the beginning of a spiral of conflict. In a small number of inactive areas a development towards more violent conflict took place, apparently irrespective of GHQ's involvement.

The policies of the authorities were another important influence on the activity and position of the Volunteers, and frequently caused a spread and intensification of conflict. The repression of forms of non-violent protest in some areas in the early years caused a radicalisation of a growing group of active Volunteers and an increasing reluctance among them to go to jail. The veto on Irish representation at the Peace Conference and the banning of the Dáil closed the avenues of political agitation and led to the official sanctioning of attacks on the Crown Forces by GHQ in January 1920. Open fighting then started in counties like Tipperary and Dublin where opposition had been strongest. The vacillating government policy of early 1920, when many active Volunteers were first arrested and then released, encouraged and radicalised the men even more. The introduction of the Restoration of Order in Ireland Act to quell the subsequent growth in violence led to a large increase in arrests throughout the country. As a result many Volunteers everywhere went on the run. Their fear of arrest was exacerbated by the brutal behaviour of some members of the Crown Forces. The Volunteers who had left home were then almost inevitably drawn into full-time involvement in violent conflict. The number of men involved in different places at each of the stages of this development varied enormously.

A clear development in the content and extent of radicalisation in the various areas has been exposed in the previous chapters. Between the Rising and the Truce, Volunteer activities developed slowly from open defiance of a fairly non-violent nature, via targeted attempts to force arms from the police, towards open attacks on the lives of many of the Crown Forces. This change had been completed to a varying degree in different areas and also took place at dissimilar speed among Volunteers within the same area. The effect of the differing relationships between Volunteers, the Crown Forces and the population in the selected counties is investigated next, exploring further the way in which some Volunteers became involved in killing, how this process took place and who were affected by it.

PART II: THEME 1

VOLUNTEERS AND THE AUTHORITIES

CHAPTER 5

Government Policy

In the description of the radicalisation of the Volunteers in the first part of this book we have seen that government policy and Crown Force violence played an important role. To understand the increasing use of violence the interaction between Volunteer activity, Crown Force reaction and government measures is further analysed. A number of writers have dealt with this previously. In one form or other, they have reiterated the development from public defiance to open conflict described before. Charles Townshend has provided a meticulous account of the changes in government policy. David Fitzpatrick, who made the first thorough assessment of the changing position of the police in Irish society between 1913 and 1921, has worded the repercussions of government policy within this development most poignantly: 'The Government's growing though spasmodic severity was largely responsible for transforming the Volunteers into a force capable of focusing indignation into systematic military resistance.' Peter Hart was the first to trace fully the interaction between government measures and radicalisation, confining himself to the activists in the most violent county of Ireland. Building on their work, this chapter takes a closer look at the way in which the development from public defiance to guerrilla fighting was affected by government policy.[1]

An important factor in the development of Volunteer activity was the changing position of the police in Irish society. The RIC had already been seriously weakened by the imminent introduction of Home Rule and the outbreak of the First World War. The impending transfer of power prevented adequate resources from being made available and the uncertain outlook caused many members to join the Army in 1914. It is argued here that between 1916 and 1920, a substantial part of the Irish population lost faith in these representatives of the British Government, who had already lost much of their authority. From respected members of society the RIC became widely regarded as a foreign force. At the same time, the IRA managed, by persuasion and intimidation, to become accepted as the defender

---

1   Quote, David Fitzpatrick (1977), 217, see also Chapter 1 & 6. Charles Townshend (1975), passim, and (1983), 334-7. Peter Hart (1992), Chapter 'The Dynamics of Violence', passim.

of the community. This meant that in some counties a polarisation could develop between the IRA as representative of the Irish people on one side, and the RIC as agents of an alien power on the other side. As a result, the two forces came to look upon each other as outright enemies. This change in perception was a crucial step in the development of bloodshed. The exclusion of the police from Irish life was partly caused by government policy which increasingly isolated the police physically from the community, and partly by active IRA strategy which stimulated a mental break between the police and the Irish population. The extent of this cleavage in each area became an important determining factor for the measure of violence that developed.[2]

RESPONSE TO THE RISING

In the period just after the Rising all organising activity was done in secret and most policemen had no direct dealings with the Volunteers. However, although initially intimidated by defeat, the internees quickly developed a non-cooperative attitude in which they discovered their power to disrupt the execution of British authority. They first realised this when they were given a questionnaire in which they were asked to list their activities at the time of the Rising:

> If few in the first two weeks knew Seamus Robinson everybody in Stafford Gaol knew the small, little man of steel with the russet stubble and the shy, retiring manner within days of the issue of the yellow form. Outside my cell door; Seamus was brought to meet Captain Allingham, the Governor, and introduced as 'this 'ere prisoner who says 'e will write nothing and sign nothing.' The Governor explained without heat or impatience be it recorded, that he cared not what was written as long as the form was signed. Seamus told him; quite courteously that he would sign no form. 'You cannot write then?' queried the Governor. 'I am reasonably well educated', said Seamus 'but I do not choose to write.' [...] This was a cypher [recte zephyr] compared to the tornado that roared down on the Gaol when Seamus refused later to sign a receipt for his internment order. [...] This was a matter of an incomplete file!

This non-cooperative attitude dismayed the wardens, who were unable to understand the prisoners' position. When the internees in Frongoch were told they were to be interned indefinitely: 'Someone near the middle of the

2   Changed position of the police in Ireland, David Fitzpatrick (1977), Chapter 1, passim.

Hall shouted – "Hip, hip" and a hurrah, spontaneous and full throated shook the hall. Burns [the soldier reading this message] stood a while silent and then "I give up", he said and went from the hall.'[3]

Outside the internment camps the majority of people initially felt that the insurgents had been foolish to attempt a rising. However, a wave of sympathy for the republicans swept the country after the executions and the severe punishment of many Volunteers. Outside Dublin and Wexford, people considered the arrests and convictions of local Volunteers, who had not engaged in any violent activity, as unjust. Admiration of those who had fought in the Rising developed, particularly among young men. Some began to show hostility towards the police when they felt safe to do so.

This attitude led to clashes with the police only months after the Rising. In the worst incidents unarmed soldiers were attacked by 'Sinn Féin mobs'. However, the police were not particularly worried by this change in attitude. They felt that the defeat of the rebels in 1916 had effectively eliminated the movement: 'After the Rising the police authorities appeared to assume that the executions, imprisonment and internment had finished Sinn Féin and the Irish Volunteers for ever, and began cutting down the number of detectives on political duty.' The lack of any serious disturbances following the release of most of the imprisoned Volunteers at Christmas confirmed this impression.[4]

DEALING WITH DEFIANCE

The reactivation of the Volunteer organisation and the nature of its operations in 1917 inevitably resulted in renewed confrontation. Initially, the illegal drilling exercises did not constitute a cause for conflict, as most were carried out indoors or in secret places. However, the increasingly defiant attitude forced the military to issue an order in July 1917 forbidding drilling, wearing of uniforms or carrying of weapons (including hurleys). Almost any overt act, such as singing nationalist songs and waving flags, could now be considered disorderly. Consequently, when widespread open drilling was started in the Southwest towards the end of 1917 more confrontation developed.[5]

Despite the ban, the authorities were uncertain about the appropriate response to these public displays. It was realised that ordinary civil prosecution would not prevent drilling. The police were reluctant to prosecute

---

3 Quote on 'forms', 'Description of Internment 1916', Sinnott Papers, Wexford Co. Library. Quote on 'cheering', 'Account of prison experience 1916', Sinnott Papers, Wexford Co. Library.
4 Quote, Broy, O'MN, P17b128.
5 Military order, Peter Hart (1992), Chapter 'The Dynamics of Violence', 12.

such minor misdemeanours, because they had no idea what to do with the large number of people involved, who could not all be imprisoned simultaneously. The military authorities explicitly refused to take any action. For the time being the government therefore declined to act, it was neither institutionally prepared nor politically willing to do so at this time.[6]

The lack of what the authorities termed 'men of importance' in the republican movement reduced its potential danger in the eyes of the government. In dealing with subversive organisations they were principally concerned with the stance taken by men of considerable social standing and political influence. This lack of alarm is evidenced in the police reports of this period which were littered with dismissive expressions: 'He is a man of good character but is not looked upon as being of much importance in the locality.' A meeting in Derry City, attended by 2,800 people and addressed by de Valéra was discarded as 'Not a representative gathering, and no persons of any importance were present.'[7]

Nevertheless, as a precautionary measure the police were ordered to keep a close eye on the parades and drilling exercises. Volunteers out on route marches or drilling in a village were often followed by constables, who would take the names of those involved but rarely made an arrest. The apparent insignificance of the men implicated in drilling was again demonstrated in their reports. The lists of participants were generously sprinkled with phrases such as: 'the most important', 'those identified' or 'remainder were young fellows [...] I did not know'.[8]

However, although relatively few people were arrested, symbols of overt defiance were suppressed. These included wearing a Volunteer uniform, waving a republican flag, carrying arms or making a public statement of sedition. This policy disturbed some Volunteers, who felt the authorities failed to take them seriously. One Volunteer whose home-made wooden gun was confiscated by the police felt insulted because they failed to arrest him. He was teased by other Volunteers, amused by the idea that he was considered less of a threat than a dummy gun.[9]

In dealing with the Volunteers the police relied on their traditional preponderance to keep the young men in line: 'There was always an RIC detailed to keep us under close observation. He would accompany us quite close on all occasions. Not a long ranged field glass business. Oh no, they must impress us that the law was watching every man.' However, the

6   Attitude to illegal displays, file marked: 'Cases not to be tried by court martial', PRO, WO35/122. See also CIs MRs 1917-1918.
7   Attitude towards 'Men of Importance', John Regan, 'Memoirs', 113, PRONI, D3160. Quote on 'good character', report on drilling in Donaskeigh, Co. Tipperary dated 9 December 1917, PRO, CO904/122. Quote on 'Derry', CI Derry MR February 1918.
8   Names taken from parades in Mayo, PRO, CO904/122/2-3.
9   Volunteer with the wooden gun, P.J. Kelly, 'One of the Men of the West'.

coherence of the organisation and the willingness to sacrifice themselves for the cause made the Volunteers less easily intimidated than ordinary boisterous youths. An almost friendly rivalry developed between the two forces in this period. This was most apparent during route marches when the Volunteers tried to shake off the often somewhat older constables by running long distances. Most Volunteers still considered the individual policeman a potential convert to the cause, and engaged in discussion with him.[10]

However, some Volunteers felt encouraged to step up their defiance of the law when they encountered what they considered to be a weak response to their drilling. In Dublin and in Derry police demanding an end to these exercises and the names of those involved were overpowered, relieved of their arms, tied up and left in a field. In 1918 this growing willingness to take on the police was most noticeable in Dublin City and in the provinces of Munster and Connacht, where public drilling was concentrated. Open defiance thus became more widespread in Dublin, Tipperary and Mayo than in Wexford or Derry.[11]

PROSECUTION OF ACTIVISTS

Large-scale prosecution being thought impracticable, the authorities thus attempted to maintain control by repressing the symbols of rebellion and arresting leading figures. Normally, this would be sufficient to keep popular support and involvement at a minimum. However, in the new circumstances such police action often led to increasing animosity. A conviction in court and a prison sentence came to be considered a measure of one's dedication to the cause and lost its deterrent effect. Court cases themselves became major propaganda events for the movement. Riots developed during these cases or during celebrations that followed bye-election successes. The violence used by the police to disperse the crowds in these protests did not subdue the young men. Aided by their organisation and inspired by the Rising, some responded in equal measure.[12]

The most serious offence in which Volunteers engaged involved attempts to seize arms from civilians or soldiers on leave. In many cases the police knew the culprits, but were unable to prosecute. Most people were unwilling to testify and jurors often failed to reach a verdict against obvi-

10 Quote, Michael Kilroy, 'The Awakening'. See also Jim O'Donnell, 'Recollections'.
11 In Dublin, Alfred Rutherford, O'MN, P17b122. In Derry, Lt. M. Sheerin, NLI, P913 A0153.
12 Clashes with the police: In Mayo, James Chambers, 'Statement'; Michael Kilroy, 'The Awakening'; Johnny Duffy, O'MN, P17b109; Ned Moane, 'Statement'. In Tipperary, Ned O'Reilly, O'MN, P17b126; Ned Prendergast, Interview.

ously guilty Volunteers, leaving the police extremely frustrated. As a result, those involved could only be prosecuted for trivial offences which had been witnessed by the police themselves. As early as 1917 some advanced Volunteers adopted radical nationalist ideology, and refused to recognise the court's right to try them. This approach soon became a general policy. However, as one of the magistrates put it: 'Unfortunately the Court recognises you.' Consequently, many were sentenced to short terms of imprisonment for offences which usually resulted in a caution.[13]

Although the refusal to recognise the court was official policy, many Volunteers continued to defend themselves. Few were really prepared to go to prison in the cause of Irish freedom, or financially able to do so. Others refused to recognise the court, but still reserved the right to interrogate the witnesses. The inconsistency of this position was pointed out by some judges, but at least one Volunteer was acquitted on basis of his questions. Nevertheless, many active Volunteers from all over Ireland were sent to prison where they met other radicals. For some of them this was a reunion having previously met in prison in 1916.[14]

Strong moral pressures were exerted on leading Volunteers to conform to the organisation's policy. Rory O'Connor, a member of GHQ, was convicted to a month in prison for refusing to pay a £10 fine. When he was released after his brother had paid the fine Rory was worried about the reaction of others in the movement. One of the wardens recalls his release:

> I gave him his outfit 'your fine is paid', I said. 'I'm not going out', he said: 'no one has authority to pay my fine, and how will I stand

13 Quote, James Chambers, 'Statement'. Attitude taken in court: In Dublin, Garry Houlihan, O'MN, P17b105. In Tipperary, Patrick Ryan, 'Statement'. In Mayo, James Chambers, 'Statement'; *Mayoman*, 13 September 1919. In Wexford, CI Wexford MR October 1918. In Derry, CI Derry MRs September-October 1918; *Derry People and Donegal News*, 22 May 1920. The refusal to recognise the court was apparently started by the Brennans from Clare, UCD AD, P7b184.

14 Volunteers asking questions in court, CI Mayo MR June 1918; CI Wexford MR December 1918; *People* (Wexford), 15 January & 5 February 1921; *Derry People and Donegal News*, 22 May 1920. A list of those arrested for political offences drawn up by Sinn Féin names 349 arrests in 1917 and 1,107 in 1918. In 1917, 38 per cent of those arrested came from Munster and 29 per cent from Dublin, while 12 per cent came from unknown places. In 1918, 41 per cent came from Munster, 17 per cent from Connacht, 12 per cent from Leinster and 11 per cent from Dublin, while the place of arrest of 2 per cent was unknown. Increases were particularly apparent in Mayo were arrests went up from 7 in 1917 to 81 in 1918, and Tipperary where arrests rose from 14 to 111. In Wexford and Derry small rises from 6 to 15 and from 2 to 7 were recorded, *Two Years of English Atrocities in Ireland* (n. d.), one copy, Gallagher Papers, TCD, 10050/626.

in the Sinn Féin organisation if they hear of it, I'm not going out.'
Take this money, and I put it in his pocket and we had to push him
outside of the gate. 'You can stand there if you like', we said.

Most activists were not deterred by their convictions. Strengthened by previous prison experience, they immediately went on hunger strike to demand
political prisoner status. After the death of Thomas Ashe in Mountjoy jail
while being force-fed in September 1917, this was granted in most prisons
and, to avoid other prisoners achieving martyrdom, many were released
before their time.[15]

From the moment the order to start public drilling had been given and
convictions had proved insufficient to subdue them, advanced Volunteers
set out to break the law deliberately. In a speech in February 1918 de
Valéra, the then president of the Volunteers and of Sinn Féin, mirrored his
policy on the success of the hunger strikers in prison: 'We will break them
[British laws] make it impossible for England to govern us as the prisoners
did in Mountjoy.' As early as January 1918 the Inspector General of the
RIC expressed his anxiety about this situation:

> The spirit of lawlessness and turbulence is daily becoming more
> embarrassing to the police, particularly in the West. It is, of course,
> nearly impossible to preserve order when there is no means of
> enforcing authority. In cases of organised illegality the lawbreaker is
> able to defeat the law by hunger-strike, and the constitutional meth-
> ods of prosecution and imprisonment no longer have any deterrent
> effect.

Nevertheless, he was still disinclined to counter the public displays of the
Volunteers. He reported that county inspectors opposed the dispersal of
massed parades of Volunteers as it might stir up more trouble than the local
police could cope with. For the moment he suggested merely imprisoning
the ringleaders.[16]

PROSCRIBING ALL REPUBLICAN ACTIVITIES

The government became increasingly worried by this increase in lawlessness, and to reactivate the deterrent effect of imprisonment the Temporary
Discharges or Cat-and-Mouse Act was put into force in March 1918. This
coincided with the Conscription Crisis which made enforcement difficult,

15 Quote, Garmon, O'MN, P17b110.
16 Quote from Eamon De Valéra, IG MR February 1918. Quote from Inspector
General, IG MR January 1918.

but when the crisis was over a tough line was adopted. Many men were arrested while leading parades, and in May several prominent Sinn Féiners and Volunteers were detained on a charge of collusion with Germany. On 3 July the Volunteers and other radical nationalist organisations, such as Sinn Féin, the Gaelic League and Cumann na mBan were declared dangerous associations, which meant that public meetings, assemblies and processions of these bodies were prohibited. The Inspector General reported that the firmer approach had been fruitful. He observed an improvement in the public's attitude towards the police in places where before they had been afraid to be seen speaking to them. However, the relations between the police and the movement now took a turn for the worst.[17]

During the Conscription Crisis many Catholic policemen sympathised with the nationalist opposition. This led to fears among the authorities that they would refuse to enforce conscription and resign. The movement's aspiration to persuade members of the police force to join the cause seemed to be within reach. However, hostility towards the introduction of conscription was often directed towards the police, who became widely boycotted by the people. In addition, the military preparations of the Volunteers led to numerous assaults on the police and to raids for arms and explosives. These attacks quickly diminished the level of sympathy for the cause among policemen, with the result that police and Volunteers became increasingly hostile to one another.[18]

The stronger government measures introduced after the Conscription Crisis ended forced the Volunteers to abandon open drilling. However, defiance was continued in other ways, and at times small moral victories were gained over the RIC which further improved the confidence and local standing of the extreme section of the Volunteers. As a result, the police found it increasingly difficult to get any information from the population regarding offences. The police gradually became used to an increased level of disrespect for the law, and although serious offences continued to be dealt with, many openly defiant acts were no longer prosecuted.[19]

As previously mentioned, attempts to obtain weapons were the cause of most political crimes, but at this stage virtually none of the Volunteers were prepared to kill in the course of doing so. Arms were obtained to resist the government in the event of a confrontation and to exert more political pressure. For most Volunteers public defiance was part of a policy to show both Britain and the wider world that Ireland was unwilling to accept British rule

17 Government measures, IG MRs March-July 1918.
18 Worries among the authorities, CI Mayo MR April 1918. During the crisis the Volunteers had called upon all DMP men to leave the force, Ernie Noonan, O'MN, P17b94. The first attack on a police barracks took place during the Conscription Crisis on 16 April 1918 in Gortalea, Co. Kerry.
19 Examples of unprosecuted expressions of republican sympathy, CI Mayo MR October 1918.

any longer. Central to this policy were the general elections of December 1918. It was hoped that a clear election victory would convince the major powers to give 'justice to Ireland' at the Peace Conference.

The government measures proved unable to deal with the increasingly daring actions of the more violent Volunteers. The prosecution of activists in 1918 had only increased the number of men radicalised by prison experience. Strengthened by their election success, they were unwilling to wait for the effects of an international campaign and began to take matters into their own hands. As a result, a string of serious assaults were committed by Volunteers in all parts of Ireland in the early months of 1919.

Although this sudden upsurge in violence unnerved the local police, the relationship between Volunteers and the police was still substantially unchanged in most districts. The majority of Volunteers, including many of the older officers, objected to the shooting of policemen and tried to control the hotheads. For the moment many of them were successful in curbing violence. The son of a local RIC Sergeant describes the hesitant attitude of local Volunteers in Tourmakeady, Co. Mayo:

> From the end of the war in 1918, there was a different feeling abroad. The younger men were not really hostile but were to some extent openly defiant, as though unsure how far they could go. They did not seem very clear as to what form this new attitude should take or as to where it would lead them. For the most part, they expressed themselves in more or less friendly discussions with my father about the day which was coming when he and his like would have to leave.

However, due to the independent nature of the local Volunteer units it was inevitable that in some places aggressive individuals took control at an early stage. In other units the moderates were later substituted by more radical men, forcing some of the former to drop out of the organisation altogether.[20]

DEALING WITH THE USE OF VIOLENCE

The introduction of 'special military areas' in clearly defined districts was the authorities' answer to the outrages of the early part of 1919. All public

20 Quote, J.R.W. Goulden, TCD, 7377/7/1. During the summer of 1919, many candidates for the Dublin Squad objected to the shooting of policemen and refused to join, Pat MacCrea, O'MN, P17b110; Frank Henderson, O'MN, P17b99; Jim Slattery, O'MN, P17b109. Volunteers dropping out after attacks resulted in the death of some RIC men, Paul Merrigan, Video made by 'Third Tipperary Brigade Old I.R.A. Commemoration Committee'; John Madden, O'MN, P17b113.

meetings, including fairs and markets, were forbidden in the districts concerned, and in areas such as south Tipperary with a market-orientated economy this hurt the people considerably. Although it minimised rebellious expressions, it further antagonised both Volunteers and the population.

In response the radical leadership of the Volunteers in south Tipperary issued a counter-proclamation declaring the South Riding a military area according to Volunteer rule. In this proclamation the police were described as 'hirelings, assassins and traitorous spies', responsible for the deportation and sentencing of thousands of Irish men. They were warned that every policeman in the area, every person on England's payroll (magistrates, jurors, etc.) 'who helps England to rule this county', and any civilian who gives information to the police or soldiery will be deemed to have forfeited his life. It added that the more notorious police would be dealt with first. Although this extreme viewpoint was not acted upon or sanctioned by GHQ, it reflected a line of thought that would become increasingly prevalent.[21]

The first targets of Volunteers who were inclined to use violence were those authorities who made themselves conspicuous by their activity against the Volunteers. The Resident Magistrate in Westport, presumably shot by Volunteers who had been sentenced by him, was an early example of this in Mayo. In Thurles, Co. Tipperary the local District Inspector of the RIC was shot at close range in a crowd on 23 June 1919. The reasons for this shooting were described by a local curate: 'He had made himself very active against Sinn Féin ever since the escape of Leahy and did not allow a week to pass without sending soldiers to stop meetings and search houses. In that way he became very unpopular and the majority of the people had turned against him.' This singling out of active opponents, initially a form of self-protection or revenge, became a general policy in 1920 to discourage the police from pursuing the Volunteers. Everywhere active policemen were warned, and in some places they were compelled to take an oath promising to leave the force. When this proved insufficient to stop their activities some were shot.[22]

21 The South Riding of Tipperary was declared a Special Military Area from January to 14 June 1919. Westport in Mayo suffered the same faith between April and 1 June 1919. Proclamation against RIC in Tipperary dated February 1919, Seamus Robinson, 'Statement', NLI, ms. 21,265.
22 Quote, Fr Michael Maher, Diary 1919, St Patrick's College Thurles. Examples of policemen forced to take an oath are found throughout the period. One of the first in a provincial area, D. Ryan (1945), 137. See also Sean Lynch, MA, Ao152. Attempts to shoot the most active policemen took place in several places, Broy, O'MN, P17b128; Seamus Fox, O'MN, P17b106. The reverse side of this policy meant that some actions were called off because a 'good' policeman might be hurt, Charlie Dalton, O'MN, P17b122.

The evolution of this policy is most apparent in Dublin. The experiences of the leading republicans there contained the seeds of the open fighting that developed between the police and the Volunteers at the end of 1920. The large concentration of wanted men in GHQ, its various departments, the branches of Sinn Féin and the Dáil, were confronted by the G-Division of the Dublin police, which consisted of a few plainclothes detectives concerned with political crime. They were well-acquainted with most of the leading IRA-officials, many of whom had been among the frequently arrested men in the period of defiance between 1916 and 1918. When the movement went underground it became imperative to prevent further arrests.

To ensure this, the detectives who were tracking down the Volunteer leaders had to be eliminated. The Squad was set up in August 1919 to deal with them. Initially they were to kidnap these detectives and warn them to stay clear of the Volunteers. However, only one of the five groups of Volunteers who were sent out to find G-men was successful. They notified the detective that if he did not give up his political work he would be shot. A few others were challenged later but most of them were unimpressed; one just laughed it off. After the warnings had thus failed to bring the desired result, attempts to execute the most committed detectives were made.[23]

Although only a few were actually shot prior to Bloody Sunday in November 1920, these executions intimidated the G-Division sufficiently to allow most IRA leaders to function in relative safety. Other victims of the Squad in this period included a spy, a financial investigator, Alan Bell, who tried to uncover money deposits of the movement, two policemen from Tipperary who had come to Dublin to look for wanted men from that county, and District Inspector Redmond who had taken over the Dublin police after the failed assassination attempt on the Lord Lieutenant, Lord French in December 1919.[24]

A similar development took place in some provincial districts. In these places the few Volunteers who engaged in illegal operations went on the run during 1919. The most serious risk they ran was recognition by RIC men who were willing to take them on. This applied particularly to the Volunteers who had been involved in the Soloheadbeg ambush in Tipperary. Although many policemen and soldiers turned a blind eye rather than risk being shot, some were extremely vigilant. To minimise the danger of capture and to discourage other policemen, the Volunteers started to

---

23 Targets of the Squad, Sean Smith, O'MN, P17b122; Patrick O'Daly, 'Statement', NLI, P4548; Frank Henderson, O'MN, P17b99; Broy, O'MN, P17b128; George White, O'MNs, P17b99, and P17b105.

24 Ibid.

concentrate on these active policemen. As in Dublin, this started with a warning, but some active law enforcers were also shot during 1919.[25]

POLICE BOYCOTT AND BARRACKS ATTACKS

The mostly spontaneous boycotts of the RIC which had started during the Conscription Crisis in areas where the IRA was strong were an important part of the movement's efforts to induce policemen to leave the force and support the cause of 'all Irishmen'. In April 1919 Sinn Féin made an attempt to coordinate this social ostracisation, and guidelines were issued: 'Police should be treated as persons, who having been adjudged guilty of treason to their country, are regarded as unworthy to enjoy any of the privileges or comforts which arise from cordial relations with the public.' The boycott and the violence against policemen antagonised those remaining in the force, and the 'friendly' rivalry of 1917 turned into open antipathy. The Volunteers, as well as a considerable section of the population, refused to talk to or associate in any way with the police.[26]

As early as January 1919, the Inspector General reported that: 'There was no improvement in the attitude of the people towards the R.I.C. who, in the more disaffected Counties, are treated with bitter hostility and are boycotted in various ways.' This boycott took several forms. In April 1919 Cumann na mBan published a leaflet forbidding members to share a church pew with a policeman. In the same month the police reported that, although at most meetings held by the movement the language was not violent, the police were always attacked. Despite the success of the boycott instituted in Tipperary in February, few attempts to harm the police or military were made during 1919. The call for a police boycott was repeated in some areas in August, when proclamations calling for a police boycott were put up in several counties. In places like Derry, most Sinn Féiners were then still reported to speak 'in a friendly way' to the police.[27]

In many communities the boycott isolated the police. As a result of the boycott, and of some cases in which activists had attacked policemen with objects ranging from stones, a flagpole to a walking stick, many policemen started to treat the entire population as hostile. Those who had been attacked tried to get retribution by claiming damages in court. If they were

25 Despite the high profile of Volunteers in Co. Cork, the first such attempt there did not take place until December 1919, Peter Hart (1992), Chapter 'The Dynamics of Violence', 39-40.

26 Quote, David Fitzpatrick (1977), 10.

27 Quote, IG MR January 1919. Policy of Cumann na mBan and tone of language at meetings, IG MR April 1919. The boycott notices, IG MR August 1919; CI South Tipperary MR August 1919. Friendly relations in Derry, 'Intelligence Notes 1919', PRO, CO903/19.

successful, the damages were then levied on the local electoral divisions. These attempt to make the entire population, in particular ratepayers, suffer for the damage done to them further polarised relations between the police and the community. This feeling was exacerbated by the inability of the police to distinguish between the IRA and civilians when open fighting developed in 1920.[28]

In the meantime relations between the Volunteers and the RIC deteriorated further. This expressed itself mainly in minor cases of intimidation of policemen, such as denying them access to a building, challenging or threatening them. During the struggle for dominance in the community some Volunteers became increasingly willing to use firearms. The failure of the case made for Ireland at the Peace Conference during 1919 strengthened the influence of the more radical Volunteers, resulting in attacks on police patrols and barracks, mainly in the Southwest. Shocked by several Volunteer successes, the authorities began to evacuate most of the more isolated police posts at the end of 1919, thus augmenting the force elsewhere for defensive purposes and enabling patrols to be strengthened.[29]

In areas where no violence had been directed at barracks many of the outlying stations were closed as a precautionary measure, to the surprise of both the local population and the police. The men were stationed in nearby barracks, but continued to patrol their beat. Showing the lack of perceived danger in some areas, the sergeant evacuated from Tourmakeady, Co. Mayo, continued to visit the village daily. Sometimes he carried his revolver, but often he left it in the barracks as it was heavy: 'He was completely confident that no local would ever interfere with him. Often they met him on the road and they used to remark: "Are you not afraid we would shoot you some night going home?" He always turned it aside as a joke and still called them all by their first names.' The evacuation nevertheless removed the police from community life and left many country areas open to the Volunteers during the evenings and the night, giving them a free hand to show their power and enforce allegiance to the Dáil.[30]

In the entire island a total of about 1,400 constabulary posts were in existence in 1914. Most of them were rural, holding only a sergeant or acting sergeant, often with his family and three or four constables who

---

28 Police claiming damages: In Mayo, *Mayoman*, 28 June 1919. In Tipperary, P.C. Power (1989), 209.

29 Evacuation of outlying posts, IG MR November 1919. According to the 'Intelligence Notes 1919', only twenty RIC stations were discontinued in that year, PRO, CO903/19.

30 Quote, J.R.W. Goulden, TCD, 3491/10.

were forbidden to marry. Most of these barracks were rented accommoda-
tions, not designed for defence, spaciousness or comfort. The son of the
RIC sergeant in Tourmakeady, described the safety precautions of such a
local barrack in 1919: 'It had at that time no defence except the bars common to all R.I.C. stations on the downstairs windows.' As a result of poor
defence works at least 447 barracks were abandoned before the summer of
1920. In Mayo almost half of the sixty-three police posts were evacuated.[31]

Confronted with such pressures many members of the RIC took early
retirement or resigned from the force, particularly in the summer of 1920.
Some were afraid; others began to see fewer prospects in the police force;
more left because of a radical conviction. The RIC in most counties now
had trouble filling the ranks as recruits were hard to find. Until January
1920 this was largely a result of the poor pay, but after a substantial
increase had improved the attractions of a career in policing, the IRA made
a point of discouraging young men from joining the police force. In
February 1920 houses of RIC recruits were visited and they were warned
not to join. The official IRA policy was described by the Chief of Staff,
Richard Mulcahy, in May 1920: 'They are to be made unfit for carrying
out the duties of the R.I.C..'[32]

Few IRA units took this approach to heart as many recruits were left
alone and others were just forced to take the oath of allegiance to the
Republic. However, few youngsters were willing to risk their life and the
hostility of the IRA and the population by joining the police. Consequently, insufficient men enlisted to meet demands. This meant that
the police could only be reinforced in more troubled counties. In Tipperary, a batch of recruits was welcomed in July 1919, while in Mayo the
County Inspector reported in November 1920 that there were still sixty-
seven vacancies. Besides a lack of manpower the police were hampered by
a shortage of transport vehicles. In November 1920 the entire police force
in Mayo had to work with two lorries and one Crossley tender, while two

31 Quote on 'defences', J.R.W. Goulden, 'Statement', TCD, 7377/7/1. See also
   TCD, 7381. For several photos of such barracks, TCD, 7380. Numbers of
   abandoned barracks, Charles Townshend (1975), Appendix V. In Mayo, CI
   Mayo MRs 1920.
32 As a result of the uncertain future of the police force a large deficiency in
   con-stables had developed during the War. In 1917, 1,400 vacancies out of an
   established strength of 10,715 were not filled, Charles Townshend (1975), 5.
   Recruitment and resignations in 1920-21, Charles Townshend (1975),
   Appendices I-III; David Fitzpatrick (1977), 37-42. Quote, Letter to acting
   Brigade Commandant Mid Clare Brigade, NLI, P911. Visits to RIC recruits,
   IG MR February 1920; Sean Lynch, MA, A0152.

others were in repair. The lack of transport seriously reduced the efficiency of the police in combating the IRA throughout the country.[33]

POLICE AND COMMUNITY

The position of the police in the community was significantly changed by these developments. For almost a century they had functioned as an integral part of Irish society. Their position as representatives of the government had given them a measure of standing sufficient to deal with most dissatisfaction. However, the political climate in the early part of the second decade, dominated by the imminent introduction of Home Rule for Ireland, had made their position unstable. Furthermore, the aspirations of radical nationalists, which became widely accepted after the 1916 Rising, challenged their source of authority.[34]

The republicans felt they represented all Irishmen, including the police, and initially called upon them to resign and join the struggle for independence. Some sympathy for the ideal of total independence was indeed present in the police force, which was particularly apparent during the Conscription Crisis. Nonetheless, the attacks on individual policemen and barracks, resulting from the urgent need for arms, seriously diminished this sympathy. The relationship became fully antagonistic when some radical nationalists started to use intimidation and violence to induce policemen to leave the constabulary or alternatively to cease operations against them.

The type of pressure exerted on the police can be seen as part of a policy to force unwilling members of the community to accept a new direction. The threats, the tying up and the taking of oaths under duress fit into this pattern. Shunning, the extreme non-violent punishment for those within a community who fail to adhere to its wishes, was started in the police boycott. Singling out those who were most overt in their opposition was an ultimate attempt to set examples. All these efforts were unsuccessful in winning over members of the police as they were caught between the mutually exclusive demands of the Volunteers and their superiors.

The large-scale evacuation of police barracks starting at the end of 1919 marked the beginning of a new phase. Concentrated in larger groups in

---

33 Lack of policemen and reinforcements, CI South Tipperary MR July 1919; CI Mayo MRs November-December 1920. The lack of transport and relief, CI Mayo MRs November-December 1920; CI South Tipperary November 1920; 'History of the 5th Division in Ireland, November 1919-March 1922', 89, IWM, 72/82/2. In the summer of 1920, the military who were better equipped with motor transport had 193 vehicles, but assessed they needed roughly double that, Charles Townshend (1975), Appendix VI.

34 A thorough treatment of the police's position in Irish society, David Fitzpatrick (1977), 1-15.

fewer barracks, contact between the police and civilians was reduced, particularly in rural areas. At the same time individual policemen became less vulnerable to the type of pressures exerted on them. Ultimately this physical separation from the community made more extreme measures against the police necessary to ensure restraint on their part, and more justifiable because policemen came to be regarded as a foreign force.

BRINGING IN THE MILITARY

The closure of outlying barracks resulted in a further decrease in the police's influence on local communities. Their inability to protect the population from intimidation by the Volunteers lost them much support. As a result, the observation and prosecution of Volunteer activity became increasingly difficult even in areas where the Volunteers had been inactive. In November 1919 the Inspector General of the RIC reported to the government: 'The police were confronted with almost insuperable difficulties in their efforts to obtain evidence for prosecution in cases of political crime owing to the state of terror organised by the republican party.' On the further spread of violence in 1919 the authorities had introduced more restrictions. The Dáil was declared a dangerous association on 10 September, and on 25 November the Volunteers, Sinn Féin, the Gaelic League and Cumann na mBan were all suppressed. In addition the population was inconvenienced further by the introduction of permits for driving a motorcar. This was considered necessary as some had been used in attacks on the Crown Forces.[35]

In order to deal with increasing attacks on the police and the inability to prosecute offenders, the government decided to bring in the military and to extend their powers to search houses and intern suspects. In January 1920 permission was granted to arrest and deport all known leaders of the Volunteers without trial. Furthermore, a list was prepared of suspects to be arrested if an outrage occurred. The seriousness of the outrage would determine the number of arrests. Those with sufficient evidence against them should be detained for trial by court martial and the others would be deported. This was intended to induce local men of influence to use their powers to stop Volunteers from acting.[36]

To alleviate the problems of deficient police the RIC was reinforced with recruits from England. Further measures were taken in the following

35 Quote, IG MR November 1919.
36 Policy changes and their effects, 'History of the 5th Division in Ireland, November 1919-March 1922', Diary, 56 & Volume I: Operations, IWM, 72/82/2; John Regan, 'Memoirs', 149, PRONI, D3160.

months, including the founding of the infamous paramilitary auxiliary police units, the Auxiliaries and the Black & Tans. In May ambush parties of military were formed to intercept suspicious persons moving around at night. These measures resulted in an increased number of raids and arrests in the early months of 1920. Up to 14 April 1920, 27 IRA brigade commanders, 13 brigade staff, 16 battalion commanders, 116 battalion staff and 145 other prominent republicans were reportedly arrested. These arrests were facilitated by the discovery of papers which revealed the names of many IRA officers.[37]

The Volunteers reacted to this with a more vigorous attempt to isolate the police socially. Individuals friendly to the police were sent threatening letters urging them to discontinue their association. The arrests and subsequent maltreatment of prisoners by the Crown Forces heightened tension, and violence began to escalate. Attitudes hardened on both sides due to several deaths resulting from sporadic attacks on police patrols and barracks. The most active members of the Crown Forces countered with threats to local leaders and sympathisers of Sinn Féin. In some cases police and Volunteers began to act on these threats and people were assassinated. The killing of policemen and soldiers often caused a violent reaction among their comrades. In extreme cases they broke out of their barracks and went on rampages, attacking local Sinn Féin sympathisers and their property. The police recruits from England were generally seen as being particularly prominent in this. The raiding, the arrests and the increased violence on both sides sharpened the conflict.[38]

The new government approach did not reduce IRA activity. The official sanctioning of open attacks on the Crown Forces by the IRA Executive in January actually led to a large increase in casualties in 1920. At Easter the

37 Figures, 'History of the 5th Division in Ireland, November 1919-March 1922', Diary, 56 & Volume I Operations, IWM, 72/82/2; Raids January-March 1920, HQ Dublin District, WO35/70. The organisation of military ambush parties, NLI, P918 A0413. Recruitment for the RIC was increasingly successful during 1920. It went up from 206 in January to 1,428 in October. Initially most were Irish born, but after May non-Irish became the majority, reaching more than 90 per cent of recruits in August. However, between a third and half of recruits dropped out, Charles Townshend (1975), 46, 55-6, 102 & Appendix I. A very high percentage of these recruits were ex-servicemen, this went up from 63 per cent in January 1920 to 87 per cent in June 1921, and they also increasingly were working class and Protestant, David Fitzpatrick (1977), 20-5.

38 Examples of threatening letters, TCD, 7377/5/4; Fr Michael Maher, Diary 25 January 1920, St Patrick's College Thurles; Paul Mulcahy, 'Statement'; NLI, ms. 8,620; 'Intelligence Notes 1919' for Tipperary South Riding, PRO, CO903-/19; *People* (Wexford), 3 April 1920; Cecilia Saunders, Diary 9 December 1920, TCD, 10055.

wholesale burning of evacuated barracks and destruction of custom and excise records further unnerved the authorities. In view of the escalating violence the government was forced to reappraise its policies again. On 3 May 1920 arrest on suspicion alone was suspended and most interned Volunteers were released. This was also a result of public pressure following a renewed hunger strike campaign by the prisoners.[39]

However, the extreme element of the Volunteers and the Crown Forces was not ready for conciliation at this point, and confrontation became even more widespread during the summer. In the most affected areas barracks attacks became a regular occurrence. The small acts of defiance which had been the main expression of Volunteer work before were now used to draw the police out of their barracks to ambush them. The deliberate policy to take on the worst opponents slowly developed into indiscriminate attempts to hurt all Crown Forces. An early example of this is witnessed in Tipperary and Derry City, where the placing of barbed wire at eye level across roads was used to catch police and military out on nightly raids.[40]

An IRA Operational Memo dated 19 July 1920 shows their general policy as it had developed during the spring. While authorising attacks on all military and police formations, it still emphasised disarmament as the IRA's main objective. The loss of life on either side was to be avoided. Yet once an operation had begun the enemy had to be 'overcome with vigour.' Although most Volunteers agreed with this approach, some leading members of the South Tipperary Brigade were more ruthless. A group of active Volunteers in the eastern half of the brigade ambushed a patrol of police and Black & Tans two weeks before this memo. After a brisk fight in which two policemen were killed the patrol was successfully overcome. Tom Donovan, the leader of the Volunteers, wanted to shoot the captured Black & Tans, but the others prevented that by stressing that if he did so no one would ever surrender again.[41]

OSTRACISING THE POLICE

The boycott of the police in 1919 was primarily confined to Volunteers and their sympathisers. In 1920 the Dáil tried to involve the entire population

39 Policy changes of British Government, 'Record of the Rebellion in Ireland in 1920-21 and the part played by the Army in dealing with it', Diary & 56, IWM, 72/82/2; Charles Townshend (1975), 58-9.
40 The use of barbed wire: In Derry, *Derry People and Donegal News*, 24 May 1920; Liam Brady, *Derry Journal*, 20 May 1953. In Tipperary, Ned O'Reilly, O'MN, P17b126; Intelligence summary week ending 29 May 1921, WO35-/71/6, 91. In Limerick, NLI, ms. 17,880, and P918 S356.
41 Operational Memo no.2, dated 19 July 1920, O'MN, P17b127. The ambush of policemen with Tom Donovan, Paul Mulcahy, 'Statement'.

when it called for an official boycott of all policemen. This was intended not only to induce policemen to leave the force, but also to ensure that the population would turn to the republican alternative as part of the movement's attempt to replace the British administration. The Volunteers were instructed to enforce the boycott. A general order was issued by GHQ on 4 June, forbidding all contact between Volunteers and the RIC and directing them to stimulate and support the boycott by the public as ordered by the Dáil: 'Those persons who associate with the RIC shall be subjected to the same boycott, and the fact of their association with and toleration of this infamous force shall be kept public in every way possible.'[42]

The initial effect of the official declaration was strong. Contact with the police was avoided by nationalists throughout the country. Few dared to be seen talking to the constabulary, and in shops and pubs service was refused. In many areas this was so successful that the police were forced to commandeer goods to survive. Usually they took the goods or a drink sometimes at gun point and paid for it themselves. This state of affairs satisfied GHQ. In answer to a query on what to do in such cases, the Adjutant General answered: 'You must at present do no more. When we have driven them to this position our boycott is a success.'[43]

The initial success of the boycott spills over in the August report of the Inspector General of the RIC, in which he paints a bleak picture of police control in the country. Many areas were without police, most people do not complain to the police, the resignations from the force had become numerous and the police had to work under poor conditions:

> Boycotted, ostracised, forced to commandeer their food, crowded in many instances into cramped quarters without proper light or air, every man's hand against them, in danger of their lives and subjected to the appeals of their parents and their families to induce them to leave the force and so put an end to the danger and annoyance to which continued service exposes them all.[44]

42 General Orders New Series no.6, dated 4 June 1920, NLI, ms. 739.

43 Quote, Letter from Adjutant General to Brigade Adjutant Leitrim, dated 18 June 1920, NLI, P911. Reports of RIC men paying market prices for goods they had commandeered, *Mayoman*, 18 September 1920; Ned Colfer, Interview; Jack Gardiner, Interview.

44 Quote, IG MR August 1920. Despite all efforts, RIC strength reached a low-point in September 1920 when 9,913 members remained. A strong influx of British recruits then started, further reinforced by the introduction of the Auxiliaries the first of whom arrived in the second week of that month. By January 1921, there were 12,755 RIC men including Black & Tans and 1,227 Auxiliaries. At the end of June 1921, there were 14,212 RIC and 1,526 Auxiliaries, Charles Townshend (1975), Appendix III.

Families of RIC members were affected by the boycott. Even the children of retired policemen were shunned, teased, called names and on occasion had stones thrown at them. The County Inspector of Limerick, who was a Catholic, recalls how many relatives of RIC personnel were threatened with outrage if the men concerned did not resign. In other areas police relatives were not directly attacked, but people refused to sell them fresh milk and they felt uncomfortable: 'There was always a sort of undercurrent to be felt, but no one was unpleasant, though we were frequently asked if we were going away soon. I think the local people did not wish us to be put on the road and just wished to know that we were going.' The IRA was well aware of the power of pressurising the family of RIC members. In one of their weekly memos they stressed that although a boycott of the family was unnecessary they must be made to bear their shame, thus hoping to force more resignations. Supplying policemen's families was permitted, but traders were ordered to 'Keep such a check on the supply in such cases, as will guard against such supplies being used by the police force generally.'[45]

Although these instructions led to a peak in the number of resignations, it was not high. Policemen never served in their native counties, and only sergeants and higher officers could marry and have their immediate family living with them. As a result relatives of policemen were not always recognised by local Volunteers. The mother and sister of the Limerick County Inspector were approached by Volunteers collecting for their Arms Fund. The Volunteers were courteous and his family was hesitant to refuse them:

> Two men arrived at our house one day and my sister went to the door to see what they wanted. They informed her that they were collecting for the IRA and requested a subscription. She at once said to them 'Do you expect me to give money to help you shoot my brother. I will do nothing of the kind.' They apologised for their request in the circumstances and then asked her would she give anything towards the widows and orphans. She wanted to know how she would be sure that anything she gave would go to that object. They gave her their promise. [...] She gave them five shillings. They thanked her politely.[46]

---

45 Quote, J.R.W. Goulden, 'Statement', TCD, 7377/7/1. Experience of police-men's relatives, Sean Clancy, Interview; J.R.W. Goulden, TCD, 3491/10. Weekly memo and orders on implementation, Boycott of RIC in West Donegal, and Weekly Memorandum No.5, NLI, ms. 739; NLI, P916 A0495; UCD AD, P7A19/170.

46 Resignation figures of RIC reached a peak during the summer of 1920, but never exceeded 54 per week, David Fitzpatrick (1977), 37; Charles Townshend (1975), 92. Stationing of RIC outside the county of origin, PRONI, D2022/1/33. Quote, John Regan, 'Memoirs', 161, PRONI, D3160.

Although the boycott was observed by most Volunteers, they were often unable to enforce adherence by non-members. In places where the IRA was only a marginal organisation the boycott never fully materialised. A RIC man who resigned from the force in Tipperary late in 1920 describes having been boycotted there. After his resignation, he went back to his native village in east Mayo: 'There was no boycott of the R.I.C. here. The Tans walked out with the best looking girls from the village of Kiltimagh.' In other places, the boycott had to be implemented by force:

> Most of the intimidation in New Ross & Enniscorthy District & to a lesser extent in Gorey is intended to prevent people from holding intercourse with the police & I always regard this as a preliminary step towards stirring up trouble. Until this month the county was free from this, now no conveyances can be hired & in some places the police have to commandeer milk etc.

Despite the initial successes, it soon became apparent that the Volunteers were unable to sustain a sufficient level of intimidation to prevent people from trading with the police altogether. In rural towns and large villages with a strong police presence, the boycott quickly petered out, and all Volunteers could do was to avoid the police as much as possible. In shops and pubs the RIC were ignored and refused service by those closely associated with the movement, but the Volunteers were unable to stop others from dealing with them.[47]

Only in rural areas with a particularly strong or well integrated Volunteer organisation could the boycott be fully enforced, and could the break between police and community, which had started with the evacuation of outlying barracks, be completed. These communities now looked on the Crown Forces as messengers of trouble, while the Crown Forces often considered all civilians to be hostile. The ostracisation of the police had turned them into outsiders, and potential targets.

EXTREME MEASURES

The growing violence and the success of the Dáil in establishing an alternative republican government during the summer of 1920 showed the authorities the failure of their policy of reconciliation. Under pressure from the

---

47 Quote from RIC man returning to East Mayo, Tom Carney, O'MN, P17b109. The haphazard implementation of the boycott in Mayo, Tom Maguire, Interview; *Mayoman*, 24 July & 18 September 1920. Quote on intimidation, CI Wexford MR June 1920. Experience of Volunteers in Wexford, John Quinn, Interview; Ned Colfer, Interview.

Crown Forces it was decided that a renewed onslaught on the republican movement was necessary. To facilitate this the Restoration of Order in Ireland Act was introduced in August. Under this act men and women could be interned indefinitely without charge and court martial was introduced, side-stepping the need for civil courts which were often unable to convict. As a result, the number of sentences by court martial rose tenfold after August.[48]

In addition to the introduction of the Restoration of Order Act, several other measures were contemplated and introduced, increasing the militarisation of the conflict. One of the first of these was an order dated 8 August 1920 to have all weapons still in the possession of civilians confiscated by the police. The authorities tried to do this secretly, using the system of arms permits they had introduced in October 1918. However, the Volunteers discovered their plans when an internal police dispatch containing this order was intercepted. A race started between police and Volunteers to capture all remaining arms, in which thousands of raids were carried out.[49]

To deal with the attacks on police barracks, which had intensified during the summer, a further concentration of the Crown Forces was ordered. In June, local police and military detachments in Cork had already been instructed to move in with each other. On 17 September the government ordered that in future police barracks had to contain a minimum of twenty men and were to be placed in areas without a military presence. This order was, however, never fully implemented as it involved a dangerous reorganisation of the force which would have meant an additional loss of control over the civilian population.[50]

The destruction of more than a third of all police posts was, of course, a serious worry to the government, but the ability of the IRA to capture occupied barracks was strongly overestimated. Its successes had largely relied on poor barracks defence, and Volunteers capable of overcoming even these were heavily concentrated in the Southwest. Of the 533 barracks destroyed in 1920, only twenty-three had been in use. Systematic attempts to reinforce the defence of existing barracks were started in November 1920, when the Board of Works was ordered to put up protection for police barracks in the disturbed areas. It was realised that this had already

48 Introduction of the Restoration of Order in Ireland Act, 'History of the 5th Division in Ireland, November 1919-March 1922', Diary August 1920, IWM, 72/82/2. Numbers of court martials and subsequent convictions, Charles Townshend (1975), Appendix X.

49 Government measures, 'History of the 5th Division in Ireland November 1919-March 1922', 59 + 63, IWM, 72/82/2. Introduction of a permit for keeping a weapon dated 9 October 1918, IG MR September 1918. Interception of despatch by Volunteers, CI Wexford MR August 1920.

50 June order to police and military to move in together, NLI, P918 A0413.

been done in most cases without the aid of the Board of Works. The extent of these fortifications is described for the barrack in Ballinrobe, Co. Mayo:

> All the windows were fitted with steel shutters. These were inside the glass, unlike the ones I have seen in some drawings. They were kept in place with iron bars fitted into cuts in the wall. They did not cover the whole window but the top was protected by a net wire frame on the outside. This was to keep out grenades and it could be lowered from inside to permit of the defenders throwing them out. The party walls with the adjoining houses were bored to the plaster in those houses so that a hole could be made in a moment if those houses were being used to attack the barracks. Floor boards were also sawn in the upper rooms so that hand grenades could be dropped into the lower rooms if they were captured.

As a result of the further concentration and the protection of the remaining barracks, only two occupied police posts were lost in 1921.[51]

During 1920 the military became more involved in police work and the police force became increasingly militarised. The Black & Tans had reinforced the RIC, while the Auxiliaries, a well-paid elite police force consisting of ex-military officers with a separate command structure, were to deal with the IRA directly. Furthermore, the Specials were introduced in the North, to curb the IRA in the six counties which were to be separated from the South in 1921. Despite misgivings expressed inside and outside the RIC, this new force was announced in October. The County Inspector for Derry had stated his fear that trouble would develop between the largely Protestant Specials and Catholics in the RIC and beyond. Nevertheless, recruiting for the new force commenced, and the first Specials were appointed in Belfast and Co. Tyrone in the second week of November.[52]

Three classes were introduced, of which the A class were full-time temporary constables intended to fill vacancies in the RIC. They were selected by the Special Constable organisation. For the B and C classes all adult

---

51 Quote, J.R.W. Goulden, TCD, 7377/7/1. Total number of destroyed barracks, Charles Townshend (1975), Appendix V; *People* (Wexford), 2 April 1921. Protection of Police barracks by Board of Works, PRONI, FIN 18/1/152; CI Mayo MR December 1920.

52 Militarisation of the police force and the involvement of the military in police duties, David Fitzpatrick (1977), 17-19. Contemplating introduction Specials and apprehensions, 'Sturgis Diary', 44, PRO, PRO30/59/1; CI Derry MR November 1920; Letter to the editor by J. R. White, 2 November 1920. The IRA reacted to this with a warning that any Catholic who joined the new Special Constabulary in the North would be seen and dealt with as traitors, Rev. T. H. Mullin (1986), 150.

men were invited to apply and did so on a large scale. The part-time B-Specials were deployed in counteracting the IRA, while the C-Specials constituted a reserve force. In the last week of 1920, all six counties had appointed some A-Specials. Derry was the last to make any appointments, possibly due to its County Inspector's reservations. By December 1920 Tyrone had already taken on 2,273 B-Specials, while Derry had only six A-Specials and no B-men. The B-Specials were soon to become notorious for their harsh treatment of the Catholic population in Northern Ireland.[53]

The events of Bloody Sunday, 21 November 1920, in which twelve military officers and intelligence men were shot in Dublin, and the subsequent ambush at Kilmichael, Co. Cork, 28 November, in which eighteen Auxiliaries were killed, made the government decide to implement the full force of the powers now available under the Restoration of Order Act. On 22 November, orders were given to intern all known officers of the IRA and other suspected men. In the following week, eighty-seven arrests took place in Dublin alone and 500 in the country as a whole. To facilitate this policy an organised system of raids was instituted, resulting in a distinct increase in the number of arrests in the months to follow.[54]

The IRA everywhere felt the effect of this renewed vigour. 'In November, the military became very active, raiding day and night in the area. Most of the officers had to go on the run permanently.' The Crown Forces were aided in their raids by discovering papers with the 'Order of Battle' of the IRA, containing the names and addresses of most IRA brigade and battalion officers. The arresting policy was indiscriminately implemented, as had been the case with the evacuation of police barracks at the end of 1919. Even in areas where the IRA had not engaged in any serious operations many were detained. As a result all IRA officers, including many inactive ones, were ordered to leave their homes and go on the run.[55]

General Macready, the Commander in Chief of the Crown Forces, had been dissatisfied with the powers introduced under the new act in August. In September he had asked the government to introduce martial

---

53 Returns for Special Constables, PRONI, FIN 18/1/11; FIN 18/1/123; FIN 18/1/157 & FIN 19/1/13. See also Bryan A. Follis (1995), 14-16.

54 The British acknowledged that on Bloody Sunday 10 of their officers, 2 Auxiliaries and 2 civilians were killed, 5 or 6 other men were wounded including one civilian. As a result, they ordered that as far as possible military officers 'living out' were to come inside the barracks, 'Sturgis Diary', 82-5, PRO, PRO30/59/2.

55 Quote, P.J. Kelly, 'One of the Men of the West'. See also Operation Summary from 1 December 1920, PRO, WO35/90; 'History of the 5th Division in Ireland November 1919-March 1922', 56 & Diary, IWM, 72/82/2. The discovery of the IRA Order of Battle, Ibid, Diary November 1920; 'Report on Cullenswood House', dated 3 February 1921, PRO, WO35/71/6/84.

law; when this was turned down he suggested the introduction of official reprisals and the carrying of prominent Sinn Féiners on lorries as a deterrent. These measures were meant to counter the feelings of powerlessness of the Crown Forces and to force the general population, especially prominent Sinn Féiners, to exercise a restraining influence on the Volunteers. The suggested introduction of official reprisals was also an attempt to repress the unofficial reprisals engaged in by frustrated members of police and military in various parts of the country. These unofficial reprisals had been widely condoned by high military and police officers, as well as government circles, but they were now regarded as a handicap in the efforts to restore order. During the summer, when the policy of conciliation was still in effect, military leaders widely dismissed it as a natural reaction:

> Macready is on very delicate ground over this reprisal business; he sees clearly that to wink at organised reprisals is the end of discipline. On the other hand he said frankly that a regiment that did not try to break out when a story – however untrue – was told them e.g. that one of their comrades had been chucked into the Liffey and shot at in the water, was not worth a damn. Having been very pious and proper he was finally guilty of the human remark that if a policeman put on a Macintosh and a false beard and 'reprised' on his own hook he was damn glad of it.[56]

After the Kilmichael ambush a system of official reprisals was indeed introduced in the south-western counties together with martial law. Under this system the property of those implicated in or cognisant of an outrage was confiscated and destroyed. Due to the lack of information at hand, this simply meant that a fixed number of houses closest to an incident were demolished. In addition restrictions were placed on fairs and markets within a twenty mile radius of an outrage. A curfew and the carrying of prominent Sinn Féiners, intended to prevent attacks on lorries, were also introduced. The use of these hostages started in the South and was extended to Dublin and Meath on 16 January 1921. The people were notified: 'Outrages against Forces of the Crown in cars if continue KNOWN REBELS will be

56 Quote, 'Sturgis Diary', 45, PRO, PRO30/59/1. See also PRO, PRO30/59/2, 26; 'Minutes of Brigade Conference held 20th January 1921 HQ Dublin District', marked B.M./33/0/2, PRO, WO35/71/6/84; Summary of 13 May 1921, PRO, WO35/71/8/117; Letter Commandant 24th Brigade dated 31 March 1921, PRO, WO35/71; NLI, P918 S356; 'History of the 5th Division in Ireland November 1919-March 1922', IWM, 72/82/2; Charles Townshend (1975), 119-23. A letter from Brig. General Prescott Decie of the 1st Munster Division of the British Army dated 1 June 1920, indicates the existence of a new government policy, NAD, CBS/Box 24.

carried as hostages for the safe conduct of the occupants in all motor vehicles the property of the armed forces.[57]

The government now considered martial law necessary to deal with the violence in more affected areas and introduced it in the four south-western counties of Cork, Kerry, Limerick and Tipperary. To facilitate raiding parties all houses in this area had to have a list on the inside of the door naming those in residence. No meetings of more than six were allowed and loitering was forbidden. Further restrictions were placed on motorcars, forbidding them to travel at night or beyond a radius of twenty miles from their place of registration. Finally, the death penalty was announced for carrying arms in the martial law area, which was extended to incorporate other southern counties in January 1921.[58]

With the introduction of official reprisals attempts to raise discipline in the Crown Forces were stepped up. In December 1920 the British Army 6th Division Commander, based in Cork, issued instructions to this effect: 'The practice by which Commanders appear in certain cases to turn a wilfully blind eye to the misdoings of those under their Command, must cease immediately.' The attempts to improve discipline by weeding out 'undesirable recruits' were judged successful in March 1921. However, despite some successes, many officers in the police and military were dissatisfied with the official reprisals which turned the population against them. They felt that the unofficial reprisals, which had terrified the population, were far more effective.[59]

As a result of this dissatisfaction Volunteers in prisons were still at the mercy of vindictive members of the Crown Forces, often from the auxiliary police forces: 'Around Christmas, we had a specially rough time. We would be disturbed by Tans running in, flashing lights on our faces and threatening us. It would all depend on the sergeant of the guard for he could stop it if he wanted to stop it.' Many Volunteers suffered mentally and physically from this treatment. Ned Lyons, commander of the Newport Battalion, went insane, while several others died young due to their prison experiences. In Dublin, the Auxiliaries were widely used in raiding. Conflicts be-

---

57 Quote, PRO, WO35/66.
58 Measures taken at the end of 1920, 'Sturgis Diary', passim, PRO, PRO30/59-/3; 'History of the 5th Division in Ireland November 1919–March 1922', 56, IWM, 72/82/2.
59 Quote, Instructions by the 6th Division Commander marked 'discipline' dated 16 December 1920, NLI, P918 A0413. 'Undesirable recruits', CI South Tipperary MR March 1921. Efforts to prevent unofficial reprisals, Major-Gen. Douglas Wimberley, 'Scottish Soldier', 146-7 + 152-3, IWM, PP/MCR/182. Some success was reported, CI South Tipperary MR May 1921. The lesser effect of official reprisals is discussed in, John Regan, 'Memoirs', 123 +188-9, PRONI, D3160.

tween Auxiliaries and soldiers over the former's treatment of prisoners are reported on several occasions. A member of the Squad arrested by the military experienced this when the lorry in which he was taken away by the military was met by Auxiliaries who demanded a transfer of the prisoners:

> The [military] officer was very angry, he called them jail birds, dirt and so on, and a lot of filthy language passed between them. The Tans[60] were getting more aggressive and seemed to be winning the argument when the little officer shouted an order to the men in charge of the Lewis gun that was mounted on the lorry to cover the Tan lorry. The man swung the machine gun around and covered the Tans. The little officer took out his watch, and, with another burst of bad language, said 'Move, or I fire in ten seconds. If you fire sooner there will be no 10 seconds.' I was surprised when the officer in charge of the military party turned round, grinned at us and said, 'I did not ask you whether you would like to go or not, but I think you would sooner stop with me', with that he handed each of us a cigarette.[61]

Some members of the RIC had became so disgusted with the behaviour of the Black & Tans and Auxiliaries that they resigned. Sinn Féin used this to their advantage by providing those who resigned for patriotic motives with alternative employment. A special bureau was set up in September 1920 to find them suitable work. This bureau also aided IRA and Cumann na mBan members who had been forced to leave their work because of their involvement in the movement. The activities of this bureau, however, always remained marginal. In 1921 it had 74 resigned policemen on its books. For 10 of these employment was found and 4 received special Dáil grants. The bureau was more successful in finding work for the Volunteer and Cumann na mBan members, but numbers remained small. Of 58 Volunteers on their books 30 found work; a further 9 were arrested and 4

60 This must have been an Auxiliary as no Black & Tans served in Dublin. Black & Tans or Tans were often confused with Auxiliaries in retrospect.

61 Quote on 'Christmas in prison', Paddy O'Halloran, O'MN, P17b114. See also Paddy Kinnane, O'MN, P17b126; Oscar Traynor, O'MN, P17b98. One of the first official attempts to reduce threats to prisoners is recorded in May 1920 when the military were instructed to treat prisoners courteously, report dated 30 June 1920, NLI, P918 S356. Quote on tensions between military and police, Patrick O'Daly, 'Statement', NLI, P4548. See also Garry Houlihan, O'MN, P17b105; Jimmy Murray, O'MN, P17b106; Sean Golden, O'MN, P17b107; Ben Doyle, O'MN, P17b96. The Chief of police notices the lack of cooperation, in a letter to the commandant of the Auxiliaries in Dublin, PRO, WO35/91. See also Private J. P. Swindlehurst, Diary 1921, IWM, 48790; David Fitzpatrick (1977), 25.

returned home. Of 37 Cumann na mBan members in this position 16 found employment.[62]

IMPLEMENTATION

The implementation of the new government measures exerted new pressures on the IRA. They responded by restating their policies towards the Crown Forces and implementing them more vigorously. In September, GHQ issued open orders to shoot on sight the 'worst and most vicious' of the RIC, and all Black & Tans. To facilitate the discrimination between good and bad RIC, records on individual policemen were to be introduced. The attacks on the Crown Forces had up till then been a direct result of the danger they presented to the survival of the Volunteers or an attempt to obtain arms. With the shooting of all 'vicious' policemen and Black & Tans as an explicit goal, the conflict became more indiscriminate.[63]

In October GHQ emphasised the importance of an all-out war against the Crown Forces. The ease with which raiding and reprisal parties had escaped the Volunteers so far was blamed on the fact that it was thought necessary that no life be lost on the side of the Volunteers and on insufficiently rapid mobilisation. It was stressed that incendiarism and the ill-treatment of Volunteers or of the people was to be punished regardless of the costs. In particular, obnoxious soldiers and policemen were to be confronted with constant warfare by sniping, ambushing and every other type of petty aggression.[64]

In the following months, further memos were issued showing the increasingly warlike conditions. As we have seen, these orders fell on fertile ground in Tipperary and Dublin, and in places like Mayo, some direct attacks now began to take place as well. In most counties, however, these orders had little effect on the few active Volunteers, and the RIC continued to live among the general population with little fear of interference by the IRA. In Dublin and Tipperary, however, precautions had to be taken.[65]

Not all Volunteers were happy with the militarisation of the conflict. The more indiscriminate violence and the singling out of the better known

62 Poor relationship between the older RIC men and the auxiliary forces, John Regan, 'Memoirs', 120-2, 154-5 + 163, PRONI D3160; 'RIC Reminiscences Xmas 1930', TCD 7378/11; E.M. Ransford, 'One Man's Tide', IWM, 80/29/1; John D. Brewer (1990), 111-16. In June 1920, the Dáil allocated a mere £350 to the Police Employment Bureau, David Fitzpatrick (1977), 39. Report on the working of this bureau, NLI, P919 A0602.

63 Orders and Memos, O'MN, P17b127. See also Kennedy, O'MN, P17b114.

64 Orders on raiding and reprisal parties, Operational Memo No. 8, O'MN, P17b127.

65 Memos, O'MN, P17b127.

officers of the IRA by the Crown Forces led to some misgivings. Leading Volunteers distanced themselves from the new tactics, or tried to suppress their implementation. A few Volunteers left the organisation on conscientious grounds when the killing of policemen became a regular feature of its activities.[66]

The authorities were anxious to take advantage of this. In October 1920 they found a letter on the dead body of Seán Treacy, in which Eamon O'Dwyer expressed his doubts about the policy of ambushing policemen. Both men were officers of the South Tipperary Brigade and had been among the few original activists in the Volunteers. When a few days later a namesake of O'Dwyer was killed, the British Press reported that he was killed by the IRA because of his weakening allegiance to the national movement. The real O'Dwyer then felt obliged to state his position in a letter to a national newspaper:

> The statement contained in that letter [...] alluded to my opposition to certain methods of warfare (notably ambushes) and I wish to make it clear that the only people whom I am in danger from are the agents of the British Government; who have already made one attempt to kill me, and failing in that mission burned my home to ashes.
>
> In a letter of mine which appeared in the Press I made the statement that I consider ambushes an unfair method of fighting. Since then the agents of the English Government have perpetrated several atrocities too fresh in the public mind to need particularising. It is nearly impossible to talk of fair play in fighting such an enemy; yet in spite of the feelings of revenge that all those deeds engender, I feel that it is best that we should remain calm but determined in the face of this provocation, and conserve our strength so that we could continue our great movement till it ends in complete victory. The English militarists hope that we will lose our heads and give them an opportunity of destroying the entire country and crushing all hopes of Irish freedom for this generation, but it will not be so.[67]

Despite these misgivings IRA policies and tactics were further militarised in reply to the additional government measures introduced in November.

66 Misgivings about the increased violence and attempts to suppress activity: In Derry City, Paedar O'Donnell and Joe Sweeney, O'MN, P17b98. In Wexford, Bob Lambert, 'Statement'. In Dublin, Andy MacDonnell, O'MN, P17b100; Dr Gaughan, O'MN, P17b122; C.S. Andrews (1979), 115-16. In Tipperary, Seamus Robinson, 'Statement'; NLI, P919, A0909; MA, Lot 1, Notebook 1921.
67 Letter to the editor, 'The Bansha Tragedies', signed Eamon O'Duibhir, *Irish Independent*, 6 November 1920.

On 2 December the Third Tipperary Brigade issued an order to destroy all main roads for heavy vehicles, and to ambush all military mending roads. This was a reaction to the restrictions placed on transport and travelling by the government. It was added that this would drive lorries on to bye-roads where they would travel more slowly and were more easily ambushed. This tactic was adopted by GHQ and became one of the major ways of involving local Volunteers in places like Wexford and Derry who were unwilling or unable to engage the Crown Forces directly. In response to the official reprisals, instructions were issued by GHQ in January 1921 to gather information on all Divisional Commissioners of the RIC in command of these reprisals in order to eliminate them.[68]

The direct attacks on the police which had been enacted by a small minority, now came to involve a much larger proportion of Volunteers. This was largely a result of the order to all IRA officers to leave their homes to avoid arrest. Many ordinary Volunteers were also forced to go on the run to protect their freedom. Up to the end of 1920 Volunteers in most areas had still felt able to express their membership openly. In the autumn many Volunteer companies still publicly trained without fear of arrest. Even on the morning of Bloody Sunday sixty Volunteers were found drilling in Merrion Square, near some of the shooting incidents. Although these drilling parties were dispersed, only those with incriminating evidence on them were arrested. However, this type of exposure of one's membership became increasingly dangerous and few such incidents are reported in 1921.[69]

The combined efforts of the authorities fell far short of halting the fighting. Instead it resulted in a large increase in indiscriminate violence and created a warlike situation in many parts of the country. Before the Truce, no further policy changes were made. Military tactics were, however, adapted to counteract the increasing violence of IRA Flying Columns. In January martial law was extended from the four south-western counties to neighbouring Kilkenny, Wexford, Clare and Waterford. Additional troops were brought in, bringing the army's strength to fifty-one battalions. A system of numerous military detachments which carried out constant foot patrols was adopted in some districts of Tipperary in March. Building on this, military flying columns aided by local policemen were introduced in Tipperary and Mayo in May to eliminate the IRA columns. In a final attempt to 'shake out' the Volunteers, whole areas were surrounded and searched: 'Encircling areas just at dawn, rounding up all the male inhabitants and making a general search of the area encircled is the latest form of activity.' In a further escalation of violence the IRA in the South success-

---

68 Order to trench roads dated 2 December 1920, O'MN, P17b127. Order to get information on Divisional Commissioners, Weekly Memo 10 dated 23 January 1921, NLI, ms. 900/21.
69 See PRO, WO35/70, and WO35/205.

fully introduced mines. After disbanding most Flying Columns, a multitude of small-scale attacks took place.[70]

This escalation of violence and the behaviour of the Crown Forces caused a total break between the police and the people in some counties. In these places the police were militarised by their isolation from the community and close association with the newly introduced auxiliary forces and the military. In many other areas the police continued to function as they had done before 1916 and IRA activists only managed to attack some of the most diligent among them. This could nevertheless lead to an escalation and a situation similar to that in more active areas.

Despite the militarisation of the conflict many Volunteers found it hard to adapt to the new conditions, and only a small number of them were willing to kill policemen. Several reports exist of active Volunteers refusing to shoot captured opponents even when ordered to do so. Crown Forces were often released unharmed after having been relieved of their arms and warned to stay out of trouble. Executions were carried out by a small group of experienced Volunteers often from outside the district. For most Volunteers, however, personal and moral constraints continued to override their republican zeal.[71]

The increased conflict also diminished the Volunteers' hold on the population. The Dáil Courts were almost eliminated in 1921, and as early as October 1920 the RIC County Inspector in Tipperary reported that the police boycott was effectively over. This, however, did not have any direct impact on the level of conflict in these counties.[72]

---

70 Quote, Report West Mayo Brigade dated 16 May, UCD AD, P7A38. See also Paddy Cannon, O'MN, P17b136; 'History of the 5th Division in Ireland November 1919-March 1922', Diary & 57, IWM 72/82/2. Use of mines, Ibid., 67 + 76; UCD AD, P7A18/175-9.

71 Examples of refusal to execute captured police and spies, Michael O'Dwyer, NLI, ms. 5,050; Thomas Morris, 'Typescript of Interview', Fr O'Kane Papers, AARC; Paul Merrigan, O'MN, P17b126; UCD AD, P7A18/127-8. Releasing captured policemen unharmed: In Derry, *Derry People and Donegal News*, 28 August 1920. In Tipperary, Patrick Ryan, 'Statement'. In Mayo, Joe Baker (1988), 32. In the South Tipperary Brigade the Flying Column men were almost exclusively responsible for executions, Tommy Ryan, 'Statement'. Confinement of the use of violence to a small group took place early on in Tipperary, Ned O'Reilly, O'MN, P17b126; Paul Merrigan, O'MN, P17b126; Sean Withero, O'MN, P17b114; Jack Gardiner, Interview. In Mayo a similar hardening took place somewhat later, Jim O'Donnell, 'Recollections'. Also in Dublin, Patrick O'Daly, 'Statement', NLI, P4548. Members of the North Tipperary Brigade were requested to come to Limerick City to shoot a number of RIC who were making themselves particularly objectionable, Seán Gaynor, 'Statement'.

72 Police boycott in Tipperary, CI South Tipperary MR October 1920.

CONCLUSION

Between 1916 and the Truce in 1921 the RIC lost its legitimacy in the eyes
of a majority of the nationalist population in many counties by a process of
physical and psychological separation between the police and the community. After the Easter Rising the police came under increasing pressure from
advanced nationalists organised in Sinn Féin to relinquish their ties with a
despised regime, and were physically attacked by Irish Volunteers who
wanted to obtain their arms. Initial attempts by the republicans to involve
the police in their struggle for independence soon proved to be futile but
nevertheless continued. The police were faced with mutually exclusive
claims of allegiance to Irish independence and loyalty to their employers.
Those who refused to bow to these pressures left themselves open to being
labelled traitors to the Irish cause. During 1917 the Volunteers and their
sympathisers began to avoid these men, and this slowly developed into local
boycotts of the police. The failure of the Volunteers to lure sufficient
policemen away from their loyalty to the government and the consequences
of growing conflict eventually led to the exclusion of policemen from the
community, particularly in rural areas where the opposition to British rule
was traditionally strong.

The successful attacks on some police barracks in 1919 intended to
obtain arms caused the evacuation of many badly defended posts. This
resulted in a physical separation between police and people in many rural
communities. In some areas the Volunteers managed by persuasion and
intimidation to bring with them a large part of the population in their rejection of the legitimacy of British rule. Between 1918 and 1920 policemen in
these areas were ostracised, through phases of warning, ignoring, and shunning, resulting in a mental rift between law-enforcers and the people, many
of whom began to consider the Crown Forces as an army of occupation.

The reactive violence of members of the Crown Forces against the population facilitated this development, and the general boycott of all Crown
Forces called by the Dáil in the summer of 1920 institutionalised it.
Successful ostracisation turned the police into outsiders and potential targets of attacks. Starting with assaults on the most diligent policemen during
1919, some Volunteers became increasingly willing to use force, and slowly
an avenue of unbridled violence directed against the Crown Forces was
opened. In this way a war of words developed into physical violence against
individual policemen, while the segregation between police and community
legitimised the killing of policemen to a community who no longer considered the police as Irish.

A direct but undesired result of the measures taken to control the IRA
in the Autumn of 1920 was the extension of violent behaviour from a small
minority to a larger proportion of Volunteers. Although most men on both
sides were primarily concerned with their own survival, small groups of

activists drew the less willing on both sides along with them into violent conflict. When many Volunteers were driven from their homes this trend increased. Nevertheless, the greater mass of cautious members who never became involved in killing also limited the activity of these small groups of activists.

Bloodshed was engaged in only after a long process of ostracising the police and increasing experience of conflict. Direct violence was therefore largely monopolised by the small number of free-ranging full-time members in the Flying Columns, who were most prominent in the Southwest. In the end their activities made all-out warfare with the Crown Forces possible, while the dynamics of violent conflict ensured an ever increasing level of casualties. In most other areas, however, little violence took place as the development towards separation of community and government lagged, hindered by a divided population and a reluctance on both sides to engage in violence. It is questionable whether this development would ever have been completed in these areas, but before it went either way it was stopped in its tracks in July 1921 by the Truce.

When the Truce came a clear differentiation had developed in the attitudes of Volunteers. The boycott of the police could only be enforced successfully in rural areas with a particularly strong or well integrated Volunteer organisation and where some Volunteers were affected to a point where they were willing to kill policemen. In this way open military conflict began in some counties in 1920. In these areas the position of the RIC had changed from a normally functioning constabulary to a para-military force often restricted to barracks in the larger towns and villages. Many of them lived in constant fear of attack when travelling on country roads. Elsewhere this process was not yet completed or was still in its infancy in 1921, and the position of the police in society remained largely unchanged.

In these places the police still functioned as it had done before 1916 and the IRA had only just started to attack the most diligent among them. In some parts of Ulster the Crown Forces had retaken lost ground by reoccupying barracks. In areas that had recently started to follow the example set in the Southwest the small number of engagements and the reluctance to get involved in the fighting prevented the struggle from developing into a brutal confrontation. In most parts of the Southwest the fight had developed into a military stalemate, but the dynamics of conflict had made violent engagement much more vicious. A large number of individual members of both forces were assassinated in the final months of the struggle. The hesitancy on both sides to take on the other meant that Volunteer violence was increasingly directed at civilians who were considered hostile to the cause.

CHAPTER 6

Crown Force Reactions to the Conflict

Having established the way in which government measures, intended to deal with the emerging violence, affected Volunteer attitudes and the position of the RIC in society, we take a closer look at the reaction of individual members of the RIC and its impact on the development of violent struggle.

POLICE RESPONSES TO VIOLENCE

Three approaches can be discerned in the reactions of individual policemen to Volunteer pressure. They either resigned, stayed but attempted to remain out of trouble, or met violence with violence. Many members alternated between these approaches at different times as circumstances demanded. Those who left the force did so under direct threats, from fear, or because they refused to accept the increased level of violence needed to maintain control. The transition from a police to a paramilitary force was disliked by many constables. The tendency among some leading police officers to answer violence with violence caused disgruntlement. Many lower officers refused to engage in such activity and restrained their men. Ordinary constables occasionally rejected their officers' command if they encouraged such forms of state terrorism. In the most publicised case, the 'Listowel mutiny' in Kerry, some RIC constables refused to serve after they were told to shoot Sinn Féiners without fear of punishment.[1]

Most RIC men, however, although frightened by the consequences and dissatisfied with developments, remained in the force. Most frequently this

---

1   Resignations, J.R.W. Goulden, 'Statement', TCD, 7377/7/1; Tom Carney, O'MN, P17b109; Pat Tohill, Fr O'Kane Papers, Tape A5, AARC; Edward O'Malley (1981), 23. Statement of two RIC men involved in Listowel mutiny, NLI, P7153. RIC Officers restraining their men, Michael Kilroy, O'MN, P17b138; J.R.W. Goulden, 'Statement', TCD, 737/7/1; *Mayoman*, 26 June 1920. An acknowledgement of the passive approval given to policemen by their superior officers, 'Sturgis Diary', 27 + 32-3, PRO, PRO30/59/3.

was a result of financial necessity. Their willingness to risk their lives was limited, and was further reduced by family and social ties with Volunteers. As a result many policemen turned a blind eye to illegal activities as long as they were not personally attacked.

This attitude was widely recognised by Volunteers. One company in Dublin, which used a granary fitted out as a gymnasium for drilling, knew the police were aware of their presence but did not fear interference:

> I am sure the local RIC were not in the least deceived as to the purpose of the gymnasium but the sergeant was on the point of retirement, one of the constables was courting the sister of one of the Volunteers and the others, except for one who was a very bad type, wanted to avoid trouble.

Fear was also a strong incentive. The violence that developed in some areas could fill policemen in entirely inactive places with, often unwarranted, fearful apprehension. This was encountered by the captain of the Monasterevin Company, Co. Kildare, who had no intention to attack the barracks:

> They were very cautious. There was one man, his name was [...]. And he was afraid actually, he was really afraid, and he came to me and he said, 'Would you ever tell me when you are going to raid the barracks.' 'What do you mean', I said. 'When you are going to raid, doing any shooting, I'll be off that night.[2]

Some policemen openly displayed this reluctance to get involved and allowed wanted men to go free. Shortly after the Soloheadbeg ambush in January 1919 proof of the involvement of one of the attackers found in his house was ignored by a policeman. In some cases, police actively intervened to avoid a clash by warning Volunteers who were waiting in an ambush site, and no attempt was made to arrest the waiting Volunteers. Initially, sympathy with the cause among those who remained in the police force was extensive. Several reports of DMP men saluting Michael Collins in the streets of Dublin testify to this.[3]

2 Quote on 'local RIC', C.S. Andrews (1979), 98. Quote on 'cautious man', Ned Prendergast, Interview.
3 Experience of one of the attackers in Soloheadbeg, Ned O'Reilly, O'MN, P17b126. Saluting Collins, Broy, O'MN, P17b128; C. MacGuinness (1934), 164; Patrick O'Daly, 'Statement', NLI, P4548. Numerous examples exist of policemen deliberately avoiding trouble by pretending not to recognise known IRA men, not reacting on guns going off in their proximity, playing along with invented stories of men held up, or not shooting when they saw Volunteers in flight: In Dublin, Harry

The IRA policy to attack only those in the force who made themselves conspicuous was intended to take advantage of this attitude. An unspoken agreement developed between the two sides; policemen who ignored the Volunteers were left alone. After the intelligence section of the DMP in Dublin had been dealt with by the Squad, the force was more or less disregarded. One of the detectives who cooperated with the IRA had warned them: 'The uniformed men didn't want to work against Irish Volunteers, but if they were shot up they would resist them.' He added that many had relatives in the Volunteers and that the majority of the younger policemen were anti-British. Even some consultation to establish rules for coexistence seems to have taken place. This effective truce between most DMP and the Volunteers held quite well throughout the struggle. In other areas such attempts to avoid trouble sometimes led to an undeclared local truce.[4]

Some policemen indeed supported the Volunteers, but were unwilling to resign. Many of them gave information to the IRA. There were contacts in the highest ranks of the intelligence sections in Dublin. Each night these people told the IRA who was going to be raided. The key to the RIC secret code and information regarding the movements of its leaders were also passed on. In the provincial areas, the information given was less useful. No systematic raiding took place and only the local sergeant

Colley, O'MN, P17b97; Patrick O'Daly, 'Statement', NLI, P4548; Jerry Davis, O'MN, P17b106; Maurice McConigle, O'MN, P17b132; Charlie Dalton, O'MN, P17b122; Liam Tobin, O'MN, P17b100; C.S. Andrews (1979), 90; 'Recollections of Col. J.V. Lawless', UCD AD, P7D148; Jack Plunkett, 'Statement', NLI, ms. 11,981; C. MacGuinness (1934), 164. In Tipperary, Ned O'Reilly, O'MN, P17b125, and P17b126; Jack Gardiner, Interview; Eamon O'Dwyer, 'Statement'; Paul Merrigan, O'MN, P17b126; Dan Breen (1981), 83. In Mayo, Michael Kilroy, 'The Awakening'; Thomas Heavy, 'Statement'; Ned Maughan, O'MN, P17b109; P.J. Kelly, 'One of the Men of the West'. In Wexford, Peter Wall, Interview. In Derry, Thomas Toner, Fr O'Kane Papers, Tape A13, AARC. In a report of the Brigade General of the Londonderry Brigade dated 10 October 1920, the absolute lack of ability and reliability of the Prison Governor and Staff in dealing with Republican prisoners is stressed, PRONI, FIN18/1/124. That this lack of enthusiasm among the RIC was induced by IRA threats was acknowledged by some British soldiers, Private J.P. Swindlehurst, Diary 20 January 1921, IWM, 48790. Policemen warning Volunteers in ambush, Seán Gaynor, 'Statement'.

4 Policy to attack the most active policemen, Seán Gaynor, 'Statement'; Jack Gardiner, Interview; Patrick Ryan, 'Statement'; Eamon O'Dwyer, 'Statement'. Quote on willingness of DMP to cooperate, Broy, O'MN, P17b98. See also Charles Townshend (1975), note 46. There were attempts by the IRA and by some RIC men to use the 'All Ireland Police Conference' to force the British Government to settle the Irish Question, UCD AD, P7A40/9. 'Understandings' between IRA and local police, Alfie White, O'MN, P17b110; Tommy Ryan, 'Statement'. In the Cahirciveen area in Co. Kerry British Military tried to arrange a truce with the Kerry 3 Brigade, UCD AD, P7A19/145; Larry Nugent, O'MN, P17b88. A similar attempt was made in Wexford in January 1921, Jim Ryan, O'MN, P17b103.

or district inspector knew where raids were going to be made. The ordinary policeman was told only at the last minute. Nevertheless in most counties there are reports of policemen giving information. This was often done in the hope that attacks on them or on the barracks might be prevented, the more frequent occurrence of this in active areas indicates as much.[5]

The third reaction came from the most diligent and aggressive of the Crown Forces, meeting violence with violence either within or outside the call of duty. Personal experience of conflict or the shooting of comrades were often the reason for this type of action. Prisoners were the first victims, but soon anyone suspected of republican sympathies was in danger. One of the first cases in which the Crown Forces took out their anger upon innocent civilians took place in Cork in September 1919, when soldiers assaulted people after a court failed to convict the attackers of some of their comrades. In other incidents, Crown Forces attacked those suspected of radical nationalist conviction in unofficial nightly forays. In the early summer of 1920, these unofficial raids became widespread when, due to the policy of conciliation, more and more IRA violence remained unpunished. In extreme cases whole towns were 'sacked' after a successful IRA ambush in the vicinity had caused casualties. In these incidents a large number of houses and shops were destroyed and people assaulted. The most notorious examples of this were Balbriggan, Co. Dublin and Cork City.[6]

5   Police with family members in the Volunteers giving information, Liam Langley, O'MN, P17b101; James Dunne, 'Statement', NLI, P4548. Information coming to the IRA from high sources in Dublin, David Neligan, RTE Radio Archives, B133/40; John Neary, O'MN, P17b122; Harry Colley, O'MN, P17b97; Liam Langley, O'MN, P17b101; Broy, O'MN, P17b98; Sean Sharkey, 'Statement'. Reports that the Irish in the Civil Service in England helped on intelligence, and that even the War Office, the Home Office, Scotland Yard and the Post Office were tapped, Markham, O'MN, P17b101; Billy Ahearne, O'MN, P17b99. Contacts among local policemen: In Tipperary, Paul Merrigan, O'MN, P17b126; Jack Gardiner, Interview; Ned O'Reilly, O'MN, P17b126; Seán Gaynor, 'Statement'. The RIC barrack in New Inn, Co. Tipperary was sniped but not seriously attacked because the sergeant gave information to the local company, NLI, P918 A0509. In Derry, Pat Tohill, Fr O'Kane Papers, Tape A13, AARC. In Mayo, Thomas Heavy, O'MN, P17b120; P.J. Kelly, 'One of the Men of the West'. In Naas, Sean Kavanagh, O'MN, P17b106.

6   The first case of unofficial reprisals in Cork, Peter Hart (1992), Chapter 'The Dynamics of Violence', 25. Reports on Crown Forces attacking civilians: In Tipperary, Mick Burke, O'MN, P17b103; Fr Michael Maher, Diary 1920, St Patrick's College Thurles. In Dublin, Sean Kavanagh, O'MN, P17b106; Lt. Col E.J.A.H. Brush, IWM, 85/8/1. Unsanctioned attempts by the Crown Forces to hurt their opponents indiscriminately included leaving live grenades in filled trenches and evacuated barracks, John Regan, 'Memoirs', 185, PRONI, D3160.

Although instilling fear in a section of the population, such actions also caused large-scale indignation throughout Ireland and abroad, resulting in more Volunteer activity and increased support for it. Most members of the Crown Forces who would usually try to avoid trouble sometimes engaged in this type of violence in reaction to a particular incident. A small number of the RIC, however, turned this into general practice. The auxiliary divisions of the RIC, less constrained by ties to the community, were most prominent in this. Their behaviour and their foreign extraction had quickly gained them a reputation for brutality. As a result, they came to be looked upon as an army of occupation to be attacked at any time.[7]

CROWN FORCE ATTITUDES DURING HOSTILITIES

Staying out of trouble without leaving the force was possible for most RIC men in the early part of the struggle. However, when violence became more common this was often impossible to sustain. The barracks attacks and ambushes of patrols involved all policemen in the hostilities. In order to defend themselves, the police and military were then given greater powers. In June 1920 the 6th Army Division received orders that in case they would:

> Meet a civilian with arms in his hands and his intention appears hostile, you are to treat him as an enemy and a traitor to his King and Country, and he should be shot. If you can first give the order 'Hands up' without endangering the lives of yourself and your comrades, you are to do so.[8]

To avoid conflict and unnecessary casualties senior officers kept the Crown Forces inside the barracks as much as possible. In some areas with a strong military or a weak IRA presence, there was no justification for this and as a result the men became bored, increasing the likelihood of disproportionate reactions to minor incidents. In the more affected areas with more cause for the Crown Forces to remain inside, morale was seriously affected by continuing fear and lack of diversion. Occasions to leave the barracks were restricted to obtaining supplies, patrolling and the relief of other stations under attack. The IRA used the relief procedures to harass and unnerve the police and the military. Frequently telegraph wires between stations were cut, rockets used by the RIC to raise the

7   Reports on how the habit of breaking out of the barracks at night attacking suspected rebels spread from the Auxiliaries and Black & Tans to a few army officers and men, Major-Gen Douglas Wimberley, 'Scottish Soldier', 146-7 + 152-3, IWM, PP/MCR/182.
8   Quote, '17th Infantry Brigade Instructions No.9', Appendix A, NLI, P918 A0413. See also NLI, P918 A0413, S356.

alarm were fired by the IRA between two police posts or feint attacks on barracks were made. These actions naturally caused considerable anxiety and excitement to those inside.[9]

Fear guided the behaviour of many in the Crown Forces. Not imbued with an ideological zeal like most active Volunteers, survival was their main preoccupation. Minor sniping attacks often resulted in an indiscriminate fusillade from the barracks. Very lights were sent up to call for help, machine guns were used and grenades fired from the barracks. The men cooped up inside, scared by stories of attacks elsewhere, were extremely nervous. When caught in an ambush, their reaction was similarly indiscriminate:

> The Tans came preceded by a small car with officers in it. A ditch that we hadn't budgeted for saved the small car. The Crossabeg [probably a Crossley] tender and Lancia car got into action and a lot of dead cattle were left in the fields – we were lucky to get out of the lane.

On several occasions sheep and cattle were killed by random fire from nervous police and military near barracks and ambush sites. This tendency to react indiscriminately when under attack occasionally led to military and police parties attacking each other, both convinced they were firing at the IRA. Even in inactive Derry City the first IRA attack, which caused two casualties, resulted in police in mufti going on a rampage, burning houses of prominent Sinn Féiners. When the military came out to protect the fire brigade they fired at plainclothes people acting suspiciously, killing one policeman.[10]

The lack of recreation and the danger of being shot reduced the enthusiasm of soldiers and policemen to serve in Ireland. The relatively large number of resignations among the RIC also extended to the auxiliary forces. This road was closed to the military. Self-inflicted wounds were one way in which soldiers attempted to get out of their predicament. This became such

9 Alarm procedures, report Mid Clare Brigade, NLI, P915 A0408; E.M. Ransford, 'One Man's Tide', IWM, 80/29/1.

10 Quote, Bob Lambert, 'Statement'. Reports of the killing of cows and sheep by young and nervous recruits, 'The Memoirs of G.W. Albin', 120-2, IWM. Shooting between police and military in Derry, CI Derry MR November 1920; Liam Brady, *Derry Journal*, 20 May 1953. The same occurred in Tipperary when a Flying Column managed to slip away. Some RIC men in Cork were too frightened to do anything against Sinn Féin, Major-Gen Douglas Wimberley, 'Scottish Soldier', 149, IWM, PP/MCR/182. In Tipperary the anxiety of the police was realised by some Volunteers, they blamed the failure of a barracks attack on too much shouting and threatening of the police which made them afraid to surrender, NLI, P919 A0509.

a frequent occurrence that court martial was threatened to anyone wounded by friendly fire, irrespective of the cause.[11]

Desertion was another popular way of avoiding service. In January 1921 seventy soldiers deserted from the Army in Ireland. In the following months this gradually fell to forty-seven in June. This lack of enthusiasm forced the authorities to bring reinforcements into Ireland without prior notice to the soldiers involved. One soldier recalls how the announcement of his unit's transfer to Ireland was immediately followed by a flying train journey to the boat. Three men 'got clean away', but the rest had no chance to desert. The fears of this soldier came true on his first day in Dublin, when he and some of his comrades were held up by Volunteers in broad daylight. Although they were released after being searched and questioned, their apprehensions were fuelled.[12]

Despite the hardening attitudes on both sides, a certain respect between the fighting men developed, particularly in areas where IRA operations were successful. This started with minor courtesies. In Derry City, a republican flag was painted on a wall in the Bogside. Soldiers of the Dorset Regiment blotted it out, but it was repainted the next night. After this had repeated itself a number of times the military one day found the wall 'Repainted in gleaming white, surmounted by two flags entwined, and under them, in fair Roman print':

> This is the flag the Dorsets hate.
>   It puts them all to shame,
> And every time they blot it out
>   It blossoms forth again.

The military patrol commandant, impressed with the artistic content of the work, then refused to take it away: 'We were not vandals and respected a work of art.' In areas where more serious fighting had developed, enemies were occasionally allowed temporary safe-conduct for humanitarian reasons.[13]

11 Resignations among Auxiliaries were much higher than desertions from the army. In the first half of 1921 desertions among military were only 50 per cent more that resignations among Auxiliaries, which was a force thirty times smaller. Desertions remained high after the Truce, which indicates that the revolution was not the major determinant, David Fitzpatrick (1977), 35. For the consequences of wounding oneself, E.M. Ransford, 'One Man's Tide', IWM, 80/29/1. The lack of enthusiasm of the military is also noticed by the RIC, John Regan, 'Memoirs', 168, PRONI, D3160.

12 The experience of soldiers coming to Ireland, Private J.P. Swindlehurst, Diary 1921, IWM, 48790. Desertions, 'History of the 5th Division in Ireland, November 1919–March 1922', IWM, 72/82/2; PRO, WO35/173.

13 Quotes, Major-Gen. G.N. Wood, 'The Military Control of Londonderry, 1919–23', 9, IWM, 78/31/1. Examples of safe-conducts, Tom Barry, in K. Griffith and T. O'Grady (1982), 220; PRONI, D2022/1/35.

OPERATION IN WARLIKE CONDITIONS

With the development of guerrilla warfare by an underground army, the Crown Forces were forced to operate more and more indiscriminately. They were increasingly unable to trace the perpetrators of violence. The knowledge of the RIC about local circumstances was constantly reduced and became less valuable when leading activists went on the run. As a result, attention during official raids and unofficial reprisals was mainly directed at the houses of well-known Volunteers and Sinn Féin representatives. Men who had been among the earliest activists, but who were not necessarily active fighters, were their main targets. Many of the less or newly prominent Volunteers were not sufficiently known to attract this kind of attention. The youthfulness of many of the most active Volunteers was also deceptive: 'I was 17 then and there was an ambush. They were holding up everyone and I was stuck up by Auxies when I had 2 attaché cases. "Where are you coming from", asked one of them. "From the Technical School", I replied. "F--off" he said.' The concentration on Volunteers who had been arrested previously and their families was evidenced in all areas. Among them were: Eamon O'Dwyer's and Dan Breen's family in Tipperary, Ned Moane's, Michael Kilroy's, Seamus MacEvilly's and Tom Maguire's homes in Mayo, the Larkins in south Derry, Paddy Hegarty in Derry City, and Dr Jim Ryan the MP for south Wexford.[14]

Without sufficient local information these houses were continuously raided even when most of the men concerned were on the run. As a result, rarely was anyone ever found there. Lack of information, but also a lack of enthusiasm on the part of the policemen, caused this. Realising they would not find anyone in these houses also meant they would avoid getting into a fight. This attitude was openly acknowledged by a RIC sergeant to the father of a Volunteer captain whose house he was about to raid: 'You're a "so and so", to bring a crowd of man to raid my house, he [the father] said, you'd get no guns there. Well, says he [the RIC sergeant], what's the use of bringing them to a house where I would get them, I would only get myself into trouble.' The same people were used as hostages to protect Crown Force lorries. This concentration on family and active sympathisers of the Volunteers fuelled feelings of

14 Quote, Paddy Rigney, O'MN, P17b105. Confirmed by, Martin Bell, private conversation; Sean Golden, O'MN, P17b107; NLI, ms. 901/99; Patrick O'Daly, 'Statement', NLI, P4548. Inactive provincial Volunteers were known to the police but were not arrested, Patrick Owen Mugan, Interview; Jack Gardiner, Interview; Peter Wall, Interview. Seamus MacEvilly, son of Michael was later killed in the Kilmeena ambush.

revenge among the Volunteers. Consequently, instead of reducing activity it led to even more active involvement.[15]

The authorities' belief that the IRA consisted of a few 'bad apples with no stake in the country' who took the law abiding part of the population along, further diminished the effectiveness of the Crown Forces. Leading men in the movement, who were seen as a restraining influence, were not always pursued as seriously as others. Arthur Griffith and Eamon De Valéra are the most obvious examples of this. Mark Sturgis, the Assistant Under-Secretary for Ireland, recorded instructions from Sir John Anderson on 2 September 1920: '[He] told them on no account to touch the Arthur Griffith lot if he could help it. [...] But of course to have a go for Michael Collins or one of that kidney.'[16]

It was also regarded as unthinkable that women or respectable people could be involved. Parties raiding were instructed to be suitably careful: 'As some of these addresses may be of considerable respectability it is most important that great care should be used by all forces concerned.' Leading IRA men like Michael Collins took advantage of this to avoid being caught simply by wearing respectable clothes and hiding in respectable houses:

> Once when I was in the Plaza the place was surrounded [...]. There were some battalion meetings there at the time and Collins was there also. I had a hard hat. Collins said come on with me. He had an attaché case, full of papers I expect. He walked straight over to a sergeant. Can I speak to the officer in charge he asked for I am a doctor on a case from the Rotunda hospital and this is my assistant here with me. [...] The officer let us go through. I was always well dressed then.

15 Quote, John Duffy, from Duneen Co. Antrim on the border of Co. Derry, Fr O'Kane Papers, Tape A20, AARC. Concentration on relatives of active Volunteers: In Tipperary, Patrick Ryan, 'Statement'; Nonie Kennedy, O'MN, P17b119; Mossy McGrath, O'MN, P17b127; Tommy Ryan, 'Statement'. See also the White Cross assessment of people eligible for support after suffering under the effects of the war in Tipperary, NLI, ms. 10,916. In Mayo, Mrs Michael Kilroy, 'Statement'; Jimmy Slattery, O'MN, P17b138; Brodie Malone and Ned Moane, O'MN, P17b120; Johnny Duffy, O'MN, P17b109; List of houses for an official reprisal, *Mayoman*, 2 April 1921. In Derry, Liam Brady, *Derry Journal*, 20-2 May 1953. In Wexford, *Life of Michael Radford* (n. d.), 11-12; Dr Jim Ryan, O'MN, P17b103; Willy Parle, Interview.

16 Quote 'Sturgis Diary', 62, PRO, PRO30/59/1. The hesitance to arrest political leaders of the Republican Movement was also a consequence of attempts at starting talks. Already on 26 August 1920 Griffith attempted to get talks with the government going, but this failed, PRO, WO35/90. Again on 2 January 1921, PRO, WO35/71/8/117. The first reference in military correspondence concerning De Valéra is found in the Operation Summary dated 24 December 1920, PRO, PRO/59/2/18.

In the spring of 1921 the military in Dublin still had to be warned that: 'It is not generally understood that the Shinner [Crown Force term for republicans] gunman is more often than not well dressed, and is not the tough-looking man standing at corners who should always be classed as disloyal.' The IRA also took advantage of the etiquette of the time which forbade men to touch a woman physically. Many women were used as messengers and to safeguard weapons and papers at roadblocks. The lack of women searchers to deal with this seriously hampered the Crown Forces in the fight against the Volunteers.[17]

VOLUNTEER RESPONSE TO POSITIONING OF CROWN FORCES

Volunteers had difficulties in responding adequately to the different approaches taken by the members of the Crown Forces. The attempts to reduce activity by eliminating the most vigilant opponents was effective when dealing with the RIC. This policy could, however, not easily be extended to the auxiliary police forces or the military, who were locally unknown. That many who continued to work for the government were in sympathy with the movement was also hard to accept. The resulting mistrust led to the discarding of information given by sympathetic policemen. At the same time, the Volunteers used the willingness of others to do anything for money. Arms were bought from servants of the Crown and some were bribed for help. Friendships between radical nationalists and policemen were abused by both sides. Occasionally the IRA was able to take advantage of tensions within the different branches of the Crown Forces. Many men on the run could escape by disguising themselves as British soldiers or Catholic priests: 'They didn't dare to stop us, for the Catholics in the ranks of the enemy were very touchy. Any indignity would be a severe boomerang, and we passed through the lines with hands at the salute.'[18]

17 Quote on 'respectable addresses' dated January 1921, WO35/71/6/84. This special treatment extended to arrested Volunteers from respectable background, Dr Jim Ryan, O'MN, P17b103; Pierce McCan, Diary. Quote on Michael Collins' imitation of a doctor, Andy MacDonnell, O'MN, P17b100. Quote on 'Shinner gunmen', letter to G.S.O.I. Dublin District dated 25 March 1921, PRO, WO35/71. Other tricks to fool the police in Dublin, Tom Duffy, O'MN, P17b105; Leo Henderson, O'MN, P17b105.
18 Quote, C. MacGuinness (1934), 163. See also D. Ryan (1945), 73. Volunteers discarding information given to them by policemen, Sean Kavanagh, O'MN, P17b106; Andy Roe, Interview; Eamon O'Dwyer, 'Statement'. Examples of confusion about how to deal with friendly police: In Dublin, Markham, O'MN, P17b101; Garmon, O'MN, P17b110; Sean Smith, O'MN, P17b122. In Tipperary, Paul Merrigan, O'MN, P17b126; Tom Smyth, O'MN, P17b103; Andy Cooney, O'MN, P17b107.

A differentiation in the treatment of the different branches of the Crown Forces established itself. Until January 1920 the military were rarely involved in dealing with the Volunteers and were consequently seldom engaged. Despite the developing confrontation between Volunteers and military, unarmed soldiers in Dublin were almost never bothered up to the end of 1920. From then on some were attacked and relieved of their uniforms. Armed soldiers were avoided in order to prevent unwanted tensions. In line with their refusal to see the conflict as a war, the authorities also tried to avoid using the military and made the RIC their main agent for dealing with the population. In the 6th Division area soldiers were ordered to interfere with neither Sinn Féin flags nor private property but to leave that to the RIC. Nevertheless, soldiers who remained walking the streets of Dublin up to the Truce, occasionally got into trouble with nationalist youths. Some of these incidents sparked off a violent reaction among the soldiers' comrades, leading to minor outbreaks of fighting.[19]

The IRA successes of 1920 increased army involvement and also led to more conflict with the IRA. Together with the Auxiliaries the military patrols became the main target for ambushes in Dublin. As indicated previously, the DMP were not regarded a target for attack, and the RIC in the suburbs of the city were approached in a more circumspect way by singling out the most active. This latter policy had evolved early on in active areas, and continued to be pursued by Volunteer units throughout the country up to the Truce. The quieter areas took up this policy only at the end of the struggle. In the active areas the RIC were eventually pushed into the background and attention was concentrated on the military and the auxiliary police forces. The latter's straightforward aggressive approach was least complicated to deal with.[20]

19 On attitude towards soldiers, Larry Nugent, O'MN, P17b88; Tom Barry, in K. Griffith and T. O'Grady (1982), 220; Patrick O'Daly, 'Statement', NLI, P4548. Towards the end of 1920 reports of attacks on unarmed soldiers, beaten up and stripped of their clothes become frequent. A great many occurred in Dublin between 23 and 26 May 1921, in one case the soldiers received a receipt from the Volunteers, PRO, WO35/205, and WO35/72. The first attack on unarmed soldiers in the West took place on 21 April 1920 at Castlebar, 'History of the 5th Division in Ireland November 1919-March 1922', 38, IWM, 72/82/2. Orders in 6th Division, GHQ Ireland Parkgate Dublin, dated 5 June 1920, MA, A0413. See also NLI, ms. 900/20; John Regan, 'Memoirs', 170, PRONI, D3160. Such an incident between Volunteers and soldiers, Paddy Rigney, O'MN, P17b105.
20 In an attempt to discourage the English auxiliary police force, attacks on their family homes in England were sanctioned by the IRA, Billy Ahearne, O'MN, P17b99; Dinny Kelleher, O'MN, P17b107; Joe McHenry, O'MN, P17b95; Hugh Early, O'MN, P17b110. A list of addresses of auxiliary RIC men was found among papers belonging to the IRA Chief of Staff, Weekly Intelligence summary for week ending 20 February 1921, PRO, WO35/70.

Volunteers everywhere were well aware that violence against the Crown Forces would engender violence against them, and many consequently remained inactive. The commander of the West Mayo Brigade had ordered his men not to attack the 'Tommies' as this would involve them in the fighting. Fear of the reaction of the Crown Forces explains the lack of activity in many areas: 'There was a good deal of raids but there was no IRA provocation. Let sleeping dogs lie was the attitude.'[21]

The attempts by many Volunteer officers to keep killings to a minimum stimulated similar diligence on the other side. This was occasionally the start of a downward spiral in the level of violence, leading eventually to an unofficial stand off. When some local radicals in these areas of undeclared truces sidelined their superiors and attacked the police, fear and confusion resulted. In November 1920 some of the local Volunteers in Newry shot a Head Constable of the RIC who had been particularly active against them, against the wishes of their superiors. The police reaction was strong and several local IRA officers, including the commandant of the South Down Battalion, fled the area.[22]

A range of different Crown Force reactions can thus be observed to which the Volunteers tried to respond. In general, attempts to keep violence at a low level dominated attitudes. Both sides were mainly concerned with their own survival. However, attempts by Volunteers to obtain arms, and the attacks on more active policemen, led to violent clashes in some areas. Occasionally this resulted in outbursts of violence by groups of enraged military and police. These incidents often sparked off small cycles of tit-for-tat attacks. Most of these cycles eventually died out when the leading figures on either side had been neutralised.

However, Volunteer successes and the often indiscriminate reaction of the Crown Forces encouraged the emergence of new cycles of violence elsewhere. Within these cycles a small number of dedicated Volunteers and diligent policemen became permanently engaged in violence. These small groups in a limited number of areas occasionally drew less willing men on both sides with them into violent conflict. For their part, the greater mass of less willing members restrained the unbridled activity of these small groups. Nevertheless, the dynamics of violent conflict ensured an ever-increasing level of casualties.

21 The policy in Mayo not to attack the military, Charlie Hughes, Interview. Quote, Tom Carney, O'MN, P17b109.
22 Events in Newry, Patrick Casey, 'Idle Thoughts', Fr O'Kane Papers, AARC. Similarly, Volunteers in Crossabeg and Killurin, Co. Wexford attacked soldiers without sanction of their officers, Bob Lambert, 'Statement'. See also Note 4.

STRENGTH OF THE CROWN FORCES PER COUNTY

Although the general direction of developments and the reaction patterns in the Crown Forces were comparable in the various brigades, clearly different relationships between Crown Forces and the IRA had established themselves in 1921. In all counties, examples of all the different attitudes on both sides can be seen, but the extent to which they were displayed and the resulting outcome differed extensively. In order to illustrate the different types of possible developments, the remainder of this chapter provides a short description of the relationship between Volunteers and Crown Forces as it had established itself in the five brigade areas in the final part of the struggle.

The Volunteers in the various counties faced different levels of opposition in their attempts to replace British rule. The local units of the RIC are a good indicator of the strength of opposition in the first stages of organisation and developing violence. The number of police barracks in each county in 1914 and the strength of the RIC in these stations in 1920 is indicated below:

Table 9: Strength of RIC in 1920[23]

	Posts 1914	Head-Constable	Sergeants	Constables	Total Police
Mayo	63	8	70	282	360
Tipperary	42	6	51	146	203
Wexford	38	4	46	121	171
Derry Co.	22	3	26	88	117
City	4	2	24	74	100
Dublin Co.	n. a.	3	29	117	149

Comparing these figures to the size of the population, it is apparent that Tipperary was unarguably the best-policed county, with one policeman to every 441 inhabitants. The other counties had much higher ratios: one to 534 in Mayo, one to 548 in Derry and one to 598 in Wexford. Relating these figures to the level of violence, there seems to have been a direct connection between the level of Volunteer activity and police strength.

From 1920 onwards the military became increasingly involved in the struggle and the police was reinforced. To estimate the total strength of the Crown Forces in 1921 we compare intelligence reports from the different IRA brigades with military records. The small presence of Crown Forces in

23 RIC stations in 1914, TCD, 7382/2. RIC strength in 1920, PRO, HO184/61.

south Wexford is recorded by the brigade in April 1921 recounting the presence of 169 policemen and 130 military. In south Tipperary the IRA faced extremely potent opposition; their reports put military strength at 2,323 in 12 barracks, and record the presence of 369 RIC in 21 barracks. The latter had been heavily reinforced and now included several Black & Tans. According to military records operational strength totalled 1,336 in south Tipperary in June 1920, while Thom's Directory of 1921 puts police strength in the South Riding of Tipperary at 327. The total strength of the Army stationed in south Tipperary more than doubled before the Truce and was further strengthened by 85 members of the Auxiliaries.[24]

A comparable IRA report in Mayo is only available from the South Mayo Brigade. This records the presence of 118 RIC men and 440 military in the brigade area in August 1921. When related to the number of policemen in Mayo in 1920, the first figure is extremely high. In November 1920 the County Inspector of the RIC in Mayo reported there were 67 vacancies in the fixed strength of the police, which had already been reduced from 436 in 1919 to 348 early in 1920. These figures make the total of 118 RIC men in south Mayo unlikely. However, from the end of 1920 the police in Mayo were also reinforced with recruits from Britain, making this figure more plausible. The IRA in south Mayo was apparently more modest about the presence of soldiers. Against its assessment of 440 soldiers two military reports state that at the end of 1920 its strength in the South Mayo Brigade area was around 600, and that in July 1921 it reached 629. The same reports put military strength in the West Mayo Brigade area at about 400 in December 1920, and 326 in July. Overall, the high number of Volunteers in Mayo were thus encountered by an average number of policemen and military.[25]

The IRA in Derry City estimated military strength at 800 and the police's at 129. In addition to this 77 A-Specials had been attached to the RIC to fill vacancies. The part-time B-Specials numbered 1,500–2,000 in the city. The 1st Battalion of the Volunteers in south Derry, covering the southeastern tip of county Derry and the area around Cookstown in Co. Tyrone, reported a police presence of 58 in the Derry part of the battalion, assisted by 63 A-Specials and 505 B-Specials. No soldiers were stationed in this area. The 2nd South Derry Battalion to the north of this area put police strength at 92, aided by 54 A-Specials. The strength of the B-Specials was reported to embody 75 per cent of all 'able-bodied Protestants'. The last

24 Intelligence reports from Wexford, UCD AD, P7a16, and P7A17/57. Intelligence reports from Tipperary, Ibidem, P7a8. Strength of military and Auxiliaries in Tipperary, Charles Townshend (1975), Appendices VIII & IX.
25 Intelligence reports from Mayo Volunteers, UCD AD, P7a11. Vacancies in Mayo RIC, CI Mayo MR November 1920. Strength military in Mayo, '5th Division War Diary', PRO, WO35/93/2; 'History of the 5th Division in Ireland November 1919–March 1922', Appendices IX & XX, IWM, 72/82/2.

government figure available for the number of Specials in Derry is for 26 March 1921. At this point 235 A-specials were appointed, aided by 1,094 B-Specials and 452 C-Specials. The latter formed a militia that was rarely used. The target strength of these forces in Derry had originally been 190 A-Specials, 4,000 B-Specials and all other available men as C-Specials. This strength allowed for the numbers reported by the IRA in July. Although Derry had thus been averagely policed until the end of 1920, it had a sizeable military presence in the city and became highly policed in 1921.[26]

Generally, a high number of Crown Forces seems to have provoked a more active Volunteer force. The measure of policing was, however, also a reflection of traditional levels of unrest. Tipperary was clearly the best controlled county, but it also contained one of the most violent Volunteer units in the country. The least disturbed part of Ireland was the Southeast. Wexford is the most south-eastern county and housed the least Crown Forces. The correlation between the strength of the Crown Forces and the level of violence by the Volunteers seems to be confirmed in Dublin. In Dublin City the unarmed DMP was about 1,100 strong and there was a considerable military presence of up to 7,726 soldiers in the Dublin District. During 1920 both forces were heavily reinforced with recruits from Britain. The fairly large number of Dublin Volunteers thus faced considerable opposition which led to much confrontation, as witnessed by the high number of recorded casualties.[27]

REGIONAL SURVEY

In Wexford neither police nor Volunteers were overtly active, and violence never reached the indiscriminate phase. The majority of the few shooting incidents involved attempts to kill active policemen, and were carried out by men from Dublin. Many of the Volunteers were known to the police, but the military insignificance of their relatively frequent actions (the cutting of all type of communications lines) prevented conflict. Although these Volunteers were harassed by the police, they were rarely seriously maltreated or arrested. Most Volunteers had little to fear and made no attempt to avoid the police, not even when their homes were raided.

26 Intelligence reports from Derry City Battalion, UCD AD, P7a10. From south Derry battalions, Ibidem, P7a11. Number of Specials in Derry, PRONI, FIN18/1/11, 13 + 144.
27 Exact figures for the RIC, DMP and auxiliary police forces recruited in England, Charles Townshend (1975), Appendix III. The Dublin District, then included the counties Dublin, Wicklow and Meath. Operational strength in July 1920 totalled 7,726 soldiers, of which 4,270 were available for mobile operations, Ibidem, Appendix VII.

Police operations in Wexford were still largely aimed at preventing offences by the use of intimidation. The IRA could continue to expose itself without fear of arrest. In October 1920 a large deputation of Volunteers openly turned out for the funeral of the victims of an explosion in an IRA bomb factory. Police presence at this funeral was limited to some police lorries driving up and down, but no one was arrested. Only a few Wexford Volunteers radicalised sufficiently to attack policemen and spies. In order to ensure the safety of some of the more active Volunteers and to set examples, a small number of alleged informers were executed in the last few months of the struggle. On the few occasions in which policemen were taken prisoner they were warned, but not treated particularly badly. On 16 April 1921 the local newspaper reported an attack in a train when a policeman in civilian clothes was relieved of some papers and his pistol and made to swear never to return to Ireland again; but he was released unharmed. None of the local IRA members interviewed could remember ever being involved in or having knowledge of the shooting of a policeman in their area besides some sniping incidents. In April the police reported that they had been successful in preventing IRA activity, and that generally speaking they had the situation well in hand. Having little cause for anger, serious breaches of discipline among the Crown Forces were practically non-existent in Wexford.[28]

In Derry, where even less Volunteer activity took place, little conflict evolved and the police became more confident during 1921. The realisation that certain precautions were unwarranted in their part of the country had led to the reopening of many evacuated barracks. After the opening of seven barracks in March only two were left vacant. Despite his initial misgivings, the County Inspector now considered the aid of the Specials helpful:

> A large number of B Specials have been enrolled, and they are now regularly patrolling in all parts of the County at night. I am glad to say that there has been no case of serious indiscipline up to the present, & the relations between them and the Regular R.I.C. are most harmonious. In some cases the old R.I.C. was at first inclined to rather throw cold water on the movement, but now they all realise how invaluable a large organised & armed force will be in the event of the I.R.A. trying to carry out a campaign of ambushes etc. in force.

Nevertheless some apprehension apparently developed among the RIC in the six northern counties when the separation of North and South became

28 Newspaper report of attack on policeman, *People* (Wexford), 16 April 1921. Confident police report, CI Wexford MR April 1921.

imminent. The IRA in Fermanagh reported that the fear among RIC men of being superseded by the Specials reduced their diligence.[29]

As seen previously, some minor military operations were attempted under the direction of the newly appointed divisional commanders in the spring of 1921. The few violent incidents were the first attempts at the removal of vigilant policemen. A sergeant who had been threatened by people from the Bogside after arresting a prominent Sinn Féiner eighteen months before, was now shot in Derry City. The ambush of a police patrol in Swatragh in June appeared to be the first expression of more indiscriminate fighting reaching Derry before the Truce. However, this was the first ambush in south Derry and can also be interpreted as a simple attempt to obtain arms. Nevertheless, two more ambushes took place here in July 1921. However, even the most violent Volunteers only hesitantly engaged in such operations. The leader of a Flying Column sent out from Derry City described their intentions: 'It was not our policy, however, in these surprise attacks, to kill indiscriminately. Our aim was to worry and harass the enemy until, in desperation, he quit.'[30]

In most areas in the North, the IRA was disregarded by police and people alike. One of the more active northern brigades in West Donegal initiated sniping attacks at barracks in 1921 with the sole object: 'a) to show the towns people (who fraternise with the R.I.C.) that there are other forces in the country besides the R.I.C. and b) to put the R.I.C. from running about a little less.' In most places in the North no escalation took place. All attempts at attacking the Crown Forces were blocked by IRA officers and Church representatives, who were afraid for the consequences. On a small scale the first steps towards violent conflict were nevertheless taken in 1921. That the conflict became far more violent in Derry in the period after the Truce indicates that further escalation had been possible.[31]

In Mayo wholesale arrests in the autumn of 1920 had forced many Volunteers to go on the run, which led to a greater measure of IRA violence. This in turn caused Crown Force brutality directed at known sympathisers and families of the Volunteers. Many column men vividly remember the unofficial reprisals against their families after the first major incident in west Mayo. After this episode, in which a sergeant and two policemen had been shot, the police retaliated by maltreating several people closely associated with the

29 Quote, CI Derry MR June 1921. Reopening of barracks, *Coleraine Chronicle*, 26 February & 12 March 1921; CI Derry MRs 1921. Report of the Fermanagh Brigade, UCD AD, P7A38.
30 Shooting in Derry City, *Coleraine Chronicle*, 9 April 1921. Quote, C.J. MacGuinness (1943), 146.
31 Quote, UCD AD, P7A20/286. Church interference in Derry, Lt. M. Sheerin, NLI, P921 No.66.

movement. They took them out of their houses and humiliated them, beat them, painted them red, white and blue, and threatened to shoot them. However, this was one of only a few incidents of this kind in the West Mayo Brigade area, and the next month the Volunteers reported little enemy activity 'of the torturing night-raiding type.'[32]

The successful ambushes in May 1921 nevertheless led to some further violence. The resulting casualties among the Crown Forces engendered strong emotions in their comrades. The officer in charge of a military party coming to the rescue of three ambushed police cars in Tourmakeady described his feelings: 'We saw one or two bodies of Constables with whom we had worked and whom we respected and I personally was filled with feelings of vengeance.' To vent their frustration some houses were burned near the ambush sites as an official reprisal in both Mayo brigades, although in Tourmakeady all houses but one were owned by Protestants. Two civilians were killed by the Crown Forces, in south Mayo, one each in reaction to the two major ambushes there. Despite the widespread maltreatment described above, just one civilian was killed in west Mayo.[33]

The Volunteers reacted to the abuse of civilians with attempts to attack the nightly police patrols. Although it never came to a fight, the police realised the Volunteers' presence and became more cautious. Most police and military showed little desire to engage the Volunteers after the latter had shown their willingness to defend themselves and their supporters. Particularly after some of the IRA ambushes had been successful, a stand off developed. Night raiding by the police was reduced and several of the remaining rural police barracks were evacuated.[34]

Although the maltreatment of their supporters infuriated the Volunteers, the officers in Mayo prevented all retribution on imprisoned members of the Crown Forces. After the successful ambush at Carrowkennedy in June

32 Examples of maltreatment by Crown Forces, UCD AD, P80/61/1 + 3; Ned Maughan, O'MN, P17b109; Jimmy Slattery, O'MN, P17b138; Johnny Duffy, O'MN, P17b109; Thomas Heavey, O'MN, P17b120; Jim O'Donnell, 'Recollections'. One of the imprisoned column men was suspected of giving information to the police. The IRA could only guess this as the captured Volunteer never returned, Michael Kilroy, O'MN, P17b138; Thomas Heavey, O'MN, P17b120. The police confirms that information was given to them by prisoners, CI Mayo MR May 1921. Quote, Report dated 16 May 1921, UCD AD, P7A38.

33 Quote, Major Geoffrey Ibberson, TCD, 3491/10. The burning of houses in Tourmakeady and the killing of a boy in Ballinrobe, *Mayoman*, 14 May 1921; South Mayo Brigade report on Tourmakeady, UCD AD, P7A38; J.R.W. Goulden, 'Statement', TCD, 7377/7.

34 IRA patrols against nightly raids, Johnny Duffy, O'MN, P17b109; Jimmy Slattery, O'MN, P17b138; Paddy Duffy, O'MN, P17b138. On the evacuation of barracks following IRA ambushes, South Mayo Brigade report on Tourmakeady, UCD AD, P7A38; CI Mayo MR May 1921.

some of the policemen, who had personally been involved in the abuse of civilians, were captured. Some column men wanted to shoot the worst offenders, but the commanding officer refused to allow it. Instead, the policemen were simply lectured on their unpatriotic stance and warned not to be seen in the RIC ranks again as they would not get off so lightly the next time. The wounded were treated and one of them was allowed to cycle to town to get help. This lenient treatment of the captured police had a calming effect; a significantly milder reaction from the Crown Forces against the population followed. The small number of engagements and the restrained reactions on both sides meant that the struggle in Mayo had no time to develop into a brutal confrontation. Mayo thus took a middle position. Although its Volunteers were involved in some ambushes, they had not reached the stage in which active policemen were singled out for execution.[35]

The most violent form of conflict developed in Tipperary. The fighting had become increasingly vicious, although large-scale engagements had become less likely in 1921. Many police and military refused to venture out of their barracks except in large numbers. Attacking these large groups was only possible by exposing the Volunteers to grave danger, and only on one occasion did the two brigade Flying Columns attempt a concerted attack on such a large grouping of enemy troops. Successful fights between Flying Columns and military parties of this size were almost exclusively limited to Co. Cork.[36]

In south Tipperary only a few successful ambushes of smaller Crown Force parties took place in 1921. This meant that the Volunteers were unable to supplement their scarce resources of ammunition, which was a further indirect blow to activity. The lack of ammunition also reduced the chances of a serious attack on police barracks and most Flying Columns resorted to simple sniping. The lack of ammunition became apparent as early as January 1921 when all Volunteer units were ordered to snipe all enemy posts and one company could only expend five rounds per person.[37]

The attempted militarisation of the conflict by the IRA was difficult to implement even in Tipperary. Many within the organisation were content with the existing situation and had little desire to provoke the other side. Most Volunteers never seriously believed that a military victory was pos-

35 The experience with captured policemen, Thomas Heavey, O'MN, P17b120; Michael Kilroy, 'ASU Operations'; O'MN, P17b136; Jimmy Slattery, O'MN, P17b138; Johnny Duffy, O'MN, P17b109; Paddy Duffy, O'MN, P17b113; Michael Hughes, 'Statement'; J.R.W. Goulden, 'Statement', TCD, 7377/7.

36 In Cork less than half of Crown Force and only 35 per cent of IRA casualties fell in combat, the others were victims of assassinations and other forms of brutality, Peter Hart (1992), Chapter 'The Dynamics of Violence', 62.

37 Unit with five rounds, Paul Mulcahy, 'Statement'.

sible. The necessity of large-scale attacks was therefore ambiguous to some column men. Sean Hogan, the commander of the second Flying Column in south Tipperary, felt the inability of the military to defeat them and thus the continued presence of the column itself justified its existence. As long as the authorities were unable to govern freely, the IRA achieved its objectives. However, as with the Volunteers in Mayo, the abuse of family and friends and their property infuriated column men, but there was little scope for venting their anger on the Crown Forces. The order to attack all enemy troops engaged in attacks at the population was impossible to enforce, because of the danger it involved to these people.[38]

Combined activity by military and police against Flying Columns which started in 1921 made all Volunteer activity, both of ordinary and Flying Column members even more difficult. The IRA columns were forced to retreat to the mountains where the military were unable to reach them. In June the County Inspector acknowledged the inability to take on the Flying Columns when he assessed the work of the Military Column: 'They have done some good, but the rebel intelligence system is exceedingly good and makes it very hard to get within striking distance of their commandos.'[39]

The Tipperary columns were disbanded. Column members were instructed to return to their units and to keep 'fairly quiet' during the summer months. A stalemate had emerged between the cautious Volunteers and the Crown Forces, who were afraid to venture far from barracks. The County Inspector of the RIC realised this when he stated: 'Our forces hold the towns and some of the villages, the I.R.A. practically holds all the country districts. It is certainly most unsafe for military or police to leave the towns except in strong force.'[40]

In southern areas like Tipperary the conflict had become exclusively

38 Attitude of the column O.C. in Tipperary, Ned O'Reilly, O'MN, P17b126.
39 Quote, CI South Tipperary MR June 1921. See also Mossy MacGrath, O'MN, P17b127; 'Conversation with Lt. Col. Tom Ryan', UCD AD, P7b179. In the 5th Division area of the British Army covering the less affected western and midland areas, no Flying Column was ever captured in its entirety, 'History of the 5th Division in Ireland November 1919-March 1922', 77, IWM, 72/82/2.
40 Quote, CI South Tipperary MR June 1921. See also John Regan, 'Memoirs', 168, PRONI, D3160; Liam Haugh, 'History of the West Clare Brigade', NLI, P915 A0363. Many examples of troops fleeing into the barrack when fearing attack or not leaving it if an attack was suspected: In Tipperary, Tommy Ryan, 'Statement'; Ned Glendon, O'MN, P17b103; Mossy McGrath, O'MN, P17b127; Kennedy, O'MN, P17b114; Ned O'Reilly, O'MN, P17b126. In Co. Dublin, Report to C/S from O.C. Fingal Brigade, UCD AD, P7A17/186. In Mayo, North Mayo Brigade report for April 1921, UCD AD, P7A18/9; Report West Mayo Brigade May 1921, UCD AD, P7A19/88. It was quietly acknowledged that the IRA controlled towns where curfew had been introduced during the night, the police patrolled only in the daytime, 'History of the 5th Division

military. Most traces of using Volunteer activity as a political weapon in order to disrupt the British administration in Ireland had disappeared. This development was epitomised by the attitude taken by arrested Volunteers in the South. In an internal IRA memo from the beginning of 1921 it was acknowledged that in Co. Cork the refusal to recognise the British courts, which was the official political line, had been replaced by arrested Volunteers repudiating the IRA. The introduction of the death penalty for carrying arms in the martial law area was an important factor in this change. Although GHQ contemplated allowing Volunteers facing capital punishment to defend themselves, it was stressed that such prisoners should not be permitted to repudiate the IRA without special reason.[41]

At the same time the conflict obtained an increasingly vicious character, caused by a lack of military targets, the anger caused by the victimisation of Volunteer families, and the increased risk attached to participation. This was shown in a sharp increase in attempted killings of members of the Crown Forces as well as civilians who were considered hostile, such as Protestants and ex-soldiers. The executions of captured Volunteers and members of the Crown Forces, in particular, caused violent reactions on both sides. This was exemplified by an IRA battalion commander in Tipperary, who reported the execution of three British officers in a letter to the military authorities: 'We are reluctant to carry out such executions but until such time as the British Government cease from executing our Prisoners of War this will re-occur.' As a result of these developments most casualties in 1921 were a result of secret murders and did not occur in open combat. Nevertheless, most Tipperary Volunteers were as reluctant to kill as those elsewhere, and performing executions was limited to a few members of the Flying Columns.[42]

in Ireland November 1919-March 1922', 58-59, IWM, 72/82/2. However, even in seriously affected cities, such as Dublin and Cork, the police and military could still walk the streets in relative safety in 1921, E.M. Ransford, 'One Man's Tide', IWM, 80/29/1; Brigadier J.V. Faviell, IWM, 82/24/1; Major B.A. Pond, IWM, 78/27/1.

41 Internal Memo, UCD AD, P7A18/40. Some Volunteers who were arrested in Dublin on 21 November 1920 claimed to be forced to join the IRA against their will or because they had no work, PRO, WO35/70.

42 Quote, Letter dated 22 June 1921, UCD AD, P7A20/137-8. The first execution of a Volunteer in Dublin also invoked much hatred against the British, C.S. Andrews (1979), 149. One Volunteer claims that the executions of Tans and British military were started after Volunteers had been executed in Cork, Andy Cooney, O'MN, P17b107. The restrained attitude of column men can be observed in the treatment of the kidnapped District Inspector Potter, Andy Kennedy, O'MN, P17b114; Ned Glendon, O'MN, P17b103; Tom O'Cannon, letter to Dan Breen dated 30 September 1966, TCD, 7377/4/7; Sean Fitzpatrick, O'MN, P17b126; Letters of Potter to his wife, TCD, 7377/4/1. A lively depiction of these type of events loosely based upon Potter's execution, can be found in a short story titled, *Midsummer Night Madness,* Sean O'Faolain (1993).

In Dublin the escalation of violence took a course similar to Tipperary, but the urban setting necessitated a different form of confrontation. Unlike the country areas, most of the fighting in Dublin took place between the Volunteers and the military in an increasingly indiscriminate fashion. The other main adversaries were the Auxiliaries, who worked closely with the military. Their rough handling of Volunteers and civilians had made them prime targets of IRA attention. The DMP continued to be ignored by the IRA as they ignored the IRA. Nevertheless, the old policy of singling out particularly active members of the Crown Forces continued to be pursued as well. Active policemen and soldiers were shot in an increasingly callous way: 'A lad on a bicycle rode by, dismounted, put his bicycle at the kerb, drew a revolver, and walked behind the 2 men and fired three shots at them. He then put his revolver back into his pocket, mounted his bicycle and rode towards Dublin.'[43]

Despite the escalation of violence, securing the safety of their own men remained the overriding consideration. Easy targets such as military cycle patrols and open parades were the first to be attacked by the IRA, but they were quickly abandoned by the authorities. Lorries travelling the streets at high speed became the main objects of attention in 1921. Men on both sides, but primarily the inexperienced company Volunteers, needed time to get used to the indiscriminate attacks. Many had difficulty getting to grips with the new situation. As in Tipperary open executions were mainly carried out by the most committed members concentrated in the ASU and Squad. Bombing a passing lorry appeared to be an act much more easily engaged in by part-time members without a particular grudge.

Towards the end of the war the death sentence for those caught with arms was largely responsible for a growing disregard for the safety of civilians. The use of private houses as bases for attacks, utilising mines, and the laying of ambushes in busy streets were, although forbidden, the best safeguard against arrest. With little knowledge of where to expect enemy lorries and the fear of being arrested with guns running high, the number of engagements remained low, but civilian casualties grew ever higher.

The Crown Forces also concentrated on relatively safe operations. To the military and Auxiliaries this meant extensive raiding. The shootings of British Intelligence officers on Bloody Sunday gave a strong impetus to this in Dublin. Of the 354 raids in November, 274 took place between the 26th and the 31st. This extremely high level, up from 66 in October, con-

---

43 Quote, report on John Brady 4 June 1921, PRO, WO35/146A. Other examples, reports dated 4 March 1921, 23 April 1921, 4 & 12 June 1921, Ibid.; Report from North Louth Battalion dated 20 June 1921, UCD AD, P7A19/148. Demonstrating the discriminate approach towards the Crown Forces, some men who had not been singled out but were found in the same room as the intended victims during Bloody Sunday were spared, Jim Slattery, O'MNs, P17b95, and P17b105.

tinued in the beginning of December with an average of 85 per night. Arrests were so frequent that raiding had to be restricted between the 12th and 24th. In addition to the 534 persons arrested in December by raiding parties, 336 were apprehended for violation of the newly introduced curfew.[44]

The large number of arrests led to congestion in civil and military prisons. Out of necessity raiding was curtailed from January onwards. Arrests were only allowed if incriminating evidence was found. In February arrests were further limited to persons found in possession of arms or ammunition; the presence of seditious literature alone was no longer sufficient. The arrests of people breaking curfew added to the problems of the prison system. In Dublin more than 600 persons were arrested each month, peaking at 978 in June. These people were usually just held overnight, but could also be sentenced to imprisonment.[45]

Table 10: Raids and Arrests by Crown Forces in Dublin 1920-1921

	Oct.	Nov.	Dec.	Jan.	Feb.	Mar.	Apr.	May	June	July
Raids	66	354	859	445	286	327	204	263	137	6
Arrests		274	534	85	96	165	173	154	127	3

Lack of intelligence remained a serious problem in targeting IRA activists. Bloody Sunday and the authority's reaction to it had seriously damaged intelligence operations in Dublin. Its effect was described by one of the British agents who had been sent over to Dublin in the summer of 1920: 'As a result of all this, those of us who had survived were shut up under guard in a hotel, from where it was impracticable to do any useful work. In fact, our job had to all intents and purposes been done, and the organisation was breaking up.' The lack of intelligence became apparent in the arrests in the early months of 1921, most of which were a result of coincidence and incidental successes. In March more than half of all the arrests were a consequence of a search of all bicycle shops, some of which were found to be a front for IRA workshops. Stumbling on IRA meetings accounted for 48 of those arrested in April, and 42 in June. In May, 70 of the 154 arrested were detained after the Custom House attack.[46]

Abortive raids for the elusive Michael Collins, and even for men who had already been arrested, continued, but the Crown Forces also had some successes. Arrests of active Volunteers as well as the capture of IRA war-

44 Raiding figures, PRO, WO35/80, and WO35/90.
45 Reasons for and figures of arrests, PRO, WO35/71-72, and WO35/90. See also Letter from 6th Division dated 15 March 1921, NLI, ms. 31,228.
46 Quote, Lt. R.D. Jeane, IWM, 76/172/1. The results of raiding, PRO, WO35/72.

material slowly increased. In order to compensate for the lack of intelligence, parts of the city were now completely cordoned off and every house searched. However, although some dumps were found in this way, few Volunteers were arrested. The military rarely knew who to look for. When an active Volunteer was asked how he avoided these searches, he said: 'Oh needless, they would have nothing on us, if we were searched, we would pretend to be innocent little boys.' The city thus provided ample opportunity for the IRA to operate in relative anonymity. The likelihood of arrest was further reduced by DMP men who did not act when they recognised wanted Volunteers, sometimes even providing them with an alibi.[47]

The loss of experienced men nevertheless hardened Volunteer attitudes further. Open orders to attack all enemies were given to the ASU and later to its successor the Dublin Guards. The company Volunteers were reminded in April that: 'All British Army Officers and British Army Dispatch Riders (Motor Cyclists) are "fair game" to be attacked by our forces.' Wholesale machine-gun attacks on large groups of police and military were planned and grand plans, like an attempt to blow up the Castle, were drawn up. The only such plan that materialised was the burning of the Custom House. The dearth of capable officers the subsequent arrests led to went unobserved by the authorities until July. However, in their opinion it did not affect the overall level of IRA activity.[48]

As elsewhere atrocities from either side were the main cause for the combatants to lose sight of the dangers and take risks in order to hurt the enemy. This mechanism was, however, readily understood by both adversaries. Whenever a serious outrage had occurred the men on the perpetrators' side wisely stayed out of sight. When this state of affairs had established itself, activity became more and more limited to soft targets. In the weekly intelligence summaries of the military in Dublin it was reported on 29 May that rebel activity was chiefly confined to molesting unarmed soldiers, followed on 19 June with: 'Attacks on Curfew patrols is a new form of outrage in Dublin. Up to the present they have been immune.'[49]

---

47 Objects and successes of raids in Dublin, PRO, WO35/71. For the hunt on Michael Collins, PRO, WO35/71; Private J.P. Swindlehurst, Diary, IWM, 48790. Quote, Sean Clancy, Interview. See also Charlie Dalton (1929), 140-3; C.S. Andrews (1979), 164; Ernie Noonan, O'MN, P17b94.

48 Quote, NLI, ms. 902/147. Large-scale schemes, UCD AD, LA9; Billy Rowe, O'MN, P17b110; Patrick O'Daly, 'Statement', NLI, P4548; Tom MacMahon, O'MN, P17b86. Lack of capable officers, summary week ending 3 July 1921, PRO, WO35/91.

49 Anticipation of reaction, Joe O'Connor, O'MN, P17b105. Quote and other examples of molesting soldiers and attacks on Curfew patrols, Intelligence summary of weeks ending 29 May, 12 June, 19 June 1921, PRO, WO35/91. See also Joe McHenry, O'MN, P17b95; Paddy Rigney, O'MN, P17b105.

CONCLUSION

The reactions of members of the Crown Forces to the activities of the Volunteers were dictated by sympathy, fear, a desire for self-preservation and anger. Sympathy for the republican ideal led to some resignations and to active and passive cooperation with the movement. Fear and a desire for self-preservation also caused some resignations and gave rise to some cooperation with the IRA to prevent conflict. Police tasks were often not executed diligently, and known Volunteers were not taken on. Local policemen gave information and occasionally attempted to come to an understanding with the IRA. However, the anger which was caused by the violence of the IRA sometimes led to virulent responses against Volunteers and their supporters, and diminished the sympathy for the republican cause among those members who had remained in the force. At the same time the violence against the population and imprisoned Volunteers by some members of the Crown Forces also led to some resignations and to attempts to curb violence by other members.

The actual behaviour of the Crown Forces during the conflict was a result of one or other combination of these motives. A sense of duty, the normal incentive for execution of police tasks, became increasingly irrelevant when violence erupted. The general approach most policemen took, to avoid getting involved in the conflict, became impossible to maintain in the most disturbed areas, where developments were forced by the actions of extremists on both sides. Despite the overwhelming desire for self-preservation, the men were increasingly influenced by their personal experience with violence, and a growing familiarity with bloodshed.

Volunteer involvement and activity were also dictated by such considerations. Fear and self-preservation caused comparable reactions to those within the members of the Crown Forces. The original acts of defiance had for the majority of Volunteers solely been a tool in reaching the widely shared object of an independent Ireland by making British administration in Ireland impossible. Intensified prosecution of those involved in these acts created a necessity for the more politically determined activists to take extreme measures to enable them to continue their work free from imprisonment. The increasing seriousness of their offences and the subsequent growth in violence needed to deter the RIC led to escalating conflict. Attempts to mobilise support within the RIC and to force them through social pressure to leave the force turned into violent attempts to diminish the effectiveness of the force.

Within the violence which developed between the IRA and the Crown Forces several patterns can be discerned. A simple tit-for-tat where violence created violence, was the most natural reaction in the areas where direct action against the police began. The feelings of revenge which fuelled this kind of escalating violence are the main explanation provided by Hart for the continuous growth in conflict and increase in casualties in Co. Cork. On basis of the experience in different areas, his assessment must however be adjusted. In many areas, the type of continuous escalation he described had a short natural life span. It often burned out within a few months when the main protagonists on either side had been eliminated one way or other. However, within these cycles of violence a small group of men was sometimes separated from their home ground and became radicalised to such an extent that they became full-time soldiers. They then extended their operations to other parts of the brigade, which was often the beginning of a new cycle of violence there. As a result of Crown Force reaction to engagements, the conflict in one district could also easily spill over to a neighbouring area. In counties where violence started it was thus more likely to escalate, making conflict a self-sustaining process.[50]

Furthermore, the violence by both sides also sparked off a reaction in inactive areas, where feelings of revenge were fuelled by these events. Volunteers and Crown Forces were inspired to follow the example set in active counties, and started new cycles of violence. In this way the conflict was transferred from one area to another, causing a continuous growth in the number of casualties despite the short life span of many of these cycles. This was exacerbated by government policies, which forced many unwilling Volunteers to participate in the conflict, particularly during 1920.

A military stalemate was, nonetheless, the most common outcome. This could follow a tit-for-tat cycle between local IRA units and the Crown Forces, but was often the result of the fear of the consequences of violence caused by events elsewhere. Apprehension and a general lack of enthusiasm made most men on both sides anxious to stay out of trouble. Consequently most areas never saw much bloodshed. A growing immunity to the consequences of violence further reduced the intensity of the reaction after a new engagement, thus restraining possible escalation.

In many areas the later period in the struggle can be described as a general stand-off, with some escalating spirals of violence springing up in different localities at different times, but usually cut short. Rarely would such a spiral develop further, as that was not in the interest of anyone on either side. The increase in casualties was a result of the violence engaged in by the growing number of full-time members roaming the countryside. They were hardened and radicalised by the fighting, and killed many government agents and alleged spies.

50 For the development of these spirals of escalating violence in Cork, Peter Hart (1992).

THEME 2

VOLUNTEERS AND THE COMMUNITY

CHAPTER 7

Mobilising Support

In the diverse and changing relationship between the Volunteers and the Crown Forces the population was constantly affected by the struggle. Measures taken by both sides directly involved civilians. The central question in this final part is how the relationship between the Volunteers and the people affected the development of violence. Coming from the Catholic community, the IRA may be seen as a strand of public opinion which gained dominance in many parts of the country in a short time. To assess to what extent the IRA continued to act as part of the community and what kind of restraints that community could lay upon the IRA's activities during the War of Independence we look at how the Volunteers dealt with the various reactions of the population towards the movement in the emerging fight. This chapter discusses the measure of the movement's success in becoming the leading nationalist party in the five counties and the ways in which the population was mobilised.

In recent historical writing, the traditional view that there existed a symbiotic relationship between the IRA and the community has been successfully challenged. Most authors acknowledge the presence of widespread support, but stress that the Volunteers often had to resort to intimidation to enforce the allegiance of all nationalists to the republican cause and to its alternative government. They draw particular attention to the victimisation of ex-soldiers and Protestants in the final phase of the struggle. However, this assessment has been based mainly on a detailed analysis of events in Cork and Clare and on some incidental evidence. Uncovering the varied development of this relationship in different counties is the final object of this part. It becomes apparent that important differences existed, and it is argued that the level of acceptance of the republican ideal among the community in different areas was directly linked to the type and measure of IRA operations.[1]

---

1 Traditional view, Dorothy Macardle (1937); Tom Bowden (1973). Recent assessment, Peter Hart (1992); Charles Townshend (1979); David Fitzpatrick (1977).

REACTIONS TO THE RISING

The 1916 Rising was rejected by the population at large. Constitutional nationalists throughout the country offered their services to the authorities against the rebels and during the Rising many inhabitants of Dublin provided the British soldiers with tea and food. Afterwards many nationalists also displayed their hostility towards the insurgents. In Derry and Dublin city arrested Volunteers were abused and spat at by the public while being led away. One of the leading Volunteers from Belfast who was taken to Dublin noticed the widespread rejection of their action on entering the city: 'Every second house, coming in, seemed to have a Union Jack flying and where I only saw about half-a-dozen friendly looks.'[2]

The main cause for the sea change in public opinion in favour of the Volunteers was the execution of the leading rebels in May:

> Most people expected that the 7 signatories to the proclamation of the Irish Republic would be shot, but when the papers came day after day and announced the death sentences on others as well besides sentences for life and long terms of years in abundance there was a rapid revulsion of feeling in favour of the Sinn Féiners on the part of the whole nationalist population of Ireland.

Public sympathy for the republicans was expressed by wearing small badges in the colours of the new flag at GAA tournaments and other large meetings, and some people displayed pictures of the executed leaders in public places.[3]

Taking advantage of this swing in opinion, most activity by aspiring rebels was aimed at severing the links between the population and the British authorities. In 1917 one of the main organisers of the Volunteers in West Mayo called on people not to deal with the authorities in any way: not to sell, pay or lend them a thing. However, anticipating the fear of socialism and violence, particularly strong among the clergy, he emphasised that the Volunteers were not out for real revolution or blood as some said, but merely for a free and independent Ireland.[4]

2 Civilians offering services to the Crown Forces during the Rising: In Mayo, Michael Kilroy, 'The Awakening'. In Wexford, CI Wexford MR April 1916; 'Intelligence Notes 1916', PRO, CO903/19. In Tipperary, CI south Tipperary MR April 1916; P.C. Power (1989), 204. On aiding military in Dublin, Charlie Dalton (1929), 39; Sean M. O'Duffy, 'Statement', NLI, ms. 21,658. Quote and rebels being spat at in Dublin, Denis McCullough, 'Statement', NLI, ms. 27,729. In Derry, Liam Brady, Oral History Project, Tape 24B, Heritage Library, Derry City.

3 Quote, Fr Michael Maher, Diary 1916, St Patrick's College Thurles. The use of badges etc., C.S. Andrews (1979), 89-90; Sean Clancy, Interview; 'Intelligence Notes 1917', PRO, CO903/19; IG MRs September & December 1916.

4 Speech in west Mayo by Ned Moane, file marked 'Midlands & Connacht District', PRO, CO904/122.

This speech emphasised one of the main aspects of Sinn Féin policy in later years; a boycott of state institutions. In a similar speech delivered by Eamon O'Dwyer in Tipperary in December 1917 the main targets of this boycott were identified as the RIC and the Crown courts. O'Dwyer encouraged people to disregard political laws dealing with drilling and such like, and to ignore the police as no one was afraid of them now. Turning to the policemen present, he warned them that if they were sensible men they would now throw in their lot with their fellow-countrymen in the struggle for freedom. A second aspect was added to this when he called on people to turn to republican alternatives. The law courts should be ignored and arbitration tribunals would be set up by republicans. However, unlike his counterpart in Mayo, he emphasised the ultimate necessity of violence to obtain an independent Ireland:

> All young men should train and make themselves efficient and be ready to act their part when the time came – as surely it would come, as the men of Easter week did. [...] That at the present time there was a great movement on foot to secure the independence of Ireland by 'passive resistance' which was all very well in its way, but that it was necessary that this movement should have the support of rifles and machine-guns.[5]

These attempts by Sinn Féin to persuade people to break with the government were reinforced by the Volunteers with intimidation. As early as the winter of 1916 threats were made to those opposing the movement. In Wexford letters were sent to people accusing them of sneering at Sinn Féiners and threatening them that they 'would be made to pay at the next rising.' Inhabitants of Enniscorthy were called on to boycott the technical school where the son of a RIC man, 'a spy and informer', was teaching. Possibly as a result of its involvement in the Rising, Wexford was one of the first counties where radical nationalists exerted themselves in this way after the Rising. In Dublin the 'separation women' (a name given to the wives of British soldiers because of the separation allowance they received), who had always actively opposed the Volunteers, were targets of much abuse, and threats were made to employers urging them to reinstate the prisoners in their employment.[6]

---

5 Quote, Report on speech by 'Edward Dwyer' dated 8 December 1917, PRO, CO904/122/2.
6 Intimidation in Wexford, CI Wexford MRs September-December 1916. Threats against employers in Dublin, Larry Nugent, O'MN, P17b88; Charlie Dalton (1929), 64. Attention to 'separation women', C.S. Andrews (1979), 90.

GAINING SUPPORT

For the time being, the political struggle took precedence. Despite the violence used to enforce non-cooperation with the authorities, most attention was given to mobilising voluntary support for Sinn Féin, first in the 1917 and 1918 bye-elections and finally in the general election of December 1918. The remembrance of slain heroes of the Rising at Easter 1917 and 1918 and the prisoners' hunger strikes, aimed at forcing the authorities to treat them as political prisoners, evoked a strong emotional response from the population and mobilised opposition to the government. Enthusiasm for the cause of Irish freedom was maintained by organising language classes, concerts and other public events to raise funds. A national spirit was not always the only reason for attending these: 'Gaelic League classes appear all over the Country. [...] it appears that the dance [...] afterwards is a greater attraction than the learning of the Irish language.' At this stage public manifestations were the main (in Derry even the only) expression of radical activity and popular support. Volunteer parades always attracted the attention of locals of all persuasions. In Ulster the home rule question had already exacerbated the existing tensions between the two communities, and marches by militia from both sides occasionally led to minor riots.[7]

Despite the election successes, the political question was of little interest to the majority of the population. Anxiety over the introduction of conscription was, however, widespread. This was observed by the police as early as September 1916. In the beginning of the War many young men had emigrated from Ireland for fear of being conscripted; others returned to Ireland when conscription was introduced in England. This concern was taken up by Sinn Féin to further the spread of the movement and to popularise its attempts to break with the British Government. Obstructing recruitment for the British Army became one of its prime objects after the Rising. Recruitment posters were torn down, meetings disrupted, and people discouraged from joining. This enhanced the feeling of disappointment among nationalists in Ireland

7   Quote, CI South Tipperary MR February 1918. See also Ned Prendergast, Interview; Liam Brady, *Derry Journal*, 8 May 1953; CI Derry MR October 1916; John Joe Philben, 'Statement'; P.J. Kelly, 'One of the Men of the West'; Sean Clancy, Interview. Public manifestations of the movement in Derry, CI Derry MRs January, February & June 1918. Effects of marching through areas inhabited by members of the other religion, Denis McCullough, 'Statement', NLI, ms. 27,729; Liam Brady, *Derry Journal*, 1 May 1953; Sean Hughes, Oral History Project, Tape 27B, Heritage Library, Derry City; CI Derry MRs February & April 1914, and May 1918.

which had already caused a reduction in recruits for the British Army even before 1916.[8]

Up to 1916 response to recruitment in Ireland had been high. In November 1916 a list was published of all men of military age in Ireland considered available for service totalling 161,239. Excluded were farmers and half of all farmer-sons and labourers, doctors, railwaymen, iron and steel-workers, explosives and chemical workers and most of those described as 'Public Administration and Professions'. Of all the 'available men', 130,241 had so far joined up; but a disproportional number came from Ulster. Although only 45,205 were considered available in Ulster, 66,674 men had already enlisted. In contrast, only roughly half of those available had joined in Munster and Leinster, outside Dublin City, while in Connacht only a quarter had done so.[9]

In Ulster counties Derry scored relatively low with 112 per cent of available men joining, compared to a 148 per cent average. In Tipperary about five out of every six had joined, far exceeding the 50 per cent ratio for Munster. Wexford slightly exceeded the 50 per cent who had joined in Leinster, with about five out of every eight joining. Mayo had one of the lowest ratios in the country, with only one in five of all available men joining the army. The high level of recruitment in Tipperary can partly be explained by the large number of military garrisons, and by the relatively high urbanisation which ensured a large pool of potential recruits. The lower ratio for Munster as a whole was probably caused by the western part of Munster, which was socio-economically comparable to Connacht.

The importance of urban areas in recruitment is shown by Dublin City, where practically all available men had joined. Despite a small increase in recruitment immediately after the Rising, overall recruitment in 1916 reached just half that of 1915. In the remainder of the War an average of 800 Irishmen joined the army each month; this represented about a quarter of the 1915 figure. Although feelings ran high, the Conscription Crisis had

8 Observation of people's anxieties, CI Mayo MR September 1916; CI south Tipperary MRs September & December 1916; IG MR September 1916. On emigration from fear of conscription in Mayo, P.J. Kelly, 'One of the Men of the West'; Patrick Owen Mugan, Interview. A government list of the number of young men of military age believed to have emigrated to America from the start of the War up to 15 June 1915 owing to rumours about conscription, gives a total of 2,211 men. In the first few weeks of the War, 885 had already left. Overall, 1,344 of them came from Connacht and 488 from Munster. Mayo dominated this list with 586 men, while the next in line were Roscommon with 218 and Kerry with 197. In Derry and Dublin, nobody was listed and in Wexford and Tipperary only 2 and 3 respectively, NAD, CBS/Box 24.

9 List, *Irish Independent*, 14 November 1916. Figures for recruitment to the British Army in Ireland differ somewhat. Fitzpatrick identifies a total of 134,158 Irish recruits throughout the War, excluding 17,804 reservists and some 20,000 Irish regular soldiers and an unknown number of Irishmen recruited in Britain, David Fitzpatrick (1977), 110-11. See also David Fitzpatrick (1989), 235.

little impact on these figures. Recruitment continued to be extremely slow in Mayo, where less than ten men joined each month, and was somewhat better in far less populated Wexford where almost twenty enlisted.[10]

Despite the successes in Ulster, recruitment was not restricted to Protestants. In February 1917 it was estimated that of those who had joined the Army since the outbreak of the war, 31,213 were National Volunteers, while during the entire war only 30,000 recruits were Ulster Volunteers. The deteriorating situation at the front in Europe in 1917 meant that many more soldiers were needed. The resulting fear that conscription would be introduced remained one of the main public issues in Ireland.[11]

Conscription was not the only concern used by Sinn Féin to mobilise public opinion against British rule. The high level of food exports to Britain in 1917 and 1918 were another sore point. Harking back to the administration's failure to deal with the famines of the 1840s, the fear that Ireland would be left with insufficient food supplies was taken up. In order to prevent another famine, Sinn Féin started to promote the extension of tillage by the breaking up of grass lands. This was taken up with enthusiasm, particularly in the West, where the sale of land to the tenants had not yet been completed and resentment over the large parcels of lands owned by ranchers was high. This was strengthened by the inability to lay to rest passionate feelings over past evictions.[12]

Apart from extending tillage, attempts were also made to impede the export of food. In Wexford potatoes and vegetables were bought from large producers and sold cheaply to the needy. In deprived areas of Mayo potatoes and flour was collected voluntarily from farmers and distributed to the poor in towns and elsewhere. The efforts soon ran into trouble in Wexford and Tipperary. The majority of the guarantors of the money for the purchase of food were merchants who were directly hit by the cheap distribution. As a result, the buying of surplus stocks had to be abandoned.[13]

10 Recruitment after the Rising, IG and CIs MRs 1916-18.

11 National Volunteers joining the Army, PRO, CO904. Ulster Volunteers joining, David Fitzpatrick (1989), 235. About one tenth of National Volunteers had joined the British Army before the end of 1915. Most of them at the end of 1914 when 48 per cent of all Irish recruits were National Volunteers. In general recruiting was strongest in 1915, but more than halved in 1916 and reduced even more in 1917 and 1918 when less than a quarter of the 1915 total joined. The share of Ulster continued to be disproportionately high. Although 36 per cent of the population lived in Ulster, 60 per cent of recruits in 1914 came from Ulster, 41 per cent in 1915, 38 per cent in 1916, 42 per cent in 1917, and 49 per cent in 1918, David Fitzpatrick (1977), 110-11.

12 Decisions of the Standing Committee of Sinn Féin on extending tillage dated 17 January 1918, NLI, P3269.

13 The distribution of food: In Wexford, CI Wexford MR February 1918; Laurence Carey, NLI, ms. 10,723(2). In Mayo, CI Mayo MRs January-February 1918; Patrick Owen Mugan, Interview. The latter remembers this as a

One unpopular aspect of the Volunteers' contacts with the population at this stage were raids for arms. Farms and the houses of the gentry were among the few places where arms were to be found at this time. Initially, the raiders concentrated on local farmers, many of whom were aggravated when they were woken up in the middle of the night and threatened by masked youths. The Volunteers involved were inexperienced and found it difficult to command the necessary respect. In their first raid, Volunteers from a Dublin company had no idea how to react when one of the women came home:

> When I told her there was a raid in progress and that she could not go in, she let loose a torrent of abuse. Blackguards, robbers, criminals, ruffians and goodness knows what else she called us in a hysterically rising voice. This we could endure, but when she tried to force her way into the house we did not know how to react. My inclination was to gag her as she was making too much noise, but neither I nor my companions could overcome the taboos which forbade us to 'lay a hand on a woman' so we just stood there in front of the door and let her push and scream her head off.[14]

This soon changed. 'Within a few months we were going into every house in the company area that we thought might have arms of any kind. At that stage we went into twos and threes, knocking at the doors and politely enquiring if we might look round for arms and were never refused.' The threat of violence was sufficient to restrain most people. One IRA veteran described people's reaction when they entered a house: 'There was no call. Their hands went up, and they stayed up. They were well enough — tutored.' Nevertheless, some people did resist. To prevent the alienation of the population Sinn Féin decided to prohibit raids for arms on private houses in February 1918. However, the Conscription Crisis of April 1918 created an urgent need for weapons and despite the order raids continued to take place. Even after the crisis was over the leadership maintained an ambivalent attitude towards raiding. Although officially prohibiting it, many military-minded leaders realised that the lack of arms required raiding and condoned them as long as the organisation was not implicated. This ambivalence continued until 1920, when the start of hostilities and the desperate shortage of arms made raiding

way to persuade people to vote Sinn Féin. In Tipperary, CI South Tipperary MR January 1918. See also David Fitzpatrick (1977), 168.

14 Quote, C.S. Andrews (1979), 116-17. See also Pat MacCrea, O'MN, P17b110. Many examples of raids on Big Houses in which the potential hostile inhabitants were treated with courtesy, Seán Gaynor, 'Statement'; Paddy Larkin, Interview.

unavoidable. To placate those having to forfeit their arms, the Volunteer leadership ordered raiders to issue receipts. This conflict between the needs of the military campaign and the desire to mobilise public support created tensions throughout the period.[15]

STRENGTH OF SUPPORT AND OPPOSITION

The Conscription Crisis gave a strong impetus to public support for Sinn Féin. Although some continued to join the British Army, the crisis changed the public standing of the Volunteers totally. From being a group of radical young activists they became the representatives of mainstream nationalist opinion. Also, the widespread defiance of the authorities scared the police. In Tipperary the County Inspector reported: 'General feeling towards police is one of hostility if not hatred leading to much anxiety in police stations.' The call by Sinn Féin to contribute to a Fund to 'indemnify against loss or injury all who suffer in the struggle' met much support. The men arrested during this period gained in prestige for their willingness to 'suffer for the cause'. Their court cases provoked riots, and their return from prison continued to lead to public expressions of revolutionary sympathy.[16]

The tougher line taken by the authorities after the Conscription Crisis reduced open Volunteer and Sinn Féin activity and people became more cautious in showing their hostility towards the police. Simply giving one's name in Irish and refusing to give the English version led to several arrests

15 Quote on change, C.S. Andrews (1979), 117. Quote on 'silent threat', John Quinn, 'Typescript of Interview', Fr O'Kane Papers, AARC. See also Thomas Toner, Tape A13, Ibidem. Order by Standing Committee of Sinn Féin against raiding of private houses dated 21 February 1918, NLI, P3269. Examples of raids in which people involved did not cooperate: In Tipperary, Ned O'Reilly, O'MN, P17b126. In Derry, *Coleraine Chronicle,* 12 February 1921. In Castlebar, Co. Mayo, Volunteers continued to raid without permission of their officers, Michael Hughes, 'Statement'; Jim O'Donnell, 'Recollections'. On the ambivalent attitude of GHQ, Martin Walton, in K. Griffith and T. O'Grady (1982), 287. An order to issue receipts was issued by the Third Tipperary Brigade on 28 August 1920, O'MN, P17b127. Receipts were also given to gun owners in Belfast. They were promised that the arms and ammunition would be returned when they desired or when the enemy had been forced to evacuate. They were warned that handing over arms to the enemy would be considered an act of treason to the Republic and dealt with as such, order dated December 1920, PRONI, D1970.
16 Quote, CI South Tipperary MR April 1918. See also CI Mayo MRs April, October & December 1918. In December most of the collected money was handed back to the subscribers, D. O'Donoghue, O'MN, P17b90; Fr Michael Maher, Diary 1918, St Patrick's College Thurles. Reaction to releases, Fr Michael Maher, Diary 1917, Ibidem; Ned Moane, 'Statement'; James Chambers, 'Statement'; CI Mayo MR October 1918.

in the latter part of 1918. Active support for the cause was a danger to many households as many employers and institutions refused to engage known republicans. The British war successes later in the year had a further calming effect. Most people again confined their expressions of sympathy to the sports and cultural sphere. Some activists associated with Sinn Féin now turned their attention to the trade unions. Their task was facilitated by the strong support Sinn Féin received from the working class. Despite the increased caution, occasional conflict between Volunteers and uncooperative civilians or policemen still erupted, more often in Tipperary and Dublin than elsewhere.[17]

Although traditional nationalists had lost much ground since 1916, they retained many followers, particularly among older people and those in urban areas. In Derry and Wexford town support for the AOH and the Irish Party remained strong. Most of these supporters felt that it was impossible to beat the might of the British Empire and that only political negotiations would achieve independence. The fact that many relied, directly or indirectly, on the government for (a supplement to) their income strengthened their resistance to revolutionary means. A Mayo Volunteer described the posi-tion in 1917:

> On the 15th of June, 1917, I myself and several of my companions joined the Newport Company, Second Battalion, West Mayo Brigade. Let nobody think that then, or in later years we had all the people on our side. A large number of the Irish people and in fairness to them I will say good Irishman and Irishwomen, thought we were mad and did not agree with our methods as they thought we had no chance against the might of the British Empire and were only stirring up trouble which would gain nothing.

Friends of this Volunteer regarded their drilling as window dressing: 'I was standing one night with a number of my school pals. They started gibing me about our drill display in the town that day. They said we were just a lot of gossoons, showing off.'[18]

17 Causes for arrest in 1917 and 1918, *Two years of English Atrocities in Ireland* (n. d.). The refusal of employers and institutions to take on declared republicans included an oath of allegiance to the Crown which civil servants were required to take in 1918, D. O'Donoghue, O'MN, P17b90; C.S. Andrews (1979), 90; Ben Doyle, O'MN, P17b101. When all public gatherings, including sport manifestations, were forbidden in July 1918 a coordinated nation-wide day of GAA matches was arranged making prosecution impossible, *Two years of English Atrocities in Ireland* (n. d.). For the relation between Labour and Sinn Féin in this period, CI Wexford MRs March, April, June & August 1918; CI Derry MR April 1918; D. Ryan (1945), 32-3.

18 Quotes, Jim O'Donnell, 'Recollections'. On the strength of the AOH in Derry, CI Derry MR March 1918. In Tipperary conflict between the two nationalist

Despite this continued support for constitutional nationalism, people found it increasingly difficult to express such feelings. The celebration of Armistice Day was one of the few opportunities to do so. In Dublin these turned into an anti-Sinn Féin demonstration, and Volunteers had to be called in to protect the Sinn Féin headquarters in Harcourt Street when the windows were broken and the building set on fire. Vehement opposition from Irish Party supporters encountered by Sinn Féin in Wexford town led to several riots. On one occasion Volunteers intervened when a Sinn Féin meeting was attacked.[19]

Most Catholics in the South did, however, support Sinn Féin during the general election in December 1918. The enthusiasm of the newly enfranchised youth organised in the republican movement had largely crippled the activities of the Irish Party. Sinn Féin took 73 out of 105 seats and obtained 48 per cent of the votes in the entire country – 65 per cent outside the six north-eastern counties. This sudden swing to Sinn Féin bewildered some constitutionalists in Tipperary:

> The strange thing is that most of the public bodies in the country have not sided with Sinn Féin nor have the older generation of farmers and shopkeepers gone over to them; yet they win the elections. The rising generation are with them mainly I think on account of their opposition to Conscription and they evidently influence the older people when the crisis comes. That and the wonderful organisation and energy of the Sinn Féin party is sweeping the country.

However, Garvin has shown that Sinn Féin received votes from all age groups. To the RIC in Mayo the explanation was simply fear: 'The intimidation by Sinn Féin agents is very great, sons are frightening their fathers as to what will happen if the fathers don't vote Sinn Féin.' Although various stratagems were used to increase the Sinn Féin poll, the clear majority

traditions erupted occasionally in some of the towns where much business depended on the presence of the British Army and many families had members in it, Patrick Ryan, 'Statement'; Denis G. Marnane (1985), 119-22.

19 The attack on Sinn Féin headquarters in Dublin, Robert Brennan (1950), 182. One British official experienced the inconsistency of the Irish reaction in the midst of the fighting on Armistice Day in 1920: 'When many flags were flown in Dame St and Grafton St "What a queer country." A lorry load of "B&T" halted in College Green at 12,- tumbled out and stood to attention for the two minutes — many Trinity College students among them, no doubt — but still the Dublin crowd, then sang "God save the King" and cheered the lorry as it went on its way', 'Sturgis Diary', 70, PRO, PRO30/59/2. In Mayo, Armistice Day led to similar public disturbances when drunken soldiers attacked a crowd, Brodie Malone, O'MN, P17b109. Clashes between Sinn Féin and Irish Party supporters in Wexford, *Life of Mick Radford* (n. d.), 7; CI Wexford MRs March & November 1918.

of votes they received in most southern counties emphasises the widespread support they had.[20]

The electoral success of Sinn Féin in the North was clearly smaller. Fearing a split vote in the face of the unity of Protestants, an electoral pact was made between constitutional nationalists and republicans before the elections, which divided most northern constituencies between the two nationalist parties. Aside from this, Irish Party support remained strong in the North. In south Derry, which later became a local hot-bed of violent nationalism, and where there had been no pact, the Sinn Féin candidate was beaten into third place by the Irish Party candidate.

To nationalists in the North the question of partition was the deciding factor in 1918. They put their trust in the Irish Party candidates who stressed the need of Home Rule for a united Ireland. They were not swayed by the Sinn Féin candidates, who emphasised President Wilson's 'Fourteen Points', and asked for a big vote for self-determination in Protestant Derry. The claim that this would take 'the whole argument of Ulster's position out of the Unionists' mouth' failed to convince Catholic voters. One researcher of these Derry elections has concluded: 'For many Northern Nationalists their fear of partition outweighed the issue of "Home Rule versus Republic" and thus, fearing the powerlessness associated with Sinn Féin's policy of abstention, voted for the Irish Party.'[21]

In Wexford in the general election in 1918 the Irish Party attracted more than 40 per cent of the votes. Wexford, Tipperary and Dublin were among the five counties outside Ulster where Sinn Féin received less than 68 per cent support. In Mayo Sinn Féin easily managed to attract more than that percentage of the electorate. These differences were confirmed in the local elections of 1920. Sinn Féin did very well despite the change in electoral system from first past the post to proportional representation intended to prevent it from taking control of local bodies. In Mayo all the seats in the county council went to Sinn Féin. In Tipperary they won more than 75 per cent, but in Dublin and Wexford less than 75 per cent of the seats. Elections for district boards showed Sinn Féin significantly less successful in towns than in rural areas. In all provinces, Sinn Féin received more than double the level of

20 Election results in 1918, Tom Garvin (1981), 118-19. Quote on elections in Tipperary, Fr Michael Maher, Diary 1917, St Patrick's College Thurles. See also CI South Tipperary MR November 1918. Quote on threats in Mayo, CI Mayo MR November 1918. Sinn Féin receiving votes from all age groups, Tom Garvin (1981), 120-2. Election rigging: In Derry, Frank Himphey, Fr O'Kane Papers, Tape 50a, AARC. In Mayo, Johnny Duffy, O'MN, P17b109. A son of an election agent described this type of election rigging as a 19th-century tradition in Ireland. According to him it was not important who had most supporters, but whose supporters could keep the others away from the polling stations would win the elections, Captain J. Horner, Boyhood in Clonmel, UCD AD, LA8.
21 Quotes, Clare Murray (1990), 58.

Map 3: Sinn Féin Votes in 1918 Election[22]

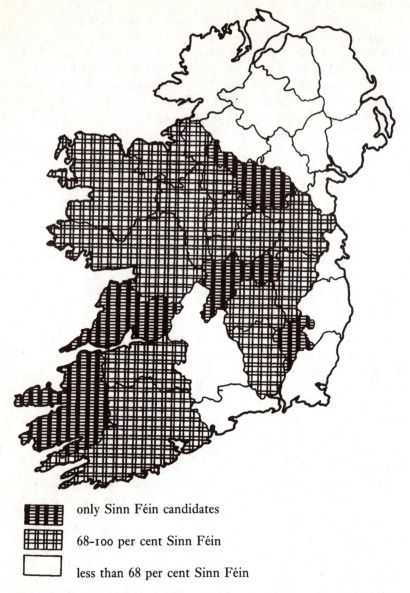

	only Sinn Féin candidates
	68-100 per cent Sinn Féin
	less than 68 per cent Sinn Féin

22 Percentages are reached by taking the average of votes casts in all electoral districts of each county together. If only Sinn Féin candidates stood in all electoral divisions in one county this is indicated. In case that in one of the electoral divisions in a county there was no opposing candidate while the other divisions had more than one candidate, the votes casts in the one candidate division are taken as 100 per cent for the party concerned. This somewhat inflates the Sinn Féin vote.

Map 4: Percentage of Sinn Féin Seats in County Councils in June 1920 Local Elections

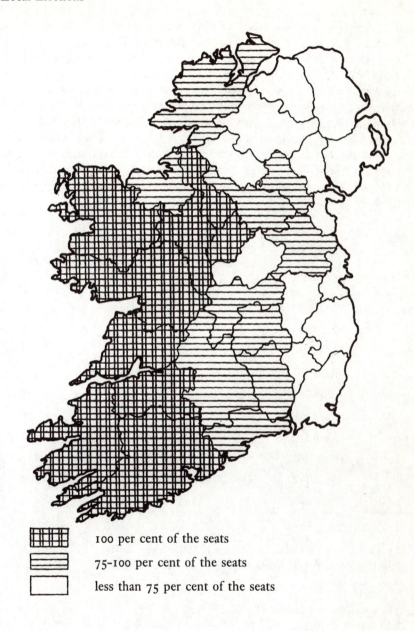

	100 per cent of the seats
	75-100 per cent of the seats
	less than 75 per cent of the seats

support in the elections for the rural district councils in June 1920 than in their urban counterparts voted for in January 1920.

In Connacht 97 per cent of seats in rural areas went to Sinn Féin but only 42 per cent in urban areas. In Munster it was 87 per cent against 43, in Leinster 67 per cent against 35 and in Ulster 42 per cent against 15. Fitzpatrick has indicated that the people in Irish towns were never so susceptible to wholesale changes in political allegiance as in the countryside, where communal pressure enforced a remarkable uniformity of loyalties and opinions. It must also be emphasised that the Volunteers were more actively involved in obtaining a good result in the rural elections after the disappointing outcome of the urban elections. The growing concentration of police and military in the towns during 1920 further hampered republican propaganda there. To a large extent the high level of urbanisation in Dublin and Tipperary therefore accounts for the strength of support for the Irish Party.[23]

Table 11: Percentage of Sinn Féin Seats in Urban and Rural District Councils in 1920

		Sinn Féin	Nationalist	Unionist	Labour	Others
Leinster	Urban DC	35	12	10	26	17
	Rural DC	67	5	1	24	3
Munster	Urban DC	43	12	1	23	21
	Rural DC	87	–	–	12	1
Connacht	Urban DC	42	14	2	24	18
	Rural DC	97	1	–	1	1
Ulster	Urban DC	15	15	47	17	6
	Rural DC	42	13	42	2	3
Total	Urban DC	30	13	20	22	15
	Rural DC	72	5	4	11	1

For a fuller understanding of political affiliations and the relative support for Sinn Féin and the Volunteers in the various counties, it is necessary

23 Maps and election results, H. van der Wusten (1977), 193 + 209-11. Local election results in Mayo, CI Mayo MR January 1920. In 1918, the Sinn Féin vote was stronger the more Catholic, the more rural, the more western and the less northern a district was, Tom Garvin (1981), 118-22; David Fitzpatrick (1977), 120. Arthur Mitchell (1995), 123-4.

to look at the membership of rival nationalist organisations.[24] The National Volunteers, the non-violent counterpart of the Irish Volunteers, are used as an indication of the strength of active constitutional nationalism before 1916. The first element that becomes apparent is that the overall strength of this organisation far exceeded that of the Irish Volunteers in all counties except Mayo. In view of the small size of its Catholic population, Derry had by far the highest membership, numbering 4,605 in January 1916, thus mobilising 15 per cent of Catholic males three months before the Rising. The strength of the National Volunteers in Derry was a result of widespread fear among Catholics in the North of the activities of the Protestant militia, but this fear had not led to support for the confrontational policies of the Volunteers. National Volunteers in Tipperary were clearly less organised, comprising about 8 per cent of Catholic males, while both in Mayo and Wexford they mobilised nearly 5 per cent. A certain inverse relationship thus existed between the strength of Irish and National Volunteers in the five counties, with the exception of Wexford whose men were least willing to join either militia. The National Volunteers organisation was practically defunct after the Rising, the police recording a slow decline in membership in all counties.

The other two organisations affiliated with constitutional nationalism used here are the Board of Erin faction of the AOH and the UIL. The AOH was the most constitutionally-minded organisation, traditionally strong in Ulster, while the UIL, the main recruiting agent for the Irish Party, had a legacy of political agitation regarding the land question. The relative strength of these organisations differed somewhat from that of the National Volunteers.

The AOH in Derry mobilised 10 per cent of Catholics in 1916. Wexford was the second best organised county, at 5.5 per cent, while Tipperary followed at 4 per cent and Mayo had only 2 per cent of Catholic males mobilised. All counties except Wexford experienced a small decline in membership over the entire period. The more radical faction of the AOH, the Irish American Alliance, was only represented in Mayo and Derry. The presence of this organisation prevented some men from joining the Irish Volunteers, and partly explains the low level of Volunteer membership in these counties in 1916. In contrast to the National Volunteers and the AOH, the UIL had by far the highest level of organisation in Mayo, mobilising around 10 per cent of Catholic males. This was a direct consequence of the organisation's involvement in land agitation, traditionally strongest in the West. Derry followed with 7 per cent, Wexford with 5 per cent and Tipperary with 4.5 per cent.

The same inverse relationship between the strength of the National

24 Membership figures of these organisations, CIs Mayo, South Tipperary, Wexford and Derry MRs 1916-21.

Volunteers representing constitutional and the Irish Volunteers representing radical nationalism is shown for the AOH and Sinn Féin. However, the widespread political support for constitutional nationalism in Wexford was never translated in a willingness to join its militia. Contrariwise the positive experience with radical agrarian agitation in the UIL in Mayo may have influenced its population's exceptional willingness to join the Irish Volunteers.

Table 12: Percentage of Catholic Males mobilised in Cultural and Political Organisations in 1921

	Nat. Vol.	Irish Vol.	AOH	Sinn Féin	UIL	Gaelic L.	GAA
Mayo	3.6	7.0	1.5	11.8	7.1	1.1	0.9
Tipperary	6.1	2.2	4.1	8.5	4.1	1.8	1.6
Wexford	4.6	1.9	5.7	6.2	5.3	2.4	2.6
Derry	10.9	1.0	9.2	5.7	4.5	-	1.7

Mayo had the most homogeneous and politically radical population; little hard support for the Irish Party was observed here, which also showed up in poor recruiting for the British Army. In Tipperary, a strong opposition to Sinn Féin and the Volunteers was concentrated in the larger towns. In many rural districts, however, the republicans enjoyed a high level of solid support. In Wexford, allegiance to the Irish Party was more resistant, which was at least partly a result of personal loyalty to John Redmond, the leader of the Irish Party. Although concentrated in Wexford town, there was also much support spread throughout the countryside. This prevented the development of large areas with solid republican support. In Dublin, the seat of government, a large part of the population was reliant on the British connection for their livelihood, while the sizeable working class provided fertile ground both for Sinn Féin and the armed forces. Both sides of nationalist politics had traditionally found good support in the city and continued to do so up to 1919. In Derry, the large presence of Protestants was supplemented with strong support for the Irish Party among Catholics fearing partition. As a result, the republican movement always remained on the fringes of the community there.

POLITICAL SUPPORT 1919-1920

In 1919 a split developed between the political and the military minded wing of the republican movement. A small group of Volunteers made the first tentative attempts to force the pace with violence. Most members of the Volunteers and Sinn Féin, however, focused their attention on setting up the machinery of the alternative Dáil government. As a result little happened to arouse either the population generally, the IRA or the Crown Forces during 1919.

In Wexford some disturbances were caused by an attempt to stop a hunt, which was seen as a thoroughly English pastime, and by the arrest of a Sinn Féin tax collector in Newtownbarry. The Wexford Volunteers, however, remained extremely cautious and consequently largely inexperienced. Similarly few offences were committed in Mayo and Derry in 1919. Derry differed from the others by the occasional clash between Sinn Féiners and constitutional nationalists, and between Protestants and Catholics. Conflicts of the latter kind often temporarily united nationalists of all shades. However, activity elsewhere, particularly in Tipperary and Cork, slowly inspired Volunteers in these counties to become more forceful. This was also translated in their attitude towards the population. In August 1919, an arms raid in Wexford could still be foiled by a maid screaming, but in February 1920 a woman resisting a raid was shot.[25]

The movement was well able to mobilise public support for matters which awakened an emotional response or issues which affected the population personally. The imprisonment of republican leaders led to large-scale protests. Commemorations of the deaths of martyr figures, and the funerals of men who had died for the cause, were occasions in which sympathy for the movement was freely expressed. The burial of Pierce McCan, the former commandant of the Tipperary Brigade in March 1919, was the first of these in Tipperary to bring out a considerable crowd.[26]

This sympathy translated itself into the refusal of many people to adhere to government regulations. The payment of levies, such as dog licences and road tax, was widely refused. The motorcar permit, introduced at the end of 1919 to prevent the IRA from using automobiles in their operations, was also widely disregarded, especially in Tipperary and Mayo. The alternatives for British rule initiated by the Dáil in 1919 the Dáil Loan and the Arbitration Courts set up to deal with disputes between civilians – also found a good response in these two counties.[27]

In 1920 the population continued to be easily mobilised for large-scale non-violent protests. A number of national strikes called in support of the republicans were widely observed. In April the three-day strike in support of the hunger strikers' demands forced the government to release them unconditionally. On 22 May a one-day strike was called to support the railway work-

25 CIs Derry, Mayo & Wexford MRs 1919-February 1920.
26 Mobilisation of public support for different issues, CIs MRs 1919-20.
27 The refusal to take out Motor permits: In Wexford, the police reported only organised opposition in New Ross, CI Wexford MR November-December 1919. In Derry, no opposition was recorded, CI Derry MR December 1919. More success in Mayo and Tipperary, CIs Mayo & South Tipperary MRs November 1919.

ers who refused to carry British war material. The last nation-wide demonstration of republican support took place on 31 October. This involved a general closure of shops as a sign of respect to Terence MacSwiney, the Sinn Féin Mayor of Cork who had died on hunger strike after seventy-four days. In Derry, these strikes were confined to the closest supporters of the movement. In other areas, these expressions of support were generally complied with or enforced by the Volunteers. Public resistance to measures which adversely affected them also continued.[28]

General observation of these nation-wide protests usually only required mild persuasion. During the hunger strike campaign in 1920 the public was easily mobilised. The harder government approach at that time meant that the prisoners were allowed to continue their strike through to the end. This caused much anxiety among the people, who came to the prisons in large groups each day, prayed publicly and expressed their anger by throwing fruit and vegetables at the wardens.

The unexpected ability of the human body to refrain from food meant that these public demonstrations continued much longer than expected by most people: 'It seems incredible that all the hunger-strikers should be still alive, but such is the case. How much longer will they last? I am getting tired of praying for them.' The willingness to suffer for the cause was widely admired. This was also used to propagate the highly successful Dáil Loan in a short propaganda film: 'It showed pictures of some well-known people buying Dáil Loan Bonds at, I believe, St. Enda's and the table used for the transaction was, as far as I remember the block on which Emmet [a revolutionary hero executed in 1803] was beheaded.' It is highly unlikely this was the actual block used to behead Emmet, but its mention shows the powerful influence of the use of such imagery.[29]

However, violence was sometimes used to enforce the observation of strikes, the non-payment of government taxes and any other form of cooperation with the authorities, Despite the spontaneous beginning of the railway strike the Volunteers had to be warned by GHQ not to force people to observe it:

> Cases appear to have occurred vastly in which Railway workers have been kidnapped or otherwise interfered with as a result of their action in connection with the munitions 'strike'. It is very important that this should not be. No action against any worker should be

28 On the railway strike, Charles Townshend (1979B).
29 Quote on 'praying', Cecilia Saunders, Diary 21 September 1920, TCD, 10055. Quote on the propaganda film, Jack Plunkett, 'Statement', NLI, ms. 11,981. A number of copies of the film went around the country but the men in charge of them did not always succeed in having them shown, UCD AD, LA9.

taken by members of the I.R.A., even at the request of local Trade Union representatives, without submitting a statement of the matter to G.H.Q. and waiting instructions in the matter.

Shopkeepers and workers refusing to strike were singled out for intimidation. Sympathy was, however, extensive and little coercion was necessary to persuade most people. Voluntary support also came from unexpected sources, such as the Catholic Archbishop of Thurles, who refused to apply for a motor permit. Whether this was because of fear that his car would be damaged locally, is a matter of debate.[30]

PUBLIC SUPPORT AND HOSTILITIES 1919–1920

The authorities had anticipated that the outrages committed by the IRA in places like Tipperary would cause considerable indignation and a rejection of the IRA. Although some resentment did follow the killings of the policemen in January 1919, it was not succeeded by a clear rejection of the IRA. In fact, the repressive measures taken by the authorities after IRA attacks often led to increased support for the Volunteers. The authorities were unable to appreciate that most nationalists had come to look on the British Government as a foreign power towards whom 'protective' violence was justified. This was combined with a strong Irish tradition of non-cooperation, and of admiring and harbouring those who defied the authorities, even if they were ordinary criminals.[31]

30 Warning not to interfere with railway workers, Weekly Memo no.6 dated 13 November 1920, O'MN, P17b127. One example of this, Sean Lynch, MA, A0152. See also Charles Townshend (1979B). The one day strike and collections made to raise money for the dismissed railwaymen: In Mayo, P.J. Kelly, 'One of the Men of the West'. In Wexford, CI Wexford MR November 1920. In Derry, *Derry People and Donegal News*, 14 August 1920. The enforcement of strikes with violence against workers and employers, Charles Gildea, 'Activities List', Fr O'Kane Papers, AARC; CI South Tipperary MR October 1920; Pat MacCrea, O'MN, P17b110. Any cooperation with government regulations dealing with civilian behaviour had to be interfered with, such as the list of occupants which was to be placed on the inside of the door of houses in the martial law area in 1921, Weekly Memo 10 dated 23 January 1921, NLI, ms. 900/21. The extent of the national strikes in Derry, CI Derry MR October and December 1920. The Archbishop joining in Motor Permit strike, Fr Michael Maher, Diary 1920, St Patrick's College Thurles. All trade unions Sinn Féin had control over were used to enforce the Motor permit strike, Cathal O'Shannon, O'MN, P17b109.
31 The experience of the men involved in the Soloheadbeg ambush, D. Ryan (1945), 82; Seamus Robinson, 'Statement', NLI, ms. 21,265; D. Breen (1981), 52–62. Similar experiences: In Dublin, Pat McHugh, O'MN, P17b110. In Monasterevin, Co. Kildare, Ned Prendergast, Interview. In Mayo, Edward O'Malley (1981), 12.

Although many people expressed their misgivings after the Soloheadbeg ambush, the perpetrators were never given away. With foresight the dangers associated with the presence of a Volunteer Army when mixed with this attitude were observed by the General Inspector of the RIC in May 1914: 'Obedience to the law has never been a prominent characteristic of the people. [...] Each county will soon have a trained army far outnumbering the police, and those who control the Volunteers will be in a position to dictate to what extent the law of the land may be carried into effect.'[32]

Unofficial reprisals were one of the most aggravating aspects of the behaviour of the Crown Forces, and became more and more prevalent when hostilities grew. During the summer of 1919 attacks on individual policemen in Thurles and Dublin and on police barracks in Cork and Clare had outraged the forces. An ambush of military in Fermoy in September led to the first uncontrolled outburst of violence, committed by the military in that town. Many shops and houses of those suspected to be sympathetic to the movement were damaged.

A similar reaction by police and military took place in Thurles after the shooting of a constable in January 1920. Initially, well-known Sinn Féiners and their sympathisers were singled out. However, when time passed these actions became more indiscriminate and several creameries, on which many farmers depended, were burned. This violence seriously damaged the image of the Crown Forces as upholders of the law. Although officially condemned by the government, it was, and was felt to be, supported by higher military and police officers. When IRA violence increased, such reprisals became common. Members of the Crown Forces became less able to distinguish civilians with good intentions from Volunteers. As a result, they started to regard the entire population as hostile. In the worst affected areas this turned most civilians against them.[33]

The use of violence by Volunteers was not popular, either within the movement or with the population. Justifying the fighting when the struggle intensified was essential to keep the support of Irish and foreign sympathisers. The less than courteous treatment of the population by some members of the Crown Forces became an ideal tool for this and was thoroughly exploited by republicans. The Crown Forces were exposed as the main aggressor by a substantial section of the national press, which was sym-

---

The admiration for lawbreakers is very well described in, G.D. Zimmermann (1967), 23-7. This attitude was particularly widespread in Irish speaking areas, Tom Garvin (1981), 116.

32 Quote, IG MR May 1914.
33 Events in Thurles, Fr Michael Maher, Diary January 1920, St Patrick's College Thurles. See also Nonie Kennedy, O'MN, P17b119. Volunteers in Tubbercurry, Co. Sligo were guarding creameries against reprisals, Charles Gildea, 'Activities List', Fr O'Kane Papers, AARC.

pathetic to the movement. In this way Volunteer violence became justified in the eyes of a majority of nationalists.

To ensure continued political support abroad a propaganda paper aimed at foreign correspondents was set up in November 1919. Part of this *Irish Bulletin* was a weekly listing of all 'atrocities' committed by the Crown Forces. This consisted of a simple but effective enumeration of: 'Acts of aggression committed in Ireland by the Police and Military as reported in the daily press.' For the week ending 14 August 1920, this reported: 445 raids, 70 arrests, 13 sentences, 2 court martials, 32 armed assaults, 15 acts of sabotage, 26 deportations, 3 murders, and 1 suppressed proclamation. These lists and the articles on particularly gruesome incidents caused widespread concern both in Ireland and abroad. The British authorities were forced to admit that Sinn Féin was better able to take advantage of these events than they were.[34]

Despite the aversion towards violence from both sides, confrontations with the government on local and national level were often an impetus for popular support to the Sinn Féin movement. The proclamation of south Tipperary as a special military area in January 1919 was widely felt to be unjust. The prohibition of fairs and markets affected many who were not implicated in the movement. Thus far, IRA operations were directed at the Crown Forces while the latter's reaction hurt everyone. As a result, negative reactions to the shooting of policemen became further limited to an ever smaller part of the population, whilst the introduction of special military areas had little impact: 'The general public is apparently prepared to suffer rather than openly condemn the criminal acts of the republican fanatics.' Nevertheless, little open disaffection was reported during the rest of 1919. Relations between police and population in most areas remained good and improved somewhat in Tipperary after the police were reinforced in July.[35]

In a similar response the suppression of the Dáil in September 1919 led to a revival of Sinn Féin clubs and Volunteer companies in many places. Even a single raid by the police could lead to a sudden substantial increase in the membership of the local Sinn Féin club. The large number of Gaelic League, GAA and Sinn Féin branches that were founded or which encountered active support in late 1919, particularly in Mayo, testifies to this.[36]

As a result of the varied impact of Volunteer activity and government response the organisation developed into an extremely localised entity, with pockets of complete dedication, a few centres of reliable support and areas where there was hardly any organisation and which were scarcely visited by

---

34 *Irish Bulletin*, August 1920. See also D.G. Boyce (1972), passim.
35 Quote, IG MR September 1919. Developments in Tipperary, CI South Tipperary MRs 1919.
36 For the public support following clashes with the police, all general and local police reports in 1919 and early 1920. The favourable reception of the movement in Mayo, *Mayoman*, October-November 1919.

activists. Areas where the Volunteers could rely on the entire population became necessary for security reasons when attacks on policemen started. Opposition or neutrality could no longer be tolerated there. The strength of the Volunteers in some places enabled them to enforce allegiance from that section of society more favourably disposed to the police.[37]

In Tipperary the police distinguished two such core areas of support in the Tipperary town and Cashel districts. These coincided with two of the original centres of the Volunteer organisation. In these areas the police experienced most hostility from the population during 1919. People were afraid to talk to them and reacted with glee to the killing of policemen in the rescue of Sean Hogan at Knocklong: 'More particularly in those parts of Tipperary and Cashel District peculiarly given to this form of showing hatred to constituted authority.' The willingness of the Volunteers to use force worried many people. In Bantry, Co. Cork, one of the local police informers was sufficiently anxious to inform his regular contact in the RIC he was giving up his work: 'One day meeting him, I asked if he had anything fresh. "I'm finished" he said. [...] "I tell you I'm finished. These fellows are serious, and if you take my tip you'll go a bit easy too." That ended my getting information from him.'[38]

However, the growing conflict and the willingness to express sympathy to the revolutionary cause did not polarise the population as much as the more law-abiding section of society feared. Even in the most affected areas apprehensions about displaying signs of loyalism were often unfounded. This was experienced by a Tipperary priest organising a bazaar for charity in the autumn of 1919. Before the event commenced he voiced his anxiety about the possible conflicts that might develop between loyalists and Sinn Féiners:

> Two things gave me concern viz. whether we should admit soldiers who were stationed in Thurles and whether I should allow any red, white and blue flags [...] to be put up. One priest gave it as his opinion that if soldiers were admitted it would mean a boycott of the bazaar. Still I decided to do nothing in the matter. When the flags were unfolded some were found to contain the three colours mentioned. They were erected by the committee for decoration many of whom were Sinn Féiners. I got 2 or 3 removed and nobody ever minded the rest. The soldiers also came to the Bazaar every day and

37 A pocket of complete dedication can be found in Rosegreen Co. Tipperary. Owenwee in west Mayo is a good example of a centre of reliable support. Veterans name areas as Drummin and Achill in Mayo, the southern part of Wexford around Bannow, the northern part of Co. Derry and some of the towns and the deep south of Tipperary as areas with hardly any organisation and which the activists scarcely visited.

38 Quote on reaction to Knocklong, CI South Tipperary MR May 1919. Quote on 'scared informer', John Regan, 'Memoirs', 114, PRONI, D3160.

nobody paid the slightest attention to them. One stall was arranged in Sinn Féin colours but they were not very prominent and no remarks were passed.[39]

The violence against civilians which accompanied the rekindled attempts by Sinn Féin in 1920 to force a break between the people and the government institutions endangered the successful mobilisation of public support. The boycott of the police and those who associated with them could only be effective if the entire population supported it. However, many were unwilling to participate in a boycott because business would be adversely affected. This inevitably led to IRA attempts to enforce it. The intricate relations between Volunteers, businessmen and the police also caused much confusion. A multitude of queries were sent to Volunteer GHQ about the exact implementation of the boycott. To what extent it was to apply to police families was a serious matter of debate in the organisation.[40]

Many civilians, including some Volunteers and their close sympathisers, were engaged in business deals with the police. People rented accommodation to them, had contracts to provide them with goods or sold their skills to them. This presented a dilemma to the organisation. Many diligent Volunteers who saw the boycott as a tool in the military struggle tried to break all these links. GHQ, however, who saw the boycott as a political weapon, an instrument to exert further pressure on the police, was afraid to antagonise the population and attempted to limit its implementation to visible forms of association. They feared that too much violence against civilians would damage their hold on the country and were satisfied if outward signs of the connection were severed. Nevertheless, the first signs of intimidation to implement the boycott were observed by the police as early as December 1919 when a resident of Hollyford, Co. Tipperary who supplied the police with goods received a threatening letter. Despite the dangers linked to intimidation, the boycott successfully helped to change the police's image in people's minds, and few were now prepared to report crime to them.[41]

39 Quote, Fr Michael Maher, Diary 1919 book II, St Patrick's College Thurles.
40 Officials, such as Resident Magistrates and Justices of the Peace, were also warned not to continue their work, Sean Lynch, MA, A0152; John Regan, 'Memoirs', PRONI, D3160; Seamus Robinson, 'Statement', NLI, ms, 21,265. The police boycott enforced with violence, G. Owens, NLI, ms. 10,723(2); UCD AD, P7A19/95-7. A long list of queries on the boycott was sent in by a Kerry Brigade. GHQ answered that medical care and milk for policemen's children should not be refused, but that anyone who was not directly reliant for their income on the police should break all contact, NLI, P916 A0495. See also UCD AD, P7A19/170; Boycott of RIC in West Donegal, NLI, ms. 739.
41 Examples of Volunteers wanting to burn houses rented to the authorities and GHQ attempting to prevent this, NLI, ms. 22,118; UCD AD, P7A20/82. In the end, GHQ stated that strategic importance of such a building should decide whether it could be demolished or attacked, NLI, P916 A0480. Despite pressure

PUBLIC SUPPORT AND HOSTILITIES 1920-1921

In 1919 increased support for the republicans, resulting from government measures and Crown Force reprisals, were largely confined to the active areas in the South. Nevertheless, the proclamation of Westport in Co. Mayo and incidental police operations in other areas caused similar but less extreme reactions. The detrimental effects of such restrictions and Crown Force actions became the most important tool in mobilising public support for the remainder of the struggle. This was increasingly backed up by violence against civilians who opposed the movement, ultimately leading to a large number of executions of alleged informers.

The lack of intelligence among the Crown Forces turned every civilian into a suspected republican, leading to arrests of anyone giving a reason to be seen as a sympathiser of the movement. The nightly raiding parties, frequently sent to the wrong addresses, caused damage and further irritation. As a result, the Crown Forces had to work in an increasingly hostile environment. Particularly after Bloody Sunday, when British intelligence was further weakened, arrests became more indiscriminate and the growing restrictions on normal public life further alienated the public.[42]

Raiding parties in Dublin quickly acquired a bad name. Cases in which houses of Volunteer sympathisers had been wrecked were widely published. Several incidents in which raiding soldiers were found to have stolen valuables are recorded by the authorities. Many innocent people, frightened by these stories, refused to open the door to military parties. The public image of the military was further damaged when the press published pictures of soldiers forcing doors of houses with pickaxes and rifles. Although the military authorities in Dublin immediately issued instructions to prevent the press from taking pictures during operations, it was too late to avoid repercussions. The military authorities received letters from civilians anxious to avoid raids. Anonymous information had for personal reasons apparently implicated persons who had no connection to the movement. Others expressed surprise when raiding parties behaved courteously. Nevertheless, every raid on an innocent person tended 'to strain a person's loyalty', as a 'most loyal Catholic' put it in a letter of complaint.[43]

   put on firms and people not to supply the Crown Forces, GHQ never forbade firms to work for them, UCD AD, P7A20/35-7 + 80; NLI, P916 A0478; UCD AD, P7A21/78. People not talking or reporting crime to the police, CI South Tipperary MR June 1919 & January 1920; John Regan, 'Memoirs', 135 + 158, PRONI, D3160.

42 Measures taken by the authorities as curfew and the order against loitering, PRO, WO35/66. In 1921, showing an acquaintance with those carried as hostages was sufficient cause for arrest, Sean O'h, O'MN, P17b100; Moira McKee, O'MN, P17b103.

43 The forcing of doors and the order forbidding press photographers, 'Raid Reports', PRO, WO35/70; Minutes of Brigade Conference, 20 January 1921

Cooperation between the population and the authorities was further diminished when raiding became a regular feature of life. The bad name the Crown Forces had acquired and the danger of being regarded as a traitor by the IRA caused many loyal civilians to think twice before even aiding a wounded member of the Crown Forces. This in turn led to much frustration among the troops, who were confirmed in their belief that the whole population was against them. The large round-ups starting in the late spring of 1921 – resulting in only a few arrests – led to further polarisation.

In a roundup in Co. Roscommon all men younger than forty-five were forced to walk past a screen which hid an informer. Out of 500 men only one was detained. When it was over they were compelled to sing 'God Save the King' and then run for it. The anger this type of action produced was taken out on the Crown Forces whenever possible. Curfew patrols in Dublin were frequent targets: 'We soon learnt that it was unwise to use the paths under the houses, from the windows we would be subjected to much abuse followed by a "bed chamber" being emptied over us. According to the language directed at us we were "All Illegitimate".'[44]

One of the problems the authorities faced in their attempts to catch IRA members were women. Because of a continuous lack of women searchers, incriminating evidence carried by a Volunteer in the street could safely be disposed of by passing it to a woman. Most Volunteers had no trouble finding willing females to perform this task. The courtesy soldiers showed to women and children saved many Volunteers from arrest. This

HQ Dublin District, file marked 'B.M./33/0/2', PRO, WO35/71/6/84. On the attitude of civilians and the behaviour of members of raiding parties, 'Order to Auxiliaries Company', dated 17 January 1921, Ibidem. Letter to military from a 'fearful civilian', dated 10 May 1921, and from the 'most loyal Catholic', dated June 1921, PRO, WO35/71/8/117, Similar letters, PRO, WO35/71; WO35/72.

44 Round up in Roscommon, 'The Memoirs of G.W. Albin', 124, IWM. See also Bryan Ryan (1969), 16. Quote, Major B.A. Pond, 61, IWM, 78/27/1. Other examples of abuse and irritation on both sides in Dublin, Private J.P. Swindle-hurst, Diary, IWM, 48790; Diary 1921, PRO, WO35/71/6/84; Lt. Col. N.M Hughes-Hallett, IWM, 86/73/1; 'Flying Officer F.C. Perry', IWM, 76/16/1. A clear case of civilians caught between the troops and the IRA took place in Kilkee, where one night the Volunteers smashed all the windows of houses having any dealings with the RIC. The Police then broke all remaining windows the next day, Liam Haugh, 'History of the West Clare Brigade', NLI, P915 A0363. Civilians running away when members of the Crown Forces were wounded in the street without helping them, PRO, PRO30/59/3; Lt. Col. N.M Hughes-Hallett, IWM, 86/73/1; Major-Gen. Douglas Wimberley, 'Scottish Soldier', 147, IWM, PP/MCR/182. The latter also reports much alcohol abuse among soldiers and that few of the local Irish girls dared to be seen with a British soldier, Ibidem, 154.

seriously impaired the effectiveness of road blocks and house-to-house searches in Dublin. The authorities were so frustrated that the commandant of the Auxiliaries in Dublin suggested using soldiers in female clothing as women searchers:

> Without the help of woman searchers the holding up of people and searching the males only is futile. It is realised that there is certain difficulty in employing women searchers, but I make the suggestion that carefully selected young men could be dressed as women for the duty. An outcry would, of course, be immediately raised were this known. [...] After all, all that is required is that muffs, handbags and coat pockets be searched, which would hardly offend the feelings of loyal women.

There is no evidence that this suggestion was ever put into practice, but the dearth of women searchers was apparently alleviated in the late spring of 1921.[45]

At the end of 1920 the authorities acknowledged the diminishing standing of the Crown Forces. They tried to raise it with a tightening-up of discipline and an increased visibility of military and police in the streets. In order to enable the officers to refute charges of misappropriation, members of raiding parties were told from August 1920 not to carry cash or valuables and were searched after raids. Officers were further reminded to use 'every possible courtesy' towards the inhabitants of raided houses, as it was realised that not all raids had good cause. In March 1921 the commandant of the Auxiliary Division in Dublin drew up several further recommendations to improve the image of the Crown Forces. This included certain measures to safeguard civilian lives and unsuccessful attempts to project a less threatening image:

> To restore confidence amongst the populace I think it would be an excellent plan to allow certain members of the Auxiliary Division RIC to stroll about Dublin in parties of three in uniform. They

45 Quote, Letter to G.S.O.I. Dublin District dated 25 March 1921, PRO, WO35/71. The special women searchers were needed because the troops were forbidden to arrest a woman, 'Record of the Rebellion in Ireland in 1920-21 and the part played by the Army in dealing with it', Volume I Operations, IWM, 72/82/2. The lack of women searchers was highlighted in the 5th Division area were there were none in 1920 and in June 1921 only about a dozen, 'History of the 5th Division in Ireland November 1919-March 1922', 50, IWM, 72/82/2. The discussion of this problem in a Dublin District Brigade Conference held 20 January 1921, file marked 'B.M./33/0/2', PRO, WO35/71-/6/84. On 6 June 1921, a special application procedure was started for raiding parties needing women searchers, PRO, WO35/71/8/117.

should make a practise of acting quite normally, such as doing shopping, visiting tea-shops, and if necessary attending public entertainment as spectators. The people watching their behaviour would soon begin to understand that we do not always look for trouble and are human beings.

The success of the movement in becoming the dominant force in southern Ireland became clear in the elections for a devolved parliament in May 1921 in which the 26 counties returned 105 Sinn Fein MPs unopposed.[46]

CONCLUSION

Overall, the movement was well able to mobilise public support throughout the struggle. Initially, this was largely an expression of the rejection of constitutional nationalism which had become largely outdated,[47] as was clearly demonstrated during the Conscription Crisis and the general election of 1918. The identification of Sinn Féin with popular issues during 1917 and 1918, also led to greater voluntary support for radical policies. Nevertheless, a measure of violence against civilians was necessary during arms raids and particularly after 1918 to enforce adherence to the various manifestations of the alternative republican administration and induce a boycott of government institutions.

Direct defiance of British rule, such as the non-payment of taxes and the boycott of state institutions, needed a large measure of enforcement and was clearly more successful in the rural areas where the Volunteers could control the community with greater ease. This violence was mainly directed at typical members of that community whose support was vital for the success of this policy. However, the need to secure grassroots support meant

46 Orders to tighten control on the behaviour of raiding parties in August and September 1920, PRO, WO35/70. The recommendations of the Commandant consisted of a long list of suggestions including a reduction in the use of machine guns, bombs and armoured cars in the streets, a reduction in the speed with which lorries travelled through the streets to twelve miles an hour and an increase of foot patrols, Letter to G.S.O.I. Dublin District dated 25 March 1921, PRO, WO35/71. Similar attempts were made in the country areas, letter Military HQ 16th Infantry Brigade Fermoy dated 17 June 1921, NLI, ms. 31,223(3).

47 In a poem entitled: 'The Ruin and Rule' this disdain for parliamentary nationalists is nicely exposed: 'The boys on Saturday nights, / Around the bars keep gatherin', / Where they tipple, as blaze the nights, / And of Home Rule still they're blatherin'. / While the boss is a patriot born, / And a Home Ruler you bet it, / And on every Patrick's morn, / Your Shamrock green he'll wet it', NLI, LOP115, item 11. See also Joseph Sweeney, in K. Griffith and T. O'Grady (1982), 33.

that they rarely inflicted serious injuries, and the focus on friends and neighbours prevented most of these incidents from being reported to the police or in the papers.

Although the violence somewhat limited their popularity, strikes in support of republican causes, commemorations and funerals were widely backed in most areas during 1920. The often indiscriminate force engaged in by the Crown Forces and the measures taken by the government aggravated the population to a much larger extent than Volunteer violence and helped to justify the military campaign. Combined with the fear evoked by the intimidation and executions of civilians in more active areas this meant that Volunteers could safely operate in many areas.[48]

It is obvious that in more affected counties the emotive effect of Crown Force violence was far stronger than elsewhere. However, the ability of the Volunteers to enforce adherence to their policies followed a different pattern. This was largely connected with the integration of the movement in the community and the continued support for constitutional nationalists. The penetration of the movement in communal life in Mayo is witnessed both by the success of the movement in the elections as well as by the success of republican institutions and the lack of violence against civilians. In Tipperary, the movement was almost equally successful in the rural areas, although a clear measure of intimidation was necessary particularly against the somewhat larger group of unionists and constitutional nationalists. The towns in Tipperary and all areas of Wexford were much more divided in their loyalty. As a result, few Volunteer operations emanated from there, although intimidation and executions of civilians were fairly common. In Dublin, the divided loyalty of the population did inspire some violence against anti-republican civilians but the anonymous urban setting ensured a relative safe functioning of the republican movement. In Derry, republicans were confronted with such an overwhelming opposition that violence against civilians or Crown Forces was almost impossible. As a result the mobilisation of public opinion was extremely difficult, and the strikes rarely extended beyond the Volunteers and their close sympathisers.

48 Volunteers who were hardened in the fighting also abused their position of power by mistreating civilians who did not readily cooperate. This included the use of physical violence to force civilians to dig trenches or put Volunteers up for the night, Bryan Ryan (1969), 40.

CHAPTER 8

Alternative Government and Civil Opposition

Having established the movement's success in mobilising nationalists behind them we can now look at the measure of public support for their alternative government and the way in which the Volunteers dealt with civilian opposition to their political and military campaign. The shape and success of the different functions of alternative government have been discussed elsewhere in detail.[1] What follows is therefore not a comprehensive survey of these themes, but an exploration of Volunteer involvement in order to obtain a fuller picture of the position of the Volunteers in Irish society. In discerning the way they dealt with opposition from within the community, special attention is given to the differences between those who actively opposed them and those who were singled out as potential enemies.

LEGITIMACY

The movement's legal claim to the existence of an independent Irish State was based on the declaration of the 'Irish Republic as a Sovereign Independent State' by the leaders of the 1916 Rising. This declaration based the existence of an Irish nation on the period before the first English settlements in Ireland and the long history of struggle against British rule. It further stated that the Provisional Government, self-appointed by this declaration, would administer the civil and military affairs of the republic until such time as a permanent national government could be elected by the suffrage of all adult citizens. In the meantime the Provisional Government claimed the right to rule Ireland and the allegiance of every Irishman and woman.

After the defeat of the rebels in 1916 their was some confusion regarding the rightful heir to this right to administer Irish affairs, between the Supreme Council of the IRB, the provisional executive of the Volunteers, and the officially elected executives of Sinn Féin and the Volunteers in 1917. However, the localised nature of reorganisation lead by Volunteer

1   See Arthur Mitchell (1995)

officers, most of whom were also IRB members, and the strong personal ties between all these bodies on a national level avoided any serious conflict between them in a period when there was little opportunity to wield such power.

The general election of December 1918 was seen as the chance to form the permanent Government of Ireland envisaged by the 1916 declaration. The election success of Sinn Féin was identified as an expression of the will of the people, which legitimised the self-proclaimed existence of a separate Irish State. All MPs elected in Ireland were invited to come to Dublin to constitute an independent Irish parliament and form a government. The establishment of Dáil Éireann in January 1919 forms an important legal base for the republicans' claim to their right to govern Ireland. The Dáil ratified the proclamation of the Irish Republic of 1916, and ordained itself as the sole power with the right to make laws binding on the people of Ireland.

The establishment of this rival government gave the republican movement a solid base to its assumed monopoly of the use of power and violence, and a moral justification for the right to raise money both at home and abroad. However, the Volunteers retained an ambivalent attitude towards the Dáil. Not until August 1919 was a serious attempt made to bring the Volunteers under the Dáil's control, and although the Volunteer Executive then reluctantly accepted that all Volunteers were to take an oath of allegiance to the Dáil, it continued to have its separate leadership. The refusal of the Dáil to sanction the use of violence and recognise the Volunteers as the 'Army of the Republic' until March 1921 made many individual Volunteers hesitate to take this oath.

The lack of clarity regarding the distribution of power between these institutions also added to the confused development towards guerrilla warfare. At the same time that bellicose members of the Volunteers began to engage the police, the Dáil initiated its non-violent campaign to set up an alternative civil administration. The success of the republican alternatives was extremely important in underpinning the Dáil's claim to be the legitimate Government of Ireland and ultimately to justify the use of violence. As a result, the Volunteers constantly had to maintain a balance between the need to enforce loyalty in a war situation and the danger of antagonising their grassroots support in the community.

ARBITRATION COURTS

From the time they had re-organised in 1917 Volunteers had become involved in settling local disputes. This was a logical consequence of the call to boycott British institutions, and it was hoped that solving local quarrels would unite the people behind the cause. In Mayo the presence of such courts is already reported in 1917. In many other areas they began in

August 1919, when Arbitration Courts were initiated by order of the Dáil. Holding tribunals for arbitration where consensus was reached between two opposing parties was allowed under British law; criminal prosecutions, however, were illegal. On their establishment the public was informed that they were expected to bring their cases to the new courts. This was often successful and in many areas people presented all kinds of grievances for arbitration. When such courts were set up in South Down in September 1920 letters were sent to both Protestants and Catholics inviting them to avail themselves of its services. In areas where the Volunteers were particularly strong many local unionists accepted this invitation. Following the spread of these courts throughout the country an official boycott of the government assizes was declared.[2]

Many of the first courts were held in the local court house and observed by public and police alike. The residing judges had to embody authority, and men of considerable local standing with sympathy for the movement were approached for this. Parish priests and captains of local companies and other IRA officers, who had been elected with similar considerations in mind, frequently presided. Cases dealt with in these courts concerned mainly agrarian matters and disputes between neighbours; they ranged from farmers who let their livestock roam, destroying milk-churns and cabbages, to minor political cases. One young man was charged with breaking the windows of a Protestant Church in Swatragh, Co. Derry.[3]

Despite the Dáil order of 1919, several places did not establish their first courts until the summer of 1920 when a more comprehensive court system was instituted. Particularly in southern and western areas where the movement found more general support, the courts were extremely successful and by the summer of 1920 they had taken over all functions of the British legal system, which was virtually paralysed. Most people brought their cases to the Dáil Courts and refused to turn up for jury duty at the British assizes:

> Sinn Féin Courts are now in full swing throughout the County, and practically put an end to Quarter Sessions and Petty Sessions. In-

2 Start of Arbitration Courts in Mayo, Tipperary and Dublin, Ned Moane, 'Statement'; Speeches reported in 1917, PRO, CO904/122; Sean Clancy, Interview. Letter in South Down, PRONI, FIN18/1/158. See also Arthur Mitchell (1995), 138-9.

3 Sinn Féin judges: In Wexford, Martin Kennedy, Interview. In Mayo, Ned Maughan, O'MN, P17b109; CI Mayo MR December 1919; 'Activities List Owenwee Company'. In Derry, Thomas Morris, 'Typescript of Interview', Fr O'Kane Papers, AARC. In Tipperary, Jack Gardiner, Interview. The type of cases arbitrated, John Quinn, 'Typescript of Interview', Fr O'Kane Papers, AARC; Paddy Larkin, Interview; Summons of Sinn Féin Court, PRONI, FIN18/1/104; Moane/Malone, Tape.

timidation is used to compel people to enter these courts in preference to the British Courts. The Sinn Féin Courts are no longer
secret tribunals. Their doings are fully reported in local papers, and
those presiding announce that the decisions will be enforced by 'the
military forces of the Irish Republic'.[4]

Although the judgements of the courts were often followed, they had little
power to enforce them. Those dissatisfied with a decision could always
refer the case to the British Courts with active support from the RIC. If
the influence of the movement was to be maintained, people who refused
to come to the court or accept its ruling had to be forced to do so:

> This fellow was convicted in the Sinn Féin Court and he told us to
> go to hell knowing that we couldn't arrest him for the police outside
> would rescue him; so we put him under open arrest. We went into
> Westport where we met Willie Malone [...] Moane and Ring and we
> told them what had happened in the Court, for Louisburgh was then
> in the Westport Battalion. They sent two carloads of men around by
> Leenane and they came in the top road by Cregganbaum. We
> marched into Louisburgh where we had 2 fellows spotting your man,
> and we arrested him the same night. We convicted him abroad in
> Louisburgh and on the following day we took him to Tom Maguire's
> of Cross and we put him working by himself for a farmer in Tuam
> for three months; as a threat we said that if he ever came back he'd
> be shot at sight, but he didn't return until his father broke his leg.
> We were often appealed to, to let him off so after a month we
> brought him to his own house. This was the first decision in the
> Court there, and after that sentence all other decisions were carried
> out after that.

4   Quote, CI Mayo MR June 1920. In Mayo, the lack of jurors at the British
    Assizes coincided with the fact that most of the cases listed had the day before
    been disposed of by a Sinn Féin tribunal, *Mayoman*, 17 July 1920; CI Mayo
    MR July 1920. The success of the courts in Mayo is emphasised by Volunteer
    officers, Ned Moane, 'Statement'; Moane/Malone, Tape; James Chambers,
    'Statement'; Jim O'Donnell, 'Recollections'. In the summer of 1920 a clear
    increase in the number of courts is reported. The first Dáil Court sessions are
    reported in Castlebar and Islandeady, *Mayoman*, 5 & 12 June 1920. Other
    western counties saw a similar success of the Dáil Courts: In Clare, Sean
    Clancy, Interview; Liam Haugh, 'History of the West Clare Brigade', NLI,
    P915 A0363. In Tipperary, many places had their first Courts in the summer
    of 1920, TSCM 1986:79; TSCM 25/5. Quote, CI Mayo MR June 1920. For
    workings of courts, J. Casey (1970 & 1974); F. Costello (1990); C. Davitt
    (1968); C.A. Maguire (1969); Tom Garvin (1981), 126-7. David Fitzpatrick
    (1977), Chapter 5; Arthur Mitchell (1995)130-54.

Reports of people kidnapped in order to try them by a Dáil Court were widespread in the summer of 1920. The acceptance of the republicans and the fear of the consequences of opposition they had been able to instil in the people were demonstrated by the fact that most who were forced to come to the courts in this way, whether convicted or acquitted, refused to inform the police about their captors. This even applied to counties like Derry where the IRA was weak.[5]

LAND AGITATION

Among the more frequent cases the Arbitration Courts had to deal with were the numerous disputes between landowners and dissatisfied tenants over rights to land. Since the foundation of the organisation Volunteers had been involved in land agitation in the South and West. The main object of this agitation by small farmers and land labourers was to force larger landowners and graziers to sell their land. The movement had used this agitation as a tool in their opposition to British rule in 1917-18. After a period of relative peace, such agitation again erupted in the spring of 1920 aided by the evacuation of barracks. In the West the agrarian agitation was often much more violent than the national struggle. Many landowners were threatened and forced to agree to sell their land. The first civilians to die in Mayo as a result of politically motivated violence in this period, were two tenants who were stoned and beaten to death after they had refused to take part in the boycott of an estate in June 1920.[6]

Many of the mostly small farmers in the West were involved in this type of agitation. The wealthier farmers in the South, better established in

5 Quote, Jack Feehan, O'MN, P17b113. See also P.J. Kelly, 'One of the Men from the West'. Threats made to people not accepting Volunteers ruling, John Quinn, 'Typescript of Interview', Fr O'Kane Papers, AARC. Reports of intimidation, CI Mayo MRs June-October 1920; CI South Tipperary MRs June-August 1920; CI Wexford MR November 1920. Many people were kidnapped in 1920, particularly during the summer. Over 100 cases of kidnap were reported throughout Ireland in July alone, IG MR July 1920. Report of kidnapped people refusing the police information in Derry, CI Derry MR November 1920. Only rarely did people resist the Volunteers in their attempts to enforce the rule of the Dáil Courts. One example in West Clare where a man used a weapon leading to his death, Liam Haugh, 'History of the West Clare Brigade', MA, A0363.
6 Violence against landowners, Arthur Mitchell (1995), 131-2. The stoning of two men refers to events on the Kenney Estate in Mayo, *Mayoman*, 12 June 1920; CI Mayo MR June 1920. In Tipperary, a herd was murdered in connection with a land dispute in July 1920, CI South Tipperary MR July 1920. An epidemic of cattle drives took place in South Mayo early in 1920, *Mayoman*, 27 March 1920.

their holdings and afraid of unrest among their labourers, were less willing to go along with it. With the emergence of violent struggle on a national basis, many people became increasingly worried lest social radicalisation of labourers and small farmers should develop. As a result, they made representations to Sinn Féin and the Volunteers Executive to control the outbreak of agitation.

Although the breaking up of grasslands tied in with Sinn Féin's policy of self-sufficiency, the resulting disruption of property relations was too threatening a proposition to consider. Attempts by evicted farmers to reclaim land they had been evicted from as long as half a century before equally threatened civil order. Despite the involvement of many Volunteers in this type of agitation, Sinn Féin found it necessary to put a stop to it. A statement was issued by Dáil Éireann rejecting this type of claim which was especially prevalent in Clare. People were warned that these claims were divisive and should be brought before the Dáil Courts.[7]

Directives were sent out to the Volunteers to distance themselves from the land question as there was a more important struggle at hand. To deal effectively with the claims that were made, a system of Land Courts was set up. The first of these was held on 17 May 1920 in Ballinrobe, Co. Mayo. Due to the involvement of Volunteers the leadership was afraid that judgements in these courts would favour the tenants. To ensure a more equitable judgement special judges were sent down from Dublin.

In line with the demands made to Sinn Féin, most of these Land Courts did indeed side with the legal owner. Although this was often an unpopular decision, the republican leadership felt it could ill afford to lose the support of the propertied classes, and judgements were enforced by Volunteers. This happened in Ballinrobe where tenants had brought a case against two landholders before the Land Court presided over by two Dublin men:

> The case was decided in favour of Hyland and Murphy [the landholders] much to the indignation of the tenants who stormed out of

7   Dáil statement, *Mayoman*, 22 May 1920. Other examples of such claims: In Leix Brigade, MA, Ao484. In Tipperary, CI South Tipperary MR June 1920. Some people in Tipperary gave up their land in favour of the old holder. The mixing of agrarian unrest and Sinn Féinism and the fear this caused in the Executive of Sinn Féin and the Volunteers was observed by the police in 1918 and 1920, IG MRs February 1918 & May-June 1920. See also Arthur Mitchell (1995), 131. The dangers involved in this mixing became apparent when a Volunteer Lieutenant in Clare was betrayed to the enemy after he had become in-volved in a land dispute, Liam Haugh, 'History of the West Clare Brigade', NLI, P915 Ao363. See also Letter to Brigade Commandant South Roscommon Brigade dated 12 May 1920, NLI, P919 Ao525.

the court claiming that it was worse than the British. Maguire relates that subsequently the Volunteers police, under the command of Tom Maguire, removed the most defiant and imprisoned them in an 'unknown destination'. His account states that after a week's detention they gave in. Other accounts suggest that the dispute was more prolonged.

Although judgements of Arbitration and Land Courts were thus difficult to implement and not always popular, their existence alone made republican government a tangible reality in many places.[8]

CRIMINALITY

The evacuation of outlying police posts at the end of 1919, and the growing reluctance of the police to venture out of their barracks gave criminals room to act. The unprosecuted arms raids of the Volunteers had given an opening to those willing to take advantage of the circumstances, and many people were robbed, some by Volunteers. Realising that a dangerous vacuum was being created which could damage the movement, it was not the police but the Volunteers who expressed their readiness to deal with the rise in crime. The republican aspiration of forming a legitimate government led them to position themselves as defenders of the community. As early as May 1919 a Volunteer company in Dublin arrested four thieves who were tried and sentenced to the lash.[9]

In a General Order of January 1920 GHQ prepared the Volunteers for action: 'In connection with this matter it should be kept in view that a definite effort may very soon have to be made by Volunteers towards the protection of the general public against the raids and robberies that have become so prevalent recently in many districts.' To prevent confusion, this order again forbade the raiding of private houses for arms without explicit GHQ permission, and instructions were given to prosecute offenders. However, local Volunteers had their own priorities and arms raiding continued, and when it became clear in August 1920 that the authorities were

8   Quote, 'The Fountainhill Case', in *Evolution of a judicial system under the jurisdiction of Dáil Éireann 1919-1921* (n. d.). Similar cases where the Land Courts decided against the incumbents, CI South Tipperary MR August 1920. See also Arthur Mitchell (1995), 135-7.

9   For a description of the large number of unpunished robberies that were taking place in Tipperary, Fr Michael Maher, Diary 1919, St Patrick's College Thurles. In Cork alone, reported robberies on businesses increased from 0 in 1917, 2 in 1918, 7 in 1919, to 47 in 1920 and 41 in 1921, Peter Hart (1992), Chapter 'The Dynamics of Violence', 55. See also Arthur Mitchell (1995), 150-2. Arresting thieves, UCD AD, LA9.

going to collect all arms in private possession, GHQ itself ordered a collective effort to obtain these arms by raiding.[10]

GHQ's desire to protect the population from robbers and thereby prove their legitimacy was strong. In some cases Volunteers were allowed to appear as witnesses in a British Court to ensure the conviction of criminals caught by the police, although this was a clear contravention of the boycott of all British civil institutions. To save face two Volunteers allowed to go forward were given instructions:

> Make it perfectly clear that they do not recognise the authority of the court, and they look on the court and those who are connected with it, as helping to prevent the proper protection of the people of this country and the proper dispensing of justice, and they should make it clear, that it is only their desire to protect the towns-people of Youghal, that makes them attend at that court.

As with their efforts to curb the effects of arms raids, republicans tried to keep a balance between the demands made by the boycott of government institutions and their efforts to represent the community as best they could. In September 1920 Sinn Féin issued a circular instructing all to refuse attending British Courts except when compelled to do so. At the same time, owners of property destroyed by the Crown Forces were allowed to claim compensation in the same courts.[11]

Local Volunteers as well as GHQ were uncertain about the appropriate steps to deal with the criminals they caught. After the arrest of some civilians suspected of a robbery in May 1920 a local IRA commander had to inquire from GHQ whether there were any official court martial procedures, or should they follow the lines of 'English court martial'. The uncertainty about possible punishments extended to GHQ itself:

> It is very difficult to deal with. There is only one punishment which we can with convenience to our selves mete out to such people, and unless it is shown clearly that such persons are a danger to society in your area, you may not carry out the extreme penalty. Some of them, however, would accept deportation. The important thing is that the

10 Quote, order titled: 'Raids and Robberies', dated 19 January 1920, O'MN, P17b127. See also NLI, ms. 11,410(11) and ms. 31.192(1). Continued raiding by Volunteers, Alfred Rutherford, O'MN, P17b122. Collective raiding effort was started at local level but became a general order, Third Tipperary Brigade Orders, O'MN, P17b127; CI Wexford MR August 1920.

11 Quote, letter from GHQ to Brigade Commandant Cork no.1 dated 5 May 1920, NLI, ms. 31,192(1). Sinn Féin circular dated 17 September 1920, NLI, P918 A0413. Claiming compensation, Weekly Memo no.1 dated 2 October 1920, O'MN, P17b127.

goods are recovered and restored. The Volunteers organisation is not in a position to take up the policing of the country.

It decided that activities against criminals should be carried out carefully, but if such people thought that 'the Volunteer forces are likely to come down on them, it may have a good effect.'[12]

Although several offenders were held for short periods, the organisation was unable to imprison anyone for a long time. The first priority was the return of the goods or their value to the original owners. The official policy was formulated in a General Order in June 1920:

> The restoration of the damage done must be insisted on as far as possible. Pending the development of a criminal department by the Dáil, no punishment will be inflicted, but the convicted parties will be retained in custody until the following Sunday, and publicly paraded after the principal Mass, their name and address and offence being publicly announced.

Most offenders got off with a warning, but later banishment and other forms of punishment were introduced by local units.[13]

Efforts to start a Dáil criminal department were already in progress. In June the Dáil Cabinet gave the Arbitration Courts civil authority and reserved the power to extend their remit to include criminal cases. To deal with the increasing demands made on the Volunteers for police services, a separate Republican Police Force was established on 19 June 1920. The IRA stated this was a reaction to: 'the destruction and evacuation of the alleged "police" force of the enemy and the rapid development of the Civil side of responsible Republican Government.'[14]

Three or four men were to be recruited voluntarily in each company under direction of special officers appointed by the brigade commandant. In November 1920 the Republican Police became a separate branch of the IRA and strength of the corps was increased to ten members per company, but it

---

12 Quotes, Letters between Brigade HQ Carlow and Quartermaster General dated May 1920, NLI, P916 A0488.

13 Quote, General Order no.9 dated 19 June 1920, NLI, ms. 739. Cases in which criminals were forced to repay their victims but with no further consequences for them, NLI, P916 A0489; Jack Gardiner, Interview. Cases where banishment was a verdict, CI South Tipperary MR July 1920; *Derry People and Donegal News*, 24 July 1920. In Clare, people who were seen to frequent a pub which served British Military were flogged after having been warned, NLI, P911.

14 Before 1920 individual Volunteers acted as Republican Police on special occasions like bye-elections and fairs for fund-raising, UCD, LA9; O'Farrell, MA, A0167; Arthur Mitchell (1995), 150. Establishment separate police force, General Orders no.4 and no.9, NLI, ms. 739.

was stressed that: 'While it must be realised that the Police will require some good men from the Army, the Army should not be unduly impoverished of good men in forming the Police. Very suitable men for Police work may be found in persons who have not actually been Volunteers.' This last order concluded with the instruction to use the IRA for police work for the present, and a request to report to what extent the introduction of the police force had progressed. This implied that despite the June order to set up a police force, many areas still did not have one by November.[15]

The replacement of the RIC by the Republican Police allowed the movement to implement the decisions of their courts. A further advantage of the execution of the civil functions of the police was the increased visibility of the alternative government. However, the prosecution of criminals also presented new problems. The jurisdiction of the Arbitration Courts had to be extended to incorporate criminal cases.

Coinciding with the start of a republican police force a system of Republican Courts was established on 29 June 1920 as an extension of the Dáil Arbitration Courts. Since criminal prosecutions by civilians was illegal under British law, all courts were increasingly regarded as illegal assemblies and broken up. The Crown Forces were taught to distinguish between the type of cases dealt with. In October 1920 the 6th Division of the British Army in Ireland drew up instructions: 'Sinn Féin Courts are not illegal except when they can be proved to exceed the functions of Arbitration Courts, and to usurp the powers of Civil Courts of Justice by imposing punishments, fines, etc.' The military were ordered to observe the proceedings and disperse the courts if they were denied access or when the proceedings exceeded their statutory rights.[16]

The continued existence of Sinn Féin Courts irritated some members of the Crown Forces and were additional causes for outrage against civilians. The increased fighting in 1920 made men involved in the various Dáil Courts targets for police attention. Many courts were broken up and those presiding arrested. As a result most courts went underground or were suspended in 1921. In some areas attendance at the British Courts was revived and even jurors re-appeared in greater numbers. In other areas the demarcation line between Dáil Courts and court martials held by the Volunteers disappeared. The sittings, under continuous threat by police raids, became shorter and were solely reliant on the judgement of the local IRA commander. Although many of its courts were thus only temporarily able to profile

---

15 Instructions from General Order No.9 and No.12, NLI, ms. 739. Reading order in Dublin, NLI, ms. 901/24. Report from East Limerick Brigade, NLI, ms. 17,880. See also Arthur Mitchell (1995), 152.

16 Quote, dated 13 July 1920, NLI, P918 A0413. In October 1920, the Assistant Under Secretary for Ireland stated he could do nothing against men signing Sinn Féin court summonses, PRONI, FIN18/1/158.

themselves publicly, they gave added support to the viability of the movement's alternative government.[17]

CIVILIAN ENEMIES

Besides arbitration between civilians and prosecution of criminals, the movement had to cope with people who actively opposed them, partly for security reasons and partly to reinforce their claim to authority. Such people were dealt with directly by Volunteer court martials. Most of this involved minor cases, such as opposing the destruction of all forms of communication, which annoyed many people in 1921. Although such action was dealt with in most brigade areas, a comprehensive list of court martials is only available for the East Limerick Brigade. The offences consisted mostly of cases in which barricades were removed or people informed the RIC of the presence of such obstructions.[18]

Most of them got off with a fine of £5, but those who challenged the authority of the Volunteers directly were punished more severely. One man who had removed a barricade after the company captain had explicitly forbidden him to do so, was fined £80. Other people were court-martialled for refusing to hand over arms, for making uncomplimentary remarks about the IRA or for physically assaulting Volunteers. At a national level attempts were made to control the expression of anti-Sinn Féin sentiment by smashing up the printing presses of newspapers which reported unfavourably on certain incidents. This was also an answer to the government's injunction on numerous newspapers because of their open hostility to British rule.[19]

The most serious offence to be dealt with was informing on the Volunteers. The proclamation put up by the IRA in south Tipperary in February 1919 as a reaction to the declaration of the riding as a special military area had already warned civilians against cooperation with the police. Those giving information or assisting the police in serious acts were deemed to have forfeited their lives and were to be executed. Although for the time this was an exceptionally extreme expression of the IRA's thinking about the role of civilians, it certainly reflected the attitude of the leadership of the Volunteers in Tipperary. At the time the Volunteers did not act on it, but

17 Attention given to members of arbitration courts in Mayo, *Mayoman*, 2 October 1920; CI Mayo MR December 1920. On the collapse of many Dáil Courts in 1921: In Mayo, CI Mayo MRs January-April 1921; Ned Moane, 'Statement'. In Tipperary, TSCM, 1986:172. In Wexford, CI Wexford MR January 1921.

18 Court martial of civilians in Limerick, NLI, ms. 17,880. See also Ned Moane, 'Statement'; Company report dated 13 May 1921, NLI, ms. 901/100; UCD AD, P7A17/270, and P7A19/146.

19 Smashing up of presses of *The Independent* and *The Freeman's Journal*, Garry Houlihan, O'MN, P17b105.

later this became Volunteer policy in areas with an extreme leadership like that in Tipperary.[20]

In practice the level of punishment for informing was supposed to be related to the seriousness of the information. A man in Limerick who informed the police of the existence of a barricade was fined £50. Others who were suspected of giving more damaging information to the police were deported from the area and warned that if they returned they would be shot on sight. Due to the lack of evidence, many suspected spies were initially merely cautioned.[21]

The more serious fighting that developed at the end of 1920 made informing increasingly life-threatening to the Volunteers. As a result the punishments became harsher, resulting in several, sometimes unwarranted, executions. The general order allowing the execution of informers issued in April 1920 made it clear that permission from GHQ had to be sought at all times, with the exception of cases in which the continued imprisonment of a spy endangered the Volunteers themselves. Nevertheless, at the end of the struggle even junior officers took it upon themselves to execute suspected spies without referring to GHQ and on little evidence. GHQ felt compelled to issue several warnings: 'It must be generally understood, that except in cases where our Forces are in actual peril and action cannot be delayed – that the Brigade Commandant's authority is necessary before a spy can be executed.'[22]

20 Volunteer proclamation in Tipperary, Seamus Robinson, 'Statement', NLI, ms 21,265, and O'MN, P17b99.
21 Civilians being deported, Tommy Ryan, 'Statement'; Sean Withero, O'MN, P17b114.
22 All association with the enemy was forbidden in April 1920, and the execution of spies was allowed on the same date providing it was ratified by the Brigade Commander. General Order No. 24 from May 1921, made it possible to relate punishment to the importance of the information, allowing for a money fine in less important cases and death in serious cases, NLI, ms. 739. Differentiation in punishment: Warning people by tying them up, Report D-Company dated March 1921, NLI, ms. 901/112; Report dated 13 May 1921, NLI, ms. 901/100; John Neary, O'MN, P17b122. A number of suspected spies were lifted, questioned and if found guilty shot, Robert Briscoe (1958), 60; Michael Chadwick, 'With the Sixth battalion', in *Dublin's Fighting Story* (1949), 185; Paddy Rigney, O'MN, P17b105; Jim Slattery, O'MN, P17b109; George White, O'MN, P17b105; Paul Merrigan, O'MN, P7b126. Those suspected of informing included all sons of the Dublin police and all touts, NLI, ms. 901/28 + 49. The confessions of spies were often made under duress, by strangling, threats and promises: In Dublin, NLI, ms. 901/109. In Cork, Letter dated 21 May 1921, NLI, ms. 31,207. In April 1921, there was still confusion whether sanction of GHQ was necessary to shoot a spy, UCD AD, P7A17/339. The shooting of spies became so frequent in Cork at the end of the war that the Intelligence officer of the First Southern Division felt forced to reassure GHQ: 'I think G.H.Q. has somehow got the idea that in the Cork Brigades, and especially in CORK No.1, men are being shot as spies more or less on suspicion. Instead of this, as I am aware myself, the greatest care is taken in every instance to have the case fully proved and beyond all doubt. As a matter of fact, the men shot have in most cases admitted their guilt before being executed.', UCD AD, P7A20/309. Quote, dated 1 June 1921, UCD AD, P7A19/1. See also UCD AD, P7A17/198.

Informing was most detrimental to the safety of Volunteers in active areas, but was more likely in Wexford and Derry where unionists and constitutional nationalists were much more numerous. Understandably, the level of participation in these counties was lower and the IRA encountered more difficulty in enforcing its rule over the population. In Mayo, with a more homogeneous population, the Volunteers experienced few problems of this kind as they had been able to gain almost complete support of the community. However, this position also made dealing with spies more difficult as most were considered fellow members of the community, and violence against them might alienate the population. In Tipperary the urban population, in particular, always remained largely opposed to the Volunteers, and it needed sterner measures to enforce acceptance of its rule. The polarisation of the people ensured that the shooting of opponents of the Volunteers was condoned by its supporters as long as they were considered to belong to the other group.

The high number of civilian informers shot in Tipperary and the fact that none were shot in either Mayo brigade area was largely a result of the different positions the Volunteers had in the respective counties. The central position they had in Mayo also constrained violence against the Crown Forces, as many Volunteers feared the reaction against the population which would follow such attacks. Despite the military insignificance of operations in Wexford, some alleged informers, all ex-soldiers, were shot in 1921. The open opposition from the community was apparently seen as a threat or an embarrassment or both to the Volunteers. In Dublin the anonymity of the city enabled the Volunteers to disregard the community. However, the IRA was unable to control the entire population, and many anonymous letters giving information about Volunteer activities were received by the authorities. To limit such informing, fear of its consequences was instilled first by beating up suspected touts and later by executions.[23]

The increasing danger and consequent growing severity of punishment for offences of this type is demonstrated by the changes in official policy concerning female informers. While their information could lead to the failure of an operation and possibly to short terms of imprisonment, they were not harshly treated. The shame connected with local exposure was sufficient to inhibit most of them: 'Mrs. Scanlon, an old woman, was taken from her bed in Emlanaughton, near Ballymote, Co. Sligo and compelled to walk two miles. She was found two hours later tied to a telegraph pole, on which there was a notice bearing the words, "Long tongues beware".' Particular

23 All type of reactions were observed in Dublin. Many civilians aided the Volunteers without knowing them, Sean Harling in, K. Griffith and T. O'Grady (1982), 159; Martin Walton, Ibidem, 287. Others were not intimidated by the Volunteers and informed on them regardless of threats, O'Sullivan, Ibidem, 205; A great number of anonymous letters to the authorities, PRO, WO35/70-90. Dealing with touts, Frank Henderson, O'MN, P17b99; John Neary, O'MN, P17b122.

attention was given to girls who 'walked with' and gave information to the Crown Forces. The visibility of their opposition was a thorn in the side of the IRA and several had their hair cut short.[24]

The way the Volunteers dealt with suspected female informants at this stage is demonstrated by the experience of a company in Dublin. During patrol duty they were warned by a woman that a local girl, who had a relationship with a British soldier, had gone out to warn the authorities of their presence. After the patrol had moved off, two lorries full of military arrived. The patrol duly reported the incident to their superiors:

> It was decided apparently by the powers that be that they'd investigate it. [...] They went back to the woman and they pressed her for informa-tion about the girl, [...] she told them who the girl was. [...] A few of us got the job of watching her and we shadowed her way up to Phibsboro. [...] We discovered she was meeting her soldier, [...] he used to come from what is now McKee Barracks, and [...] we followed them out to Glasnevin passed the cemetery. [...] There were bushes and trees there which led into a field, and it was a place for courting couples [...] at night, and we just followed them [...] and the Kerry man produced this huge big scissors he brought them especially for the job. [...] The sol-dier got a hide in the park and was told to go away about his business, which he did. He was lucky to get away. [...] Your man produced the huge big scissors, I think it must have been a sheep sheer, and cut the two plaits of the girl and told her to go to her mother.[25]

The continued defiance of the Volunteers by some women led to frequent requests for instructions as to how to deal with them. The existing treat-ment was formalised in a General Order issued in November 1920. A woman who was found guilty of spying by a Court of Inquiry was, in the case of a non-Irish woman, to be ordered to leave the country in seven days and to be informed that only consideration of her gender prevented the infliction of the death penalty. A formal public statement of the facts about the conviction was to be issued as a warning. In the case of an Irishwoman it was hoped that simply bringing publicity to her actions would neutralise her. In dangerous and persistent cases of this kind full particulars were to be placed before GHQ and instructions sought. However, these instructions were not sufficient to deal with the problem. In 1921, the destruction of property and banishment were introduced as alternative punishments.

24 Quote on 'Mrs. Scanlon', *Tipperary Star*, 22 January 1921.
25 Quote from Dublin, Sean Clancy, Interview. Another soldier courting a local girl in Dublin in 1921 was threatened by two men, but was let go in the end, Major B.A. Pond, IWM, 78/27/1.

Eventually, a few women whose alleged informing had led to loss of life were executed in 1921, notably in Cork.[26]

CIVILIAN VICTIMS

Besides some blatant cases of informing, those accused of informing were mainly people who were not representative of the community. As proof was extremely hard to establish, suspicion was generally the only basis for such allegations. This often fell on those who made themselves into outsiders by their general behaviour. Killing people considered to be 'outsiders' has always been easier than shooting 'one of your own'. The first to come under suspicion in this way were ex-soldiers and ex-policemen who had remained in contact with their old comrades. In Wexford, all those shot as informers fell in this category. The lifestyle of travelling people made them both suspicious as well as a possible victim. When many Volunteers went on the run, their presence became increasingly threatening. Uncertain of their political allegiance, all were considered to be potential spies. Some indeed provided the Crown Forces with information for money; but these were exceptions. Information leading to arrests was often given by unsuspected sources closer to the Volunteers, but most were unwilling to consider these people for execution.[27]

26 General Order on 'Female Spies', NLI, ms. 739. On destruction of property and banishment, Letter to East Clare Brigade dated 12 April 1921, UCD AD, P7A17/197; Letter from South Roscommon Brigade, UCD AD, P7A38. During 1921, many brigades remained uncertain what to do in these cases, UCD AD, P7A17/198; Letter from South Roscommon Brigade dated 14 February 1921, UCD AD, P7A38. Unauthorised shootings of female spies continued, Oscar Traynor, O'MN, P17b98; Letter to QMG dated 27 February 1921, NLI, ms. 31,223(1); UCD AD, P7A21/155.

27 In a list titled: 'Civilians accused of giving information to and associating with British Forces in War of Independence', recorded during the Truce for the counties Cork, Waterford, Kerry and Limerick 258 males are named. Of this a high number (44) were ex-military or ex-RIC, and three were Protestant ministers or rectors. Out of a total of ninety females, eight were direct family of police men. Most of the others had jobs which involved direct contact with the Crown Forces. Most stated offences were innocent in itself 'associating with', or 'being friendly to the Crown Forces', 'keeping the pub open', 'has openly expressed his opinion of the IRA and styled them the Murder Gang', or 'has entertained RIC or Black & Tans'. Some more serious offences included people 'phoning RIC about trenches', 'speaking to the enemy', 'seen to point out several young men to the Tans with the result that the men were flogged afterwards', and 'told constable [?] that Constable Berger was in communication with IRA, which was true'. The evidence was thin and consisted mostly of: 'anyone can state this' or 'he has a permit after curfew', MA, A0897. The frequent victimisation of travellers and other wandering people, Letter from HQ 1st Battalion Cork no.2 Brigade dated 21 May 1921, NLI, ms. 31,207; Andy Cooney, O'MN, P17b107; Diarmuid MacManus, O'MN, P17b94; Paul Merrigan, O'MN, P17b126. Description of the victims of revolution, Peter Hart (1992), Chapter 'Spies and Informers'. A somewhat overstated account of the victimisation of ex-soldiers, Jane Leonard (1990).

Travellers and strangers in general thus became a target of suspicion. Local IRA units in active areas wanted to remove all strangers. As early as June 1920 the Kerry No.1 Brigade banished travellers from their brigade area. However, GHQ felt that this was no solution; the problem was only transplanted to the neighbouring unit. In the spring of 1921 the East Clare Brigade ordered that 'All strangers walking or cycling through any part of the Brigade must be placed under arrest and held until they can prove who and what they are satisfactorily.' After having banned them from their own area, the Second Southern Division suggested a General Order prohibiting the presence of 'Tramps, Tinkers, etc.'. GHQ having become convinced of the danger they presented, now stated that it was an excellent suggestion which had already successfully been tried in Clare. One Volunteer in the South Tipperary Brigade, part of the Second Southern Division, with a particular anxiety about the potential danger these people presented, remembers an order to treat all 'beggars' as spies and not to allow them to travel the country.[28]

The police, who were traditionally considered to be members of the community, could only be shot after they were ostracised. When applied to core members of the community, the long drawn-out workings of the process of ostracisation explains the small number of them executed by the IRA. Up to 1921 only those with solid proof against them were considered for this. However, even then some were saved by family ties with local Volunteers. In 1921 the conflict had escalated and the hard-core of the Volunteers were less inhibited to kill anyone who threatened their safety. However, their victims continued to come mainly from outsiders in the groups mentioned above.

PROTESTANTS

As the Volunteers were most vulnerable to information given by members of their own community, the Protestants, who remained largely aloof from the struggle, were initially not targets for intimidation. As a result of the dynamics of violent conflict, however, they became increasingly targeted by the Volunteers. In the first stage of the struggle, a small number were raided and forced to give up their arms as were many Catholics. One Volunteer in Wexford remembers Protestants being prevented from threshing; but any other interference with larger landowners or Protestants was stopped by higher officers. The Church of Ireland Bishop of Derry and Raphoe, who

---

28 Policy Kerry Brigade No.2, letter dated June 1920, NLI, P916 A0495. Quote, Report HQ East Clare Brigade dated 12 April 1921, NLI, ms. 10,916. Request from Second Southern Division, UCD AD, P7A21/168. GHQ answer, UCD AD, P7A22/15. On beggars as spies in Tipperary, Paul Merrigan, O'MN, P17b126. On those seen as enemy agents in this brigade, Report Third Tipperary Brigade dated July 1921, UCD AD, P7a8.

made frequent tours through largely Catholic Donegal, admitted that he was almost universally well-treated by the Volunteers when they learned who he was. Nevertheless, realising their own vulnerable position, most southern Protestants made every effort not to oppose the Volunteers openly. Some larger Protestant landowners in the South were believed to pacify the most violent members of the IRA by sending gifts into prison.[29]

Relations between Catholics and Protestants had already been polarised in the North since the introduction of Home Rule had become likely in 1912. The increasing attacks on the police after 1916 further antagonised the Protestant population in the northern counties and set a spiral of escalating violence in motion. When perpetrators of attacks in the South were sent to prisons in Belfast and Derry, they were the target of much anger:

> We got a terrific reception from the workers in the Belfast ship-yards. Bolts, nuts, pieces of metal and everything they could lay their hands on were thrown at us. One of the prisoners walking in front of me was Father Durbage from Waterford, and when the mob saw him he came in for all their violence. They spat in his face, they struck him, and their language was vile. Every spit seemed to be followed by 'To hell with the Pope'. The military guard were shoving the crowd back as well as they could.

In Derry, the arrival of republican prisoners led to violence between the two communities, culminating in a serious outbreak of rioting in June 1920 in which nineteen people died. In Belfast the polarisation led to serious conflict in August and September 1920. Relations between Protestant and Catholic workers were already strained and when the economic downturn

---

29 Example of raiding Protestants, P.J. Kelly, 'One of the Men of the West'. Volunteers stopping threshing, Andy Roe, Interview. Preventing attacks on landlords and Protestant, Ned Glendon, O'MN, P17b103; Seamus Robinson, 'Statement', NLI, ms. 21,265; *Tipperary Star*, 30 July 1920; Ned Moane, 'Statement'; Carlow Brigade letter dated 1 June 1920, NLI, P916 A0488; 2nd Battalion 2nd Cork Brigade letter dated 19 March 1920, NLI, P917 A0499; David Fitzpatrick (1977), 78. Ignoring Protestants, Paul Merrigan, Interview; Jack Gardiner, Interview; Ned Maughan, O'MN, P17b109; James Harkin, Fr O'Kane Papers, Tape A9, AARC; Willy Parle, Interview; Ned Colfer, Interview. Protestants making efforts not to antagonise the Volunteers, John Regan, 'Memoirs', 132 + 157, PRONI, D3160; Jack Gardiner, Interview; Patrick Casey, 'Idle thoughts', Fr O'Kane Papers, AARC; Liam Brady, *Derry Journal*, 13 May 1953; Lt. Gen. A.E. Percival Papers, 'Guerrilla Warfare - Ireland 1920-21, I'. One of the few Protestant Irish Volunteers in Belfast, Rory Haskins, 'Statement', Fr O'Kane Papers, AARC. The experience of the Church of Ireland Bishop, *Peacocke of Derry and Raphoe* (1946), 37.

Map 5: Percentage of Protestants in District Electoral Divisions in 1911

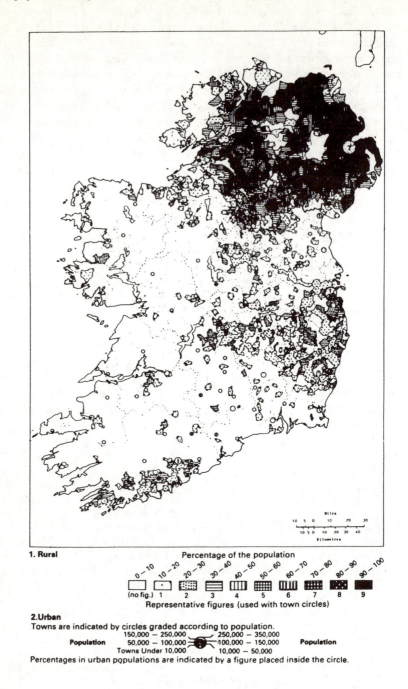

1. Rural   Percentage of the population

0 – 10   10 – 20   20 – 30   30 – 40   40 – 50   50 – 60   60 – 70   70 – 80   80 – 90   90 – 100

(no fig.)   1   2   3   4   5   6   7   8   9

Representative figures (used with town circles)

2. Urban

Towns are indicated by circles graded according to population.

	150,000 – 250,000		250,000 – 350,000	
Population	50,000 – 100,000		100,000 – 150,000	Population
	Towns Under 10,000		10,000 – 50,000	

Percentages in urban populations are indicated by a figure placed inside the circle.

affected employment, attack on Catholic worker communities resulted in many deaths and left thousands homeless.[30]

In January 1921, Sinn Féin reacted to the violence directed at Catholic workers with a boycott of goods from firms in Belfast and other northern towns. The Volunteers were called on to enforce this boycott, which was later extended to goods from England. The increasingly hostile attitude taken by GHQ became apparent in a policy document drawn up in April 1921, instructing the 4th Northern Division: 'The general aim underlying all operations in Carsonia [republican name for present day Northern Ireland] is to disorganise the economic structure of the territory, and make the hostile inhabitants realise that aiding and abetting the Enemy does not pay.'[31]

Protestants in the North were thus increasingly alienated from the aims of the movement, finally resulting in armed attacks on Volunteers by organised groups of Protestants. Operations by these bands in 1920 are supposed to have been the basis for founding the Special Constabularies. In general the violence between the two religious groups overshadowed IRA activities in the North from the summer of 1920 until the Truce. Cycles of revenge attacks developed between nationalists and unionists. The Volunteers, realising this type of violence distracted men from the 'real struggle', tried unsuccessfully to prevent the Catholic community

30 Quote, Patrick O'Daly, 'Statement', NLI, P4548. See also Tom Smyth, O'MN, P17b103; Paul Mulcahy, 'Statement'. Reception in Derry leading to riots, Desmond Murphy (1981), 254; Liam Brady, *Derry Journal*, 13 May 1953; CI Derry MR June 1920. Frequent riots are reported in Derry City from the spring of 1920 onwards, *Derry and Donegal News*, 1920; CI Derry MRs 1920. On a few occasions Unionists shot at policemen when they interfered or were seen with Nationalists, CI Derry MRs October & December 1920. Development of communal violence, *Derry People and Donegal News*, second half of 1920. See in particular: 18 September 1920 for threats made to Protestants during an arms raid; 20 November 1920 for an attempt to burn a Catholic Church near Derry City; 4 December 1920 for a Protestant employer in Cookstown who was threatened that if he did not fire his Catholic employees either he or his employees would be shot. Pogroms in Derry, Rev. T.H. Mullin (1986), 150. In the Belfast Pogrom figures of 184 killed and 1,213 wounded are reported, UCD AD, P80/100. Armed opposition to the IRA by Protestants, PRONI, FIN18/1/144, and D2022/1/31.

31 Belfast Boycott, CI Derry MR January 1921; Report on enforcement 10 July 1921, UCD AD, P17a105; Dáil Eireann receipt for fine of £5 for contravention of the English Boycott, TCD, 7377/5/4; Black list of firms in Belfast Boycott, UCD AD, P7A22/132. Quote, dated 26 April 1921, UCD AD, P7A17/238-40.

from retaliating. In Belfast a Volunteer attempting this was maltreated by the Catholic crowd.[32]

For Volunteers in the South the communal violence in the North legitimised their attacks on Protestants, who had become one of the few easy targets in a struggle which had severely limited military contact with the Crown Forces. Houses of loyalists were burned in response to the official reprisals and the fear that the police would reopen barracks, and many Protestants were accused of spying and shot. The burning of houses started in different areas throughout Ireland during 1921 and was officially authorised by GHQ in June. As in drawing up many other policies, GHQ only reacted to these burnings taking place in areas like Tipperary before it issued a general order. This order allowed the destruction of houses on every occasion in which the enemy destroyed house property or house contents, whether from military necessity or not. The following counter-reprisals were permitted: 'A) A similar number of houses belonging to the most active Enemies of Ireland may be destroyed, in Battalion area in which the original destruction takes place. B) An equal number of houses belonging to the most active Enemies of Ireland may, in addition, be destroyed.' If the Crown Forces persisted in these actions the Volunteers were to stop only when the district concerned had been entirely cleared of active enemies of Ireland.[33]

32 Development of retaliations between the two communities in the North concentrated on the destruction of Protestant owned creameries and bread vans, Thomas Toner, Fr O'Kane Papers, Tape A13, AARC; *Coleraine Chronicle*, 16 April & 9 July 1921; CI Derry MR May 1921. Remarkably, seeing the communal violence, 6 people whose first preference was for a Unionist in the North Derry constituency in the parliamentarian elections of May 1921, had their second vote go to the Sinn Féin candidate. While 37 first preference voters for Sinn Féin gave their second preference to the Unionist candidate, *Coleraine Chronicle*, 28 May 1921.

33 Quote, dated 21 June 1921, NLI, ms. 739. Development of reprisals on Protestants in the South, CI South Tipperary MRs April & June 1921; Cavan Brigade, UCD AD, P7A19/49; Athlone Brigade, letter dated 6 July 1921, UCD AD, P7A21/64; Nt. Wexford Brigade, UCD AD, P7A21/154, and P7A20/77-9; Tom Barry, in K. Griffith and T. O'Grady (1981), 221; Louth, UCD AD, P7A19/148; 'History of the 5th Division in Ireland November 1919-March 1922', 77, IWM, 72/82/2. A suggestion to burn enemy houses as a reprisal for the burning of republican's houses was already made but not accepted in July 1920, NLI, ms. 11,410. Again in October, *Mayoman*, 2 October 1920. In the final month of the struggle, six shops owned by nationalists in Cork City were forced to close and their owners were banished by the Crown Forces, as a retaliation the local IRA was instructed to close six English firms and order the director or manager: 'to England or Carsonia as the individual deserves.' This order was not acted upon before the Truce came, HQ 1st St Division to Chief of Staff dated 5 July 1921, UCD AD, P7A21/129. The lack of combat in the last few months of the struggle in Cork City is demonstrated by the fact that there were only eight successful attacks by the IRA on patrols and barracks, but 131 shootings of helpless victims, Peter Hart (1992), Chapter 'The Dynamics of Violence', 72.

GHQ attempted to control the implementation of these reprisals and to prevent it from developing into a general onslaught on Protestants by adding a warning to this order: 'No one shall be regarded as an Enemy of Ireland, whether they may be described locally as, Unionist, Orangeman, etc., except (when) they are actively anti-Irish in their actions.' Until the Truce, some loyalists' houses were burned and a small number of Protestants were shot in Tipperary. Most of these were justified by the Volunteers with clear military reasons, as the houses concerned were about to be used as billets for troops. Before this could develop into a systematic attack on Protestants the Truce came. However during the Civil War this policy became a carte blanche in some areas for wholesale attack on Protestants and other loyalists who were widely regarded as supporters of the newly established Free State.

EMIGRATION

Apart from giving information Irishmen could betray the cause by withdrawing from the struggle altogether, which became quite prevalent in 1920. Emigration had long been extremely common in Ireland, but during the War it had virtually come to a halt. Recruiting for the army took most of these men away, but it led to a steep rise in the number of young men in areas where recruiting was weak. In the boom years of the War and shortly after it these men had little trouble finding employment. However, during 1919 some short-term unemployment developed in many parts of the country, and a post-war recession hit Ireland mainly in 1921. Combined with the growing violence, this rekindled emigration in 1920. The authorities, realising that a surplus of young men with nothing to do strengthened the IRA, favoured this.[34]

The IRA felt that all Irishmen leaving the country at this time were guilty of treason, and tried to stop them. Early in June 1920 the Minister of Defence of the Dáil Government issued a public manifesto against emigration. He stated there was no excuse for this desertion as there would be plenty of employment for everyone in Ireland in the future. Shortly after this, GHQ issued a General Order against emigration of Volunteers:

1. Ordinarily emigration at the present time must be regarded as desertion in the face of the enemy.
2. No Volunteer shall leave the country or apply for a passport to any other country for the purpose of emigration without trans-

34 The absence of emigration increased the population of Ireland by 110,000, but enlistment took 150,000 away, David Fitzpatrick (1977), 242.

mitting particulars of his case through his superior officer to
Headquarters Staff and receiving their formal written authority.[35]

Under new regulations all men of military age were supposed to apply for
written permission from the Dáil and pay one shilling and six pence (7.5
pence). Emigration was only to be allowed if it was the solution to definite
hardship, defined as stemming from medical causes, educational reasons or
unemployment. However, emigration was an economic necessity for many,
including Volunteers, and it continued unabated. Some people did indeed ask
permission, but most did not bother. Some of the latter were picked up by
Volunteers and sent home after their passports and tickets were confiscated.[36]

When fighting had become more serious the Volunteers showed less consideration for those wanting to leave. In March 1921 the Cork No.1 Brigade
requested GHQ to issue a public notice threatening Volunteers who emigrated with execution and civilians with severe measures. The Chief of Staff,
writing to the Minister of Defence, acknowledged that it was hard for men
fighting in the country to come to terms with a wave of emigration developing around them. Nevertheless, he felt it was impossible to deal with this at
the ports. However, Volunteers continued to prevent people from leaving. In
Ulster the IRA drew up plans to attack even those who had already emigrated as a deterrent. This occurred in Liverpool and elsewhere, where Irish
emigrants were assaulted.[37]

35 Quote, NLI, ms. 739. See also Manifesto dated 5 June 1920, NLI, ms. 739;
   Sean M. O'Duffy, 'Statement', NLI, ms. 21,658. The order on emigration was
   again a reaction to question from units in the country. See the answer to Kerry
   No.2 Brigade dated June 1920, NLI, P916 A0495. Some emigration had continued from Derry City until December 1916, but had come to a total standstill
   from then on. The first 34 emigrants were again recorded in August 1919, and
   an average of about 150-200 emigrants left Derry in 1920, CIs MRs 1916-21.
36 Decision to allow emigration only in cases of definite hardship dated 16
   September 1920, NLI, ms. 10,916. Volunteers stopping emigrants: In
   Tipperary, *Tipperary Star*, 9 July & 24 September 1920. In Mayo, *Mayoman*,
   14 August 1920; Thomas Heavey, 'Statement'. In Dublin, 'Raid on Seville
   Place 100', dated 24 March 1921, PRO, WO35/71; George White, O'MN,
   P17b105. An IRA officer serving Dáil orders prohibiting emigration on ship-
   ping agents, CI Derry MR May 1921.
37 The letter from Cork No.1 Brigade to GHQ dated 26 March 1921, UCD AD,
   P7A17/146. Note from the Chief of Staff to the Minister of Defence dated 31
   March 1921, UCD AD, P7A17/145. Idea in 2nd Ulster Division to deal with
   emigrants abroad, UCD AD, P7A48.

LABOUR

The intricate relationship between Volunteers and community extended to two major interest groups in Irish society. Both organised labour and the Catholic Church were important factors in the political orientation of nationalists. Inevitably, the new claim to authority that the republicans asserted during these years challenged both. The success of the republican movement forced these institutions to fall in with their demands without either losing sight of its own interests.

In most of the nation-wide demonstrations and in the general elections of 1918 and 1921, Sinn Féin had cooperated closely with Labour. Despite some misgivings, this cooperation worked well on a national level, as demonstrated in 1918 when Labour parliamentary candidates stood down in favour of Sinn Féin. On a local level, however, relations were less harmonious, with the two organisations often standing at opposite sides in labour conflicts. Signs of a rift between Sinn Féin and Labour were detected in Mayo and Wexford as early as 1919. In Mayo Labour declared some strikes against Sinn Féin employers, detecting an anti-labour tendency within Sinn Féin in July 1920: 'Whether the denial of labour's rights comes from men under the Union Jack or the Green, White and Gold we shall challenge that denial and resist it to our last penny and last worker.' The local Sinn Féin branch had previously expressed its doubts about the sincerity of Labour's nationalism when the ITGWU lent one of their halls to the 'Comrades of the Great War' in July 1919.[38]

The social struggle also led to conflict between the two organisations in rural areas. The successful attempts of the ITGWU to organise land labourers antagonised the large farmer representation in the Volunteers and Sinn Féin. In turn, Labour complained about the high number of middle-class candidates, particularly shopkeepers, put forward by Sinn Féin in various elections. In many counties cooperation was nevertheless close. In Tipperary the police was unable to distinguish between Labour and Sinn Féin, and believed Sinn Féin was dominated by Labour activists. Despite their differences, Labour frequently opposed actions taken by employers against the movement. Some-times they ordered strikes when men were dismissed because of their membership of the Volunteers.[39]

38 Quote, *Mayoman*, 31 July 1920. See also *Free Press*, 10 January 1921. Sinn Féin's doubts about Labour, *Mayoman*, 26 July 1919.

39 For relations in different counties, CI Wexford MRs June 1919 & August 1920; CI Mayo MR May 1919; Tom Maguire, in U. MacEoin (1980), 281; CI South Tipperary MRs April-May 1919; Seamus Robinson, O'MN, P17b99. Conflict between employers and labour could have a strong effect on relations within the IRA. When a labour organiser became brigade commandant he was not accepted by the battalion officers in Derry City, UCD AD, P7A18/284. Strikes in support of dismissed members of the movement, William Nolan (ed.) (1985), 397-405. Tensions between the movement and shopkeepers and ratepayers, 'Intelligence Notes 1919', PRO, CO903/19.

Since both organisations were coalitions built around one issue, any involvement in another issue was potentially divisive. The need to represent their own interests inevitably antagonised the other organisation. Most Sinn Féiners saw the conflict between labour and employers as secondary to the national struggle, and felt it should be ignored as it threatened to divide the movement. To alleviate some of the resulting tensions, republicans tried to mediate in labour disputes. Although not always successful, the large overlap in membership at every level prevented serious conflict between the two organisations.[40]

The electorate of Sinn Féin and Labour had much in common. In urban elections transfer votes between Labour and Sinn Féin were high, as urban Volunteers were predominantly working-class. In rural areas the Volunteers had no recruits from the wealthiest classes either, but did take in poor as well as better-off farmers. The reasons for joining the IRA followed a slightly different pattern there. In most counties the Volunteers found that they always relied on the poor for support. The high proportion of working-class Volunteers disappointed some female admirers of the IRA when they came out in the open during the Truce: 'I saw an obviously slum youth in uniform. I almost got a shock. I had never pictured his type in the I.R.A. I always thought of the tall dark, black haired & flashing eyes I.R.A. of my imagination.' Michael Collins's poor grammar was another sore point with her.[41]

Successes in the local elections in 1920 had given Sinn Féin and Labour control over most boards in the country. Sinn Féin dominated most rural areas, while Labour was strong in urban areas. However, besides the decision to strike from the records the resolutions condemning the 1916 Rising, they did little. A policy of non-cooperation with the British authorities was hampered by the financial dependency of the local bodies. Only a few local assemblies separated themselves from the state's Local Government Board

40 Internal division in both organisations concerning the other, Letter from Cork dated 10 November 1919, NLI, ms. 13,955; Lt. M. Sheerin, NLI, P915 A0394. The role of IRA officers in mediating between tenants and the Artisans Dwelling Company, UCD AD, LA9. The Labour Department of the Dáil Government reports that it mediated in 68 Labour disputes, 46 times successfully and eight times unsuccessfully, 'Report of the working of the Labour Department', NLI, P919 A0602.

41 On transfer votes in local elections, *Mayoman*, 24 & 31 January and 7 February 1920; *Coleraine Chronicle*, 28 May 1921. Reliance on the poor: In Mayo, Paddy Cannon, O'MN, P17b136; Ned Moane, O'MN, P17b136. In Tipperary, Ned Glendon, O'MN, P17b103; Bryan Ryan (1969), 20. In Dublin, Eamon O'Dwyer, 'Statement'; Pat MacCrea, O'MN, P17b109; Fr Michael Maher, Diary 1916, St Patrick's College Thurles. In Derry, C.J. MacGuinness (1934), 141-4. In Wexford, Mark Killilea, O'MN, P17b109. Quote from female admirer, Celia Shaw, Diary 3 March 1922, NLI, ms. 23,409.

immediately on their election, thus giving up all financial aid from central government.[42]

To bring loyalties out in the open, the British authorities demanded a clear show of allegiance from all local councils on 29 July 1920. In August the Dáil responded with an attempt to enforce a 'clean break' of all local councils from the Local Government Board. This was facilitated by the fact that the government had put a levy on the rates to pay for damages caused by republican violence. This meant that the grant from the board was substantially lowered, diminishing the financial consequences of a break. Although many boards refused to give the allegiance demanded by the British Government and the clean break was quite successful, the Sinn Féin Executive was forced to continue efforts to convince their own councillors to disconnect themselves from the government until the Truce, stressing that they were not as dependent as they believed.[43]

Reliance on Labour to give Sinn Féin a majority in many urban councils made a break more difficult. The subsequent cut in government subsidy to the council meant a lack of employment for local labourers. Nevertheless, by the spring of 1921 most local bodies had broken their ties with the Local Government Board. All but the six Protestant-dominated County Councils in Ulster had changed their allegiance to Dáil Éireann. The different levels of support for Sinn Féin in the rural and urban areas is also reflected in this. Of 201 Rural District Councils only 42, of which 37 were from Ulster, still recognised the Board, while of the 94 Urban District Councils only 33 had switched allegiance to the Dáil.

Table 13: Allegiance to Local Government Board by Local Bodies, Spring 1921[44]

	Ulster			Other Three Provinces		
	Declared	Rejected	Doubtful	Declared	Rejected	Doubtful
Co. Council	6	3	0	0	24	0
Co. Borough	2	0	0	0	4	0
Urban DC	32	5	3	22	28	4
Rural DC	37	12	6	5	125	16
Union	31	10	1	4	105	3
Town Com.	3	0	3	2	3	17

42 Local bodies striking the condemnation of the Rising of the record: In Innishowen, *Derry People and Donegal News*, 15 May 1920. In Enniscorthy, Richard Roche (1966), 58.
43 Separation from the LGB, 'Dáil Éireann Local Government Department', report dated 15 March 1921, UCD AD, P7A16/28-9. See also UCD AD, P7A16/30, and P7A17/72-3; David Fitzpatrick (1977), 184-97; Arthur Mitchell (1995), 157-9.
44 Figures taken from, *Tipperary Star*, 16 April 1921.

Although Labour frequently complained about their victimisation by the government, the activities of Sinn Féin and the Volunteers were a larger burden on people paying rates than on the average worker. Damage done by the Volunteers had to be paid for by local bodies; later the uncontrolled violence of police and military, angered by Volunteer actions, was directed at property owners, particularly shopkeepers. The demands made by the movement for financial support further alienated the wealthier classes. As a result, support for the movement was more likely to be given by the working class or poorer farmers who had less to lose by their association with republicans. Some indication of the validity of this point is given by the changes in social composition of the IRA in different periods of the struggle (see the appendix).

CATHOLIC CLERGY

Comparable to the position of labour, the Catholic clergy were caught between the demands made on them by republicans, law-abiding Catholics and the authorities. The official position of the Church was determined by the necessity to maintain good relations with all sections of society. The natural tendency of the bishops to support the upholders of law and order was somewhat diminished in Ireland by a long history of discrimination of Catholics. Traditionally, the Hierarchy had strong ties with the leadership of the Irish Party, in whom they had invested their hopes of bringing Home Rule to Ireland. Consequently, the request for support by the insurgents of 1916, addressed to all bishops individually, was rejected. All of them condemned this 'foolish attempt'.[45]

During most of 1916 and 1917 the Hierarchy remained entrenched in their opposition to the Sinn Féin movement. Remembrance Masses for 1916 men were refused in many places or only allowed after strong representations. Some of the lower clergy, however, had changed their allegiance and actively supported the republicans. Others still spoke out openly against them. Trying to keep a balance between both demands, the Bishops issued an open letter to the clergy in June 1917. They reminded all priests in Ireland of the regulations made by the National Synod regarding the attendance at meetings of a political or public character. Parish Priests could freely attend the meetings held in their own parish, but curates needed their consent. For meetings in another parish all priests needed the express per-

45 A young boy from Castlebar was one of those sent to the Bishops with this letter: 'When the Bishop had read the contents of the letter he looked at me and said, "Go home and don't be such a foolish young man" or words to that effect,' James Chambers, 'Statement'. See also CI Mayo MR April 1916. The Archbishop of Cashel advised his priests to exercise their influence to restrain any hot-headed young men that might show any tendency to commit rash acts, Fr Michael Maher, Diary 1916, St Patrick's College Thurles.

mission of the local Parish Priest. In Dublin City the bishop of the priest wanting to attend had the power to authorise this, unless the Archbishop of Dublin objected.

The priests were also reminded that it was strictly forbidden to speak of political affairs in church. They were ordered to avoid 'words that could wound the queenly virtue of charity, or give reasonable course for offence to any member of his flock.' These measures affected Sinn Féin more than the Irish Party. Overall, the younger curates were more often supporters of the former, while the older Parish Priests were more tied up with the latter.

Advanced Volunteers were frequently angered by the clergy's refusal to say Mass for dead Volunteers or to support their actions. Priests who opposed the movement were threatened or openly attacked. After a priest attacked the Easter Week men in church a Volunteer officer spoke out against him after Mass: 'I began my address by referring to the statement of Fr. Laurence. He, accompanied by Fr. Moloney, the C.C. of the parish, were just going out the gateway from the church premises when I made the statement that what Fr. Laurence said was a bald and a damnable lie, and the crowd cheered my words to the echo.'[46]

In 1917, with the death of Thomas Ashe and Sinn Féin's success in bye-elections, the clergy started to rethink its policy towards the movement. It could not permit itself to lose control of its flock and had to try and work with those representing the population politically. The Archbishop of Cashel privately admitted this in 1917:

> The Archbishop said that it would be right to watch this movement, because the [Irish] Party was evidently losing hold of the country and if the convention [The Irish Convention of 1917] failed there would be nothing but Sinn Féin to fall back upon therefore it was incumbent on us to maintain such an attitude that, should circumstances arise, we could throw in our lot with Sinn Féin as far as our conscience would allow us to do so.

The shift in attitude of the clergy became apparent when they took an active part in organising opposition to conscription in April 1918, uniting all Catholics.[47]

In the period after the Conscription Crisis the priests became more openly divided in their approach. The majority kept their political prefer-

46 Quote, Eamon O'Dwyer, 'Statement'. Threats made to priests and a bishop in Tipperary, P.C. Power (1976), 144-6; Ned O'Reilly, O'MN, P17b126.

47 Quote, Fr Michael Maher, Diary 1917, St Patrick's College Thurles. This Archbishop refused to have a Mass said at the first anniversary of the Rising in April 1917, but said Mass himself for Thomas Ashe in September 1917. In January 1918, the General Inspector felt that De Valéra's loss in the South Armagh bye-election was a result of Cardinal Logue's refusal to meet him, IG MR January 1918. The support of the clergy in the Conscription Crisis, CI Derry MR April 1918; Brodie Malone, O'MN, P17b109; Martin Kennedy, Interview.

ences to themselves in an attempt to prevent confrontation. For the time being, most went along with the growing dominance of Sinn Féin, but a small number started to oppose or support the movement actively. The election committees of both parties were full of these priests. Some clerics, often having a personal connection with Britain, refused absolution to men on hunger strike or opposed them in other ways.[48]

Other priests clearly expressed their sympathy for Sinn Féin in church. One young priest in Mayo told his parishioners in August 1918 that he hoped they would keep their pledge and not join the Army, as it was better that all would die than for one man to join the British Army. He added that anyone who took part in the recruiting scheme had no self-respect, and he hoped that no one in his parish would have anything to do with it. He added that the few who gave information to the police were free to join, as they would be no loss to the parish.[49]

The fear that Sinn Féin was connected with socialism deterred some priests. The presence of a declared socialist in the leadership of the 1916 Rising had fuelled their apprehension. The successes of the Bolsheviks in Russia further exacerbated this fear. The Dean of the Cashel diocese called Sinn Féin a reckless and dangerous organisation, terrifying and unholy because it was identified with socialism, the 'pest and the curse of modern society.' The association with Labour in the elections, and the Democratic Program adopted at the first meeting of the Dáil, which had strong labour overtones, strengthened their concern. In reaction to this, the Church made representations to Sinn Féin in the summer of 1919 urging them not to allow Liberty Hall (the headquarters of Labour in Dublin) to take control, as its inhabitants were irreligious and socialistic. However, few church men genuinely feared a socialist take over of Sinn Féin.[50]

The first killings of policemen in 1919 created a new dilemma for the bulk of the clergy who had started to condone and quietly support Sinn

48 Priests as leading members of local Sinn Féin clubs: In Tipperary, Eamon O'Dwyer, 'Statement'. In Mayo, James Chambers, 'Statement'; CI Mayo MRs May 1918 & December 1919; Brodie Malone, O'MN, P17b109; *Mayoman*, 6 September 1919. In Derry, Liam Brady, Oral History Project, Tape 24A, Heritage Library, Derry City. David Fitzpatrick states that 73 priests associated themselves with the separatist cause, particularly curates, David Fitzpatrick (1977), 138. Priests using their influence to stave off violent conflict, Fr Michael Maher, Diary April & December 1918, St Patrick's College Thurles; CI South Tipperary MR April 1918; CI Mayo MR April 1918. Priest actively opposing Sinn Féin, Ned Prendergast, Interview; Report on priest in Killaloe dated 14 December 1917, NAD, CBS 13580, and DE 2/135; Mark Killilea, O'MN, P17b109.

49 Speech of priest in Mayo, IG MR August 1918.

50 Dean's speech, Deaglan O Bric, in *Tipperary Historical Journal* (1990), 105. This view was opposed by the Archbishop who himself voted for Sinn Féin in 1918, Fr Michael Maher, Diary 1918, St Patrick's College Thurles. Church representations to Sinn Féin, IG MR August 1919.

Féin. Their support did not extend to the shooting of policemen, which was frequently criticised even by the most radical priests. Nevertheless, most were forced to follow public opinion in a similar condemnation of the attitude of the Crown Forces and the British Government. Violence from both sides was denounced by the clergy, including most bishops.[51]

Although this satisfied most people, it antagonised extremists on both sides. On the one hand passionate Volunteers were seriously insulted by the attitude of some churchmen and refused to attend services or confession. Dan Breen, one of the leading Tipperary Volunteers, was outraged when the body of a Volunteer, who died in an attack on the Lord Lieutenant of Ireland in December 1919, was denied entrance to a church by the Archbishop of Dublin. On the other hand, when the clergy condemned the police actions, Catholics closely connected to the force left church.[52]

Most priests tried to balance the interest of all sections of the community and, regardless of their own persuasion, refused to speak out in support of either side. Nor would they allow violence to erupt in their parish. The polarisation this might cause in the community endangered their influential position. Reports of priests interfering with the Volunteers to stop actions from taking place come from all over the country. Some priests opposed those aiding violence by threatening active supporters of the Volunteers: 'In 1920/21 Fr. Geoffrey Prendergast told the people that if they harboured any column, he wouldn't say the stations in their houses.'[53]

51 The first murders by the IRA in Tipperary and in Wexford were condemned by clergy even of distinctive Sinn Féin tendencies, CI Wexford MR February 1920.

52 Dan Breen refusing to go to confession, Seamus Robinson, 'Statement', NLI, ms. 21,265. See also Paddy O'Halloran, O'MN, P17b114; Ned O'Reilly, O'MN, P17b126; Mark Killilea, O'MN, P17b109. Extreme reactions to church condemnation of violence from both sides, IG MR August 1919; Fr Michael Maher, Diary 18 March 1919, St Patrick's College Thurles.

53 Quote, Johnny Duffy, O'MN, P17b109. Priests trying to stay out of trouble by not voicing any particular viewpoint, Tom Maguire, Interview; Andy Roe, Interview; Willie Parle, Interview; John Quinn, Interview. David Fitzpatrick claims that this unwillingness to rock the boat was also dictated by the need for funds to repair leaking churches, David Fitzpatrick (1977), 140-1. Examples of priests interfering in Volunteer actions, Peter Wall, Interview; Bob Lambert, 'Statement'; Lt. M. Sheerin, NLI, P921 No66; John Regan, 'Memoirs', 174-5, PRONI, D3160; PRO, PRO30/59/3. Volunteers objecting to this interference, Letter from Sligo Brigade dated 30 July 1920, NLI, P911; UCD AD, P7A21/146. The Parish Priest in Aughagower was found writing to the authorities denouncing his curate who was actively aiding the Volunteers, Thomas Heavey, O'MN, P17b120, and 'Statement'. Another was found to have warned the police after a Volunteer had told him of a planned attack during confession, Brodie Malone, O'MN, P17b109. Others were blamed for turning a whole area against the Volunteers, Pat Fallon, O'MN, P17b109; John Duffy, Fr O'Kane Papers, Tape A20, AARC. The clergy in Derry made efforts to unite both nationalist sides to avoid defeat by the Protestants. First in the elections of 1918, CI Derry MR November 1918. In June 1920, they tried to unite the Catholics against Protestants during the riots, Lt. M. Sheerin, NLI, P915 A0394; Liam Brady, Oral History Project, Tape 24B, Heritage Library, Derry City.

The open support for Sinn Féin in the local newspaper in Mayo was a thorn in the side of one of these opponents of the movement. The Parish Priest of Cong/Neale wrote a letter complaining about the space given to the 'fledgling' politicians of Sinn Féin whom he described as 'The little clique of upstarts who imagine that they are the alpha and omega of Nationality here.' He further denounced them as: 'These writers of local columns, most if not all, are corner boys without any business.' The local columnist gave his ironic answer to this letter: 'We are extremely anxious to preserve the few rare specimens still remaining of the "men who stood in the gap" and blocked the progress of the cause for Irish Freedom for years.'[54]

As early as August 1919, the police feared the Church was losing its control of the extremists: 'The Irish Republican Brotherhood, however, was never submissive to Clerical control and there is good reason to believe that already the priests have to a considerable extent lost influence over their parishioners.' Most Volunteers were indeed unaffected by the condemnation of their actions by certain sections of the church. Active Volunteers who had broken the physical ties with their home parish when going on the run, in particular, widely ignored them. Traditionally, radical nationalists had opposed the meddling of the church in political affairs. In June 1919 a priest warned a RIC sergeant that he detected a widespread rejection of church interference: 'There are a class of men going about who don't care for priests or anybody else. They think it is no sin to shoot a policeman.' Indeed, when the Bishop of Cork excommunicated those who organised or took part in ambushes or kidnapping, or were otherwise guilty of murder or attempted murder in his diocese, few people expected the Volunteers to take much notice of this.[55]

In every county there were priests who actively supported the Volunteers. They ran messages, hid weapons in churches, gave shelter to fugitive Volunteers, bought arms and even joined in their operations. In contravention of their vows, two priests in Clare joined the Volunteers. On some occasions priests also sanctioned the execution of spies, relieving Volunteer officers from their moral responsibility. A man who had been arrested for spying and was told he had one day to leave the county was arrested again when he refused to do so. A priest was then fetched before the man was to be executed:

> After he had his confession told. The Priest [...] asked me did I hold a Court Martial on him and I told him I did, he said that was right

54 Quotes from newspaper, *Mayoman*, 27 March & 3 April 1920.

55 Quote on 'loss of control', IG MR August 1919. Quote on 'rejection of church interference', IG MR June 1919. The excommunication order was read at all the Masses in the Diocese of Cork on Sunday 19 December 1920, NLI, ms. 31,148. See also Frank Henderson, O'MN, P17b99; D. Ryan (1945), 112-13; Celia Shaw, Diary, NLI, ms. 23,409. A description of the lack of church control on the movement in Derry, Desmond Murphy (1981), 238-9.

that I was doing my duty. The Priest then gave him the blessed sacrament and he told me to take him out. Immediately out of his sight. Concluding, I think myself perfectly right in shooting him as myself and my men were in danger, considering I had the Priest's advice as well in the matter.[56]

The Church was never able to follow a single policy regarding the republican movement in the War of Independence. Churchmen from bishops to curates took their own approach. The Irish bishops had traditionally been independent in their own dioceses and reacted differently to the changing circumstances; from the excommunication in Cork to open condemnation of the government. Local priests also felt free to follow their own consciences. All bishops, however, were aware of the potential danger of open support for the republicans, while future developments were uncertain. Consequently, some of the most active propagators of Sinn Féin among the lower clergy were transferred to parishes outside the country. Nevertheless the divided stance of priests had allowed a 'pick-and-choose' attitude to develop among Volunteers concerning the Church's attitude towards their activities.[57]

CONCLUSION

The involvement of Volunteers in the alternative government during 1919 and 1920 added substance to their claim of representing the legitimate

56 Quote, UCD AD, P7A18/264-7. Priests passing messages and giving shelter in several counties, Garry Houlihan, O'MN, P17b105; Ned O'Reilly, O'MN, P17b126; Martin Kennedy, Interview; Jimmy Swift, O'MN, P17b136; Batty Cryan, O'MN, P17b120. Hiding arms and fugitives by priests was greatly aided by instructions to the Crown Forces not to search 'Convents, Monasteries and Churches', order from Divisional Commissioners Office Cork dated July 23 1920, NLI, ms. 31,225; 5th Division War Diary December 1920, PRO, WO35/93/2. Nevertheless, cartridges and the butt of a shotgun were found in a church in Kilmeena, Co. Mayo, Report week ending 11 December 1920, PRO, WO35/93. Arms were hidden by a clerk of the chapel in St Joseph's statue in the church in Shough, Co. Tipperary. The directions for finding it were: 'put your hand up his hole and you'll find a revolver. Then go over to the Blessed Virgin's hole and you'll find 400 rounds of .45 ammunition,' Michael Fitzpatrick, O'MN, P17b114. See also P.J. Kelly, 'One of the Men of the West'. Priest buying arms for Volunteers, Jack Gardiner, Interview. The priest who joined an arms raid in Derry in 1919, Pat Tohill, Fr O'Kane Papers, Tape A5, AARC. Priests attending to column men in private houses before an ambush, Michael Kilroy, O'MN, P17b138; Thomas Heavey, 'Statement'. Priests as member in Clare, David Fitzpatrick (1977), Chapter 6, note 5.
57 Active supporters of Sinn Féin being transferred, Fr Michael Maher, Diary 1919, St Patrick's College Thurles; CI Mayo MR January 1921; CI Wexford MR March 1919.

Government of Ireland. Many people were willing to follow them and switch their allegiance from the British authorities. In their dealings with the population the movement continuously vacillated between the needs of their political and military campaign against the British and the need to ensure continuous support. As a result they managed to find a modus vivendi with most groups in society and with other institutions representing Irish nationalists. Although tensions occasionally came to the surface at a local level, no one was willing to risk losing the support from its own grassroots by directly clashing with the others.

However at the end of 1920, military confrontation increasingly interfered with the functioning of the alternative government. Relations between Volunteers and the population became particularly strained in active areas where the Volunteers were hunted by the Crown Forces and informing became life-threatening. As a result, more and more violence was used against the population. Fearing a loss of support and reluctant to attack those who were considered to be part of the own group, the main victims of this type of violence were 'outsiders' such as Protestants, ex-soldiers, and travelling people. Taking these groups as the main targets also allowed for a more aggressive approach, and many suspected spies were killed. Although few of the real informers came from these groups, the example set was sufficient to deter most informers more closely associated with the movement. Consequently, the initial claim to represent all Irishmen became increasingly confined to those who shared the same beliefs or refused to cooperate with the British authorities. Apart from the Irish members of the police who were excluded at an early stage, ex-soldiers, travelling people and Protestants failed the acid test of republicanism in 1921.

Early examples of this increasingly restrictive image of Irishness were particularly evident in Mayo. Taking up the role of policing and controlling the local community allowed some local Volunteers to make themselves guardians of morality. The experience of power gained in the courts made them feel they were justified in determining right and wrong in all areas of public behaviour, and they suggested measures in line with a boycott of all that was British or foreign. Eradicating foreign elements from the 'Gaelic Culture' and a wish to uphold moral standards made them attack certain books, 'non-Irish' fashions, music and dance. Because of the realisation that this would damage their universal appeal GHQ generally rejected such attempts, but they were nevertheless tempted to suppress aspects of public life which they considered undesirable. In Dublin and Cork Volunteers were ordered to act against people betting on GAA matches, a practice that body had long frowned on. Occasionally taking the moral high ground was combined with the idea that all previous risings had failed because of alcohol abuse; as a result, many poteen stills were destroyed and public houses were forced to close on time. This defence of public morality represents one of the first expressions of a narrow conservative interpretation of Irishness and morality, which is still alive today among many Irish nationalists.[58]

58 Campaign against foreign fashion, *Mayoman*, 15 November 1919. Against jazz, foxtrot and other 'immoral foreign importations', *Mayoman*, 3 January 1920. Against foreign school books, Query dated 7 August 1920, NLI, P911. Against betting: In Dublin, UCD AD, LA9; Patrick O'Daly, 'Statement', NLI, P4548. In Cork, Letter to Brigade Commandant Cork no.1 dated 10 May 1920, NLI, P917 A0498. Volunteers cutting people's clothes for smoking foreign cigarettes, NLI, ms. 902/151. On the closing of pubs and the destruction of poteen stills: In Derry, Thomas Toner, Fr O'Kane Papers, Tape A13, AARC; Frank Himphey, Tape 50a, Ibidem; Thos O'Neill, Tape A13, Ibidem. In Mayo, CI Mayo MR November 1920; Joe Baker (1988), 16; *Mayoman*, 25 September 1920. In Dublin, George Gilmore, O'MN, P17b106. In British Army 5th Division area, 'History of the 5th Division in Ireland November 1919-March 1922', 43, IWM, 72/82/2. GHQ had given open permission to deal with poteen stills, Communication with Longford Brigade dated 22 June 1920, NLI, P916 A0492. GHQ forbade Volunteers to issue regulations governing the conduct of licensed premises in the Dublin Brigade area, Weekly Order No. 2 dated 6 September 1920, NLI, ms. 900/16. Sometimes the closing of pubs had ulterior motives, such as on days that ceilidhs and dances to raise money for the Volunteers were held, Thomas Toner, Fr O'Kane Papers, Tape A13, AARC. In a more static form Peter Hart has first presented the idea that the Volunteers saw themselves as embodying 'the people' or 'the nation', directing their violence towards outsiders or deviants, Peter Hart (1992), Chapter 'Youth Culture and Rebellion', 31. Tom Garvin sees this positioning as defender of the community and its values as the expression of resistance to a process of transformation, of a community threatened by alien political, economic and cultural forces. Within this context taking such a position was a characteristic of revolutionary fervour, and was directly connected with areas of widespread social change and declining economic sectors, which he places in Cork and Tipperary. However, the defence of morality seems to have been strongest in Mayo where the Volunteers formed a more integrated part of the community, Tom Garvin (1987), 6-8.

CHAPTER 9

The Restraining Influence of the Community

In all their dealings with civilians the movement's balancing act to ensure as much support as possible has become apparent. However, the escalation of violence towards the end of 1920 substantially changed the relationship of the Volunteers with the population in many areas. The intensity of the struggle had always been varied, but now its nature began to differ. In this final chapter, it is argued that the respective positions of the Volunteers in the various counties largely determined the type and level of violence in which they engaged.

CONDITIONS IN WEXFORD

In Wexford the Volunteers enjoyed limited popular support. Although they had sufficient manpower in certain areas to engage in operations, they were unable to control the local community. The politically more divided population forced them to function largely in secret. As a result the population was caught between two sides without being clearly dominated by either. Enforcement of the different aspects of alternative government was haphazard. Following the start of the official police boycott and the introduction of Republican Courts in 1920, some reports of intimidation of civilians become available; but in many areas people were hardly affected at all. Nevertheless they were inconvenienced by the implementation of the policies of both sides. In 1921 this became a physical reality to them when some were used as commandeered labour first in digging trenches by the IRA, and later in filling trenches by the Crown Forces. Occasionally the same people who were forced to dig a trench or cut down a tree were later forced to undo their own work.[1]

Despite the intimidation and the use of forced labour by the IRA, civilians were generally more affected by the often indiscriminate measures of

1   Effect of struggle on civilians, *People*, 15 January, 19 & 26 February, 9 April, 4 & 25 June 1921; Andy Roe, Interview; Ned Colfer, Interview; CI Wexford MRs June, August & November 1920, and February 1921. Cases where civilians were forced to fill in trenches in Mayo, Paddy Duffy, O'MN, P17b138; Ned Moane and Brodie Malone, O'MN, P17b120.

the government. In executing their operations the IRA tried to ensure as little inconvenience to the population as possible. This was partly a consequence of their assumed position as guardians of the community and partly inspired by the fear of losing support. As shown, the actions of the Wexford Volunteers in 1921 mainly involved non-violent operations. GHQ directives had emphasised the need to cut all lines of communications, i.e. roads, telegraph and telephone.

Interception of mail delivery was the only obstruction of communication which had been engaged in previously. The Volunteers had always concentrated on mail for police and other government institutions; post for civilians was left alone and returned to the post office for delivery. In cutting roads and later in cutting telegraph wires they again attempted to target the Crown Forces. When roads were trenched a small passage was generally left open sufficient for a farmer's cart but too small for a lorry. Differentiating between civilians and Crown Forces in the cutting of wires was harder. Although GHQ made attempts to teach Volunteers to single out the wire going to the police or military barracks, this attempt at protecting ordinary citizens from the effects of their actions was only implemented on a small scale.[2]

It was, however, impossible to safeguard the population completely from the consequences of IRA operations. Due to the large number of disruptions, certain postal and telegraph services in Wexford were suspended in June 1921, demonstrating the success of the emphasis put on non-violent operations in Wexford. When, as a result of British counter-measures, blocking roads with trenches or trees became less effective, bridges were demolished. This was sometimes done by hand, but with the greater availability of explosives in 1921, several were blown up. In both cases attempts were made to leave a small part of the bridge standing, too narrow to let a motorcar pass. In contrast to this attitude, the Crown Forces displayed their alienation from the population by occasionally demolishing the remaining part of the bridge.[3]

The consequences of government policy became most apparent when martial law was introduced in Wexford in January 1921. The relatively non-violent operations of the IRA in Wexford hardly necessitated it, but the authorities were afraid that active Volunteers from neighbouring counties

2 Leaving space for smaller vehicles when trenching roads, NLI, ms. 900/30. Weekly Memo dated 31 October 1920, stressed that wires should be cut only to police and military barracks not indiscriminately as is still being done. Weekly Memo 12 dated 7 February 1921, calls for precautions to safeguard the ordinary traveller against accident in road cutting. This memo also allowed the ordinary public to repair roads if they were forced to do so, O'MN, P17b127.

3 Suspension of services, *People* (Wexford), 4 & 11 June 1921. Police in Tipperary were ordered to destroy all bridges which were irreparable but where enough was left for an ordinary cart to cross, CI South Tipperary MR May 1921.

would divert their attention to areas without martial law. As a result few people saw any justification for the imposed restrictions, which were often more of an irritation to the public than to the IRA. The constraints on markets and travel impaired economic activity and people's freedom. The restrictions on the use of motorcars, and later on the use of bicycles, resulted in widespread discontent. The targeting of local representatives of the Dáil Government and their sympathisers by the Crown Forces did indeed make people hesitant to associate in public with the movement. Arrested Volunteers who were taken around as hostages noticed that people were afraid to show signs of recognition, and more friendliness was shown to the police after the boycott had ended in failure. Nevertheless, contrary to the authorities' expectation, there was little understanding of the government's actions and few people changed their allegiance. Even declared supporters of the government refused to give Volunteers away.[4]

In 1921 when the conflict had become almost entirely military, large-scale expressions of political support and adherence to the institutions of alternative government had become less important. The Volunteers acted only against civilians when they endangered their operations or showed clear signs of support for the authorities. In the few ambushes and sniping attacks on barracks that took place in Wexford civilians who might interfere or inform the police were restrained by either confining them to their homes or holding them up until the operation was over. No excessive violence was used against these people. Only those who openly showed sympathy for the Crown Forces were targeted. This was limited to women who associated with soldiers or policemen, and to persons who were clearly friendly towards them. A number of ex-soldiers who publicly mixed with the Crown Forces, were shot. Their previous service to the Crown and continued association made them prime targets of assassination with a high symbolic value. The police acknowledged

---

4 Volunteer experience in Wexford, *The Life of Mick Radford* (n. d.), 11–14; Jim and Mairn Ryan, O'MN, P17b103; Mrs. Bridie Quirke, Interview; *People* (Wexford), 15 January & 19 February 1921; Andy Roe, Interview; Willie Parle, Interview; John Quinn, Interview; Ned Colfer, Interview; CI Wexford MRs August 1920, and January, March & May 1921. Attention given to Sinn Féin Rate Collectors, communication dated 11 April 1921, PRO, WO35/71/8/117. In June 1921, the County Inspector acknowledged that the rebels had sympathisers everywhere and had no difficulty in obtaining food, shelter and support even from persons who are opposed to their aims and activities, CI Wexford MR June 1921. In Tipperary, the police boycott was virtually over in November 1920. This followed the tougher approach taken by the authorities in August, CI South Tipperary MRs September & November 1920. The success of the carrying of hostages is shown in Clare when the members of the ASU refused to fire at Crown Forces who used their family and friends as a shield, Report Mid Clare Brigade dated 4 June 1921, UCD AD, P7A19/24–26.

that all civilians shot in Wexford had been overtly friendly to the Crown Forces; some of them had even joined them in raids on republicans.[5]

CONDITIONS IN DERRY

In the less violent period of the struggle the IRA in Derry had participated in most of the nationally coordinated actions. In the areas where they enjoyed strong support, in certain parts of the city and in the south-eastern portion of the county, the response to this was satisfactory. Some evacuated barracks were burned, income tax offices were raided and many nationalists joined in the nation-wide strikes. In 1921 no nationally coordinated actions were initiated and consequently contact with the population was reduced. Unable to challenge the Crown Forces militarily, the Volunteers practically disappeared from the stage. In the few operations the Volunteers staged in 1921 they relied heavily on directions from GHQ. Under the influence of the organiser sent to them attacks on lines of communications became apparent from April 1921 onwards. These attacks were, however, executed on a much smaller scale than in Wexford, and had only an extremely limited effect on the population.[6]

The small number of Volunteers in Derry was a direct result of the widespread hostility of the population. Large parts of rural Derry were dominated by Protestants, while the Hibernians were strong in most areas with a religiously mixed population. In such a hostile environment radical nationalists often felt unable to come out and organise themselves. It was difficult to admit membership when even one's own family might actively oppose one. In these circumstances it was extremely difficult to organise. Consequently Volunteer units remained confined to a few areas dominated by radical Catholics, leaving large parts of the county completely unorganised. In Wexford, where the Volunteers had to operate in an environment with similarly divided loyalties, the number of Catholics was much higher

5   Examples of girls who had their hair cut, *People* (Wexford), 12 February & 23 April 1921; CI Wexford MRs November 1920 & February 1921; W.G. Roberts, 'Memoirs', 42, IWM, PP/MCR/98; Major-Gen. Douglas Wimberley, 'Scottish Soldier', 147, IWM, PP/MCR/182. Precautions taken to restrain civilians by the IRA, Peter Wall, Interview; Ned Colfer, Interview. Shooting of ex-soldiers and the reasons for it, CI Wexford MRs January-May 1921; Ned Colfer, Interview.

6   Nationally coordinated actions in 1920, *Derry People and Donegal News*, 15 & 22 May and 28 August 1920. Activity in 1921, *Coleraine Chronicle*, 12 February, 9 April & 9 July 1921. Most of the few ambushes in Derry and Tyrone were led by the GHQ Organiser, Thomas Morris, 'Typescript of Interview', Fr O'Kane Papers, AARC; W. Loughran, NLI, ms. 17,506.

and companies had already been organised in most parishes during 1917, when support was widespread.[7]

The Volunteers in Derry were thus confined to an extremely small section of the population for recruiting and support. The silent acceptance of the Volunteers as the sole representatives of the Catholic community, which crossed most sections of the community in the South, was limited to a few small pockets of hard-core support. Operating in an overwhelmingly hostile environment also limited the effectiveness of threats made to civilians. Activity was extremely low, and the only direct dealing with the population took place in the few arms raids. Most targets of raids were Catholics, as the Volunteers were too weak and were too unfamiliar with the Protestant community to raid them. Despite this inactivity most Catholics were sufficiently intimidated by the reports of IRA dealings in other areas, to be appropriately fearful during these visits.

Association with the Crown Forces was so widespread in Derry that it could not be seen as sufficient reason to charge anyone with spying. The 2nd South Derry Battalion considered all Protestants and some Catholics as enemy agents, but had no definite information on any particular person. The treatment of the few informers who were exposed through captured mail showed the inexperience and low level of radicalisation of the Volunteers in Derry. The first of these spies taken by a unit in south Derry was not shot but was imprisoned at its headquarters. When he escaped and took shelter in the local police barracks, the Volunteers panicked and swiftly relocated their headquarters. The second informer arrested by this unit left the county after he was tried and told to clear out or death would ensue. Ex-soldiers were never singled out as a target by the IRA in Derry. A high proportion of the IRA and its officers in south Derry and Derry City were ex-soldiers themselves. Only on one occasion was an ex-soldier attacked on his record in a brawl: 'You have worn the coat for Britain for four years. You think you are a brave man.' The ex-soldier made short shrift of this accusation; he allegedly bit off his attacker's ears.[8]

7   Tension between Volunteers and Hibernians, William John Himphey, Fr O'Kane papers, Tape A20 & A23, AARC. Non-cooperation of parts of the Catholic population causing the failure of a train ambush, Report South Derry Brigade March 21, UCD AD, P7A39. Among the local pockets of hard-core support for the Volunteers were the Bogside in Derry City and a number of townlands in south Derry along the shores of Lough Neagh, Major-Gen. G.N. Wood, 'The Military Control of Londonderry, 1919-23', 10, IWM, 78/31/1; CI Derry MRs 1916-21; Paddy Larkin, Interview, John James McGee, Interview.

8   Spies caught in south Derry, Thomas Morris, 'Typescript of Interview', Fr O'Kane Papers, AARC. The raids on the mail were often the only highlight in many units' existence, W. Loughran, NLI, ms. 17,506. Those considered to be enemy agents in the Second South Derry Battalion, UCD AD, P7A11. Ex-soldiers in the IRA in Derry, Paddy Larkin, Interview; William John Himphey, Fr O'Kane Papers, Tape A20 & A23, AARC; CI Derry MR May 1921. Quote, *Derry People and Donegal News*, 5 June 1920.

Those who went on the run in Derry and Wexford had to be particularly careful. The presence of so many opponents made informing on their whereabouts probable, particularly of those travelling the countryside with arms. The flatness of south Wexford made it almost impossible to do this unnoticed. These circumstances made the functioning of a Flying Column in these counties extremely difficult. Consequently few men went on the run, and if they did so they left the county altogether or stayed close to their own home and mainly engaged in non-violent activities. The executions of civilians in Wexford in the spring of 1921 involved ex-soldiers who closely associated with the Crown Forces, and were meant to protect the safety of wanted Volunteers and warn others not to inform. In Tipperary the Volunteers operated in a socio-political environment comparable to that in Wexford. The rural areas were, however, more prone to supporting the Volunteers and the presence of mountain ranges provided them with safe areas. More importantly, the level of fear caused by the harsh treatment of suspected spies enabled them, unlike the Volunteers in Wexford, to travel the countryside safely.

CONDITIONS IN MAYO

Until 1921 the Volunteers in Mayo had operated strictly within the confines of their community. The relative homogeneity of the population had enabled them to dominate most aspects of life, particularly in the rural areas. This is shown by their success in organising the Dáil Courts and in enforcing adherence to its decisions. The popular response to the Dáil Loan and the Police boycott had also been good. However, the greater interaction between Volunteers and the population also gave the community a greater constraining influence on the IRA. This largely explains the low level of activity in such a well-organised county before 1921. An undesired consequence of the success of the alternative government was that many Volunteer officers had become well-known. The extremely high number of arrests in Mayo at the end of 1920 demonstrates the familiarity of the police with the organisation.[9]

Despite the Volunteers' success in penetrating community life, some civilians had to be 'persuaded' to conform to the new norm. However, most of this type of intimidation did not reach the headlines as it was relatively non-violent and directed at people who were unwilling to report it to the police. In this respect Mayo contrasted with Tipperary where much

9 The relatively high number of arrests in Mayo after the introduction of the Restoration of Order in Ireland Act is demonstrated in the reports of the different County Inspectors from August to December 1920.

intimidation was directed at loyal Catholics, who were numerous enough to be undeterred by the possible consequences of contact with the police. In Mayo the central position of the IRA in the community also made many people less fearful of the Volunteers. Few expected direct violence to be used against them by fellow members of the community, and were not easily intimidated. In one of the first ambushes in Mayo a local man deliberately walked up and down in front of the ambush position in an attempt to prevent the action from taking place close to his home. It took a locally unknown member of the column, who was more likely to enforce a threat, to intimidate him sufficiently to comply: 'Michael Kilroy sent me down as I was a stranger to threaten him, and then he cleared back to his house.' A similar effect was shown in relation to establishing authority within the developing organisation; authority over local people was more easily established by an outsider.[10]

The formation of Flying Columns in Mayo had significant consequences for the relationship between Volunteers and ordinary civilians. For the column members it implied a break with the immediate environment of family and friends, which made attempts on the life of policemen possible without directly endangering those with whom they had grown up. Although forced upon them by the increased vigilance of the Crown Forces, this was a vital step in the development of violent conflict in Mayo. Released from the restraining influence of their environment, these men were free to decide their own course of action. Mixing exclusively with other radicals meant that the parameters of acceptable behaviour were widened to take in ambushes and possibly executions. From the outset it was clear that ambushing policemen was the main objective of these men. As indicated before, this endangered people living near an ambush site who were often the victims of reprisals by the Crown Forces. This was, however, not an overriding consideration once these men had left their family and work. As a result the columns found there were only a few places where they were enthusiastically received. Nevertheless the population was unwilling to cooperate with the police and little informing took place in Mayo. Although occasionally people on the fringes of the community gave information to the police about the columns' whereabouts, this rarely caused any serious danger. The column members were unaware of local loyalties, and never fully investigated these cases. As a result neither in the West nor in the South Mayo Brigade area was any civilian shot as a spy or informer. Men who associated closely with the

10 The persuasion included tarring a number of girls to stop them from going with members of the Crown Forces, Johnny Duffy, O'MN, P17b109; Charlie Hughes, Interview; *Mayoman*, 24 July & 18 September 1920; CI Mayo MRs July-August 1920. Quote, Paddy Cannon, O'MN, P17b136. A similar case involving a postman, *Mayoman*, 11 June 1921.

police were looked upon with suspicion, but were not singled out as targets.[11]

The columns travelled from one entirely reliable area to another and rarely spent the night in other places. On the occasional visit to less trusted areas they occupied the houses of people hostile to them. In the areas where they were most welcome, they were extremely well treated. The locals willingly vacated their beds for them and provided them with food. Some people were famous for their willingness to slaughter animals every time the column came by. Others went out of their way to support them, risking their own lives in the process. The column men were aware of the sacrifices and dangers these people endured. One Volunteer concerned with their inability to engage the police felt somewhat embarrassed: 'For a month we did nothing except wait in ambush positions during the day, then plenty of dancing and singing at night. I began to feel ashamed of being quartered on the people.' Some attempts were made to ensure the columns would not needlessly aggravate or endanger the civilians by their behaviour, both during their stay with them, but also in the targets they chose for their operations. This, however, remained only a secondary consideration to the columns as the national struggle was all-important.[12]

11 Limited number of entirely safe areas, Ned Maughan, O'MN, P17b109; Tom Maguire, O'MN, P17b100; Michael Kilroy, O'MN, P17b101, and 'ASU Operations'; Johnny Duffy, O'MN, P17b109; Paddy Cannon, O'MN, P17b136; Jimmy Swift, O'MN, P17b136; John Madden, O'MN, P17b113; Joe Baker (1988), 19. All Volunteer officers state that no civilians were shot in these parts of Mayo despite the fact that most of them had some suspicions, Ned Maughan, O'MN, P17b109; Ned Moane, 'Statement'; Tom Maguire, O'MN, P17b100, and Interview; Michael Kilroy, O'MN, P17b101; Thomas Kettrick, 'Statement'; Pat Fallon, O'MN, P17b109; Jack Connolly, O'MN, P17b120; Paddy Cannon, O'MNs, P17b109, and P17b136; Joe Baker (1988), 19; CI Mayo MRs 1916-21. In only one case a Volunteer was arrested by the police as a result of information given to them, Thomas Heavy, O'MN, P17b120. An example of the view taken of people associating with the Crown Forces, Tom Kettrick, O'MN, P17b136.

12 Quote, Thomas Heavey, 'Statement'. Use of hostile houses, Johnny Duffy, O'MN, P17b109. Eagerness to feed the Column, John Madden, O'MN, P17b113; Johnny Duffy, O'MN, P17b109; Thomas Kettrick, 'Statement'. The Column found that many locals were willing to support the movement with large amounts of money and goods, Ned Maughan, O'MN, P17b109; Ned Moane, 'Statement'; Thomas Kettrick, 'Statement'; Ned Moane and Brodie Malone, O'MN, P17b120. Nevertheless, a levy of ten shilling was put on every half barrel of beer in Castlebar and the surrounding countryside to pay for the appointment of Republican police, James Chambers, 'Statement'. The police reported in June 1921 that the Volunteers had committed twenty robberies to obtain funds to keep the Flying Column supplied. They also stated that the farmers felt that between the stoppage of fairs and markets which prevented them selling their cattle, and the IRA who 'ate them out of house' they were unable to manage to live, CI Mayo MR June 1921. On measures taken to limit the burden on civilians, Michael Kilroy, 'ASU Operations'; Ned Moane and Brodie Malone, O'MN, P17b120, and Moane/Malone, Tape.

After some reprisals by Crown Forces took place in Mayo open support for the IRA diminished and the willingness to cooperate with or at least talk to the Crown Forces grew. This was particularly apparent in the towns, where most of the remaining police barracks were situated, and the population had always been more hesitant to support the Volunteers. Most column men in Mayo came from the towns, and several complained about the lack of support they got from townspeople. The higher risk of informing in towns had forced many Volunteers on the run, and had largely been the cause of the high proportion of urban Volunteers in the Flying Columns. The rural areas, abandoned by the police and economically less dependent on the presence of the British, were and remained more supportive. However, the danger incurred by associating with the column meant that more and more of them also tried to prevent their visits. One of the more striking examples of the effects of an official reprisal in which the houses of the brigade commandant and adjutant were destroyed took place in the West Clare Brigade:

> The Brigade Adjutant returned to view the wreckage a week later, and then proceeded to the nearest dug out to spend the night. Alas! the moral effect had materialised. The dug-out had been destroyed by local residents in frenzied panic – two others a distance off had been denuded of their furnishings and left bare. [...] Nor was all this without its due reaction on the people. The wanted man was in many cases furtively received. The usual procedure was the immediate setting of the tea table, regardless of protests, while some member of the family watched from the roadway. When tea was finished, holy water was immediately produced. And excuse for further delay there was none.[13]

Some of the most friendly locals also became more hesitant to harbour Volunteers when they were confronted with police reaction. A Mayo Volunteer who contemplated joining the column was strongly but unsuccessfully urged by his friends not to do so: 'One man particularly complained to father that I was bringing danger to the home.' After their first major ambush the West Mayo column was advised by one of its most loyal supporters: 'As we had justified our stand by all the fighting we had taken part in, we should now go easy until the harvest was gathered, and perhaps a settlement might soon be made.' Nevertheless support continued to be given to the columns. The inability of the Crown Forces to distinguish between ordinary civilians and Volunteers played an important part in this:

> It was a vicious circle whenever there were raids or small round ups of the population. Men ran away as soon as they saw either the mili-

13 Quote, Liam Haugh, 'History of the West Clare Brigade', NLI, P915 A0363. The change in attitude towards the police, CI Mayo MRs October-December 1920.

tary or the police, for they were afraid of being beaten and questioned. Then whenever they were seen as they ran away they were fired on. The Tans, the RIC, the Military and the Auxiliaries took anyone whom they met with (outside of those who had stringent Anglo-Irish voices), as the enemy: and they certainly behaved towards them as if these men and women before them were their enemies whom they were armed against.[14]

The disappearance of the Mayo columns in May 1921 and the unwillingness of local Volunteers to endanger themselves and the community led to a virtual paralysis in June and July. The resulting lack of operations was common for many other parts of Mayo. In the East Mayo Brigade the Volunteers were completely paralysed by the fear of police reaction and the infighting of the local IRA, and no action was taken. When some officers of the West Mayo Brigade visited the area they had to leave hurriedly as their presence terrified the locals. A similar lack of operations, caused by disputes between officers and petty jealousies, were found by them in Foxford, Swinford and Charlestown.[15]

CONDITIONS IN TIPPERARY

In Tipperary some of the most active brigade officers had already been separated from the restraining influence of their communities in January 1919, but they were forced to leave the county after the Knocklong rescue

14 Quote, on Volunteer whose father was approached, Jim O'Donnell, 'Recollections'. Cases where formerly friendly people became reticent, Tom Kettrick, O'MN, P17b136; John Madden, O'MN, P17b113; Neligan, in K. Griffith and T. O'Grady (1982), 179 + 208. Quote, on 'telling them to stop fighting', Michael Kilroy, 'ASU Operations'. See also Jack Connolly, O'MN, P17b120. The refusal of civilians to give away the Volunteers even when under serious threat, Johnny Duffy, O'MN, P17b109; Joe Baker (1988), 19; Tom Maguire, O'MN, P17b100. Quote, on the 'self-fulfilling prophesy', Michael Kilroy, O'MN, P17b138. An example of the resulting distrust of the police, Jimmy Slattery, O'MN, P17b138. In other areas, people ran away when the Crown Forces arrived for fear of being taken as hostages, Paul Merrigan, O'MN, P17b126; Sean O'h, O'MN, P17b100. Police outrages, UCD AD, P80/59, 61/1-3, 69 + 75; Tom Maguire, O'MN, P17b100; Brodie Malone, O'MN, P17b109; Jimmy Slattery, O'MN, P17b138. Acknowledgement of the inability of the military to distinguish between friend and foe, 'History of the 5th Division in Ireland November 1919-March 1922', 73, IWM, 72/82/2.
15 Situation in East Mayo, Ned Maughan, O'MN, P17b109; Paddy Duffy, O'MN, P17b136; Tom Carney, O'MN, P17b109. Similar situations in Donegal and Kilkenny, report dated May 15 1921, UCD AD, P7A18/277; Tommy Ryan, 'Statement'; Jack Gardiner, Interview.

in May. Violent action became widespread only after their reappearance in
the spring of 1920. Many willing Volunteers from all over the brigade area
joined in these attacks, together with the local company and battalion officers. As a result of this most active spirits in the brigade became sufficiently involved during the summer of 1920 to join the main officers in
their wandering existence and became free to engage in more activity. This
early separation of many Volunteers from their home grounds set in motion
a cycle of retaliating violence, and explains the early foundation of a Flying
Column and the high level of casualties in South Tipperary.

Although the growing violence was initiated by the IRA, it led to deteriorating relations between the Crown Forces and the population, while the
IRA often became more popular. The violence the Crown Force used
against civilians in Tipperary was an important factor in this development.
Many in the Crown Forces were frustrated by the inability to prosecute the
perpetrators of attacks on them and the favourable reaction of the population to those who killed their comrades.

> These young men, when being escorted to gaol were applauded as
> heroes by a great many of the townspeople and when they came out
> got what looked like a civic reception. [...] We knew the leaders and
> could lay our hands on them but, apparently we had to wait till they
> shot us and then they might be tried for murder before a Jury if
> anyone could be found brave enough to give evidence.[16]

The reactive violence of the Crown Forces was directed at relatives and
close sympathisers of the movement whom most people considered as their
own, and consequently it antagonised a majority of nationalists. This first
became apparent after the murder of a number of local activists in the early
part of 1920. The inquiries that followed two separate incidents near
Thurles caused much public indignation. On both occasions general opinion considered the police guilty of the killings. Most felt that one of the
victims had been mistaken for his brother, a Labour councillor who had
aggravated the Crown Forces by his continual demands for an investigation
into the damage done to the town on the night of 20 January following the
wounding of a local constable.[17]

During the inquest into his death policemen came forward to account
for themselves. Several of them were challenged in court and the public
did not hesitate to show their hostility: 'the crowd applauded any point
made against them.' Despite public opinion the jury refused to assign
responsibility to the police as was done in the other inquest. This caused

16 Quote, John Regan, 'Memoirs', 115, PRONI, D3160.
17 Events in Thurles, Fr Michael Maher, Diary 1920, St Patrick's College,
   Thurles; CI North Tipperary MRs January–April 1920.

much disappointment leading to attempts to force the population to close ranks behind the republicans: 'There is a good deal of talk going about over the failure of the Thurles jury to saddle the blame on the police. Some of them [members of the jury] are mentioned as having got threatening letters and there is talk that the shopkeepers amongst them will be penalised by being boycotted.' Contrary to feelings around the inquests the shooting of two policemen during the proceedings failed to arouse public condemnation.[18]

The confrontation which emerged in 1920 was largely a kind of personal feud between active Volunteers and diligent policemen, by which the bulk of Volunteers, Crown Forces and the population was only indirectly affected. Blame for the growing violence was largely ascribed to the Crown Forces. The relative immunity from violence of most people meant that they were able to express and develop republican sympathies without fear of possible consequences. The tactics of the IRA in Tipperary reinforced the perception that they were defenders of the community against the onslaught of foreign forces. Many of its measures were a direct attempt to counter Crown Force violence against civilians, often their own families. This began in February 1919 when the IRA answered the proclamation of Tipperary as a special military area with a similar proclamation. When violence grew, this development became more pronounced. All Crown Forces known to be guilty of carrying hostages on their lorries to prevent attacks were threatened with death. When houses of republicans were burned under official and unofficial reprisals, the IRA retaliated by burning the houses of local loyalists.[19]

The official reprisals of 1921, in which the houses of wanted Volunteers and of those who lived close to an ambush site were blown up, further alienated the people from the authorities. The arbitrary aspect and the long period between the ambush and the reprisal seriously diminished its acceptance by the population as a legitimate response. The lack of intelligence meant that the Crown Forces were unable to get to the perpetrators, and innocent civilians were made to suffer. This became official policy and was spelled out in January 1921 when seven houses were burned near an ambush site: 'The inhabitants were bound to have known of the ambush

18 Quotes, Fr Michael Maher, Diary April 19 1920, St Patrick's College Thurles. See also CI North Tipperary MRs January–April 1920.
19 Due to the polarisation simple situations, such as people refusing to take a drink from soldiers, could lead to maltreatment, Tom Smyth, O'MN, P17b103. Order on 'hostages' dated 16 January 1921, O'MN, P17b127. Burnings and murder as reprisal by Crown Forces, Mossy McGrath, O'MN, P17b127; Fr Michael Maher, Diary 1920, St Patrick's College, Thurles. As early as July 1920, the IRA considered the destruction of enemy houses as a means to prevent destruction and commandeering of Republican houses, but it was not accepted then, NLI, ms. 11,410.

and attack, and they neglected to give any information.' The occupants of the houses received notice that they had one hour to clear out their valuables, but not their furniture. The furniture was taken out by the military and burned and then the house was demolished by bombs. The large military drives instituted at the end of the struggle, in which all males were rounded up and some were arrested without cause, confirmed people's perception.[20]

The Tipperary Volunteers also attempted to minimise inconvenience to civilians, but any cooperation with the Crown Forces was severely dealt with. The 4th Battalion, for instance, tried to prevent accidents after demolishing a bridge by building little walls on both sides to warn the traffic and put up a red lamp for the train underneath. In the burning of barracks civilians directly endangered by Volunteer operations were aided. In extreme cases attacks were called off if too many people would be endangered. Both GHQ and the Tipperary brigade officers were well aware of the burden which the existence of the Flying Column put on the population. Particularly the less well-off made many sacrifices for them. A string of measures were taken at the end of 1920 to lessen the impact on the population. A general order was issued forbidding the commandeering from civilians of goods which could be bought, except under compelling necessity. To pay for the columns' supplies the South Tipperary Brigade introduced a levy on each company. To reduce the exposure of sympathisers, dug-outs were made to hold goods and more permanent Volunteer offices. For more adamant column members, however, the military struggle prevailed and they refused to take much notice of these arrangements.[21]

20 Quote, *Tipperary Star*, 21 January 1921. Other reprisals in which houses of known rebels (15 and 6 respectively) were officially destroyed, CI South Tipperary MRs February & May 1921.

21 Avoiding trouble for civilians, 4th Battalion order dated 6 July 1921, UCD AD, P17a105; Order dated 2 December 1920, O'MN, P17b127; *Derry People and Donegal News*, 22 May 1920. Volunteers who failed to shoot when civilians were in the line of fire, Sean Fitzpatrick, Lecture in *Nationalist*, and *Tipperary Star*, 27 October 1951, UCD AD, P7D109; Report on South Tipperary Brigade offensive action 10 May 1920, NLI, P919 A0509; UCD AD, P7A17/272-5, P7A19/24-6, 163 + 184. Civilians passing through ambush sites often caused problems, Mossy McGrath, O'MN, P17b127; Kennedy, O'MN, P17b114; Tommy Ryan, 'Statement'; Paul Merrigan, Interview. Orders on commandeering and dug outs, General Order No 4 dated 4 November 1920, South Tipperary Brigade Orders dated 11 October 1920 and 11 January 1921, O'MN, P17b127. See also Artie Barlow, O'MN, P17b114; Kennedy, O'MN, P17b114; Ned O'Reilly, O'MN, P17b126; Tom Murphy, 'Statement', NLI, ms. 31,225; Seamus Robinson, 'Statement', NLI, ms. 21,265. To deal with the increasing lack of accommodation, all battalion commandants in the South Tipperary Brigade were ordered to compile a list of houses that would put up Volunteers for a night, O'MN, P17b127.

From the beginning of the struggle anyone associating with the police socially was pressurised to refrain from this. In certain rural parts of the county and occasionally in some of the towns those showing themselves sympathetic to the Crown Forces, encountered the wrath of the community. Public exposure of these people was considered a sufficient deterrent in most cases. As a result of the increasing pursuit of Volunteers relations became more strained. The presence of 'men and boys roaming aimlessly through the country' in areas where dug-outs were made or near ambush sites endangered and irritated the Volunteers. Occasionally Volunteers lost their temper and maltreated those who did not readily cooperate. Farmers were forced to pay a levy on their livestock in support of the IRA, and if they refused their cattle was seized and sold. Especially towards the end of the struggle some Volunteers in the active areas were willing to abuse their position of power and steal for their own benefit.[22]

As in Mayo, the Flying Columns stayed with people who were friendly to them in areas they could rely on not to inform on them. The people with whom they mixed admired their bravery and willingness to put their lives at stake for the freedom of the country. The stories of their experiences attracted much interest. Nevertheless some grumbling was voiced behind their backs in the villages they visited: 'They wouldn't say to the like of us but they might say it to others, that the men hadn't much to do at home when they go around like this.' More open opposition was encountered from parents and wives of men who joined the columns. They

22 Warning people not to associate with the police, and shunning of those who were seen to associate, *Tipperary Star*, 14 May 1920; Paul Merrigan, Interview; Jack Gardiner, Interview; CI South Tipperary MRs June, July & September 1920, and February 1921. Cutting or the threat of cutting girls hair when associating with Crown Forces, *Tipperary Star*, 30 July 1920, and 22 January & 7 May 1921; *Tipperary People*, 16 April. Order to stop people from hunting, ferreting etc. unless they obtained a written permit from the battalion commandant dated 8 December 1920, O'MN, P17b127. Civilians forced to dig trenches, Bryan Ryan (1969), 40; UCD AD, P7A19/95-7; Order on 'commandeered labour' dated 5 December 1920, O'MN, P17b127. Levy on farmers, Paul Merrigan, Interview; UCD AD, P7A21/144-5, and P7A23/22-3. Levy on other well-to-do people, P.C. Power (1976), 150; Eamon O'Dwyer, 'Statement'. The commandant of the brigade remembers asking GHQ to order such a levy, which became General Order No. 15, Seamus Robinson, 'Statement', NLI, ms. 21,265. The quartermaster of this brigade remembers discussing the lack of discipline in the IRA with Michael Collins at an early stage, Eamon O'Dwyer, 'Statement'. Only at the end of the struggle were serious measures, including executions, contemplated against looting by Volunteers, UCD AD, P7A21/10-11 + 168, and P7A22/14. The Order introducing a levy on Volunteer companies contained the phrase: 'I would suggest that the money be got if possible by means other than collection.' Some local commanders took this as a license to rob, Order dated 11 January 1921, O'MN, P17b127. Examples of mistreatment of civilians, Bryan Ryan (1969), 40.

expressed their concerns and tried to dissuade the men from going out. One young Volunteer who was called out at 2 o'clock one night to help in the attack on a barrack, experienced this from close quarters:

> My mother locked the door. I didn't know what to do but my father opened it. [...] Pat said, 'We have to call Martin Dwyer.' Your man stayed at Dwyer's gate and sent me in. I hadn't my wits about me. I knocked at his window. For I knew where I was, his mother started giving out — such a lacerating. 'Wait till I meet your mother, calling people out of their beds to commit murder, and get killed yourselves. Well if you have nothing else to do Martin has. Clear off.'

One of the original Volunteer organisers, well known in the area, was receptive to the approaches made by concerned relations, thus demonstrating his sensitivity to the continued dependency of the Volunteers on the community:

> A good deal of the time — when it was known that I was home — I had women callers who wanted to get their sons or brothers or husbands out of danger's way. They were good people, staunch enough to the cause and ready to make any sacrifices of money, means, imprisonment, but they wished to save the lives of their dear ones, and who could blame them. Those were heartbreaking ordeals for me, and sometimes I had to intervene and bring fellows home against their will.[23]

Despite the high level of sympathy and support for the IRA, few civilians were willing to assist Volunteers in actions against the police. The higher level of active opposition to the IRA in Tipperary towns and villages was demonstrated on several occasions when policemen were protected by civilians:

> Donovan, Clancy and I then went to the front door and knocked. There was some delay about opening the door. In fact, we had to knock long and persistently before it was opened to us. There was no sign of the two policemen in the shop and a lady who was there said that they had left. We searched the office and tap-room but no sign of them. The lady in charge of the shop shouted and screamed that they had left, that they were not there. Donovan opened the back

---

23 Quote on 'grumbling', Jack Gardiner, Interview. Quote on 'parents reaction', Bryan Ryan (1969), 15. Experience of column men with locals, Paul Merrigan, Interview; Mossy McGrath, O'MN, P17b127. Quote on the officer approached by Volunteer's families, Eamon O'Dwyer, 'Statement'. He also states that another officer, Michael Sheehan, was approached by relatives of Volunteers.

door and Tommy Lee, who was outside, assured him that no one had left by the back. We tried to calm the lady by telling her that we did not intend to shoot or harm the R.I.C. men, but to no avail. She became so violently hysterical that we abandoned our idea of searching the upstairs part of the house for them.

Other people refused to give information: 'The lads in the village wouldn't give us any information about the RIC or their movements. (They were afraid I expect of the murdergang visitation or of the destruction of houses by the military.)' Even in Tipperary the IRA was hesitant to antagonise the population needlessly and did not feel it was necessary to deal with these cases of non-cooperation. Only those who actively opposed or people who informed on them were taken on. Nevertheless, even in such cases other considerations influenced their reaction: 'In Ballylanders [Co. Limerick] the names of the lads were put into a postbox. This fellow [?] had the names of the lads and he went to the Grange ambush. The Volunteers raided the box and they found this list in it. This man had 2 nephews in the column so we couldn't shoot him and he was transported.'[24]

CONDITIONS IN DUBLIN

In the more impersonal urban setting in Dublin City the at times symbiotic relationship between Volunteers and community was absent. Their activities could be carried out all over the city without directly implicating family and friends. The checks and balances that contained violence within a rural community were consequently less operative in Dublin. Nevertheless large-scale violence began only in January 1921. The need to use violence to prevent arrest was not as strong in a city as it was in rural areas where wanted men were harder to hide.

Most civilians in Dublin City, as in most country towns, were ignored by Volunteers. Some efforts were also made to safeguard civilians from the consequences of the fighting. Cathal Brugha, the Minister of Defence, made a particular point of this concerning the use of grenades and mines in street

24 Quote on 'woman shielding the police', Patrick Ryan, 'Statement'. Quote on 'refusal to give information', Ned O'Reilly, O'MN, P17b126. See also Paddy O'Halloran, O'MN, P17b114; Mossy McGrath, O'MN, P17b127. Quote on 'informant', Paddy Kinnane, O'MN, P17b125. Other examples of experienced Volunteers unwilling to shoot spies outright, Ned O'Reilly, O'MN, P17b126; Paul Mulcahy, 'Statement'; Jack Moloney, Interview; Jack Gardiner, Interview; Bryan Ryan (1969), 43; Tommy Ryan, 'Statement'. Cases of people shot because of spying or active opposition, Ned O'Reilly, O'MN, P17b126; Mossy McGrath, O'MN, P17b127; Paul Merrigan, O'MN, P17b126, and Interview; Kennedy, O'MN, P17b114; Brigade report dated 4 July 1921, UCD AD, P17a105.

ambushes. After a woman trader, the mother of three children was killed in an ambush in Camden Street, the commandant of the Dublin Brigade was summoned by the Minister:

> I was asked to see Cathal Brugha by himself, and I didn't relish that. Always I got a lecture, or what seemed to be a lecture from Cathal Brugha. [...] 'It shouldn't have taken place on Saturday night', he said. It's a very busy night for the housewives of Dublin, now the poor children are motherless and we don't know what damage has been done. I tried to reason with him, but it was no good. 'The enemy', I said 'will strike wherever and whenever they can.' 'It doesn't matter he said tell your men not to plan ambushes on Saturday night', and I had to issue the order. The men had a good joke about it: 'The weekly Saturday night ambush is postponed to Monday'.

Brugha also forbade shooting from inside houses as that would implicate the inhabitants. The fair prosecution of spies was a particular concern of the Minister, and he ordered convincing proof to be brought forward in every case. However, the more violent members, including Michael Collins, frequently ignored these instructions. As a result, many alleged informers were killed without referral in 1921.[25]

Towards the end of the struggle the Dublin Volunteers started to use their power more freely, as in most active country areas. More civilians were shot as spies and in a few cases people were robbed. The violent attitude towards civilians shown by members of the ASU and the Squad, and by Michael Collins himself shocked more conscientious Volunteers. In one case misbehaving Volunteers were mistaken for Black & Tans. The tension between the theoretical approach of the Minister and the more practical approach of the fighting men shows up clearly in an incident in Dun Laoghaire in which a civilian was shot:

> Once I was brought before him [Michael Collins] for Pearse Beasley reported that my men had killed a civilian in Dun Laoghaire.

25 Quote, Oscar Traynor, O'MN, P17b98. Order to select quiet localities for bombing lorries, Letter from Department of Organisation to Chief of Staff dated 22 March 1921, UCD AD, P7A47. Order not to snipe from buildings and the breaking of that order, Paddy Rigney, O'MN, P17b105. Tendency to abandon actions when innocent people might be hurt and the attitude taken by the Minister of Defence, Tom Duffy, O'MN, P17b105; Oscar Traynor, O'MNs, P17b96, and P17b98; Jim Slattery, O'MN, P17b109; George White, O'MN, P17b105; Michael Crummins, O'MN, P17b98; UCD AD, P7A19/163; Jimmy Murray, O'MN, P17b106; Mick O'Hanlon, O'MN, P17b106. Instructions of the Minister of Defence concerning spies and Michael Collins breaking them, Larry Nugent, O'MN, P17b88; Frank Thornton, O'MN, P17b100; Oscar Traynor, O'MN, P17b98.

> There was a raid on the mails as they came off or went to the mail boat. [...] I was instructed to hold up part of a street in Dun Laoghaire and I was told not to let anyone pass whilst the job was being brought off. Suddenly I saw a cyclist dash through. Why didn't you hold up that man I shouted. We did I was told we halted him but he dashed through. I knew that if this continued we would be powerless to carry out such an operation again. There was an IRA man near me with a rifle. He had been in the British Army as were many of the company there and I knew he was a good shot. 'Shoot at him,' I said, 'and shoot to kill.' The lad fired. I saw the man fall of the bike: he went one way and the bike went another way. Ginger [J. J. O'Connell] stood up for me at the inquiry, for I had to carry out my orders he said. 'He was quite right,' he said. It was his duty to shoot and the man was shot. Collins was trying to placate Beasley. 'Get out you bastard,' he said to me pleasantly.[26]

With the high population density and greater anonymity in the city, a wide variety of reaction to the Volunteers was possible. Some people were more than willing to cooperate with the Volunteers and helped them in many different ways. As in Tipperary, admiration for those engaged in the struggle was mixed with a desire to stay out of trouble. This was relatively easy in the city due to its size and the inability of the Crown Forces to assign the blame for IRA actions to anyone in particular. In the Camden Street area, where frequent ambushes took place, the street traders were so familiar with the Volunteers that they left as soon as they saw them or they asked ambushing parties to shift their position to prevent endangering them. Most people ignored the struggle as much as possible. However, the atrocities of the Crown Forces in other parts of the country which were well covered in the newspapers led to much indignation in Dublin as well. As a result, many IRA operations were well received, sometimes to the surprise of the Volunteers involved. When Volunteers tried to slip away after burning military goods in a railway station they were cheered and applauded by the public and the railway workers. To those opposing the movement it was relatively safe to give information to the police, witnessed by many

26 Quote, Andy MacDonnell, O'MN, P17b100. Brutal behaviour of members of the Squad and Michael Collins, C.S. Andrews (1979), 153; Alfie White, O'MN, P17b110. Dealing with robberies by Volunteers, NLI, ms. 902/151; General Order dated 7 July 1921, NLI, ms. 739; Order against raiding of private houses 19 January 1920, NLI, ms. 11,410; Letter from Cork 2nd Brigade dated March 1920, NLI, P917 A0499; UCD AD, P7A18/286-8 + 310, and P7A22/48-52 + 77-87.

anonymous letters reaching the authorities in Dublin; but some resisted the Volunteers more openly.[27]

There was also strong pressure from family members on Dublin Volunteers to remain at home. Married men in particular experienced this and often hid their involvement. Consequently some families were unaware to what extent their relatives were mixed up in the movement. The wife of a prominent member of the Squad only discovered the true depth of his involvement when he came home after having been involved in the shootings of Bloody Sunday:

> Members of my family inquired as to where I had been and I told them I was out with the boys, fishing, as this was a practice with the local boys, and was at Mass. My wife said she had not been to Mass, and I had been thinking of going to the 11-30 Mass, the one evidently she proposed attending. Up to this point my wife did not think I was deeply involved. When I said I had been out fishing she asked me where was the fish. This remark caused me to stumble and I could not think of a satisfactory reply. In order not to give myself away, after breakfast I took the tram into town and went to the short 12 o'clock Mass in Marlboro St. [...] I lay on the couch in the room and fell asleep. I was awakened that evening about 4 o'clock. My wife came into the room crying, with a 'Stop Press' in her hand. I woke up and asked her what was the matter. Before speaking she handed me the 'Stop Press' and wanted to know was this the fishing expedition I had been on. Seeing that there was no use in concealing things any longer from her, I said 'Yes, and don't you see we had a good catch,' or words to that effect. She then said, 'I don't care

27 Attitude of street traders, Paddy Rigney, O'MN, P17b105; Joe O'Connor, O'MN, P17b105. Public indignation, particularly after the execution of Kevin Barry, and the inflated stories about the casualties after several events, Celia Shaw, Diary 1920 and 1921, NLI, ms. 23,409; C.S. Andrews (1979), 149. Burning of military goods, Pat MacCrea, O'MN, P17b110. People helping or shielding Volunteers, Pat MacCrea, O'MN, P17b110; Michael O'Reilly, O'MN, P17b115; Sean Smith, O'MN, P17b122; Ben Doyle, O'MN, P17b96; John Neary, O'MN, P17b122; Tony Woods, O'MN, P17b95; George White, O'MN, P17b105; Joe O'Connor, O'MN, P17b105; Jimmy Green, O'MN, P17b92; Charlie Dalton (1929), 163-64; Michael Lynch, 'Statement', NLI, ms. 22, 117/1; Sean Harling, in K. Griffith and T. O'Grady (1982), 159. Many people in Dublin tried to stay out of trouble and were unwilling to aid the Volunteers, Jimmy Murray, O'MN, P17b106; Moira McKee, O'MN, P17b103; Michael Noigh, O'MN, P17b128. Volunteers uncertain about attitude of civilians, Michael Lynch, 'Statement', NLI, ms. 22,117/1; Patrick O'Daly, 'Statement', NLI, P4548. Civilians wilfully trying to prevent Volunteers from acting, Harry Colley, O'MN, P17b97; C.S. Andrews (1979), 164; Jim Slattery, O'MN, P17b109; Paddy Rigney, O'MN, P17b105.

what you think about it I think it's murder.' I said: 'No, that's non-sense: I'd feel like going to the altar after that job this morning,' and thus I tried to calm her. I don't think she put out any lights in the house during the following winter. I did not stay at home then for about a week.[28]

Prior to 1921 a lot of attention was given to mobilising public support in the nationally coordinated activities of the movement. The Dáil Loan in 1919, the several strikes in 1920 and the Belfast Boycott from January 1921 received a good response in Dublin. Shops in Dublin were visited and warned not to stock goods from firms on the 'black list'. If the shops continued to do so they were fined, and if they refused to pay the fine, goods to that amount were taken from the premises. Stocks of listed goods found on railway stations and in trains were taken out and burned in all parts of the country.[29]

The only direct demand made on the population was for money. In December 1920 a General Order was issued to the Volunteers to start a collection. A leaflet was to be distributed asking the people to give generously. The example of such a leaflet accompanying this order, explicitly named the object for which the money was to be used:

A collection is being made in this area, by authority of General Headquarters of our Army, to enable me to carry on the work of arming the Volunteers in this Brigade, and so sustaining and increasing the fight waged against the enemy.

You are asked to subscribe a fair amount. It is for your own protection, as well as for the national good. The enemy forces are running loose wherever they get an opportunity. They are murdering defenceless people. They are pillaging, burning, outraging, wherever they go. Arms are needed to meet them and to beat them. Money is required to get the arms. That is the plain statement of the case. It is no Appeal. It is just a request to every man and woman who believes in Ireland to help the Army of Ireland to carry on the fight.

During the next week collectors appointed by the Officer in charge of your area will call on you.

The collection was to be made thoroughly; everybody with the exception of declared enemies was to be approached. In instructions given to the West

28 Quote, Pat MacCrea, O'MN, P17b110. Other Volunteers opposed by their family, Garmon, O'MN, P17b110; Frank Henderson, O'MN, P17b99.
29 Weekly Memo 10 dated 23 January 1921, called upon Volunteers to enforce the Belfast Boycott strictly as a big 'push' by Belfast traders to get rid of their stock was expected, NLI, ms. 900/21. Enforcement of this boycott, Tom Duffy, O'MN, P17b105; UCD AD, LA9; NLI, ms. 901/112.

Connemara Brigade it was stated that: 'Assistance from those who have the means to assist should be boldly asked for as a right, without leaving yourselves open to any great charge of threatening or intimidation.' When the brigade funds did not allow the payment of the ASU, such a partially voluntary collection was made in Dublin. A note signed by the O.C. Dublin Brigade was put in every door of a particular street, simply stating: 'You will be called on on behalf of a collection in next 5 minutes.' This collection is supposed to have raised £470, and only one Volunteer was arrested after a person who was raided rang up the police. Later collections were made without notice. The Volunteers simply knocked on every door in a particular street where they expected money, and asked for a subscription. On entering a house they would first disconnect the phones to prevent people from warning the police. Most people gave something, and rarely did they meet any hostility.[30]

CONCLUSION: REGIONAL SPREAD

Until the autumn of 1920 most Volunteers in Ireland lived at home and were mobilised only for simple IRA operations which did not involve violence. Only a tiny section of the IRA in a few areas had been willing to engage in anything more serious. Violence against the Crown Forces would put the Volunteers involved and the population in the immediate vicinity of the action at risk. Reluctant to endanger those close to them, most of the Volunteers refrained from acting. The few Volunteers who had left their home areas while evading arrest felt more free to engage in offensive actions. They considered the danger this brought to the population in areas other than their home ground to be subordinate to the cause. The first to make such a break were a few bellicose activists in the South.

In an attempt to contain the increasing conflict the authorities introduced the Restoration of Order in Ireland Act in August 1920. As a result Volunteers everywhere were forced to go on the run and make a similar break with their home ground. Initially most of these Volunteers stayed with family and friends near their homes. In this way their relationship with the community did not fundamentally change. In the few areas where men on the run broke the physical ties with their homes, by moving around and engaging in activity elsewhere, real violence developed which then

30 Continuation of the Dáil Loan until early 1921, D. O'Donoghue, O'MN, P17b90. Quote from General Order No.15 dated 3 December 1920, NLI, ms. 739. Quote from instructions to West Connemara Brigade dated 18 April 1921, UCD AD, P7A19/198. Quote from instructions in Dublin, Oscar Traynor, O'MN, P17b96. Experience of ordinary Volunteers collecting, Sean Clancy, Interview. On 9 January 1921, 16 girls between 15 and 20 years of age were seen by the police to collect at Church gates, DMP report dated 9 January 1921, PRO, WO35/71/8/117.

involved more Volunteers. In Tipperary a few men had left their homes immediately after the Soloheadbeg ambush, and during the summer of 1920 this group expanded. In Mayo this took place after the founding of Flying Columns in the early months of 1921. This followed the relative success of the measures of the Crown Forces there at the end of 1920. The high public profile of the Volunteers in Mayo had made many of them known to the authorities, making arrests more likely and forcing many to leave home after the authorities had decided to arrest all known republicans. The inability of Volunteers on the run in Wexford and Derry to separate themselves from their direct environment explains why a stage of open violence did not develop in either county.

The differences described above between the counties was largely a result of the differing extent to which the Volunteers managed to control their community. In Mayo the Volunteers had found a good response among the population in most areas from the beginning. As shown earlier, they had mobilised an extremely large proportion of the population in the organisation. As a result of this widespread support there was no need for active Volunteers to leave the home area even when they were wanted by the police. This meant that these men continued to be restrained by the fear of the consequences of violence. The disconnection between activists and their homes was forced upon Mayo activists, particularly from the towns, at the end of 1920 when police pursuit became too strong.

In the other counties Volunteers experienced more opposition from the Catholic community. In Tipperary this opposition was concentrated in the numerous towns. Even in January 1921 a military unit leaving Clonmel was played to the station by a local band and seen off by a large and cheering crowd. In the rural parts of Tipperary the IRA found more response and could silence existing opposition with violence. The high level of urbanisation and opposition to radical nationalism had forced some of the activists to go on the run at an early stage. They could function safely in the more supportive rural areas, although some violence was needed to control their opponents. The confrontational environment in Tipperary was therefore an important factor in the early radicalisation of its Volunteers.[31]

In Wexford and Derry large parts of the population in urban as well as rural areas were hostile to the movement. This made it extremely unsafe to travel around as many people were liable to inform the authorities. The lack of natural shelter in Wexford further restricted this. Although the Volunteers in Wexford had many members who also became increasingly active during 1921, the introduction of permanent Flying Columns was practically impossible. In Derry the Volunteers were too few and their support too small to allow anyone to go on the run and engage in operations without an overwhelming fear of informing. Important support for these differences between

31 Band playing in Clonmel, CI South Tipperary MR January 1921.

the five counties comes from the election results, the response to recruiting for the British army, the number of the Volunteers' civilian victims and their social and religious background. The predominantly urban background of active Volunteers throughout Ireland further confirms this.

In 1921 the link between active Volunteers and the population was broken in several areas. At the same time the nation-wide schemes of the Dáil, like the courts and the police boycott, were ended by the stronger line taken by the government under the Restoration of Order in Ireland Act, and gradually the IRA lost control over the behaviour of many civilians who were intimidated by the Crown Forces. In areas where constitutional nationalism was still well supported people resumed communication with the police and more information about the IRA started to reach the authorities. In the warlike circumstances that had developed more violence was therefore needed to ensure that the population would not inform on the Volunteers. Suggestions were made by local units confronted with this to deal severely with those cooperating with the authorities. GHQ was asked to issue orders forbidding all to aid the Crown Forces even when forced to do so. The subsequent execution of many civilians in areas like Tipperary, Wexford and Dublin in the spring of 1921 frightened the population to such an extent that cooperation with the police was significantly reduced again. However, the Volunteers still had to operate between the need to keep public support and the necessity to enforce total reliability. On the one hand, this led to attempts, often initiated by GHQ, to limit all kinds of violence. On the other hand, the need to stop informing stimulated the level of violence against civilians.[32]

The success of the movement and the level of violence directed at the Crown Forces and civilians in different areas therefore depended on two factors: its ability to organise people behind them and the capacity to deal with the opposition it encountered within the community. Each of the five chosen counties showed a different relationship between Volunteers and the community. This was largely connected with the integration of the movement in the community and the continued support for constitutional nationalism or unionism. The varying position of the Volunteers within the community resulted in the distinctly different types and levels of activity they engaged in. It is apparent that within rural Ireland the separation of Volunteers from the direct environment they grew up in was the essential step to large-scale violence and killing, the ability to do so depending on the number of Volunteers and the strength of local opposition. The looser social ties and anonymity in a large urban area like Dublin City constituted another set of circumstances in which indiscriminate violence could grow, once a sufficient level of support for it existed.

32 Changes in the attitude towards the police in Tipperary, CI South Tipperary MRs January & April 1921. Suggestions to forbid people to be commandeered to fill trenches, UCD AD, P7A18/108, and P7A20/33-34.

Summary and Conclusion

ACCEPTANCE OF A REPUBLICAN GOVERNMENT IN IRELAND

Studying patterns of radicalisation among Volunteers in Ireland between 1916 and 1921 provides us with a diverse picture. The revolutionary nationalism of Sinn Féin and the Irish Volunteers was the latest expression of a long-felt desire for independence among a majority of the Irish people. This desire enjoyed considerable sympathy from English political parties. From 1885 onwards, Home Rule for Ireland was on the political agenda of the English Liberals, but was constantly blocked by a conservative-dominated House of Lords. After the power of the House of Lords was curtailed in 1911, the political readiness of the British Government to grant some form of self-government to Ireland finally became a reality in 1912. The Home Rule Bill would have come into operation in 1914; but opposition by the Ulster Unionists and the outbreak of the First World War prevented this. The exceptional circumstances which then evolved discredited constitutional nationalism and ensured the emergence of widespread support for the revolutionary ideology of Sinn Féin and the Volunteers.

To turn the republican campaign into a success it was imperative for the movement to convince a majority of the population of the necessity and legitimacy of the growing use of violence. The Volunteer campaign of 1920-21 was indeed made possible by the spectacular change of political allegiance from constitutional to revolutionary nationalism between 1916 and 1918. The basis for this change lay in the postponement of the introduction of Home Rule in 1914. Events during the War further demonstrated the impotence and irrelevance of traditional nationalist politics. This provided radicals with an opportunity to convince nationalists of the necessity of their road to independence. The virulent British reaction to the failed rising in 1916 swayed the allegiance of many and, by identifying with popular issues such as the opposition to conscription, the republicans established themselves as the main representatives of nationalists in 1918.

After the Conscription Crisis of April 1918 the political campaign was largely aimed at making the right to an independent Ireland a reality in the international arena, notably at the Peace Conference in Versailles. However, although mobilising growing support, the international political campaign

335

for independence soon ran out of steam. None of the Allies was prepared to force the issue and allow Irish representations to be put forward at the conference. To generate new pressures on the British Government the leadership of the movement then concentrated more and more on making its alternative government a reality to the Irish population. This campaign was only temporarily successful, but the introduction of Dáil Courts, the take-over of local government, the issue of Dáil Bonds, and the establishment of a republican police force nevertheless made the republican administration a tangible fact in the life of many Irish people. This in turn strengthened the legitimacy of the call to boycott the institutions of British rule, i.e. the police, the courts, and the payment of tax. It also justified the enforcement of adherence to the alternative institutions. This form of loyalty to the Republic, particularly from nationalists, was crucial and was often enforced by the Volunteers with intimidation aimed at those who stood at the centre of community life.

Although the movement's legal claim to the existence of an independent Irish Republic was widely accepted in Ireland, the growing violence engaged in by the Volunteers had to be justified at various stages. In the preceding pages it has been shown that although the majority of nationalists supported Sinn Féin's policies in 1918, this was not a declaration of support for violence. Many of the former supporters of the constitutional nationalists had switched allegiance to Sinn Féin under pressure of the growing conflict. The violence engaged in by the Crown Forces appalled the majority of nationalists and formed an important element in the switch of support to Sinn Fein and the Volunteers. Ultimately the political campaign provided the basis for acceptance of the military campaign. It had forced many nationalists to reject the legal basis of British rule in Ireland, turning the conflict into a struggle between two states, justifying all violence engaged in by their own side. Despite the intimidation used against the population during this struggle, the IRA managed to position itself as the defender of the community against Crown Force brutality, while the Crown Forces left themselves open to being labelled as the army of a foreign power who occupied Ireland illegally.[1]

The political campaign was increasingly underpinned by a military campaign which eventually overshadowed it. The violent acts were initially restricted to a few impatient radicals who were unwilling to wait for the possible fruits of international political pressure, and who acted without their leaders' authorisation. These extremists refused to believe in a voluntary withdrawal of England from Ireland. Their grievances against centuries of British rule and their admiration for the sacrifice made by the 1916 insurgents pointed the way to violent confrontation. The two campaigns thus operated side by side during a large part of the struggle. Although creating an uneasy balance between the

1   A persuasive description of this switch in allegiance from constitutional to revolutionary nationalism, David Fitzpatrick (1977), passim.

requirements to make both a success, they reinforced the acceptance of the Dáil Government by the population. Originally favouring mobilising political support, the IRA leadership became dominated by those who promoted military conflict. The slowly increasing severity of government measures provided the Volunteers with the opportunity to convince a substantial section of nationalists to go along with them in their violent opposition to the British right to govern Ireland.[2]

However, the willingness of a section of the Volunteer membership to commit themselves to the increasingly violent acts was lost at each stage of further radicalisation of the conflict. The same applied to the support of a part of the nationalist population for this aggression. Thus the more violent the conflict became, the smaller the group of potential supporters became, and the more difficult it was for the IRA to justify further escalation both to its own members and their supporters. Such contraction of support is most clearly demonstrated by the decrease in reported membership in south Tipperary as soon as violence erupted in the spring of 1920. At the same time the potential for almost complete support was shown by the continuous growth of membership in Mayo where no serious violence took place until the spring of 1921, and the renewed growth in membership in Wexford and Derry when more non-violent activity was initiated in 1921. The requirements of violent confrontation also led to a shrinking definition of the Ireland the republicans represented, first losing Irish policemen and later all citizens who failed to conform to their picture of a fully Gaelic Roman Catholic Ireland.

The militarisation of the conflict tipped the balance in favour of the physical force party. The political campaign had to be largely abandoned as a result of the violence. The nation-wide schemes of the Dáil, were ended by the tougher line taken by the government under the Restoration of Order in Ireland Act. Gradually the IRA lost control over the behaviour of many civilians who were intimidated by the Crown Forces. The resulting threat of informing was countered with more violence against civilians; many suspected spies and informers were killed. Since the Volunteers dependent on continued support from civilians, and due to a general reluctance to kill those considered to be part of their own community, the victims of this were those who were already seen as outsiders either by their behaviour or their background, such as Protestants, ex-soldiers and travelling people. The threshold of violence against these 'outsiders' was also much lower. The civilian targets of the IRA thus changed from intimidation of core members of the community, whose support had been necessary for the success of the alternative government, to outsiders whose death functioned as a warning to any member of the community who stood in the way of the militarists.[3]

2 The accumulation of grievances against British rule, O. MacDonagh (1983).
3 The targeting of 'outsiders', Peter Hart (1992), Chapter 'Youth and Rebellion', 31.

Although radicalisation was an internal process, the Irish struggle cannot be understood without its international context. Revolutionary nationalists had frequently sought and obtained support from other countries. The Rising in 1798 had received military aid from the French Republic, and moral support from the recently independent United States, which was fervently anti-colonial. During the nineteenth century support for Irish nationalism grew further in the United States, particularly among the large Irish immigrant population. In the early part of the twentieth century the strong anti-colonial feeling in the United States was translated into the assertion of each nation's right to self-determination. This became one of the pillars of its foreign policy during and after the First World War, and provided the republican movement in Ireland with the opportunity to mobilise external pressure on the British Government.

The unrest in Ireland, combined with the strength of the Irish-American lobby, was an important factor in postponing full participation by the United States in the War, and forced the British Government to deal with the 'Irish Question'. Partly in response to American opinion, the Irish Convention was established in 1917 to draw up an all-Ireland constitution. A few days after the United States entered the War President Wilson informed Lloyd George that the only obstacle in the way of full cordial cooperation with Great Britain was its failure to find a satisfactory method of self-government for Ireland. However, once the USA was fully committed to the War, it was neither able nor willing to dictate a solution to its ally. The failure of the Irish Convention did not cause any repercussions, and despite the acceptance of a resolution calling for Irish self-determination by the American Congress in March 1919 the British Government managed to avoid any discussion of this 'internal affair' at the Peace Conference. The lack of willingness in American government circles to force this issue upon an ally was partly a result of the collusion between Irish rebels and Germany in 1916. This had come about through Irish-American mediation and discredited the revolutionary nationalists in the USA.[4]

American pressure upon England to cease waging a 'savage' war upon the Irish, as well as unfavourable international opinion, were nevertheless important factors in the success of Irish republicans in forcing Britain to grant Ireland a large measure of independence in 1921. The eventual willingness of the British Government to come to an understanding with the Irish rebels was, however, no fundamental change of policy from the Home Rule Bill prepared by the Liberals in 1912. The fact that Britain was not prepared to wage a full-scale war against the IRA seemed to have been the main reason for the attempt to find a peaceful solution. This apparent republican victory set an example for many other nationalist movements in

4   Influence of American opinion on Irish affairs, F.M. Carroll (1978), Chapter 4-5, passim.

British colonies and elsewhere. The drive towards Irish autonomy had always had wider implications for the British. They feared that granting such autonomy would fuel a similar desire in all British colonies, and would thus affect the entire make-up of the Empire. After 1921 the Irish experience began to function as an important touchstone for the British Government, as well as for nationalist organisations in the colonies. In the decolonisation process, partition has also been used in a number of other areas as an often unsuccessful solution to ethnic and religious tensions. The most notable example of this strategy can be found in the Indian subcontinent and in former Palestine. The further development of the Commonwealth into an association of independent states paved the way for many other nationalist movements in the colonies to gain an acceptable form of independence without breaking all ties with England. Finally, the military experience of the IRA has become one of the first examples of a guerrilla movement which gained political success in modern times, and has therefore functioned as a point of reference for guerrilla organisations throughout the twentieth century.[5]

We have seen that Sinn Féin and the Volunteers were successful in winning the political battle with Britain, forcing it to give a substantially larger measure of independence than intended in 1912. However, the movement failed to settle its differences with the unionists. Neither did it manage to win the hearts of all Irish nationalists. The repercussions of its failure to convince the unionists of their good intentions, exacerbated by the increasingly brutal treatment of Protestants during the War of Independence and the subsequent Civil War, led to the institution of Northern Ireland and the violence which has continued to characterise it ever since its creation in 1921. The failure to preserve unity within the movement over the treaty with Britain in 1921 was to some extent a resurfacing of the differences between constitutional and revolutionary nationalists of the nineteenth century. Politics in southern Ireland since the end of the War of Independence has been dominated by the controversy between those who were willing to accept a compromise and those nationalists who were radicalised by the polarisation during the struggle and refused to settle for anything less than complete independence. These differences led to the Civil War in 1922–23 and continued to divide politics in southern Ireland for many decades after the Treaty. The decrease in support for the use of violence, which had set in during the final phase of the War of Independence, continued after 1923. The remaining revolutionary republicans nevertheless continued to form an extremely visible section of Irish society.

5   The lack of willingness in the British Government to wage full-scale war in Ireland in 1921 has recently been uncovered in the release of government papers, *The Irish Times*, 29 & 30 December 1993. The use of partition in the British decolonisation policy, T.G. Fraser (1984).

THE CAUSES OF VIOLENT CONFLICT

The use of violence was a crucial element in the success of the republican movement. A number of questions relating to the growing willingness to engage in this have been dealt with in the foregoing pages. The central point of attention was the identification of general trends within the various forms of radicalisation which occurred among the members of the Irish Volunteers. The study of a wide range of circumstances has also enabled the distinguishing of factors which could account for the widely differing levels of violence throughout Ireland, testing the validity of those put forward by other authors and formulating alternatives.

We have seen that so far historians have been unable to provide a comprehensive explanation for the differentiated development of violence. It has been argued here that a number of psychological and social mechanisms can account for this. These include the importance of a threshold of violence, the localised attempts to ostracise the police from the community who thereby became legitimate targets of physical attack, the importance of outsiders in the organisation and the development of violence, and the link between leaving the familiar setting of work and home life and the level of violence individual Volunteers engaged in. Furthermore, in the final part of the struggle GHQ played an important role in initiating the use of violence in some of the inactive IRA units.

The main driving forces behind the escalation which took place after 1916 were the Volunteers' attempts to obtain arms, the reaction of the Crown Forces to their operations and the indiscriminate government policies to quell the upsurge in defiance and violence. In order to become a viable military threat to British rule after the failed rising of 1916, the Volunteers had to obtain large numbers of arms. For this purpose some members began to collect arms with vigour shortly after the re-establishment of the organisation in 1917. Few could be bought, so the Volunteers were forced to turn to raiding civilians and members of the Crown Forces. Although these raids were not part of a general attack on the Crown Forces, the small number of engagements resulting from them set in motion a process of escalation. Obtaining arms in this way became increasingly difficult as the government took counter-measures which restricted the possession of arms, forcing the IRA to attack barracks and the strengthened patrols of police and military. Eventually even these avenues to obtaining arms were closed and a military stalemate established itself in 1921. A more vicious type of violence then became mainstream in active areas.

The initial willingness to collect arms by increasingly violent means was strengthened by the radicalisation of activists after 1916. The authorities' policy of imprisoning the ringleaders and all others who publicly defied them failed to subdue these men, who had gained the admiration of their peers. During two years of political resistance, often with the explicit object of getting arrested, many of these activists became reluctant to undergo further incarceration and were prepared to defend their freedom with force. They then became increasingly involved in military preparations, adding to the spiral of violence.

The violent reaction of the Crown Forces to the initially small-scale IRA operations and public defiance has been recognised as an important element in the escalation of the conflict in 1920. David Fitzpatrick has recently identified it as the overriding cause: 'The rapid intensification of violence after 1919 was largely caused by the disorganization and savagery of the "occupying" forces.' The violent reaction of the Crown Forces, which was often prompted by their frustration regarding the inability to convict the perpetrators of attacks upon them or their comrades, was mainly directed at the original activists and their families, but could affect everybody. This form of state violence antagonised both the population generally and those Volunteers who were directly affected by it. Peter Hart has characterised the feelings of revenge on both sides as the main motivating force behind the escalating violence. The resulting familiarity with the use of physical force amplified the developing spiral of conflict between the Crown Forces and a limited number of radicals. The violence engaged in by the Crown Forces also created widespread support for Volunteer operations and thereby involved more Volunteers in the conflict.[6]

The indiscriminate policies of the government sometimes restrained the development of the Volunteers temporarily, but often augmented the long-term strength and aggression of the movement. The growing though spasmodic severity of the government's measures alienated the population and transformed the Volunteers into a successful guerrilla force. The persecution of radical nationalists after the Rising, and the proposed introduction of conscription were two of the main causes for Sinn Féin's success at the polls in 1918. The banning of republican organisations and the punishment of entire districts after the first acts of violence further alienated the local population from the government. The abandonment of police barracks in 1919-20 gave Volunteer units free reign in rural areas, which were often disorganised by the strong line taken by the government after the Conscription Crisis. The radicalisation of Volunteers was intensified by the large-scale arrests and the subsequent release of many leading Volunteers in early 1920. Fitzpatrick recently reiterated how the introduction of the Restoration of Order in Ireland Act in August 1920 led to the formation of the Flying Column, and involved many more people in conflict: 'The slide towards terrorism was largely precipitated by increasingly brutal repression, which forced armed Volunteers to "go on the run" and band together for

6   Quote, David Fitzpatrick (1989), 250. See also Charles Townshend (1983), 350; Peter Hart (1992), Chapter 'The Dynamics of Violence', 52, 69, 87 + 107-09.

protection. After reintroduction of massive internment under the Restoration of Order in Ireland Act (August 1920), these groups began to crystallize as "flying columns" plotting pre-emptive ambushes against "enemy" parties.' Swaying government policy thus polarised the conflict.[7]

DIFFERENTIATED RADICALISATION

One of the main causes for the wide variation in levels of activity and violence was the lack of central coordination in the initial phases of conflict. This meant that the impetus for the military campaign depended on local activists who were ready to act without authorisation from the national leadership. Charles Townshend has emphasised the significance of this: 'The sporadic opening of the campaign of violence was a function of wide local variations in organizational strength and attitude.' He added that GHQ had no means of enforcing activity, and that the performance of IRA units in 1920-21 depended entirely on the initial impetus in 1918-19: 'thereafter no amount of prodding from above could spur on slow starters to make up lost ground.' Although we have seen that this assessment is not entirely correct, the first impetus was indeed exceedingly important in inducing the use of violence.[8]

In all selected areas a cadre of radical nationalist activists was present long before the establishment of the Irish Volunteers. Most of them had joined the IRB shortly after 1910. These men seized the opportunities presented by the turmoil which followed the preparations to introduce Home Rule and the 1916 Rising to establish themselves as the leading political grouping. Their prison experience in 1916 radicalised them and gave them sufficient local standing to command support. However, only a minority of activists, heavily concentrated in the South, began to engage the police after 1916. The important role of widespread support and active leadership first became apparent with the start of open drilling in 1917, which was one of the first signs of defiance. This was centred in areas such as Dublin, Tipperary and Mayo, with little taking place in Wexford and Derry. This early defiance eventually led to further radicalisation in these areas. After the Conscription Crisis the most bellicose among the leading activists feared that the success of the political campaign would push the military campaign into the background. This fear inspired them to initiate a number of attacks on the Crown Forces. Such men were more numerous in the South. Their

7   Government measures leading to widely supported guerrilla struggle, Peter Hart (1992), Chapter 'The Dynamics of Violence', 107-9; David Fitzpatrick (1977), 216-17. Quote, David Fitzpatrick (1989), 249. For effects of punishment of districts, Ibidem, 250.
8   Charles Townshend (1979), 321-2.

uncoordinated activities ultimately resulted in the development of a full-blown guerrilla campaign in these areas and also brought about the spread of violence throughout the country.[9]

The initiative to engage in violence taken in some localities set in motion a process in which action and reaction led to a spiralling severity of conflict. The self-sustaining nature of conflict thus allowed for ever-increasing differences, even after GHQ sanctioned the use of violence. Support for the importance of the first impetus comes from the strong correlation between early activity of the Volunteers and the propensity of violent confrontation in 1920-21. The consequences of early activity can be best illustrated by looking at the personal experience of those arrested in 1916. Every time something illegal of a political nature occurred in their area after their release the police harassed them or their family. This continued attention augmented their radicalisation. As a result the original centres of organisation often remained the focus of activity in the War of Independence. Although the IRB became less important after 1916 and some of the early activists dropped out of the organisation, the original cadre would dominate the violence in many places. The radicalisation process thus affected only a small part of the adherents of revolutionary nationalism.[10]

An important obstacle to the diffusion of violence was the presence of a high threshold which had to be overcome before people were willing to shed blood. Although a small number of radicals was often sufficient to set an escalation in motion, only in an odd individual did the experience of conflict during the period of defiance erode this psychological barrier sufficiently, by growing personal feelings of anger, frustration and revenge, to make killing possible. Furthermore, the overwhelming desire for self-preservation remained an important factor in containing the level of violence and limiting its extension from the core areas of conflict. Sporadic attempts to alleviate the dearth of arms set in motion a spiral of conflict in some areas, but this deficiency also limited the use of violence in other areas.

Some physical force was nevertheless used by most units during 1919, but this new direction was only seriously pursued in 1920 by the Volunteers in counties like Tipperary and Dublin. Although a lack of willingness and courage pervaded the ranks of the Volunteers everywhere, some places became involved in growing violence while others were paralysed. In the preceding pages it is argued that two crucial factors in overcoming the threshold of violence and making the transition to military conflict were the

9 The fear among militarist to be sidelined by the political campaign, Charles Townshend (1979), 320-1; Peter Hart (1992), Chapter 'The Dynamics of Violence', 42-3, & Chapter 'The Rise and Fall of a Revolutionary Family', 22; David Fitzpatrick (1977), 215-16.

10 Correlation between early activity and later violence, David Fitzpatrick (1978), 122. Peter Hart has showed that this correlation was strong but did not always exist, Peter Hart (1992), Chapter 'The Dynamics of Violence', 87.

ostracisation of the police from the community, and the separation of active Volunteers from the restraining hand of that same community. The importance of these developments has been indicated by other authors, but a comparison of how the extent to which these developments had taken place influenced the level of violence has not been undertaken before this.

The separation of the police from local communities provided the Volunteers with 'legitimate' targets. This segregation had two main causes. As a result of the conflict, which resulted in the abandonment of many outlying barracks, a physical separation between police and community took place in many areas at the end of 1919. At the same time the ostracisation of the police from Irish life became a conscious policy of the Volunteers. After a process of ignoring, warning, threatening and shunning, those who remained in the police were pushed out of the community. In this process of mental separation the police were transformed from valued members of the community to hostile outsiders who were acceptable targets of attack, politically as well as psychologically. Some of the most actively anti-republican policemen were then killed to set examples and eventually all members of the Crown forces became acceptable targets. Nevertheless, few Volunteers actually engaged in this type of violence. In many areas, the ostracisation of the police never began, failed or was not yet concluded. As a result the local police were not considered to be legitimate targets or only those who were overtly anti-republican were attacked. Even in areas where the police had become outsiders, many were willing to attack patrols and barracks from a distance, with the clear likelihood of casualties on the other side, but refused to kill captured and imprisoned enemies, either military or civilian. This was left to a small elite of hardened fighters concentrated in the Flying Columns.[11]

The successful ostracisation of the police was a precondition for open violence, but whether an area actually became engaged in it depended on the Volunteers at local level. The relationship between activists and the community played an important part in the emergence of radical organisations and the development of violent conflict. It has been demonstrated that outsiders played an essential role in the establishment and extension of the organisation, both before and after the Rising. Outsiders played a similar role in the growth of violence. The great majority of Volunteers were sensitive to the restraining influence of their direct environment. They were often prevented from engaging the Crown Forces by the fear of the consequences for their family and friends, or by an active attempt by influential members of the community to contain activity. As a result the transformation from defiant action to shooting enemies was most easily made and completed by those who had broken the physical ties between themselves and the community in which they had grown up. The importance of the lifting of the

11 Ostracisation, David Fitzpatrick (1977), 106-11.

restraining hand of the community was first indicated by David Fitzpatrick. In the preceding pages we have seen that it was an essential step in the development of violent conflict. The measure to which Volunteers actually severed these ties accounts for the varying levels of violence in the selected counties. Only Volunteers who had gone on the run, often after initial involvement in operations, engaged in further violence and started a cycle of escalating conflict.[12]

The main activists and officers in south Tipperary were some of the few examples of Volunteers who left their work and homesteads in 1919. This freeing from the constraints of communal life meant that these men felt free to engage in violent attacks, irrespective of the consequences for others. A high level of support from the local population and a general refusal to cooperate with the police were necessary to sustain their operations for a considerable period. However, even these men had to go through a lengthy process to overcome the high threshold of violence. Due to injury and time spent in Dublin, it took about a year after their forced break before the Tipperary officers again initiated attacks on the police in their home county. This was facilitated by the change in GHQ's policy in January 1920 when it sanctioned the use of violence against the Crown Forces, particularly aimed at barracks. The operations of these men involved and stimulated many other Tipperary Volunteers who were often forced to leave home as well, thus establishing a large pool of men with some fighting experience who could become more involved.

Within provincial Ireland the separation of Volunteers from the direct environment in which they grew up was the essential step towards large-scale violence and killing. The introduction has dealt with some of the reasons which have been suggested to account for the differing extent to which this break was made. David Fitzpatrick has dealt with Erhard Rumpf's proposition that the absence of Flying Columns was a reflection of a lack of demand for this from among the local Volunteers. Rumpf argued that rebels on the run rely for their survival and success upon general support for their struggle and general disparagement of opponents and potential informers, and that the level of revolutionary violence in each district was thus associated inversely with the power of economic interests or political traditions setting the people against the practice of guerrilla warfare. We have seen that this can indeed account for the lack of activity in areas like Wexford and Derry, where economic ties with Britain and opposition to the use of violence by nationalists were traditionally strong. It also explains the propensity to violence in Tipperary, where economic ties were

---

12 David Fitzpatrick (1977), 218. The importance of the restraining hand of the home community had long been realised by the British Government, who had forbidden policemen to serve in their own county or a county where close relatives lived.

weak and a strong tradition of violence prevailed. However, it fails to explain the long-standing inactivity of a county like Mayo with similarly weak economic ties and a long legacy of violent agitation. Rumpf's arguments to explain this are discounted by Fitzpatrick, while evidence for Fitzpatrick's suggestion that police efficiency in Mayo could account for this has recently been found inconclusive by Peter Hart.[13]

Tom Garvin has suggested a socio-political cause for the predisposition of Volunteers in the South over those in the West to become engaged in violent activity after 1916. On the basis of the experience of nationalist resistance movements in the nineteenth century, he has linked the level of violence to the detrimental impact of capitalist change on the pre-industrial middle-class of artisans and farmers in relatively prosperous areas. These groups resisted the growing competition from industrial products for their artisanal and cottage industry with most fervour. He has also argued that below a certain material level no IRA activity could be sustained. Peter Hart's findings that IRA activity in Co. Cork thrived in more urbanised areas with better land and was hampered by poverty and physical isolation support this assessment. However, the socio-economic background of Volunteers found by Hart and the inconclusive proof for downward economic pressure on artisanal and cottage industry in Munster disclaim it. Conversely, one could argue that the recent sale of land to tenants in Connacht, which improved the standard of living and gave hope for an increased standard of living in the future, dampened the general willingness to risk the consequences of violence. Although Garvin's arguments thus cannot be unequivocally supported or disclaimed, its general approach fails to explain the way the process of radicalisation took place in individuals. The question to be answered here is under what circumstances did active Volunteers leave their domestic existence and start to engage in violence.[14]

In the preceding pages it is argued that, provided there was a substantial group of radicalised activists present, the balance between the measure of support for and opposition to revolutionary nationalism was a decisive factor in initiating this break. The presence of local adversaries actually intensified the development to violence in certain circumstances. Activists from places where republicanism was less popular were more likely to radi-

---

13 Discussion of Rumpf's ideas, David Fitzpatrick (1978), 117-18. See also Charles Townshend (1983) 368-71. Assessment of correlation between Volunteer activity and police efficiency, Peter Hart (1992), Chapter 'The Dynamics of Violence', 85. The tradition of violent nationalist activity in an area as precursor of action, H. van der Wusten (1977), 288; David Fitzpatrick (1978) 117-21 + 137; Tom Garvin (1981) 124.

14 Impact of capitalist society, Tom Garvin (1987), 6-8. Economic threshold, Tom Garvin (1981), 124-5. IRA activity in Co. Cork, Peter Hart (1992), Chapter 'The Dynamics of Violence', 84. Background Volunteers, Peter Hart (1992), Chapter 'Volunteers', 29-31.

calise through confrontation with their political opponents and the police, and were more likely to go on the run as a result of the danger of informing. In the South political opposition to the Volunteers was stronger than in the West and largely concentrated in the more numerous towns and villages, and came from both within the population as well as from the larger garrisons of Crown Forces. When coinciding with extensive support in rural areas, like in Tipperary, the mainly urban activists, who were driven from their homes, could operate in relative safety in the countryside. The large number of such radical activists and the continued possibility of informing forced these men to form Flying Columns to ensure their freedom. In this view, radicalisation was the consequence of the actions of determined activists and the level of opposition they encountered. The stronger financial position of the Volunteers and their supporters in the South over those in the West may have facilitated the ability to leave home and become fully involved in Volunteering. However, the fact that Mayo Volunteers also left home later on discounts this.

The different levels of support for the movement in the selected areas have been demonstrated by the success of the police boycott, the adherence to the institutions of alternative government, the public demonstrations of support for the republicans and the election results. Support was much stronger in rural than urban areas, and it increased farther away from Dublin and Belfast. The low level of urbanisation and the westerliness of Mayo thus ensured an extremely high level of support for revolutionary nationalism. In highly urbanised Tipperary we have witnessed the presence of strong opposition in the towns and solid support in the countryside. In Dublin and Wexford the population was politically more divided, while in Derry opposition to republicans was general. The widespread support for revolutionary nationalism in the West was connected with a lesser acceptance of British rule in these areas. The mental distance between the British Government and its Irish 'subjects' was considerably greater in rural and western areas than in urban and eastern areas. Economic independence, a high number of Irish speakers, few Protestants, and poor recruitment figures for the British Army are main indicators of this.

The fact that Volunteers in Tipperary were most easily radicalised is thus a result of the level of local opposition which was particularly prevalent in the numerous towns. The extensive loyalty to revolutionary nationalism and the low level of policing in predominantly rural counties such as Mayo blocked the separation of activists from the community. There was only a small group of radicalised activists in Mayo who avoided their homes, most of whom also came from the towns. However, most of these men did not engage in the use of violence and were able to continue to work or travel the countryside without fear of detection. Yet, as a result of government policy, they were also eventually forced to form Flying Columns. The small number of radicalised activists and the general opposition to the use of violence in Wexford and Derry, combined with unfavourable geo-graphical features, made going on the run exceedingly dangerous and accounts for the absence of Flying Columns there. In Wexford small groups of Volunteers on the run were indeed also observed by the police in 1921, but they were unable to form a permanent column. In Derry only the city provided the confrontational circumstances in which a small num-ber of activists were forced to go on the run. Due to the small number of republican sympathisers they were however also unable to remain in the city and transferred their operations to the rural areas in Donegal where support from the local population was extensive. The large urban area in Dublin with widespread support for republicanism provided an alternative set of circumstances where radicalisation took place, and where operations could be safely carried out.

The initial concentration of IRB activists in towns and the continuous opposition they experienced there thus explain the prominence of urban backgrounds among Flying Column members and arrested Volunteers found by Peter Hart. The lesser urbanisation in Mayo was therefore an important aspect in the weaker impetus to the campaign of violence. Hart also argued that the relative decline in urban membership in Leinster and Ulster in the latter part of the struggle was linked with their inactivity. The correlation between violent conflict and the level of policing further supports this argument.[15]

The relative dominance of outsiders, either recently migrated or sent down by GHQ, which we found among active Volunteers again indicates the importance of a lack of emotional ties with the local population for the development of violence. However, the socialising aspect of Volunteering was also extremely important to men who had recently come into a com-munity. The more impersonal setting of large cities, which attracted most migrants, and the importance of socialising to all urban members is also demonstrated by the narrow age bracket of the Volunteers in Dublin.

THE SPREAD OF CONFLICT AND THE ROLE OF GHQ

The interaction of the elements discussed above accounted for the differen-tiated development of radicalisation and resulted in the widely varying levels of violence in Ireland. We have seen that radical nationalists were active in most areas prior to 1916. Varying numbers of these men were arrested in 1916. Imprisonment improved their local standing and strengthened their resolve to further the cause of Irish freedom. The willingness to defy the police openly after the release of these prisoners was largely concentrated in Munster, Connacht and Dublin City, where the movement could rely on

15 Peter Hart (1992), Chapter 'Volunteers', 22-3 + 28; Tom Garvin (1981), 124-5.

extensive support. The arrest of men leading illegal drilling parties and raiding for arms set in motion a radicalisation which led to escalating conflict. The growth of confrontation was continuously checked by the problematic step towards the use of violence. This barrier was overcome in some areas after a polarisation between Crown Forces and the local community had resulted in the ostracisation of the police.

The concurrent denial of the legitimacy of British rule turned all members of the Crown Forces into potential targets of attack. Successful ostracisation was most likely to evolve in areas of solid support where the population was relatively united in their opposition, such as rural areas in the South and West. The final step that had to be taken before widespread violence would emerge was the separation of active Volunteers from their workplace and domestic responsibilities. Going on the run was most likely in places where localised opposition to republicanism from civilians and the Crown Forces was strong and where many Volunteers had been radicalised during the period of defiance. Such circumstances were prevalent in the South. The violence eventually spread to other areas, partly as a result of a similar but later escalation, but mainly as a direct consequence of the conflict in the South, notably by direct intervention of GHQ who attempted to activate other units, and through the indiscriminate policies of the British Government to curtail lawlessness. The evacuation of police barracks and the introduction of the Restoration of Order in Ireland Act in particular forced many well-known Volunteers in inactive areas to go on the run and make the break, eventually leading to the emergence of some violence in these areas.

Radicalisation was an individual as well as a collective process, and took many shapes and forms. The driving force was formed by the attempts to obtain arms which brought active Volunteers into growing conflict with the Crown Forces. The reality of conflict gave it a self-perpetuating and increasingly violent nature. The unbridled extension of conflict was constrained by the high threshold of violence and the influence of the home community on activists. This threshold was lowered by labelling certain sections of the community as enemies. After the police, Protestants, ex-soldiers and travellers were so labelled they became legitimate targets. The restraining hand of the community was lifted by leaving home and work. This was prevalent among activists in the South, where a concentration of Crown Forces, strong internal opposition in urban areas, and large support in a countryside provided favourable circumstances. The fact that more of these activists were financially able to become full-time Volunteers may be an additional factor.

Although self-preservation was the overriding characteristic of most combatants on both sides, violence continuously escalated and became increasingly widespread. This was largely a result of the interaction of Volunteer activities, Crown Force violence and government policies. Minor engagements could develop into cycles of tit-for-tat violence between Crown

Forces and bellicose Volunteers. Most of these were cut short or died a natural death when the main protagonists on either side had been eliminated in some way. However, within these cycles of conflict a small group of Volunteers radicalised to such an extent that they were willing to leave home and become full-time soldiers. They then extended operations to other parts of their brigade area. These operations and the often harsh reaction of the Crown Forces then involved other Volunteers in these places and often sparked off new cycles of violence. In this way violence spilled over from one locality to an adjoining district, causing conflict in an ever-widening area. At the same time the example given by Volunteers in active areas, together with the indiscriminate government policies and the emotional response Crown Force violence aroused in non-participants elsewhere, initiated some operations by Volunteers in all parts of the country. This could then again lead to an eruption of new cycles of violence. Conflict could thus be transplanted from active to inactive areas without direct involvement of experienced radicals. Together with a growing familiarity with bloodshed and an increasing lack of targets which made conflict more vicious, these developments ensured a continuously growing level of violence within Ireland, despite occasional successes of the Crown Forces.

The role of GHQ in these developments has often been underestimated in recent historical writing. Charles Townshend has stated that Volunteer companies never entirely accepted the hierarchical control implicit in the term 'Army', and although a certain level of central control was established in the final part of the struggle through the process of military professionalisation, the most substantial function of GHQ was one of political propaganda. David Fitzpatrick has identified the existence of a certain understanding between GHQ and the local units in which: 'Headquarters provided advice, instruction, a little equipment and a welcome sense of national togetherness. In return provincial units accepted the dismissal and appointment of commandants, provided the families of local importance were not seriously inconvenienced; and to some extent they modified their military activities to accord with headquarters' preferences.'[16]

Although the Volunteer leadership was indeed hesitant in allowing the use of violence and unable to introduce a regular army style discipline, the threat of violence was always an integral part of their policy which could be taken up by individual members. The hesitancy of the Volunteer leadership stemmed from a fear that the use of violence would lose them support both at home and abroad. As we have seen, this left the development of violent conflict in the hands of local radicals. The refusal of GHQ to control and coordinate the unfolding of conflict allowed the considerable variation in levels of violence and activity to emerge. Nevertheless the major increase in

16 Quote, David Fitzpatrick (1977), 208-9. Charles Townshend (1983), 334-7, and
   (1979), 336.

engagements and casualties which followed GHQ's sanction of violence in 1920 is a clear indication of its influence over local units.

Although they experienced several set-backs, GHQ managed to obtain a measure of control over the radicalisation and institute an increasing professionalisation of the organisation by taking up military developments in active units and introducing them in others. Without GHQ's controlling influence violence could have become an object in itself, as it did for some Volunteers who abused the power they had gained to further their own interests. Contrary to Townshend's assessment, GHQ was also able to increase involvement in inactive areas, such as Wexford and Derry in 1921. By concentrating its attention it could stimulate local Volunteers to become increasingly involved in non-violent operations. Getting engaged in killing was again a difficult step to take for the great majority of these Volunteers, and was hesitantly stimulated by GHQ. More violence might have evolved in these areas as a result of the dynamics of conflict as seem to occur in Derry in July 1921, but the Truce prevented this.[17]

The lack of central control was a consequence of the tension between the movement's claim to represent an independent Irish Government with a regular army and local realities. From the period of reorganisation in 1917 onwards an important section of the Volunteer Executive attempted to create a regular army in line with its view of itself as the legitimate Government of Ireland and the Crown Forces as the invaders of the country. Peter Hart has indicated that arms were initially seized in anticipation of open conflict, and that among the leadership visions of a second rising persisted well beyond the end of the Great War. However, a regular army structure was impossible to implement as the reorganisation was not initiated by central command but the result of initiative of local activists. Similarly, violence was begun by extremists within the organisation without the official sanction of the leadership. Charles Townshend has shown that the style of warfare which developed was created by the slender resources of the Volunteers, rather than by a conviction that it held any hope of ultimate success. The localised and haphazard development of conflict and GHQ's failure to sanction violence until 1920 meant that an extremely independent attitude developed in many active units, which resulted in a form of conflict based on local initiative and mobile fighting groups which we now know as guerrilla warfare.[18]

---

17 Role of GHQ, Charles Townshend (1983), 332-7. Role of GHQ in initiating activity, Charles Townshend (1979), 322.
18 Peter Hart (1992), Chapter 'The Dynamics of Violence', 36-7. Charles Townshend (1979), 320-1.

Guerrilla struggle was thus the unplanned consequence of the profession-alisation of a small but substantial and influential part of the Volunteers under the pressures of confrontation and the influence of often ill-directed government policy and Crown Force brutality. The lack of central control combined with the hesitant approach of GHQ provided some of the ingre-dients which allowed local radicals to make the military campaign a success. Nevertheless GHQ played an important role in extending operations after 1919. The struggle for control between local Volunteer officers and the IRA leadership was never satisfactorily settled, but the local freedom to ini-tiate operations, combined with GHQ's ability to regularise the organisation and develop general tactics, did provide the necessary conditions in which a small group of radicals could force the start of military conflict while cen-tral command was able to extend this to other areas.

The question whether the IRA could have successfully continued its campaign after July 1921, has been a bone of contention in and outside the organisation ever since the Truce. Many top Volunteers thought that the forced disbanding of many Flying Columns in the spring of 1921 witnessed the end of the Volunteers' military challenge. In their view the IRA was unable to continue and they felt forced to accept the terms of the Treaty which were negotiated during the Truce of 1921. However, it can be argued that further escalation was more likely than these men thought. The increasing activity in places like Wexford and Derry and the continued growth of casualties among the Crown Forces in all areas after the end of the Flying Column in the South indicate a vitality contradicting the nega-tive assessment of many members of GHQ. A large elusive and ruthless fighting force, capable of threatening British authority even further, could have established itself.

The potential for the development of a willingness among a section of the population to use force against the authorities is present in many his-torical situations. Whether this development actually takes places depends on the conjunction of a number of circumstances of which we have encountered one particular example, and although the conditions in which such a radicalisation can take place vary widely we can still see many of the radicalising elements which existed in the first two decades of this century at play in Ireland today.

Social Composition of the IRA

The main aim of this analysis is to determine the background of the people who joined the IRA, and how they differed from the general population. To do this I have compared some characteristics of the entire membership of a number of chosen Volunteer companies to the characteristics of all males who lived in the company area concerned.

The absence of addresses and the greater mobility in cities and larger towns made a detailed analysis of urban membership impossible. However, although active members, particularly those in Mayo, had a predominant-ly urban background, the larger part of the rank and file in the provinces was rural. The choice of rural companies for analysis therefore gives a representative picture of ordinary IRA membership in relatively active areas.

This analysis is made on basis of membership lists for July 1921 drawn up in the early 1930s. The nature of the lists used presents two major problems in determining the social background of the IRA mem-bers. The first is a direct consequence of the date at which these lists were compiled. Drawn up in the 1930s, they had to be collated with the census records of 1911. This meant that, particularly in areas with a higher social mobility, it has been impossible to retrace all members and obtain a full match between list and census. However, the farming back-ground of the majority of members ensured that a large proportion of them had continued to live in the same place. The number of men in each company who could not be traced with reasonable certainty in the 1911 census records are enumerated in Table 14. The second problem was establishing the exact borders of company areas. Parish boundaries soon proved to be unsatisfactory guidelines, and only the rough borders could be established. Taking these problems into account the results given below can only be seen as indications rather than absolute figures.

In south Derry only the pensions list of the Belagherty Company could be traced; but a list of all active members of this and the New-bridge Company was obtained. For the Belagherty Company, the latter differed on several points from the pension list. This was partly because the active-members list included some battalion officers and members of nearby outposts, and also because some inactive members were added to

the pension list. To allow for these differences, the pension list is included as Belagherty, and the active members list as Belagherty 2.

For the occupation and date of joining of the Dublin IRA, I had to rely
on lists of two extremely small companies of the 4th Battalion. These lists
provide little information, and to make a useful comparison for occupation
and developments over time, the full membership of the Second Battalion
of the South Dublin Brigade has been added. This brigade was founded
shortly before the Truce and was based on the 6th Battalion of the Dublin
Brigade. It comprised the harbour town of Dun Laoghaire and most of the
small villages around it. For the age and occupation of Volunteers in
Dublin City, figures for the IRA in the Dublin District compiled by Peter
Hart have been used. Due to his basis of compilation, an over-representation of active members is unavoidable in these figures.[1]

AGE

The first aspect treated here is the age of Volunteers. In Table 14, the
percentage of the members of the selected companies in age-groups of ten
years is given. The most interesting age-groups, 20-24 and 25-29, are indicated separately. The total membership of each company and the number
for whom an age could not be traced, are given in the first two columns.
The latter have been disregarded in all further calculations. Looking at this
table, the first thing catching the eye is the large disparity in the number of
members per company, ranging from 15 to 165, which might be compared
with the preferred size of 100 members per company. Mayo clearly stands
out for the large size of its companies, Tipperary takes a middle position.
Wexford and Derry in particular had extremely small companies. The figures for Dublin show the findings from a sample of active Volunteers from
all units of the Dublin Brigade divided between officers and rank and file,
and do not relate to one particular unit. This explains the absence of unknowns.

The Volunteers in Mayo and Tipperary had the biggest range of ages.
Aughagower Company tops this with members from 13 to 71 years of
age. The oldest member was a RIC pensioner who had a son in the company and possibly only fulfilled an advisory role. Generally, the largest
percentage of members was aged between 20 and 24 years. Especially in
Wexford and Derry, the 20-29 category dominated the companies. In

---

1   The figures for Dublin relate to the Dublin District area, which include the
     suburbs of Rathmines, Blackrock etc. and is roughly co-terminus with the
     Dublin Metropolitan Police District, Peter Hart (1992).

Mayo there was a tendency to join at an even younger age.[2] The dominance of the young is particularly apparent in Dublin City. In Killenaule and Newbridge companies, Volunteers were somewhat older. For Killenaule this is borne out by the highest average age. This could have something to do with the fact that Killenaule Company was dominated by a large village. Although few IRA members came from the village itself, it provided work for adult men from the countryside who were generally older. In Newbridge the IRB members who joined around 1911 dominated the small company. This in contrast with Belagherty Company, which was organised after the Rising.

Table 14: Ages of IRA members as a percentage of the Company in 1921

	Total	Unknown	10-19	20-24	20-29	25-29	30-39	40-49	50+
Owenwee	68	9	31	25	47	22	19	3	0
Aughagower	165	8	29	22	35	13	22	8	5
Moyglass	68	24	27	24	35	11	24	9	5
Killenaule	35	11	8	17	38	21	38	17	0
Laffansbridge	56	4	31	31	46	15	15	8	0
Crossabeg	17	1	0	63	76	13	19	6	0
Glynn	28	3	16	28	52	24	24	4	4
Adamstown	65	13	23	27	48	21	25	4	0
Belagherty	28	3	24	36	60	24	8	8	0
Belagherty 2	23	1	23	50	73	23	0	5	0
Newbridge	15	2	15	31	70	39	8	8	0
Dublin Officer	-	11		18			19	2	1
Dublin Men	-	20		68			9	2	0

A final observation is the small appeal the IRA had to men over 30 in Derry and Dublin. It has been established that older IRB members in south Derry were left out of the Volunteers after the Rising. I have attributed this to the higher risk IRA members ran in the more hostile environment in Ulster. The traditionally strong support for the Ancient Order of Hibernians among older people in the North provides a further explanation. In Dublin the IRA was less integrated in society, initially mainly providing a leisure activity for young men. The wide age-range in Mayo and Tipperary indicates a better integration of the IRA into rural life.

To gauge the appeal of the IRA to the different age-groups, the number of

2   The youthfulness and the large age range of the members in Mayo is confirmed by police reports of drilling in 1917, File marked 'Midlands and Connacht District', PRO, CO904/122.

Volunteers in each age bracket is compared with the total number of Catholic men in that age bracket living in the company area. In Table 15 the percentage of each age-group that joined the IRA in the different counties is indicated for the chosen companies. The total number of Catholic men in each age-groups is based on the census of 1911.

To give a more exact indication of the appeal of the IRA, only Catholics are included. The disparate numbers of Protestants living in the selected areas would distort the figures. The three Protestant members of the IRA, two in Tipperary and one in Wexford, are not included in these mobilisation figures. The few IRA members under 15 and over 60, confined to the companies in Mayo, are also excluded.

It must be realised that, as indicated in Table 14, not all ages of company members could be traced. The percentages provided can therefore only be tentative, and only apply to these relatively active companies. The mobilisation figures in these companies are much higher than those for the entire counties provided in Table 12. This is due to a number of factors. Firstly and most importantly the fact that males under 15 and over 59 are excluded. Secondly the choice of companies all of which concern particularly active parts of the respective counties. Mobilisation was distinctly lower in urban areas excluded from this analysis. Thirdly the fact that the lists were drawn up to establish people's right to a pension ensured a certain amount of exaggeration. Finally these assessments are based on the IRA's own lists while the figures in Table 12 are based on police figures, which include only those people who publicly exposed their membership in 1921. The figures nevertheless provide a useful indication of the proportion of males within each age-group who joined the IRA in the relatively active parts of these counties. Unfortunately, it has been impossible to make a useful similar comparison for Dublin.

Two conclusions emerge from these figures. First the extremely high grade of organisation in Mayo in all age-groups, bringing 34 per cent of all Catholic men between 15 and 60 into the IRA. Aughagower Company stands out with a more than 50 per cent level of mobilisation in all groups from 15 to 40. In Tipperary, Laffansbridge and Moyglass Company have a level of organisation that exceeds Owenwee's company in Mayo in the age-groups under 25. Killenaule, however, had a comparatively insignificant level of organisation, especially in the lower age-groups. This probably has to do with the same factors indicated with Table 14. The hostile environment in Derry and the resulting need to operate in secret were added factors in the low level of mobilisation there, which have been discussed before.

Another prominent feature is the appeal the organisation had to men of all ages. Tipperary and Mayo show the highest mobilisation in younger age-groups, while in Wexford and Derry the Volunteers' appeal is concentrated among those in their mid-twenties. The fewer older members in Wexford and Derry, and to a lesser degree Tipperary, is a measure of the acceptance of the organisation by the communities there. It has become apparent that the IRA in rural Mayo stood at the heart of the community. This was somewhat less strong in the rural areas in Tipperary. In Wexford and Derry, where the penetration of the IRA in the different age-groups rarely exceeded 10 per cent and was more concentrated among the young, its role was a more peripheral one.

Table 15: The proportion (in percentages) of males living in selected company areas who were members of the IRA in 1921, in six age-groups

Age:	15-19	20-24	25-29	30-34	35-39	40-59	Total
Mayo	43	38	38	31	36	12	34
Tipperary	17	20	13	12	9	3	13
Wexford	7	16	10	9	4	1	7
Derry	5	8	7	2	1	1	4
Derry 2	5	9	7	1	0	1	4

OCCUPATION

Next we look at the occupation of the Volunteers, as a percentage of those in the company and as a percentage of all men in that occupation. As the data for most members dates from 1911, the occupations used for most young members are those of their fathers. To a certain extent this therefore represents a measure of their personal assessment of their social position rather than their true occupation in 1921.

The labourer category in the provincial brigades consists mainly of farm labourers. The small artisan category includes skilled workmen and tradesmen. The merchants category consists of shopkeepers, dealers and commercial traders. The section 'Others' incorporates mainly teachers, civil servants and fishermen. Teachers featured strongly in the rural areas, while fishermen are confined to the coastal companies in Wexford and Derry. The Glynn Company had three, the Crossabeg Company two, and the Newbridge Company also two. Under the heading 'Sample' the percentage of each unit's members for which the occupation was available is indicated: for total membership see Table 14.

From Table 16 it is clear that the IRA in Mayo was entirely dominated by farmers. The dominance of farmers is to a lesser extent true for Derry and Wexford. The larger farms in Tipperary with a substantial need for labourers explains the almost equal representation of farmers and labourers there. In most companies some artisans, merchants, and others, mainly fishermen and teachers, were also included.

Table 16: Occupation of IRA members in Percentages

	Farmer	Labour	Artisan	Merchant	Others	Sample
Owenwee	97	0	3	0	0	88%
Aughagower	95	4	0	0	1	97%
Moyglass	55	31	8	4	2	75%
Killenaule	43	39	7	7	4	80%
Laffansbridge	50	39	7	0	4	96%
Crossabeg	47	18	6	6	24	100%
Glynn	44	32	8	4	12	89%
Adamstown	67	21	4	2	7	92%
Belagherty	69	27	4	0	0	93%
Belagherty 2	78	17	4	0	0	100%
Newbridge	71	0	0	14	14	93%

The urban setting of Dublin provides a completely different social make-up, in which farmers naturally do not figure. In Table 17 the occupation of the 1921 members of two small city companies and of the entire membership of the 6th Battalion is compared to a sample taken by Peter Hart from the active membership in the capital. The last two groups are divided into officers and rank and file. The category of low or semi-skilled labourers includes general labourers, gardeners, dairy workers, porters, messengers, vanmen, and dockers, either working or unemployed. The skilled labourers category in the city includes carpenters, bricklayers, hairdressers, smiths, mechanics, van and motor drivers, etc. The white-collar workers include clerks, shop assistants, civil servants, bookkeepers, agents, etc. The professionals category includes doctors, accountants, etc. The merchants include shopkeepers, dealers and traders. The others category includes a gas company official, a tram conductor, a water inspector, a fireman, a bank guard, a farmer, an engine driver, some railway employees, and, almost incredibly, a criminal investigator in the police.

Although the IRA in Dublin drew its support mainly from the lower and lower middle classes, a distinct difference can be detected between the social status of officers and rank and file. Men employed as labourers in particular, but also white-collar workers, were over-represented among the rank and file. On average Dublin officers were drawn from a higher social stratum, with relatively few labourers and a high proportion of white-collar workers, while skilled labour, professional and shopkeepers were also better represented among officers than among the rank and file. The urban membership of the IRA thus reflected the social divisions in that society.

Table 17: Occupation of IRA members in Dublin District in Percentages

| | Labour | | White- | | | | | Sample |
	Low	High	Collar	Proffes.	Merchant	Student	Others	Size
City	19	26	44	4	4		4	27
6th Off.	5	30	45	5	5		10	20
6th R&F	49	23	19	0	1	1	9	172
Officers	27	23	32	9	6	1	2	86
R&F	46	23	18	2	3	3	4	507
1926 Census	36	30	15	5	5	2	3	

Table 18 provides a picture of the proportion of the different occupational categories which joined the IRA in the provincial areas. To provide the clearest picture of the group to whom IRA membership appealed most (Catholics of military age), the Catholic Volunteers in the selected company areas are compared to all Catholics living in the selected areas in the age-group 15 to 40. In the first column all farmers of military age who lived in the area are numbered. In the second column the percentage of these who had joined the IRA is indicated. Similarly, this is done for the other occupational groups. In this way the under or over-representation of each category in the IRA is shown. Thus the higher the percentage of a category which joined the IRA, the greater its relative representation.

Table 18: The proportion (in percentages) of each occupational group living in selected company areas who were members of the IRA in 1921, for the age-group between 15 and 40

| | Farmer | | Labourer | | Artisan | | Merchant | | Others | |
	Total	% IRA	Total	% IRA	Total	% IRA	Total	% IRA	Total	% IRA
Mayo	452	40	11	54	6	33	0	0	5	20
Tipperary	258	24	353	12	54	15	29	14	35	11
Wexford	432	13	433	5	37	11	7	29	42	26
Derry	347	7	214	3	37	3	15	13	41	5
Derry 2	347	7	214	2	37	3	15	13	41	5

The most important conclusion to be drawn from this is that the IRA everywhere had roughly twice as much appeal to farmers as to labourers. Only in Mayo were labourers better represented; however, their numbers there were so small that this was hardly significant. The 11 labourers of military age living in the area of the two Mayo companies together formed less than 3 per cent of the number of farmers. An over-representation of farmers over artisans is significant in all areas, but somewhat less apparent. The merchants are the best organised group in Wexford and Derry and also figure strongly in Tipperary; but again this concerns only small numbers of people.

The high mobilisation of 'others' in Wexford and Derry is explained by the presence of fishermen. In Wexford this accounts for nearly half of the member from this category (5), and in Derry all (2). Furthermore, teachers also featured strongly among them. In total, 6 of the 11 non-fishermen in this group from all areas together came from a teaching background. Three of these were brothers who had a labourer as father and a teacher as mother. The other 3 were part of a total of 8 teachers and their sons, giving a mobilisation of 54 per cent among teachers.

Generally IRA membership appealed to all sections of society apart from the most well-to-do, and disproportionately least to the lowest social strata. Labourers had on the whole probably less time for such activities, and were perhaps economically too dependent on the larger farmers to join the IRA. Contrary to the image of the IRA portrayed by its enemies as people with no stake in the country, the IRA clearly appealed more to people who did have a stake in the country, if not necessarily the largest.

WEALTH

Although not always the highest mobilised group, farmers thus formed the bulk of IRA members in all provincial areas. To assess to whom the IRA appealed most, or to see how the 'stake in the country' of the members of a farming background compared to the stake of all Catholics listed as farmers or as farmers' sons, we look at the level of mobilisation in the IRA among groups of farmers who possessed holdings which were roughly equally valued; in cases of farmers' sons, the value of their father's holding is taken. This indicated their relative wealth, as a local property tax was struck as a percentage of this valuation. Tables 19 and 20 show the proportion of all farmers living on similarly valued holdings which joined the IRA. These percentages are calculated by comparing the number of farmers and farmers' sons in the IRA living on a holding valued at a certain level with all the farmers and farmers' sons in the company area living on such holdings. Again only Catholics who worked as farmers or were farmers' sons in the age bracket 15 to 39 are included. Examining this group, which consisted of men most likely to join, provides the clearest picture of the profile of people to whom the IRA appealed most, and does not really differ from that of the males in the age bracket 15 to 60.

The valuation system used was related to the fertility of the land and consequently to the possible income of the farmer who owned it. It does not, however, directly reflect the income of the farmers concerned. This depended on the way they used and improved the land. Although revisions of the valuation were periodically made, many of them were based on out-dated assessments. Nevertheless, these figures do provide a measure of their relative wealth and income within the community as unreasonable local differences were likely to be contested. The figures relate to the valuation of the land they possessed, and differences in the value of the buildings on their land have generally been disregarded. As explained, the value of the land is taken whether the Volunteer concerned was the head of the family or the farmer's son. The social status the latter experienced growing up is taken as equal to that of his father, and in some cases the sons would actually have inherited the farm between 1911 and 1921. The valuation bands used for Mayo are much smaller than those for the other counties, as the land in Mayo was much poorer and the holdings relatively small.[3]

Table 19: Percentage of People who lived on Equally Valued Holdings Mobilised in the IRA in Mayo

£-Value	1-2	2-3	3-4	4-5	5-6	6-7	7-8	8-9	9-10	10-20	20+
Mayo	13	28	43	58	35	33	57	50	38	38	15

The results for Mayo demonstrate that 'below average' farmers, whose land was valued at around £4, were more likely to join the IRA than the poorest. A dip in representation appears among those whose land was valued at around £6, and another peak occurs at values around £8. After £9 the relative percentage of IRA membership drops again. Although no explanation for this spread can be suggested, it can be assumed that the poorest farmers were, like labourers, too busy earning a living to join the IRA, while those with a little more appeared to possess the time and resources to engage in this type of activity. The wealthiest part of the farming community was financially more depended on the economic ties with Britain, and had probably more to gain from preserving the status quo. A possible explanation for the two-peak phenomena could be that those just beneath the wealthiest might aspire for more and therefore view membership of the

3 The valuation and ownership of land is recorded for each townland separately. I have tried to trace all the land that was owned locally by the people living in that area. However, as the name of the owner and previous owners were the only indicators of identity it has not always been possible to make certain who owned it. Also it is possible although generally unlikely, that families owned land further afield in parts of the county I have not checked. This would however mainly apply to the wealthier classes who are already identified as members of the highest earning class on basis of the value of their homes.

IRA as a way to fulfil that aspiration, while the middle group wanted to go up in status but were at the same time restrained by their fear of going down. Their main interest might have been to maintain the status quo.

Table 20: Percentage of People who lived on Equally Valued Holdings Mobilised in the IRA

£-Value	0-5	5-10	10-15	15-20	20-25	25-30	30-35	35-40	40+
Tipperary	4	55	38	9	24	20	33	50	13
Wexford	6	21	13	11	24	19	17	0	9
Belagherty	3	6	17	7	20	17	100	33	0

In the other areas the average value of the holdings was considerably higher. The high percentage of farmers who joined the IRA in Tipperary, when compared with Wexford and Derry, is evident. Nevertheless, mobilisation in Derry[4] is relatively high, reaching a level similar to Wexford among those with higher valued holdings. A comparable two-peak phenomena as in Mayo is apparent in all areas. In Tipperary there is one peak around valuations of £10 and another around £35. The importance of the second peak is somewhat deceptive, the small number of farmers with holdings valued between £35 and £40 considering, only 6 in the 3 companies together. Nevertheless, this indicates a similar trend.

With small adaptations, the position is similar in Wexford: few rich or poor farmers and modest peaks around £10 and £25. Belagherty in Co. Derry shows a smaller two-peak effect, one between £10 and £15 and one for the higher bands. Again few small farmers joined, but unlike the other areas a clear over-representation of richer farmers is noticeable. A total of 28 per cent of the eighteen farmers with holdings of more than £20 had enrolled. However, few Catholics in Derry possessed holdings with such a high value, which makes clear conclusions problematic. Nevertheless, the image of the IRA in Derry consisting of independent farmers is confirmed by their relative wealth.

CHANGES IN SOCIAL COMPOSITION

Having established the social composition of the IRA in 1921, we can now look at its development over time. Unfortunately, except for Mayo and Dublin, there is only incidental information available about the date of join-

---

4   Unfortunately, collating the valuation records with the 1911 census in Newbridge Co. Derry presented insurmountable problems in obtaining a reliable picture.

ing the Volunteers. In Owenwee those joining in 1917 are compared with those enlisting in 1918-19 and in 1920-21. The measure in which the recruits from a farming background differed in the value of the holdings they came from is used as an indication of the changing type of recruit. Non-farmers are too few for conclusions to be drawn from the time they joined. In 1917 the overall two-peak phenomenon is again noticeable, but at a somewhat higher level at £5 and £9, instead of £4 and £8. In the period 1918-19 only nine farmers or farmers' sons joined, while the two-peaks shifted downwards to £3 and £7. For the final period 1920-21, when serious military action began, it is obvious that poorer rather than richer farmers joined in Owenwee. This indicates that poorer farmers, like labourers, were less inclined to join when membership was considered a 'luxury', while they were less inhibited to join when life and possessions were at stake.

In Aughagower a different set of years are compared, due to the nature of available information. Most pre-Rising IRA members came from higher middle income men, with holdings around £8. A couple of poor farmers were also involved, but none from holdings with a higher value. Those who joined between 1916 and 1918 came disproportionately from three valuation bands, around £3, £7 and more than £10. In the period 1918-21, farmers from all groups joined with a peak around £4 and £9. The different periods used for Aughagower makes a comparison with Owenwee difficult. However, the strong growth among the richer farmers in the period 1916-18 in Aughagower can be partly accounted for by the higher average valuation and does not alter the conclusions drawn above. Despite recruitment coming from all income groups, it is remarkable that all seven labourers in the Aughagower Company joined in the final period, thus supporting the conclusion that poorer farmers only joined when something real was at stake.

The small companies in Dublin City for which the date of enrolling is known reveal one clear tendency. The organisation originated mainly among skilled labourers, but became more popular with the lower working class when hostilities began. A similar pattern shows itself for the suburban and small town area of the 6th Battalion, later South Dublin Brigade. I have used the occupations of the entire membership, officers and rank and file. When compared to the size of occupational groups in the Dublin City area in the 1926 census the following emerges. The organisation was set up disproportionately by skilled and white-collar workers, professionals and shop assistants. After 1916 few professionals, merchants, students and others joined. The main groups attracted to membership were semi- or unskilled labourers and white-collar workers. Shop assistants joined mainly in 1919, while skilled labourers were somewhat below average in numbers.

Looking at the date of joining of the battalion officers separately (numbering 20 in 1921) there are 6 white-collar workers, 6 skilled workers, 3 shop assistants, 1 labourer, 1 shopkeeper, 1 professional, a railway investigator and 1 without work. A clear relative dominance of white-collar workers, and to a lesser extent of skilled labourers, appears. The professional was the only officer with pre-1916 experience, illustrating the traditional picture of 1916 men as poets and scholars. After the Rising skilled workers were the first among future officers to join, with men from the other groups joining from 1918 onwards. White-collar workers mostly joined at the height of the fighting; many of them soon became officers.

The general figures for the IRA in Dublin City, favouring active members, present a similar picture. Among the rank and file the relative position of skilled workers declines sharply after 1919, while the relative position of the other groups remains substantially the same. The unskilled or semi-skilled labourers were always over-represented among the rank and file. Both groups of labourers are under-represented among the officers, who show an over-representation of professionals. The importance of social standing in the election of officers is indicated by the absence of professional rank and filers. The late growth in membership from the lower social strata in Dublin confirms the conclusions drawn for the provincial areas concerning the lack of their representation there. However, the increase in the relative strength of the lower classes in Dublin could also be a result of middle-class members dropping out when hostilities started.

OTHER CHARACTERISTICS

In Table 21, I test the assumption that it was less likely for a first-born farmer's son to become involved in the IRA because it would endanger his inheritance. The figures show that this is untrue. Except in Wexford, the number of first-born is roughly equal to the number of other sons. In areas where the IRA stood more in the centre of communal life – rural Mayo and in parts of Tipperary – first-born sons were not prevented from joining. Apparently first-born were more restricted in Wexford than elsewhere; this ties in with the position of the IRA as a peripheral organisation. They also experienced more opposition from the AOH, which was popular among older people, many of them parents of Volunteers. However, the figures for Derry, where the organisation had an even more peripheral position, contradicts this. This confirms a difference between Wexford and Derry suggested before. In Wexford the Volunteers were peripheral but acted in the open, while in Derry the IRA had to act in secret, thus making it less vulnerable to family pressure. One conclusion can be drawn from the difference between the official Belagherty Company list and the active members list; first-born sons were less likely to engage in active operations. In this way the assumption considering first-born is strengthened.

Table 21: Percentage of First and Later Born sons from farming
background in the IRA

	First-born	Second or Later	Unknown
Mayo	41	46	13
Tipperary	35	29	36
Wexford	28	45	27
Derry	40	44	16
Derry 2	32	58	11

Another distinct characteristic that came to the fore during my research was the large number of IRA men whose father was absent when they joined. Of the 8 veterans I spoke to in Mayo, 5 had no father alive at the time, while 2 of the other three stressed they had a politically radical father or mother. In Tipperary the 3 young farm labourers that I talked to lived on the farm where they worked without any parental control. The fathers of 2 main organisers in south Tipperary, Seán Treacy and Dan Breen, were also dead. In Table 22 the IRA members who were living independently, or whose father was absent in 1911, are recorded. One has to bear in mind that in the following 10 years this percentage must have grown. The significance of these figures as an indicator of parental control is lessened by the fact that many of the members of these companies were older and already economically independent by 1911.

Table 22: Percentage of socially independent IRA members

	Independent	Dependent	Unknown
Mayo	22	72	6
Tipperary	38	47	15
Wexford	34	55	11
Derry	21	72	7
Derry 2	18	79	3

Notable is that in Tipperary and Wexford the number of independent Volunteers is significantly higher. This partly confirms the lesser integration in communal life in these areas. However, Tipperary having the highest level of independent members contradicts the conclusion that it was better integrated in the community than Wexford. This might be explained by the higher number of labourers in Tipperary, who worked and lived independently from an early age. In Derry and Mayo most members were farmers, explaining the low level of economically independent members.

Some poor farmers' sons worked on their father's land as well as for larger farmers, but unlike labourers they often lived at home.

Besides working and living away from home, the mortality rate among labourers seems to have been higher than that among farmers, ensuring the presence of fewer fathers of the labourers' class. This is borne out when the absolute numbers of labourers and farmers of advanced age are compared with their younger counterparts, and becomes even more apparent when looking at those older than 60. In Moyglass the number of farmers and labourers in the different age-groups was roughly equal, but in the over 60s category the labourers are less than half the number of the farmers – 33 to 68. In Laffansbridge, labourers are an obviously larger group among the age-groups under 40. Between 40 and 60 they are equal in numbers, but among those over 60 the farmers are 75 strong against 41 labourers. In the different areas in Wexford and Derry the same tendencies are observed. Alternatively, high emigration among labourers who were over 60 in 1921 might account for this.

When comparing the number of independent members with the size of the occupational groups in the IRA, the picture becomes blurred. Laffansbridge Company in Tipperary, for instance, with the lowest percentage of independent Volunteers, has a high percentage of labourers. The Mayo companies and Adamstown in Wexford, the other companies with a low percentage of independent Volunteers, however, have low numbers of labourers.

Despite this, the high level of independent Volunteers leads to the conclusion that the presence of a father as a figure of authority and control had a dampening effect on young men's enthusiasm to join the IRA. The comparatively low percentages in Mayo and Derry are a consequence of the position of the IRA in these counties. In Mayo they stood at the centre of the community, while in Derry they worked in secret. The high level in Tipperary contradicts an integrated position in rural Tipperary. However, the large number of labourers in their ranks offers a possible explanation for this. Nevertheless, when considering the peripheral position of the IRA in Wexford, the smaller number of labourers cannot entirely account for the lower level of independent Volunteers there.

A final aspect of the IRA traced here is the percentage of members with a brother or father active in the IRA. A high level of family involvement becomes apparent from Table 23. In Mayo and Derry this was strongest. The high level of organisation in Mayo – over 40 per cent in the age-group between 15 and 20 – inevitably leads to this. In Derry the confinement to family can be explained by security reasons and by the strong link between membership of a particular family and political allegiance. The connection between family politics and membership, which was supposedly strong in Wexford as well, is not borne out by the figures. However, in the Cushingtown Company, 21 out of 32 members in 1917 had brothers in the company. In Tipperary the percentage was higher in the two country companies and significantly lower in the Killenaule Company. This again reflected the social composition of this company, with a higher percentage of labourers, who were more likely to live or work separated from their families. This is also supported by the figures for the Second Battalion of the South Dublin Brigade, where the overall percentage of men with an active brother in the same company is 26 per cent. Again the high number of independent-living labourers in Dublin would be the cause of a clearly lower (but still significantly high) level of active brothers. Generally, the undoubted importance of relatives in organising the IRA is shown by these figures. It can be concluded that having an active family member was an important, but not a deciding reason for joining the IRA.

Table 23: Percentage of IRA members with an active Brother

	Active Brothers	Inactive Brothers	Unknown
Mayo	58	36	6
Tipperary	38	48	14
Wexford	36	59	5
Derry	51	47	2
Derry 2	55	42	3

Bibliography

I: UNPUBLISHED PAPERS

National Archives, Dublin (formerly the Public Record and State Paper Offices)
RIC Crime Branch Special Papers; Dáil Éireann Papers; Census 1911; Sinn Féin Funds Case

National Library of Ireland
Dr F.S. Bourke Papers; Collins Papers; Joseph McGarrity Papers; MacKenna-Napoli Papers; Edward MacLysaght Papers; J.J. O'Connell Papers; Florence O'Donoghue Papers; Sean T. O'Kelly Papers; George Noble Plunkett Papers; Dr Dorothy Price Papers; Several loose statements and collections relating to the IRA

Military Archives, Dublin
Papers Relating to the War of Independence

Trinity College, Dublin, Manuscript Room
Frank and Cecilia Gallagher Papers; J.R.W. Goulden Papers

University College, Dublin, Archives Department
A-Company 1st Battalion Dublin Brigade IRA. Concise history of the company's activities during the years 1916-1922; Elizabeth Bloxham Papers; Ernest Blythe Papers; Margaret Burke and Fr Thomas Burke Papers; Con Moloney Papers, concerning the Second Southern Division; Richard Mulcahy Papers; Ernie O'Malley Papers, including Ernie O'Malley Notebooks

Irish Valuation Office, Dublin
Valuation Lists

Public Record Office of Northern Ireland
Several loose items relating to 1916-1921

Imperial War Museum, London
Jeudwine Papers, Includes 'Record of the Rebellion in Ireland in 1920-21 and the part played by the Army in dealing with it', and 'History of the 5th Division in Ireland, November 1919-March 1922'; Lt. Gen. A.E. Percival Papers, two lectures on 'Guerrilla Warfare - Ireland 1920-21'; Several memoirs of British Soldiers who served in Ireland between 1916-1921

Public Record Office, London
   War Office Papers; Colonial Office Papers; Home Office Papers

Wexford County Library, Wexford
   T.D. Sinnott Papers

Wexford County Museum, Enniscorthy
   Several items and diaries relating to 1916 and later

Tipperary County Library, Thurles
   Statement by Sean Gaynor; I.R.A. Intelligence Notes

Tipperary County Museum, Clonmel
   Several items relating to the IRA and the Dáil Courts

Heritage Library, Derry City
   Oral History Project

Clew Bay Heritage Centre, The Quay, Westport
   Papers relating to Westport Battalion, West Mayo Brigade owned by Jarlath
   Duffy, Carrowholly, Westport

Mayo County Library, Castlebar
   Several items relating to the IRA

Archdiocese of Armagh, Records Centre, Armagh City
   Fr O'Kane Papers

Killenaule Community Project - Teamwork (Local History), Killenaule
   Papers relating to South Tipperary Brigade

II: UNPUBLISHED SOURCES MENTIONED IN THE NOTES

'Activities list A-Company New Ross', in possession of James Doyle, New Ross
'Activities list Cushingstown Company', in possession of Andy Roe, New Ross
'Activities list Owenwee Company', CBHC
'Activities list Dualla Company', in possession of John Hassett, Cashel
Chambers, James (also known as Brod), 'Statement', in possession of Michael
   MacEvilly, Dublin
Gaynor, Sean, 'Statement', Tipperary County Library
Heavey, Thomas, 'Statement', in possession of Michael MacEvilly, Dublin
Hughes, Michael, 'Statement', in possession of Michael MacEvilly, Dublin
Kelly, J., 'One of the Men of the West', CBHC
Kettrick, Thomas, 'Statement', CBHC
Kilroy, Michael, 'The Awakening', CBHC
Kilroy, Michael, 'ASU Operations', CBHC
Lambert, Bob, 'Statement', in possession of Bob Lambert (son), Wexford

Maher, Rev. M., [Diary] 'Annals 1910-1926', St Patrick's College, Thurles

McCan, Pearse, 'Arbour Hill. Three Months in England's Prisons', in possession of Frank McCan, Dualla

Moane, Edward, 'Statement', in possession of Michael MacEvilly, Dublin

Moane/Malone, [Tape], Moane, Brigadier E., and Malone, Vice Comdt. B., 'Transcript of tape recordings made in Dublin by the above in January 1967' (Transcribed by Michael MacEvilly - Dublin 1983), in possession of Michael MacEvilly, Dublin

Moran, M., 'With Michael Kilroy during Easter Week 1916 and the years before', CBHC

Morrissey, Peter, 'Memoirs', in possession of Peter Morrissey (nephew), Rosegreen

Mugan, Patrick Owen, 'Statement', CBHC

Mulcahy, Paul, 'Statement', in possession of Sean Hassett, Cashel

Murphy William, 'Statement', Killenaule Community Project - Team Work (local history).

O'Donnell, Jim, 'Recollections based on the diary of an Irish Volunteer 1898 to 1924', CBHC

O'Dwyer, Eamon (O'Duibhir), 'Statement' (in two parts), Tipperary County Museum

Philben, John Joe, 'Statement', in possession of Michael MacEvilly, Dublin

Roe, Edward, 'Statement', in possession of Andy Roe, New Ross

Ryan, Patrick, 'Statement', Killenaule Community Project - Team Work (local history).

Ryan, Lt. Col. Tommy, [Statement] 'One Man's Flying Column. The Story of South Tipperary Column No.2', Tipperary County Museum

Stafford, Thomas, 'Statement of the Activities of Thomas Stafford 1916 to 1923', in possession of Bob Lambert, Wexford

'Statement of Michael Kilroy's Wife', CBHC

Video, 'Memories of the Third Tipperary Brigade', commissioned by Third Tipperary Brigade Old I.R.A. Commemoration Committee, December 1986, original footage in possession of John Hassett, Cashel

III: INTERVIEWS WITH VOLUNTEERS AND RELATIVES

From Derry: Liam Brady, Derry City; Gerry Doherty (The Bird), Derry City; John Lagan, Limavady; Patrick Larkin, Magherafelt; John James McGee, Belagherty; Paddy Donnelly, Maghera.

From Dublin: Martin Bell; Sean Clancy; James Henry; Ned Prendergast.

From Mayo: Thomas Conroy, Neale; Luke Gilligan, Taugheen; Thomas Heavey, Dublin City; Charles Hughes, Lankill; Tom Maguire, Cross; Patrick Owen Mugan, Cloonskill; Edward O'Malley, Owenwee; J.P. Quinn, Ballyglass; Dan Sammon, Murrisk.

From Tipperary: Mrs May Davin, Loughtally, Clonmel; Jack Gardiner, Callan, Co. Kilkenny; Patrick Hunt, Moglass; William McGrath, La Paloma, Cahir; Paul Merrigan, Golden; Jack Moloney, New Inn; Matt Morrissey, Newcastle, Co. Dublin; Ms. Elizabeth Plant, Moyglass; Frank Purdue, Cashel; Mike Purdue, Rosegreen.

From Wexford: Ned Colfer, New Ross; R. Dunphy, New Ross; Jim Fahardy, Gorteens; Martin Kennedy, Duncannon; William Parle, Clover Valley; John Quinn, Wellington Bridge; Mrs Bridie Quirke, Hayestown; Andy Roe, New Ross; Philip Tobin, Kilmacoe; Peter Wall, Newbawn

IV: NEWSPAPERS AND PERIODICALS

The Capuchin Annual; The Coleraine Chronicle; The Derry Journal; The Derry People and Donegal News; The Free Press; Irish Bulletin; Irish Independent; The Mayoman; The Nationalist (Clonmel); The People (Wexford); Tipperary Historical Journal; Tipperary People; Tipperary Star; An tÓglach.

V: BOOKS, ARTICLES AND THESES

Andrews, C.S., *Dublin Made Me: An Autobiography* (Dublin/Cork 1979)

Augusteijn, J., 'The Importance of Being Irish. Ideas and the Volunteers in Mayo and Tipperary', in Fitzpatrick D., (ed.), *Revolution? Ireland 1917-1923* (Dublin 1990)

Baker, J., *My Stand for Freedom. Autobiography of an Irish Republican Soldier* (Westport 1988)

Barry, T., *Guerrilla Days in Ireland* (Dublin 1949)

Béaslaí, P., *Michael Collins and the Making of a New Ireland*, 2 Vols. (Dublin 1926)

Beckett, J.C., *The Making of Modern Ireland, 1603-1923* (London 1966)

Bennett, R., *The Black and Tans* (London 1970)

Bonner, B., *Derry an Outline History of the Diocese* (Dublin 1982)

Bowden, T., 'Bloody Sunday - A Reappraisal', *European Studies Review*, II. No.1 (1972)

Bowden, T., 'The Irish Underground and the War of Independence 1919-1921', *Journal of Contemporary History*, VIII. No.2 (1973)

Bowden, T., 'The IRA and the changing tactics of terrorism', *Political Quarterly*, XLVII (1976)

Bowden, T., *The Breakdown of Public Security. The Case of Ireland 1916-1921 and Palestine 1936-1939* (London 1977)

Boyce, D.G., *Englishmen and Irish Troubles: British Public Opinion and the Making of Irish Policy, 1918-1922* (London 1972)

Boyd, D.G. (ed.), *The Revolution in Ireland 1879-1923* (Basingstoke 1988)

Breen, D., *My Fight for Irish Freedom* (1981)

Brennan, M., *The War in Clare, 1911-21* (Dublin 1980)

Brennan, R., *Allegiance* (Dublin 1950)

Brennan-Whitmore, W.J., *With the Irish in Frongoch* (Dublin 1917)

Brewer, J.D., *The Royal Irish Constabulary: An Oral History* (Belfast 1990)

Briscoe, R., *For the Life of Me* (London 1958)

Browne, C., *The Story of the 7th. A Concise History of the 7th Battalion Cork No. 1. Brigade I.R.A. from 1915-1921* (n.d.)

Butler, E., *Barry's Flying Column* (London 1971)

Butler, T.C., *A Parish and its People. History of the Parish of Carrig on Bannow* (1985)

Carroll, F.M., *American Opinion and the Irish Question, 1910-23* (Dublin 1978)

Carroll, F.M., *The American Commission on Irish Independence 1919. The Diary, Correspondence and Report* (Dublin 1985)

Casey, J., 'Republican Courts in Ireland, 1919-1922', *Irish Jurist*, V (1970)

Casey, J., 'The Genesis of the Dáil-Courts', *Irish Jurist*, IX (1974)

Colmcille, Fr, 'Tipperary's Fight in 1920', *The Capuchin Annual* (1970)

Coogan, O., *Politics and War in Meath, 1913-1923* (privately published 1983)

Coogan, T.P., *Michael Collins* (London 1990)

Costello, F., 'The Republican Courts and the Decline of British rule in Ireland', *Eire-Ireland*, XXV Vol. 3 (1990)

Counahan, G., 'The People Backed the Movement 1920', *Capuchin Annual* (1970)

Cronin, S., *Kevin Barry* (The National Publication Committee, n.d.)

Dalton, C., *With the Dublin Brigade 1917-1921* (London 1929)

Davis, R., 'The Advocacy of Passive Resistance in Ireland, 1916-1922', *Anglo-Irish Studies*, III (1977)

Davis, R., 'Ulster Protestants and the Sinn Féin press 1914-1922', *Eire-Ireland* XV Vol. 4 (1980)

Davitt, C., 'The Civil Jurisdiction of the Courts of Justice of the Irish Republic', *Irish Jurist*, III (1968)

Deasy, L., *Towards Ireland Free: The West Cork Brigade in the War of Independence, 1917-21* (Cork 1973)

Dublin's Fighting Story 1916-21 (Tralee 1949)

Evolution of a Judicial System under the jurisdiction of Dáil Éireann 1919-1921

Figgis, D., *Recollections of the Irish War* (London 1927)

Fitzpatrick, D., *Politics and Irish Life 1913-1921: Provincial Experience of War and Revolution* (Dublin 1977)

Fitzpatrick, D., 'The Geography of Irish Nationalism, 1910-1921', *Past and Present*, LXXVII (1978)

Fitzpatrick, D., 'Ireland Since 1870', in Foster, R., *The Oxford Illustrated History of Ireland* (Oxford, New York, 1989)

Fitzpatrick, S., *Recollections of the Fight for Irish Freedom and of the part played therein by the 3rd (South) Tipperary Brigade Irish Volunteers, more colloquially "I.R.A." as from the Spring/Summer of 1920* (privately published n.d.)

Foster, R.F., *Modern Ireland 1600-1972* (London, New York 1988)

Fraser, T.G., *Partition in Ireland, India and Palestine, theory and practise* (London 1984)

Garvin, T., *The Evolution of Irish Nationalist Politics* (Dublin 1981)

Garvin, T., 'Priests and Patriots. Irish separatism and fear of the Modern', *Irish Historical Studies* (1986)

Garvin, T., 'The Anatomy of a Nationalist revolution: Ireland 1858-1928', *Contemporary Studies in Society and History* (July 1986)

Garvin, T., *Nationalist Revolutionaries in Ireland, 1859-1928* (Oxford 1987)

Gaughan, J.A., *Austin Stack: Portrait of a Separatist* (Dublin 1977)

Gevers, A.M., *De Ierse Paasopstand van 1916: politieke bedoelingen, vermogens en gelegenheid* (Amsterdam 1987)

Gleeson, J., *Bloody Sunday* (London 1962)

Gough, Gen. Sir H., 'The Situation in Ireland', *Review of Reviews*, LXIII (Feb. 1921)

Greaves, C.D., *Liam Mellows and the Irish Revolution* (London 1971)

Greaves, C.D., *The Irish Transport and General Workers' Union. The Formative Years: 1909-1923* (Dublin 1982)

Griffith, K., and O'Grady, T., *Curious Journey: An Oral History of Ireland's Unfinished Revolution* (London, Melbourne, etc. 1982)

Hart, Peter, 'The Irish Republican Army and its Enemies' (PhD. thesis, Trinity College, Dublin 1992, in the references the page numbers of a draft are used)

Hennessy, P., *Davidstown Courtnacuddy (A Wexford Parish)* (1982)

Hindley, R., *The Death of the Irish Language, a qualified obituary* (London 1990)

Hobson, B., *A Short History of the Irish Volunteers, 1913-1916* (Dublin 1918)

Hogan, D., (pseud. F. Gallagher), *The Four Glorious Years* (Dublin 1953)

Holt, E., *Protest in Arms. The Irish Troubles 1916-1923* (London 1960)

Kerry's Fighting Story 1916-21 (Tralee 1949)

Laffan, M., 'The Sinn Féin Party', *Capuchin Annual* (1970)

Laffan, M., 'The Unification of Sinn Féin in 1917', *Irish Historical Studies*, XVII, 67 (1971)

Leonard, J., 'Getting them at Last. The I.R.A. and Ex-Servicemen', in Fitzpatrick D., (ed.), *Revolution? Ireland 1917-1923* (Dublin 1990)

Life of Commandant Mick Radford (n.d.)

Macardle, D., *The Irish Republic: A Documented Chronicle of the Anglo Irish Conflict* (London 1937; new edn. London 1968)

McCann, J., *War by the Irish* (Tralee 1946)

MacCarthy, Col. J.M. (ed.), *Limerick's Fighting Story 1916-21* (Tralee 1949)

MacDonnell, K., *There is a Bridge at Bandon. A Personal Account of the Irish War of Independence* (Cork 1972)

MacEoin, G., 'The Irish Republican Army', *Eire-Ireland* IX Vol. 2 (1974)

MacEoin, U., (ed.), *Survivors* (Dublin 1987)

MacEvilly, M., 'Sean MacBride and the Republican Motor Launch St. George', *Irish Sword* (1984)

MacGuinness, C.J., *Nomad* (London 1934)

McKenna, K., 'The Irish Bulletin', *The Capuchin Annual* (1970)

Macready, C.F.N., *Annals of an Active Life*, 2 Vols. (London 1924)

Maddock, J., *Rosslare Harbour. Past and Present* (Rosslare Harbour n. d.)

Maguire, C.A., 'The Republican Courts', *The Capuchin Annual* (1969)

Maguire, G., 'Mayo and Sligo 1920', *The Capuchin Annual* (1970)

Maher, J., *The Flying Column - West Kilkenny 1916-1921* (Dublin 1987)

Marnane, D.G., *Land and Violence - A History of West Tipperary from 1660* (The Author 1985)

Martin, F.X., *The Irish Volunteers 1913-1915. Recollections and Documents* (Dublin 1963)

Martin, F.X., *Leaders and Men of the Easter Rising: Dublin 1916* (London 1967)

Mitchell, A., *Revolutionary Government in Ireland. Dáil Éireann 1919-22* (Dublin 1995)

Mulcahy, Gen. R., 'Chief of Staff 1919', *The Capuchin Annual* (1970)

Mulcahy, R., 'The Development of the Irish Volunteers, 1916-1922' (address to *Irish Military History Society*, 9 November 1978)

Mullin, T.H., Rev., *Ulster's Historic City Derry Londonderry* (Coleraine 1986)

Mullins, B., *Memoirs of Billy Mullins Veteran of the War of Independence* (Tralee 1983)

Murphy, D., *Derry, Donegal and Modern Ulster 1790-1921* (Londonderry 1981)

Murphy, S. & S., *The Comeraghs Refuge of Rebels (Story of Deise Brigade I.R.A.) 1914-1924* (Clonmel n.d.)

Murray, C., 'The 1918 General Election in the Three Derry Constituencies' (Unpublished thesis, Queen's University of Belfast, May 1990)

Neligan, D., *The Spy in the Castle* (London 1968)

Nolan, W. (ed.), *Tipperary: History and Society* (Dublin 1985)

Ó Bric, D., 'Pierce McCan, M.P. (1882-1919) Part 2', in *Tipperary Historical Journal* (1990)

Ó Broin, L., *Revolutionary Underground. The Story of the Irish Republican Brother-hood, 1858-1924* (Dublin 1976)

Ó Broin, L., 'Revolutionary nationalism in Ireland: the IRB, 1858-1924', in Moody T.W. (ed.), *Nationality and the Pursuit of National independence* (Belfast 1978)

Ó Broin, L., *Michael Collins* (Dublin, 1983)

O'Casey, S., *The Story of the Irish Citizen Army* (Dublin 1919)

O'Connor, B., *With Michael Collins in the Fight for Irish Independence* (London 1929)

O'Connor, F., *The Big Fellow – Michael Collins and the Irish Revolution* (Swords, Co. Dublin 1986)

O'Doherty, L., 'Dublin - 1920', *The Capuchin Annual* (1970)

O'Donnell, P., *There Will Be Another Day* (Dublin 1963)

O'Donoghue, F., *No Other Law: The Story of Liam Lynch and the Irish Republican Army, 1916-1923* (Dublin 1954)

O'Donoghue, F., 'Guerrilla Warfare in Ireland', *An Cosantóir*, XXIII (1963)

O'Donoghue, F., *Tomas MacCurtain. Soldier and Patriot* (Tralee, County Kerry 1971)

O'Faolain, S., *Vive Moi: An Autobiography* (London 1965)

O'Faolain, S., *Midsummer Night Madness and other stories* (Penguin 1993)

O'Farrell, P., *The Ernie O'Malley Story* (Dublin, Cork 1983)

O'Hegarty, P.S., *The Victory of Sinn Féin: How it won it and how it used it.* (Dublin 1924)

O Mahony, S., *Frongoch: University of Revolution* (Killiney, Co. Dublin 1987)

O'Malley, C.K.H., 'Ernie O'Malley Autobiographical Letter', *Cathair na Mart. Journal of the Westport Historical Society*, Vol. 9 No. 1 (1989)

O'Malley, Edw., *Memories of a Mayoman* (Westport 1981)

O'Malley, E., *On Another Man's Wound* (London 1936)

Peacocke of Derry and Raphoe. An Autobiographical Sketch (1946)

Power, P.C., *Carrick-on-Suir and its People* (Dun Laoghaire 1976)

Power, P.C., *History of South Tipperary* (Cork 1989)

Roche, R., *Here's Their Memory. A Tribute to the Fallen of Republican Wexford* (1966)

Roche, R., 'Events in Wexford - 1920', The Capuchin Annual (1970)

Rumpf, E., *Nationalismus und Sozialismus in Irland. Historisch-soziologischer Versuch über die Irische Revolution seit 1918* (Meisenheim am Glan 1959)

Ryan, B., *A Full Private Remembers the Troubled Times* (Hollyford, Co. Tipperary 1969)

Ryan, D., *Seán Treacy and the Third Tipperary Brigade, I.R.A.* (Tralee 1945)

Snoddy, O., 'The Midland Volunteer Force, 1913', *Journal of the Old Athlone Society* (1968)

Street, C.J.C., *Ireland in 1921* (London 1922)

Talbot, H., *Michael Collins's Own Story* (London 1923)

Tierney, M., *Eoin MacNeill, Scholar and Man of Action, 1867-1945* (Oxford 1980)

Townshend, C., *The British Campaign in Ireland, 1919-21: The Development of Political and Military Policies* (Oxford 1975)

Townshend, C., 'The Irish Republican Army and the Development of Guerrilla Warfare, 1916-21', *English Historical Review*, XCIV (1979)

Townshend, C., 'The Irish Railway Strike of 1920: Industrial Action and Civil Resistance in the Struggle for Independence', *Irish Historical Studies*, XXI, 84 (1979B)

Townshend, C., 'Bloody Sunday - Michael Collins Speaks', *European Studies Review*, IX (1979C)

Townshend, C., *Political Violence in Ireland: Government and Resistance since 1848* (Oxford 1983)

Two Years of English Atrocities in Ireland (1919)

White, T. de V., *Kevin O'Higgins* (London 1948)

Walsh, L.J., *On my Keeping and in Theirs* (Dublin, London 1921)

Wilkinson, B., *The Zeal of the Convert* (Washington 1976)

Williams, T.D. (ed.), *The Irish Struggle, 1916-26* (London 1966)

Williams, T.D. (ed.), *Secret Societies in Ireland* (Dublin 1973)

With the IRA in the Fight for Freedom, 1919 to the Truce (Tralee 1955)

Wusten, F.H. van der, *Iers verzet tegen de staatkundige eenheid der Britse eilanden 1800 1921; een politiek geografische studie van integratie- en desintegratieprocessen* (Amsterdam 1977)

Zimmermann, G.D., *Songs of Irish Rebellion. Political Street Ballads and Rebel Songs 1780-1900* (Dublin 1967)

Index